THE BLACK
INTELLECTUAL
TRADITION

THE NEW BLACK STUDIES SERIES

Edited by Darlene Clark Hine
and Dwight A. McBride

*A list of books in the series appears
at the end of this book.*

THE BLACK INTELLECTUAL TRADITION

AFRICAN AMERICAN THOUGHT IN THE TWENTIETH CENTURY

EDITED BY
DERRICK P. ALRIDGE, CORNELIUS L. BYNUM,
AND JAMES B. STEWART

UNIVERSITY OF
ILLINOIS PRESS
Urbana, Chicago, and Springfield

Library of Congress Cataloging-in-Publication Data
Names: Alridge, Derrick P., editor. | Bynum, Cornelius L., 1971–
   editor. | Stewart, James B. (James Benjamin), 1947– editor.
Title: The Black intellectual tradition : African American
   thought in the twentieth century / edited by Derrick P.
   Alridge, Cornelius L. Bynum, and James B. Stewart.
Other titles: African American thought in the twentieth century
Description: Urbana : University of Illinois Press, [2021] |
   Series: The new Black studies series | Includes bibliographical
   references and index.
Identifiers: LCCN 2021012137 (print) | LCCN 2021012138 (ebook)
   | ISBN 9780252043857 (hardcover) | ISBN 9780252085840
   (paperback) | ISBN 9780252052750 (ebook)
Subjects: LCSH: African Americans—Intellectual life—20th
   century. | African American intellectuals—History—20th
   century. | African Americans—Race identity—History—
   20th century. | Blacks—Race identity—United States—
   History—20th century. | Black nationalism—United
   States—History—20th century. | African Americans—
   Social conditions—20th century. | United States—Race
   relations—History—20th century.
Classification: LCC E185.89.I56 B56 2021 (print) | LCC E185.89.I56
   (ebook) | DDC 305.896/0730904—dc23
LC record available at https://lccn.loc.gov/2021012137
LC ebook record available at https://lccn.loc.gov/2021012138

CONTENTS

THE BLACK
INTELLECTUAL
TRADITION

INTRODUCTION

DERRICK P. ALRIDGE, CORNELIUS L. BYNUM,
AND JAMES B. STEWART

This volume sets out to delineate a distinctive Black intellectual tradition rooted in the understandings and experiences of people of African descent living in the United States and their perspectives on race, systematic racism, and the world. Following the 1896 *Plessy v. Ferguson* ruling wherein the US Supreme Court gave constitutional sanction to racial segregation, Black people acted with particular diligence to fashion new theories of race, identity, and culture that served to validate Black humanity. The result was a comprehensive system of thought specifically designed to challenge Jim Crow, lynching, disfranchisement, discrimination, and other forms of racial oppression that were now facts of law, not just facts of Black life. The essays collected here concentrate on the ideas that Black artists and intellectuals, performers and protest activists, institutions and organizations, and educators and religious leaders developed to fight against the persistent waves of racial oppression sweeping over generations of Black people in the United States. Indeed, these ideas animate the long struggle of Black people for equal justice.

Notions about race, racism, discrimination, and Black equality that emanated from just about every quarter of Black life in the United States after the turn of the twentieth century especially cut against the skepticism of those that eschewed the existence of a Black intellectual tradition. Harold Cruse's *Crisis of the Negro Intellectual: A Historical Analysis of the Failure of Black Leadership* is a good example. Here, Cruse offers an insightful critique of Black leadership and thought from the 1920s to the 1960s. His study moved the discourse on Black thought beyond the early twentieth-century focus on "race uplift" to topics like Black nationalism, socialism, and literature. But his criticisms of pan-Africanist and Black Power theorists as lacking any meaningful authentic or organic philosophical underpinnings are rooted in a myopic view of Black thought. Stanley Crouch extends these miscalculations and misunderstandings in his introduction to the 2005 edition of Cruse's book. Crouch asserts, "There has never been a substantial body of thought on any Afro-American subject that was formed of deep studies, original theories, probing cultural examination, complex religious assessment, and schools of philosophical concern that raised questions about essences as opposed to superstitions, hearsay, and propaganda."[1] What the authors gathered in the current volume demonstrably proves is that such skepticism about a cohesive system of Black thought is simply wrong.

Cruse, Crouch, and others miss the deeply impactful ways that the experiences of Black people in the United States and their long struggle for social justice produced innovative strategies for challenging systematic racism at home and abroad. Emphasizing the twin objectives of defining and defending Black humanity and of demanding social justice and the dismantling of racial apartheid, this volume examines the ideologies, theories, interpretative studies, and cultural productions and reproductions Black people created to affect change. The volume demonstrates how Black people communicated their ideas about race, racism, discrimination, and equality and transmitted these ideas from one generation to another and how post–civil rights generations have extended the ideas of their predecessors while charting new intellectual terrain.

While skeptics like Cruse and Crouch questioned the existence of a Black intellectual tradition, others, like philosopher Lewis R. Gordon, assert just the opposite: there is no one definitive Black intellectual tradition. In his book *Existentia Africana: Understanding Africana Existential Thought*, Gordon provides a comprehensive examination of Black existential thought across the African diaspora that emphasizes its broad complexity and diversity. He subsequently argues in the essay "Black Intellectual Traditions" that there are "more properly black intellectual traditions . . . formed from a diverse set of ethnic groups . . . rather than a single black intellectual tradition."[2] In both these important works, Gordon identifies a set of themes, among them liberation, Black nationalism, Black feminism, and Afrocentrism, that define Black thought throughout the diaspora. Gordon's studies provide an important lens for examining the particular ways that Black people in the United States adapted and incorporated these diasporic perspectives into a set of ideas and beliefs uniquely framed by their experiences in North America.

The themes that Gordon highlights are central to the system of Black thought that emerged around the turn of the twentieth century. As the progressive impulses of the era focused increasing attention on pressing social concerns, such as child labor, urban vice, and workers' rights, Black Americans gave new voice to their determination to challenge their racial oppression. When Ida B. Wells presented her findings on racial lynching in 1895 followed by the publication of W. E. B. Du Bois's seminal study, *The Philadelphia Negro*, in 1899, both applied the emerging social scientific methodologies at the center of the Progressive movement to the problem of race. In both instances, Wells and Du Bois used the new tools of social science to debunk beliefs about inherent Black deviancy and criminality that underlined White supremacy and justified racial segregation and discrimination in the minds of many Whites. But Wells's and Du Bois's efforts also reflected a long-standing determination among African Americans to assert and defend their basic humanity. Indeed, these efforts to articulate and defend Black humanity as well as to claim the same rights of self-determination that White Americans took for granted largely defines how Black intellectuals and activists approached the problem of race in the New Negro era and beyond.

Du Bois, Charles S. Johnson, and Alain Locke together initiated and largely directed the New Negro literary era of the Harlem Renaissance. Each came to see Black artistic expression as a vital mechanism for defending Black humanity and, thus, challenging racist myths undergirding Jim Crow segregation. The term "New Negro" comes from "Enter the New Negro," an essay Locke published in 1925 in *Survey Graphic*. Explaining that the days of old where the Negro was "more of a formula than a human being" were fading, Locke proclaims the arrival of the New Negro on a "mission of rehabilitating the race in world esteem from that loss of prestige for which the fate and condition of slavery have so largely been responsible."[3] Johnson expresses similar sentiments in his reflections on the periods. For him, this time was both a "self-conscious and race-conscious" one. The artistic endeavor that drove the Harlem Renaissance, he notes, was "not only [one] of the quivering search for freedom but a cultural, if not a social and racial emancipation."[4] Du Bois makes plain Locke's and Johnson's ultimate point, asserting that in Black people's push to contest racial subjugation, "all art is propaganda." In "Criteria of Negro Art," published in the *Crisis* magazine in 1926, Du Bois insists that "until the art of the black folk compels recognition, they will not be rated as human" or accorded the full measure of human freedom.[5] As the literary outpouring to the Harlem Renaissance flowed steadily in the decade or so following World War I, these ideas about the role of Black artistic expression defining and defending Black humanity against the onslaughts of American White supremacy became a central feature of Black intellectual thought.[6]

Marcus Garvey and the mass movement he sparked in 1918 with the Universal Negro Improvement Association headquartered in Harlem reflect another key feature of Black thought and activism during this period. Arriving in New York in 1916, Garvey quickly came to recognize the unique character of Harlem: a self-contained but growing Black community with discernable disposable income and largely unbothered by White New Yorkers.[7] Moreover, Garvey's arrival coincided with the early beginnings of the New Negro literary movement connected to Black newspapers especially popular in Harlem at the time.[8] The relative prosperity and cultural liveliness of the Black community at the outset of the Renaissance fascinated Garvey partly because he fervently believed that "the Negro will have to build his own government, industry, art, science, literature and culture, before the world will stop to consider him."[9] At its core, Garveyism—Garvey's racial and political ideology—viewed Black self-determination as the most likely avenue for Black people to achieve liberation. "No Negro," Garvey declares, "shall be truly respected until the race as a whole has emancipated itself through self-achievement and progress."[10] Garvey gives almost no time to arguing in defense of Black humanity. Unlike Du Bois, Johnson, and Locke, Garvey never invested cultural or racial capital in what he viewed as mimicry of White Western norms. Instead, he saw the struggle for racial liberation in much more stark terms. Although the cultural arguments Du Bois, Johnson, and Locke outlined were meaningful, Garvey determined that Black people "must strike out for ourselves in the course of material achievement, and by our own effort and energy present to the world those forces by which the progress of man is judged."[11]

Another notable feature of Garvey's racial thinking is his internationalism. The problem of racial oppression was a global one in his mind, and, thus, he cast his program of racial liberation through self-determination in global terms. "It seems that the whole world of sentiment is against the Negro," Garvey notes in arguing for broad racial organization, "not on domestic-national lines only, but universally."[12] Indeed, Garvey addresses his message to "the Negro people of the world," declaring that "wheresoever [Black people] form a community among themselves [they] should be given the right to elect their own representatives to represent them in legislatures, courts of law, or such institutions as may exercise control over that particular community."[13] Although contemporaries and successors would share elements of Garvey's international perspective on the problem of racial oppression and its solution, this kind of international Black nationalism at the heart of Garvey racial messaging is essential to grasp in considering the intellectual landscape of the New Negro era.

Black Marxists, such as A. Philip Randolph and Frank R. Crosswaith, and the political thinking of others writing and organizing in Harlem and elsewhere during this period represent another strain of Black thought on the problem of race. Reasoning that racism was endemic to the American system, Randolph, Crosswaith, and their Marxist brethren viewed alternatives to American industrial capitalism as necessary to alleviating racial oppression. Indeed, they insisted that the raw individualism and naked competition that fundamentally drove capitalist systems incentivized White supremacy. The "path" of capitalism, Crosswaith points out, was that of "competition and human exploitation for private gain" and, thus, made it "futile and meaningless" for Black people to pursue "equality, democracy, liberty and other such myths under the capitalist system."[14] Randolph proposed a system of democratic socialism as the remedy to the inherent racism bred by capitalism. He insisted that injustice and racial oppression were so deeply embedded in the competitive structures of capitalism that only "a socialized economy and a democratized society" that "constituted" a genuine "break with the old political and economic order" could produce the full liberation that Black people sought and deserved.[15] Although other Black Marxists in Harlem pursued other solutions to the problems of race and White supremacy, few, if any, quibbled with the basic diagnosis that Randolph and Crosswaith outline.

New Negro women raised their voices and mobilized to exert influence on discussions of Black liberation and the problem of race in these years as well. In newspapers like Randolph's *Messenger* and Garvey's *Negro World*, Black women express their views on the proper courses of race advancement and liberation. Writing in the *Messenger* in 1927, for example, Alice Moore Dunbar-Nelson explains in "The Negro Woman and the Ballot" how newly enfranchised Black woman were a key source of support for the Dyer Anti-Lynching bill passed by the US House of Representatives in 1922. She recounts how Republican representatives that opposed the bill from New Jersey, Delaware, and Michigan were voted out of office and "properly castigated by being kept home" largely because of the political mobilization of Black women in those states. Party loyalty, she notes, was an insufficient shield against the political wrath of Black women voters who "unquestionably had the deciding influence" on these outcomes.[16] Amy Jacques Garvey, Marcus Garvey's wife, was equally vocal in 1925 about her prescriptions regarding race and gender: "The exigencies of this present age requires that women take their place beside their men." In "Woman as Leaders," published in the *Negro World*, Amy Garvey encouraged Black women, who as the "backbone of the home" had demonstrated "their economic experience and their aptitude for details" to "participate effectively in guiding the destiny of the nation and race." In pursuing the goals of racial liberation through self-determination, Amy Garvey urges Black women to sally "forth to help their men establish a civilization according to their own standards and to strive for world leadership."[17]

In these and other ways, Black intellectuals and activists of the New Negro era articulate a broad set of ideas that defined and inspired the goals and struggle for Black liberation well beyond just the years following World War I. In explicit and implicit ways, their ideas informed the various civil rights campaigns African Americans initiated in the United States and the efforts of Black people throughout the Atlantic world to overthrow colonialism and other forms of racial oppression. Indeed, understanding the ideas and thinking about defining and defending Black humanity and Black self-determination that emerged out of the postwar New Negro years is vital. They elucidate both the momentous changes that occur in the status of Black people throughout the world in the second half of the twentieth century and the stubborn racist structures that have, nonetheless, persisted.

In the years following the New Negro era, the effort to bridge disparate approaches to knowledge creation associated with social science and humanistic scholarship harkened back to the historical nondisciplinary explorations of the major themes discussed by the likes of Wells, Du Bois, Garvey, and Randolph. The search for "authentic" Black intellectual work sparked distinctive movements in both the social sciences and the humanities. In the early 1970s, a group of Black social scientists called for the creation of a "Black social science." They proposed research terminology that rejected sanitized descriptions of racial oppression, brought oppressive relationships into sharp relief, and reinforced political commitments to undertake social science research to counter racism and discrimination as well as improve the life circumstances of people of African descent. They insisted that such transformative linguistic convention would challenge racism and improve the lives of African-descended people.[18]

The Black Arts Movement (BAM) that roughly spanned the period 1964 to 1976 was the humanistic counterpart to the Black social science movement and was linked closely to the Black Power movement. BAM sought to challenge Western notions of ideal exemplars of form and beauty and catalyzed the creation of a large body of poems, plays, and essays. Much of the creative production employed distinctive expressive modes, including hyperbolic language, used to attack racism. Many works celebrated African American folk and urban lifestyles.

BAM artists developed innovative linguistic conventions, including coining new terms and using words and phrases taken from various African languages. Many works explored historical themes as, for example, in tribute poems celebrating heroic historical figures. Other materials celebrated how African Americans have continually struggled to overcome oppressive conditions. Some BAM artists adopted techniques borrowed from various musical genres, especially jazz. These artists often prioritized the militant dimensions of jazz, reinterpreted the music, and disseminated these interpretations through poetry.[19]

The concept of a "Black Aesthetic" constituted the theoretical foundations undergirding BAM. Academic critics, including Addison Gayle and Stephen Henderson, cultural workers, such as Larry Neal and Hoyt Fuller, and poets, such as Amiri Baraka and Carolyn Rodgers, all contributed to refinement of the Black Aesthetic. These theorists sought to develop coherent standards and processes to enable judgments regarding content and aesthetic appeal. Consistent application of these standards would presumably promote refinement and maturation of both the artistic and political aspects of cultural production.[20] The various Black Aesthetics formulations along with the critical discourse examining BAM writ large constitute important but typically undervalued contributions to the Black Intellectual Tradition.

Africana Studies poses a unique challenge for conceptualizing the boundaries of Black intellectual thought. The construct of "Afrocentricity," as articulated by Molefi Asante, has offered an interesting critique of Eurocentric scholarly traditions.[21] Asante links the construct of Afrocentricity to a theory of inquiry characterized as "Africalogy," defined as "the Afrocentric study of African concepts, issues, and behaviors," and claimed to constitute "a separate and distinct field of study from the composite sum of its initial founding disciplines."[22] This is one among many efforts to challenge complex ontological and epistemological assumptions embedded within Western intellectual traditions. Specifically, claims that Africana Studies is interdisciplinary, multidisciplinary, nondisciplinary, or transdisciplinary dispute the value of existing disciplinary demarcations.

Africana Studies has also been critical for reasserting the linkage between intellectual thought and political activism. Maulana Karenga, who founded the nationalist organization US in 1965 in the wake of the Watts Riots, is illustrative of this trajectory. As leader of US, Karenga developed the Kawaida philosophical system, which foregrounds the importance of cultural authenticity and promotes cultural nationalism as the necessary foundation for efficacious liberatory praxis. Guided by Kawaida philosophy, US developed community-based programs to address concrete problems that precipitated the Watts Riots. When Karenga later became involved in Africana Studies research, teaching, and instruction, he emerged as a major theorist whose scholarship reflected a variety of influences including Kawaida philosophy, studies of African ethical systems, and experience leading US. Notably, US continues to be active under Karenga's leadership, while he serves as a professor in the Department of Black Studies at California State University, Long Beach. Karenga's intellectual-activist profile illustrates how activism can be an important incubator for intellectual production.[23]

As a final comment on Africana Studies and the Black intellectual tradition, it is important to note that Africana Women's Studies is one of the most vibrant subfields. Africana Women's Studies contributors are in continuous engagement with the expanding body of womanist scholarship, including ideas articulated in this volume. Two different schemas have been competing for visibility within Africana Women's Studies, broadly defined. One school of thought foregrounds cultural nationalist ideology and emphasizes the need for partnership between Africana men and women in pursuit of antiracist political objectives.[24] A competing approach prioritizes feminism and tends to be more connected to traditional academic disciplines than their counterparts, with a special connection to literary criticism and creative writing.[25]

In recent years, the emergence of Black public intellectuals and Hip-Hop intellectuals has reshaped the contours of Black intellectual production. Adolph Reed suggests that the term "Black public intellectual" emerged in the 1990s when "several youngish black professors with ties to and visibility within the cultural studies/cultural politics precincts of the academic left began to use it to refer to themselves and one another" who have achieved significant public visibility that has generated substantial financial benefits. Reed launches a blistering critique of this cohort, asserting that the public intellectual label has devolved into a "justification for an aversion to intellectual or political heavy lifting." Elaborating, Reed insists that Black public intellectuals' style "has baleful effects on the scholarly examination of black American life," in part, because they reject "all considerations of standards of evidence and argument as expressions of naïve positivism" enabling them to "make the story up as they go along."[26]

In a less vitriolic assessment of Black public intellectuals, Michael Hanchard argues that the "category black public intellectual should be expanded to include a class of committed people whose books (if they have them) and speeches may never reach the bookstores or your local video shop. . . . Grassroots activists and organizations who fit into this latter category run the continuous danger of being ignored and neglected by an amorphous public whose intellectuals are already defined for them. What is at stake here are definitions of leadership (another category that overlaps with public intellectual but is not its coeval) and who makes these definitions."[27]

Although not examined in this volume, Hanchard's formulation provides a context for appreciating the emergence of "Hip-Hop intellectuals." A. Shahid Stover enthusiastically champions Hip-Hop culture as a potential site of intellectual discourse and foregrounds the intellectual production of Hip-Hop emcees.[28] Specifically, he maintains, "Hip Hop culture, when resolutely cultivated, potentially serves as a redemptive artistic and intellectual vantage point from which the socio-politically oppressed, the culturally marginalized, the spiritually dehumanized, the globally dispossessed, the racially outcast, the outsiders, the wretched of the earth—the postmodern lumpenproletariat can critically engage an oppressive society."[29] Within this space, "[t]hrough the efforts of the EMCee as Hip Hop intellectual, Hip Hop music in its totality becomes an accessible cultural reservoir of African American thought and lived historical experience for the postmodern proletariat who has become disenchanted with socially sanctioned models of education."[30] Further, Derrick P. Alridge argues that Hip-Hop is part of the long Black intellectual tradition that has carried on and revised ideas of self-determination, liberatory education and pedagogy, economic solidarity, and Pan-African connections.[31]

The essays collected herein explore four categories of inquiry to reveal a system of Black thought that has largely guided Black people's struggle for freedom in the twentieth century and beyond: scholarship and education, arts and letters, social activism and institutions, and racial identity and ideology. Moreover, by foregrounding the important contributions of Black women, this volume is also a needed corrective to an area of study heavily focused on the lives and work of Black men. What results is a more comprehensive and persuasive presentation of the ideas that continue to animate Black people's strivings for full participation in American life. Indeed, if Du Bois was correct that the problem of the twentieth century is the problem of the color line, then the systematic examination of the kind of Black intellectual tradition this volume explores is vital to understanding how African Americans have confronted issues of race and racial discrimination.

Several important works serve as guideposts and exemplars in the study of Black thought. In 1983 philosopher Leonard Harris in his anthology *Philosophy Born of Struggle* helped establish the existence of a Black intellectual tradition. The volume features previously published essays by Locke, Lucius Outlaw, William Fontaine, Cornel West, Bernard Boxill, and other philosophers whom Harris found had common and disparate streams of thought in their writings. This pivotal work has often been overlooked in contemporary discussions of Black thought, but since the 1990s, *Philosophy Born of Struggle* has continued to play a pivotal role in shaping the understanding of the Black intellectual tradition, and it has influenced the construction of this volume.[32]

The emphasis of the current volume's editors on an expansive understanding of intellectualism is informed by the eclectic collection of essays in *Black American Intellectualism and Culture: A Social Study of African American Social and Political Thought*, edited by James Conyers. In this volume the status of "intellectual" is conferred on contributors associated with various specialties, including historians, novelists, poets, artists, lawyers, and activists. Also influencing the current volume, *Contemporary Critical Thought in Africology and Africana Studies*, edited by Molefi Asante and Clyde Ledbetter Jr., offers a synthesis of key constructs undergirding Afrocentric scholarship. In the third chapter Asante provides valuable bibliographic references useful for understanding important theoretical controversies, including Afrocentricity and the Classical African Base, Afrocentricity and Critical Theory, Afrocentricity and Culture, Afrocentricity and Historical Interpretation, and Afrocentricity and Radical Educational Transformation.[33]

Mia Bay, Farrah Griffin, Martha Jones, and Barbara Savage's *Toward an Intellectual History of Black Women* fills a significant void in the literature in the Black intellectual tradition. The study of Black thought has historically focused on the ideas of Black men and does not engage comprehensively the significant impact of Black women on Black thought. This volume, wide-ranging but also succinct, uncovers the ideas of lesser-known Black women activists and ushers in what we hope will be a floodgate of scholarship on Black women and the Black intellectual tradition. Brittney Cooper's *Beyond Respectability: The Intellectual Thought of Race Women* also makes an extremely important case that Black women have been largely overlooked as contributors to Black thought. Identifying and explicating the work of Anna Julia Cooper, Pauli Murray, Mary Church Terrell, and others, Brittney Cooper extends the argument that Black women must be central to the study of Black thought to gain an accurate understanding of the Black intellectual tradition. These and other recent works on Black women have been highly influential in our thinking.[34]

Brian Behnken, Gregory Smithers, and Simon Wendt's *Black Intellectual Thought in Modern America: A Historical Perspective* provides examinations of key topics in Black thought. The contributors explore Black intellectuals, Black nationalism, Black Marxism, and Black feminism during the civil rights and post–civil rights periods in a highly accessible and thoughtful way. The volume affords an excellent introduction to the history of Black thought.[35]

Keisha Blain, Christopher Cameron, and Ashley Farmer's *New Perspectives in the Black Intellectual Tradition* offers fresh insights on Black thinkers and thought in the nineteenth and twentieth centuries. Covering an array of issues, such as Black thought and sexual politics, Black women's cultural theory, and slave resistance, the volume provides deep historical contextualization and analyses of largely underexamined areas in the Black intellectual tradition. One of the most significant contributions of *New Perspectives* is its attention to Black thought within a Black internationalist framework. Chapters in the volume address this issue with great precision.[36]

The current volume extends the existing literature by offering systematic interdisciplinary inquiry into Black intellectual life and thought. This book also offers examinations of Black thought grounded in Black historiography and literature and outlines major historical and intellectual patterns in the Black intellectual tradition. Offering a chronological, thematic, and selective examination of the ideas and thought in Black life, the volume editors set forth Black thought fashioned to address racism and racial discrimination in the twentieth century and beyond.

Notes

1. Stanley Crouch, introduction to *The Crisis of the Negro Intellectual: A Historical Analysis of the Failure of Black Leadership*, by Harold Cruse (1967; New York: New York Review Books Classics, 2005), x–xi. Ross Posnock has also taken issue with the idea of a Black intellectual and argues that Black intellectuals were the "first modern American intellectuals." He attributes the categorizations of ideas along racial lines as "identity politics." See Ross Posnock, *Color & Culture: Black Writers and the Making of the Modern Intellectual* (Cambridge, MA: Harvard University Press, 1998), 2.

2. Lewis R. Gordon, *Existentia Africana: Understanding Africana Existential Thought* (New York: Routledge, 2000), and "Black Intellectual Tradition," in *Encyclopedia of American Studies*, ed. Simon J. Bronner (Baltimore: Johns Hopkins University Press, 2018), https://eas-ref.press.jhu.edu/.

3. Alain Locke, "Enter the New Negro," *Survey Graphic*, March 1925, repr. of *The Making of African American Identity* 3 (1917–68), *National Humanities Center Toolbox*, http://nationalhumanitiescenter.org/pds/maai3/migrations/text8/lockenewnegro.pdf.

4. Charles S. Johnson, "The Negro Renaissance and Its Significance," in *The Portable Harlem Renaissance Reader*, ed. David Levering Lewis (New York: Penguin, 1994), 206–218.

5. W. E. B. Du Bois, "Criteria of Negro Art," *Crisis* 35 (1926): 293.

6. Cornelius L. Bynum, "The New Negro and Social Democracy during the Harlem Renaissance," *Journal of the Gilded Age and Progressive Era* 10, no. 1 (2011): 91; Ernest Allen, "The New Negro: Explorations in Identity and Social Consciousness, 1910–1922," in *1915, the Cultural Moment: The New Politics, the New Woman, the New Psychology, the New Art, and the New Theatre in America*, ed. Adele Heller and Lois Rudnick (New Brunswick, NJ: Rutgers University Press, 1991).

7. Cary D. Wintz, *African American Political Thought 1890–1930* (New York: Routledge, 1995), 11.

8. The *Amsterdam News* (1909), *Crisis* (1910), and *Messenger* (1917) were all headquartered in New York City, and their editors would write about and respond to Garvey and Garveyism. *Opportunity* (1923) was founded at Fisk University in Nashville, Tennessee, but was deeply influential in New Negro Harlem. And, of course, Garvey founded his own newspaper, the *Negro World*, in Harlem in 1918.

9. Marcus Garvey, "An Appeal to the Conscience of the Black Race to See Itself," in *Philosophy and Opinions of Marcus Garvey*, ed. Amy Jacques Garvey (New York: Atheneum, 1992), 24.

10. Ibid.

11. Ibid., 23.

12. Ibid., 22.

13. Marcus Garvey, "Declaration of Rights of the Negro Peoples of the World," in A. J. Garvey, *Philosophy and Opinions*, 137.

14. Frank R. Crosswaith, "The Negro at the Crossroads," 5, box 2, Frank R. Crosswaith Collection, Schomburg Center for Research in Black Culture, New York Public Library, New York.

15. A. Philip Randolph, "Statement to Educational Political Conference in Chicago, Illinois, at the International House," Speeches ND, box 2, A. Philip Randolph Papers, Schomburg Center for Research in Black Culture, New York Public Library, New York.

16. Alice Moore Dunbar-Nelson, "The Negro Woman and the Ballot," *Messenger*, April 1927.

17. Amy Jacques Garvey, "Women as Leaders," *Negro World*, October 25, 1925.

18. See Abd-l Hakimu Ibn Alkalimat [Gerald McWorter], "The Ideology of Black Social Science," in *The Death of White Sociology*, ed. Joyce A. Ladner (New York: Random, 1973), 173–189; Robert Staples, "What Is Black Sociology? Toward a Sociology of Black Liberation," in Ladner, *Death of White Sociology*, 161–172; Ronald W. Walters, "Toward a Definition of Black Social Science," in Ladner, *Death of White Sociology*, 190–212.

19. James B. Stewart, "Riddles, Rhythms, and Rhymes: Toward an Understanding of Methodological Issues and Possibilities in Black/Africana Studies," in *Ethnic Studies Research, Approaches, and Perspectives*, ed. Timothy P. Fong (Lanham, MD: AltaMira, 2008), 179–218.

20. Ibid.

21. Molefi Asante, *The Afrocentric Idea* (Philadelphia, PA: Temple University Press, 1987).

22. Molefi Asante, *Kemet, Afrocentricity, and Knowledge* (Trenton, NJ: Africa World Press 1990), 12.

23. Two books have been published about Maulana Karenga's scholarship and activism: Scot Brown, *Fighting for US* (New York: New York University Press, 2005), and Molefi Asante, *Maulana Karenga: An Intellectual Portrait* (Cambridge, UK: Polity, 2009). Karenga's own perspective on these issues is provided in Maulana Karenga, "Us, Kawaida, and the Black Liberation Movement: Forging the Future in Struggle" (unpublished manuscript, 2005); a slightly different version is published in *Engines of the Black Power Movement, Essays on the Influence of Civil Rights Actions, Arts, and Islam*, ed. J. Conyers (Jefferson, NC: McFarland, 2007), 95–133.

24. See, for example, Clenora Hudson-Weems, *Africana Womanism: Reclaiming Ourselves*, 5th ed. (1993; New York: Routledge, 2020).

25. See, for example, Gloria Hull, Patricia Scott, and Barbara Smith, *All the Women Are White, All the Blacks Are Men, but Some of Us Are Brave: Black Women's Studies* (1982; New York: Feminist, 2015).

26. Adolph Reed, "What Are the Drums Saying, Booker? The Current Crisis of the Black Intellectual," *Village Voice*, April 11, 1995, 31, 35, 35. Reed specifically identifies Cornel West, Henry Louis Gates Jr., bell hooks, Michael Dyson, and Robin Kelley as highly visible Black public intellectuals.

27. Michael Hanchard, "Cultural Politics and Black Public Intellectuals," *Social Text* 48 (Autumn, 1996): 107.

28. A. Shahid Stover, *Hip Hop Intellectual Resistance* (Philadelphia, PA: Xlibris, 2009).

29. Ibid., 24.

30. Ibid., 30.

31. Derrick P. Alridge, "From Civil Rights to Hip Hop: Toward a Nexus of Ideas," *Journal of African American History* 90 (Summer 2005): 226–252.

32. Leonard Harris, ed., *Philosophy Born of Struggle: Anthology of Afro-American Philosophy from 1917* (Dubuque, IA: Kendall Hunt, 1983).

33. J. L. Conyers Jr., *Black American Intellectualism and Culture: A Social Study of African American Social and Political Thought* (London: Emerald, 1999); Molefi Kete Asante and Clyde Ledbetter Jr., *Contemporary Critical Thought in Africology and Africana* (Lanham, MD: Lexington, 2017).

34. See, for example, Hudson-Weems, *Africana Womanism*.

35. Brian D. Behnken, Gregory D. Smithers, and Simon Wendt, *Black Intellectual Thought in Modern America: A Historical Perspective* (Jackson: University Press of Mississippi, 2017).

36. Keisha N. Blain, Christopher Cameron, and Ashley D. Farmer, *New Perspectives in the Black Intellectual Tradition* (Evanston, IL: Northwestern University Press, 2018).

PART I

SCHOLARSHIP AND EDUCATION

Introduction

DERRICK P. ALRIDGE, CORNELIUS L. BYNUM, AND JAMES B. STEWART

Since enslaved Africans landed on the shores of the Americas in the 1600s, Blacks have viewed education as a form of resistance and liberation. Enslaved Blacks possessed a strong desire to read and write and sought to learn the language of the enslavers. The enslaved appropriated the enslavers' religion to form their own religious belief system to explain their existential situation and chart their future possibilities.

After Emancipation, Blacks adamantly pursued education by building their own schools, which laid the foundation for public education in the American South. Throughout the twentieth century, they made great strides in education. Black colleges and universities were established, education as a profession provided a solid foundation for the rise of a Black middle class, and Blacks reaffirmed the value of education as a form of liberation.

Yet, despite the reverence African Americans have had for education and the central role of education in the Black freedom struggle, the study of Black education has been largely absent from the discourse on Black thought and the Black intellectual tradition. The chapters in this section illuminate the thought of Black historians, educators, and intellectuals. The chapters also examine twentieth-century debates in Black thought that animated larger conversations in the Black intellectual tradition.

The first chapter, "African American Intellectual History: The Past as a Porthole into the Present and Future of the Field," is a historiography of African American thought in the twentieth century. Although not specifically about the practice of education as an intellectual enterprise, Pero Gaglo Dagbovie's chapter provides a historiography of the Black intellectual tradition based on the work of historians. Dagbovie offers a well-rounded analysis of historical literature that broadly reflects Black thought in the twentieth century.

For instance, Dagbovie reflects on how Blacks responded to notions of Black inferiority through the scholarship of historians, such as Carter G. Woodson, W. E. B. Du Bois, and V. P. Franklin, among others. These historians, who were also educators, saw it as their responsibility to provide a corrective or "vindicationist" scholarly response to the miseducation promulgated by White supremacists and revisionist historians of the early half of the twentieth century. In addition, Dagbovie posits that Black women historians have challenged scholars to be much more inclusive in their thinking about the role of women in the Black intellectual tradition.

Aaron David Gresson III's chapter, "Afrocentricity and Autobiography: Historiographical Interventions into Black Intellectual Traditions," examines the debates around Afrocentricity, arguing specifically that Afrocentric education remains a viable means of educating African American youth. Gresson teases out the themes in Afrocentric education, including agency, collective consciousness, dialectics, and liberation, among others. The chapter also provides an examination of Afrocentric educators and thinkers. such as Molefi Asante, Asa Hilliard, and James Stewart. Drawing from the fields of psychology, communication, and the sociology of knowledge, the chapter employs an autobiographical approach that places Gresson at the center of the narrative.

Dagbovie and Gresson offer historiographies that explore the complexity, nuance, and variety of African American thought in the twentieth century. Whereas Dagbovie presents a sweeping overview of the currents in African American thought, Gresson provides a granular and autobiographical explication of one current in African American thought. Together, these two chapters, along with the introduction, provide the foundation upon which the volume stands.

CHAPTER 1

AFRICAN AMERICAN
INTELLECTUAL HISTORY

THE PAST AS A PORTHOLE INTO THE
PRESENT AND FUTURE OF THE FIELD

PERO GAGLO DAGBOVIE

Intellectual history—in unembellished terms, the history of ideas and of those who formulated, articulated, and documented their thoughts in different time periods and varying contexts—is a foundational subspecialty of African American history that has expanded by leaps and bounds since the mainstreaming of the study of African American history sometime during the Black Power era. Since its earliest expressions, those who have practiced Black intellectual history have, broadly speaking, been concerned with explaining how African American spokespersons have thought and written about their people's unique status, which has been primarily characterized by varied forms of racial oppression. It may seem that we are now existing in an era during which old-fashioned African American intellectual history—once widely known as "Negro thought" scholarship—is steadily being superseded by what many social and cultural historians of the Black past understandably hold to be more fascinating and enriching subject matter. Even so, African Americanists continue to creatively interpret the beliefs and writings of well- and lesser-known Black leaders, activists, thinkers, and theorists, predominantly those operating from the late nineteenth century through the Black Power era. On a refreshing note, new generations of Black scholars, like those belonging to what Michael Eric Dyson has called "an emerging black digital intelligentsia," have challenged and expanded upon long-standing canonical interpretations of the Black intellectual enterprise. More symbolically, in the twenty-first century, various scholars have evoked the notion of *Black thought* in their book titles.[1] African American intellectual history, by name, has also recently been institutionalized and reinvigorated. Approximately two decades after the establishment of the International Society for Intellectual History and several years after the founding of the Society for US Intellectual History, in January 2014 a group of talented and enthusiastic African American historians founded the African American Intellectual History Society (AAIHS). The purpose of this scholarly organization is straightforward and, as its name signals, revolves around Black intellectual history. AAIHS conceives Black intellectual history as "African American and African diasporic intellectual history." The society encourages recognition of "interdisciplinary approaches to black intellectual history" and by explicitly evoking the concepts of African American intellectual history and African American and African diasporic thought, AAIHS—which disseminates important scholarship online and convenes dynamic annual conferences—is helping to popularize the still undertheorized subfield of African American intellectual history. It is also refreshing that in early September 2020, the *Chronicle of Higher Education* published an interview with an active member of AAIHS, historian Brandon Byrd, on the marginalization of Black intellectual history. With "The Rise of African American Intellectual History," Byrd has published one of the first substantive articles that seeks to define, theorize, and contextualize this undertheorized field.[2]

A voluminous amount of scholarship has been published by African Americanists on what today could be construed as *African American* or *Black* intellectual history. Focusing on the ideas of an assortment of scholars (mainly historians), this chapter discusses what I perceive as being an important (by no means comprehensive) body of scholarship, salient characteristics and trends, and key turning points in Black intellectual history during the first three quarters of the twentieth century.[3] The chapter does, however, delve a bit into the late twentieth and early twenty-first centuries. Given the abundance of scholarship in Black intellectual history for close to a century, like all historiographers I have had to make some sagacious decisions about which of the field's major practitioners and publications to include. Further, because Black intellectual history should not be viewed in vacuo, the chapter also surveys some basic trends in mainstream US intellectual history, highlighting a group of its leading practitioners' general disregard for African Americans' contributions to the saga and evolution of American thought. The essay closes with a reflection upon what it might mean to be a practitioner of Black intellectual history and what the not-too-distant future of the field could entail. Central to my approach is Adolph Reed Jr. and Kenneth W. Warren's perceptive observation: "The academic practice of intellectual history is itself a historical phenomenon."[4]

In 1961 intellectual historian, clergyman, and longtime professor at North Carolina Central University Earl E. Thorpe (1924–1989) authored *The Mind of the Negro: An Intellectual History of Afro-Americans*, a relatively inconspicuous and largely ignored yet cerebral, ambitious, and far-reaching book.[5] The prevailing concept behind the title of Thorpe's book had noticeable antecedents in US historiography. In 1926 Carter G. Woodson released the volume *The Mind of the Negro as Reflected in Letters Written during the Crisis, 1800–1860.* "The mind of a people, the development of the public mind," Woodson remarks in passing, "has become a new factor in historical interpretation."[6] This anthology of primary documents offers readers a medley of letters from antebellum-era African American leaders that collectively serve as vital windows, Woodson reasons, into "the mind of the Negro." In the same year that Woodson's edited volume appeared, philosopher John Herman Randall Jr. published *The Making of the Modern Mind*, a heralded and bird's-eye history of Western thought from the medieval age until modern times. Randall was one of a multitude of American philosophers who contemplated the history of ideas during the first half of the twentieth century. Other tomes authored by White American historians who endorsed the once largely conventional belief in consensus history similarly evoked the existence of a prevailing "American mind."[7]

Approximately a decade after Thorpe's *Mind of the Negro* appeared, notions of the existence of an overarching "American mind" and the preoccupation with elite or nonordinary American spokespersons' ideas and worldviews were being increasingly challenged by an array of historians and scholars who were influenced by the growing popularity of social history or history "from the bottom up." That the title of Thorpe's study implies the actuality of "the Negro mind" during a decade when claims about an "American mind" were eroding is not surprising. With the exception of Merle Curti, dubbed the dean of American intellectual historians by some of his progeny in the 1970s, White US intellectual historians like those who contributed to and read the *Journal of the History of Ideas* (founded in 1940 by philosopher Arthur O. Lovejoy) did not genuinely integrate African Americans into their syntheses of the "American mind" or "American thought" during the first half of the twentieth century that coincided with a so-called golden age of American intellectual history. The recognition that Blacks possessed intuitive opinions and ideas of substance often materialized in the form of occasional token nods to Booker T. Washington, Frederick Douglass, and W. E. B. Du Bois. From the 1950s through as late as the first decade of the twenty-first century, leading White intellectual historians regularly ignored and marginalized the existence of a Black intellectual tradition.[8] Founded in 2004 with a focus on Europe and the United States, the journal *Modern Intellectual History*, with the exception of Byrd's thoughtful and lengthy 2020 piece, has published close to nothing on African American history.[9] Even in his accessible 2007 overview of one century of American intellectual history in the *OAH Magazine of History*, seasoned intellectual historian David A. Hollinger totally passes over African American intellectual history and the Black historians who have shaped this vibrant field.[10] Hollinger's and his predecessors' and contemporaries' dismissal of African American intellectual history is most likely the byproduct of their Eurocentric orientations and lack of knowledge about African American history.[11] Nevertheless, such a disregard for Black intellectuals in US intellectual history contributes to what philosopher Lewis R. Gordon has called "the tendency to deintellectualize African and Black intellectual history."[12]

Generally speaking, Blacks' beliefs, attitudes, and thoughts have, of course, differed significantly from Whites because of how race has been constructed in the United States. Beginning with the era of US slavery (1789–1865), the periodization of African American intellectual history is starkly different than that of its mainstream American counterpart. Adding African Americans to the pantheon of American intellectuals significantly complicates how the totality of US intellectual history is understood and described. Black intellectual history has its own distinct creation story, evolution, and subfields. It possesses what Du Bois called a sense of "two-ness," or duality. It can be considered a part of American intellectual history, yet its distinctiveness warrants that it be its own freestanding field. Still and all, in order for US intellectual history to be complete, African American subject matter must be considered and in some cases even centered.

In retrospect Thorpe's *Mind of the Negro*, a byproduct of the civil rights movement, was certainly an expression of what Alan K. Colon and later Manning Marable describe as the "corrective" principle of the Black intellectual tradition. Similarly, historians engaged in African American intellectual history in the twenty-first century could also be considered, albeit to a lesser degree, vindicationist in their appeal. Those active in Black women's intellectual history have overwhelmingly participated in rehabilitative scholarly endeavors. As Brittney Cooper has recently argued, Black women thinkers must be taken seriously, and their works must be theorized. For Thorpe, Black intellectual history essentially amounts to the thoughts and ideas of African American men from the "age of slavery" through contemporary times. He acknowledges that enslaved African Americans and their descendants in the South represented the majority of the Black population through the first half of the twentieth century, and, therefore, the history of "the Negro mind" largely constituted the history of the perceptions and ruminations of the Black masses who were most impacted by slavery, Reconstruction, and Jim Crow segregation. Because like his White American counterparts he focused on the written record, Thorpe placed a spotlight on the documented beliefs and viewpoints of "articulate" Blacks.[13] As a result, the origins of the "intellectual history of Afro-Americans" for Thorpe began primarily with those free Black men who were active in the abolition and Black convention movements. Like his male predecessors and contemporaries, he perpetuated a male-centered view of Black intellectual history that remained largely unchallenged until Black women scholars launched the Black women's studies and history movements during the 1970s and 1980s.

In *The Mind of the Negro*, Thorpe explores how African American men have pondered and grappled with various issues, in some cases for more than a century, including Africa, slavery and freedom, religion, family, history, segregation, education, politics, democracy, the US presidency, capitalism, socialism, communism, materialism, war, myths, and, in broadest terms, the meaning of their existence. At the most basic level, Thorpe surmises that there were two central themes of Black intellectual history: the "quest for freedom" and "defending the race against the charge of biological and racial inferiority." He identifies the end of the Reconstruction era as signaling a major shift in African Americans' collective consciousness and approaches to dealing with racial oppression. By this time, he deduces, African Americans had largely adopted self-help ideologies and programs. Reinforcing the problematic dichotomies and categories advanced during the 1940s and 1950s by political scientist Ralph Bunche, sociologist Gunnar Myrdal, and historian August Meier, Thorpe argues, "Negro thought is basically accommodation and attack thought."[14] He recognizes some of the tendencies, variations, and faults of "Negro thought," highlighting class divisions and the impact that slavery and Jim Crow segregation had on the Blacks' cumulative psyches. Yet, he does not provide a penetrating definition of Black intellectual history as a specific subfield. A close reading of *The Mind of the Negro* reveals that Thorpe subtly identifies two different conceptualizations of Black intellectual history as a field, which are still instructive. On the one hand, it was the history of African Americans' collective consciousness, impulses, mindset, temperament, and thoughts about their conditions during slavery, Reconstruction, the era of Jim Crow segregation, and the early years of the conventional civil rights movement. On the other hand, Thorpe envisions Black intellectual history as constituting the history of the beliefs and ideas of leading African American male thinkers who left behind meaningful writings.

Ergo, by focusing on how Blackness and racial oppression shaped African Americans' worldviews, Thorpe's study diverges significantly from previous celebrated studies on the "American mind." He also argues that African Americans' beliefs were diverse, and the notion of the singular "Negro mind" per se did not, and never would, really exist. "The existence of groups or classes" within African American society, Thorpe cautions, "indicates that one might more rationally entitle an intellectual history of the race, 'The Minds of the Negro.'" Thorpe confesses to his readers that his book is loaded with generalizations concerning how African Americans in different time periods and contexts made sense of their realities. Yet, he insists that his lengthy narrative is the first study to attempt to "analyze the Negro mind in the United States."[15] Thorpe maintains that US intellectual history was in its infancy, and he draws attention to the fact that

White historians active in this emerging subfield had, by and large, neglected African American thinkers' ideas.

Thorpe is correct in observing that in 1961 intellectual history—for him simply defined as "the tracing and analyzing of ideas"—was "a fairly new field" in US history. As practitioners of the "Great (White) Man" historical tradition, US male historians, philosophers, and literary critics had produced sweeping narratives on Americans' (mainly educated White males') minds, thoughts, and ideas since the early twentieth century. Thorpe was familiar with these books authored by Vernon Louis Parrington, Henry Steele Commager, Merle Curti, John Herman Randall Jr., Perry Miller, Louis Hartz, and others. In the late 1970s John Higham described the 1930s and 1940s as representing the "heroic age" in American intellectual history. As a categorical subfield in US historiography, intellectual history seems to have blossomed from the 1940s through the 1960s.[16] From the 1950s through the first decade of the twenty-first century, "intellectual history has flourished within the ranks of United States history specialists."[17] At the same time, in the early 1990s, several leading scholars within the field of White-centered US intellectual history debated the state of their démodé field.[18] The fate of US intellectual history since its romanticized heydays (from between the 1940s and 1950s) until the present can certainly be interpreted in numerous ways. One thing is clear. Increasingly since the 1970s, US history as an aggregate field has become hyperspecialized, and intellectual history is now one of countless subspecializations in US history. Similarly, Black intellectual history is also a subfield of African American history. Black intellectual history may share with US intellectual history "the belief that texts and the discourses in which they are embedded are multiple points of entry into human creativity in its profuse variety of historical forms, and that their study is essential to understanding the nature of cultural life and the meaning of civilization itself."[19] At the same time, practitioners of Black intellectual history are often inevitably most concerned with how Black thinkers throughout the ages have responded to the enduring oppression of Black America.

African American scholars have certainly battled each other concerning the roles and responsibilities of "the Black intellectual" for more than a century, especially since the post–World War II era. During the 1960s a group of scholars, most notably Harold Cruse, discussed the "dilemma," "failures," and "crisis" of the "Negro intellectual." In 1987 Cornel West recycled many of these debates in his popular essay "The Dilemma of the Black Intellectual." Michael Eric Dyson's critique of West and West's attack on Ta-Nehisi Coates are recent and somewhat entertaining examples of this tradition. Yet, debates about the meaning, state, and future of intellectual history among African Americanists have not been nearly as prevalent and intense as those debates in the mainstream (White) US historical profession. For instance, the accommodationist-protest dichotomy paradigm of "Negro thought" popularized by August Meier in the 1960s flourished for decades and still often informs how African American history is taught in high schools, colleges, and universities.

That Thorpe did not concentrate on formulating a nuanced philosophy of African American intellectual history in *The Mind of the Negro* published more than five decades ago is unsurprising. Such theorization would come later in the evolution of African American historiography. Even though there is an abundance of scholarship on what could be classified as constituting Black intellectual history in the broadest sense of the field's scope, it could be argued that the field of Black intellectual history per se in the twenty-first century is still undertheorized. The delayed evolution of explicit theorizations of African American intellectual history, when compared to mainstream American intellectual history, has much to do with the peculiar evolution of African American history, what I call its movement from "the margins to the mainstream" of US history.[20] Simply put, prior to the civil rights–Black Power movement, explicit theorization of subfields was not a crucial task for Black historians. They had much more pressing concerns.

The specific term "Negro intellectual history"—later referred to and known as *Afro-American* intellectual history, *Black* intellectual history, and *African American* intellectual history—seems to have first entered the lexicon of scholars during the late 1960s in a lengthy review of Cruse's *Crisis of the Negro Intellectual* in the journal *Freedomways*.[21] Cruse's exhaustive study is an unapologetically critical exercise in Black intellectual history meshed with contemporary social commentary and remains an important document in Black intellectual history and one of the most well-known works by an African Americanist dealing with the history and often discussed "dilemma" of Black intellectuals.[22] He was not the first Black scholar to publicly indict the Black intelligentsia who more often than not were members of the Black middle class and elite. Booker T. Washington, Carter G. Woodson, E. Franklin Frazier, and Nathan Hare, among others, had launched similar attacks on "highly educated Negroes." Cruse also endorsed the dichotomy of Black leadership between accommodationists and nationalists and, unlike many of his predecessors and colleagues, celebrated Washington's contentious worldview and tactics.

Historians have been engaged in Black intellectual history—without identifying it as a clear-cut, precise field—since the early Black history movement that spanned from approximately 1915 until 1950. The Black biographical genre, perhaps, the oldest and most sustained expression of Black intellectual history, is more than a century old and developed into a distinctly scholarly field in the first half of the twentieth century. Biographies often take the form of inventive analyses of individuals' minds and psyches. When executed properly, psychohistory and/or psychobiography is a compelling expression of intellectual history.

In 1985 historian Waldo E. Martin Jr. captured this with his appropriately titled *The Mind of Frederick Douglass.* One of the first, major identifiable forms of Black intellectual history beyond the biographical tradition is "Negro thought" scholarship that peaked during the 1960s when books and articles with "Negro Thought" in their titles were common.[23] Scholarly discourse on what has been called Negro thought (most often a synonym for the ideas of Black leaders and spokespersons) dates back to the early twentieth century.

In *The Souls of Black Folk* (1903), Du Bois offers a concise history of how African Americans, particularly Black leaders, reckoned with their oppression. He identifies three prevailing attitudes that he believes African Americans espoused since the eighteenth century, ranging from "revenge" and "revolt" to assimilation to "self-assertion" and "self-development." Du Bois the historian explains that Blacks' ideas instinctively shifted with the changing times. He evokes the term "Negro thought" specifically in reference to Washington, who, in Du Bois's opinion, epitomized "in Negro thought the old attitude of adjustment and submission."[24] Other prominent Black writers during the early twentieth century—like longtime Howard University professor and dean Kelly Miller and teacher, community activist, and amateur historian Leila Amos Pendleton—also allude to "Negro thought," often subdividing Blacks' approaches to the wrongly named "Negro Problem" and sociopolitical ideologies into two major camps, radicals and conservatives.[25]

During the Harlem Renaissance, African American intellectuals consistently distinguished themselves from ideologies of "the Old Negro." "There is ample evidence of a New Negro in the latest phases of social change and progress, but still more in the internal world of the Negro mind and spirit," Alain Locke declared in 1925. He underscores that "the younger generation" and "new intellectuals" were vibrant with a new psychology," a "new outlook," a "new social understanding," a "new mentality."[26] In the early 1930s Woodson claimed that "we do not find in the race a large supply of thinkers and philosophers" and that "the Negro's mind has been all but perfectly enslaved." Woodson, the polemicist, purposely denied the existence of Black intellectual history in this case. The prolific Bunche did not. In the late 1930s, he harkened back to the existence of "two great schools" of Black thought: "The two principle historical schools of Negro thought had as their ideological leaders Booker T. Washington and W. E. B. Du Bois."[27] Washington was the poster child for conciliation and appeasement, while Du Bois embodied an advocacy for complete social and political rights.

Scholarly discourse on Negro thought that flared up during the 1940s represents a concrete precursor to or intriguing early manifestation of Black intellectual history. In his 1940 *Journal of Negro History* essay, "An Interpretation of Negro Thought from the Standpoint of the Sociology of Knowledge," philosopher William Fontaine critiques more than a few leading Black scholars at the time and argues that until the dawning of the World War II era, African Americans, namely, scholars, accepted the idealistic American "democratic way of life" worldview because they had for centuries been socialized to do so. In other words, he postulates that African Americans had been passive thinkers and engaged in "the defense psychology of the race."

Political scientist Bunche arguably shaped Negro thought scholarship in the first half of the twentieth century more than any other scholar. His ideas were paramount to Myrdal's 1944 opus and Meier's scholarship from the 1950s through the 1970s. Bunche's "Memorandum on Conceptions and Ideologies of the Negro Problem"—an at times understandably disjointed manuscript that he prepared for *An American Dilemma* from which Myrdal sampled directly and liberally—focused on the then present state of what he viewed as African Americans' responses to racial discrimination.[28] When dealing with how African Americans approached the so-called Negro Problem, Bunche suggests that deciphering "the thinking of 'the Negro'" was burdensome for a host of reasons, especially since in his mind "the Negro" was a calculated social construction of White America. As Thorpe observes as well, Bunche calls attention to the "extreme diversity" in the Black population. He also deduces that when analyzing Black thought, we are, in essence, focusing on "the intellectuals, professional men, the Negro middle and upper classes" because the "man on the street" is "inarticulate" and purportedly did not contemplate his status in an explicitly decipherable manner.

Bunche divides Black thought into two major arenas. "Roughly speaking, all Negro ideologies on the Negro question fall into one or the other of two rather broad categories: 'accommodation,' and release or escape," he states. "Perhaps the most characteristic feature of Negro thinking is the striving after release from the confines of lower class and color caste status." He perceives the diversity within the two major ideological categories and critiqued accommodationism (synonymous with "appeasement," the "adoption of white conceptions," and Washington) and celebrates the "Negro civil libertarian ideology" epitomized by Du Bois. For Bunche, the latter represented a "dire threat to the hegemony of the South." He points out other streams of thought, such as "radical" ideologies that prioritized "class consciousness," "class unity," and critiques of capitalism as well as Black nationalism, which he believed was on the rise.[29]

The most popular historical monograph in the "Negro thought" genre of the 1960s was Meier's *Negro Thought in America, 1880–1915: Racial Ideologies in the Age of Booker T. Washington* (1963). Unlike Thorpe's *Mind of the Negro*, Meier's book was widely and for the most part positively reviewed. Meier focuses his analysis on the ideas "expressed by the articulate members of the race" during the height of Washington's reign as the most powerful African American spokesperson, homing in on the strategies and philosophy of Washington himself. Like Thorpe, Meier emphasizes the convention movement as embodying a quintessential early "vehicle of Negro thought." Also like Thorpe, but for different reasons, Meier held that Reconstruction sparked a shift in the trends of prevailing African Americans' ideologies. In his view, African Americans adopted certain prevailing American ideals "to their own racial situation." He comments: "We have no direct evidence on what the masses were thinking."[30] Yet, he did attempt to penetrate what historian L. D. Reddick in the late 1930s dubbed the "feelings and thoughts of the common folk." He did make distinctions between the beliefs of "the masses" and "elite leaders" and, focusing on the latter, deduced that during the "Age of Booker T. Washington," most articulate Black spokespersons were either supporters or critics of Washington and advocated self-help, racial pride and solidarity, Black humanity (as expressed in challenges to lynching and anti-Black violence), and complete citizenship rights.

In the final part of his study, "The Divided Mind of the Negro, 1895–1915," Meier argues that a sense of "ethnic dualism" characterized Black thought and that "precise generalizations" were problematic because of the "wide variety of thought patterns." Nonetheless, he endorses a limiting dichotomy of Black thought between "conciliators" and "agitators" or, like Kelly Miller and Pendleton proposed half a century earlier, "radicals" and "conservatives." This dimension of Meier's work has been the most long-lasting. In the 1970s, several scholars challenged Meier's approach. Political scientist Hanes Walton Jr. criticized those like Meier who sought to characterize "Black political thought" with typologies.[31] Similarly, Judith Stein effectively challenges Meier's categorizations of Black (political) thought: "The dominant American historians have used formal categories—accommodation and militance, self-help and protest—to describe the course of Black history. But viewing Black movements as mechanical successions of protests against racism and withdrawal into self-help only mystifies the historical process." Stein concludes, "The language of mechanical oscillations between protest and withdrawal, integration and nationalism, is inadequate."[32] In the late 1990s, Adolph Reed Jr. evoked Stein's argument, encouraging scholars to challenge "procrustean, ahistorical typologies" and other such "abstract" and "formalistic constructions" when describing and explaining African American political thought. He preferred for scholars to probe into the multiple "significant substantive distinctions among kinds of political action."[33]

Although the terminology "Negro thought" seems to have faded away from historians' vocabulary during the Black Power era (even though it was later evoked and known as *Black* and *African American* thought), this catchphrase was in a sense replaced with the then somewhat vague label "Black nationalism." From the 1920s through the 1960s, different groups of scholars, namely, sociologists, political scientists, and historians, examined "Negro nationalism." In the 1970s the editors of *Black Nationalism in America*, John Bracey, Meier, and Elliott Rudwick, defined "Black nationalism" as constituting diverse "body of social thought, attitudes, and actions" spanning from (in four periods of time) the late eighteenth century through the first half of the Black Power era. They identified at least half a dozen expressions or categories of Black nationalism, each of which possessed its own subcategories and degrees of vehemence. As revealed by the long list of Black leaders included in the volume, almost any major Black leader, in the editors' minds, could have been considered a Black nationalist in some way or another. Bracey, Meier, and Rudwick were, in effect, challenging scholars like T. G. Standing and others who in previous decades simplistically equated Black nationalism with Black radicalism. Howbeit, in broadening the parameters of Black nationalism, they also watered down its meaning. During the Black Power era, historical scholarship on historically rooted Black-nationalist ideologies flourished. Several examples demonstrate the contributions of this expression of Black intellectual history.

In *The Ideological Origins of Black Nationalism* (1972), perhaps titled such in response to Bernard Bailyn's classic *Ideological Origins of the American Revolution* (1967), historian Sterling Stuckey directly challenges Cruse, maintaining that the "flowering of black nationalist thought" emerged decades before Martin R. Delany's 1852 Black-nationalist manifesto. Stuckey argues, first, that enslaved Blacks were Black nationalists even though that they did not "frame their thoughts into statements calling for a transformation of values and the creation of institutions"; second, that Robert Alexander Young, author of *The Ethiopian Manifesto* (1829), and abolitionist David Walker, author of *Appeal to the Colored Citizens of the World* (1829), sparked great controversy and "created black nationalist ideology"; and, thirdly, that Black nationalist theory was born in the north because "the narrow limits of freedom there, broader than in the South, afforded black men more time in which to theorize on the condition of their people." For Stuckey, antebellum-era Black nationalists validated their Africanity and African identity, embracing Pan-African unity, racial solidarity, self-determination and self-reliance, a belief in a glorious African past, and the development of Black institutions. Stuckey also reiterates that Black nationalism was not monolithic and that nationalist and integrationist leanings often overlapped: "It becomes evident that with few exceptions the terms 'black nationalists' and 'integrationists,' when thought of as mutually exclusive, are not simply inadequate as a means of understanding the individuals being labeled but prevent us from understanding major ideologies and movements." He adds, "The view advanced by Harold Cruse that Martin Delany was the prototype black nationalist and Frederick Douglass the prototype black integrationist is not merely a rank oversimplification but a barometer of the extent to which he lacks familiarity with the sources."[34]

In *The Golden Age of Black Nationalism, 1850–1925* (1978), Black intellectual historian Wilson Jeremiah Moses disagrees with his colleagues whose research agendas and inclinations were in many cases molded by the Black Power era. He sought to spark debate and even controversy by suggesting that during its golden age, Black nationalism was "civilizationist," "assimilationist," and "conservative." Fundamentally recognizing that Black nationalism was expressed variously and that Black leaders meshed ideologies of "cultural assimilation" and "political nationalism," Moses ultimately argues that during its formative years, Black nationalism was a "prime vehicle for acculturation processes." For him, "the distinction between nationalism and assimilation is a false one, since the two ideas are not mutually exclusive." Those Black nationalists from the golden age whom he discusses include Delany, Douglass, Alexander Crummell (the quintessential Black Victorian civilizationist), Washington, members of the National Federation of Afro-American Women and its successor, National Association of Colored Women (NACW), Du Bois, Sutton Griggs, and Marcus Garvey, who blended golden-age, Black nationalism with New Negroism. According to Moses, Black leaders began to increasingly shift away from a civilizationist stance in the aftermath of World War I. During the Harlem Renaissance, Black intellectuals, unlike their predecessors, began to celebrate and romanticize the culture of the Black masses. "It was not until the twenties," argues Moses, "that black intellectuals envisioned and rejoiced at the possibility of creating a counterculture. . . . The basic difference between Afro-American thought of the Golden Age and that which has occurred since 1960 is that nineteenth-century leaders, unlike their recent counterparts, seldom saw acculturation to Western norms and values as undesirable."[35]

In the mid-1970s when scholarship on Black nationalism was somewhat in vogue and popular, when African American history was gaining unprecedented, though by no means universal or uncontested, mainstream interest, and when US intellectual history was arguably seeking revitalization, slavery historian John W. Blassingame suggested to readers of *Reviews in American History* that African American intellectual history was a "neglected field."[36] How he specifically defined this supposedly overlooked field is unclear. Was he referring to the history of how Blacks from all walks of life contemplated their existence, or was he alluding to the history of the ideas and lives of those groups of Blacks who were more deliberately classified as being intellectuals? Whatever the case may have been, he could have justifiably made such a comment about more than a few other subfields in African American history at this juncture. By the end of the Black Power era, in addition to longue durée studies, the most noticeable and popular subspecialties in African American historiography were without a doubt slavery, Reconstruction, Black labor history, Black life in the so-called ghettos, and biographies of Black leaders. During the 1970s, 1980s, and 1990s, numerous historians were active in Black intellectual history even though the field's scope was not perspicuously debated during these decades.

In the mid-1990s John Hope Franklin echoed Blassingame, commenting that the historical scholarship on African American intellectuals was still underdeveloped. For Franklin, Black intellectual history entailed the "critical examination of what the group—historians, novelists, theologians, sociologists, psychologists, and others—were thinking and saying" in the past. In the mid-1990s William M. Banks wrote *Black Intellectuals: Race and Responsibility in American Life* (1996), a study that Franklin dubbed a "major" contribution to the history of Black intellectuals.[37]

Banks's book is a chronologically organized narrative that touches upon how different generations of Black intellectuals were inevitably shaped by the times during which they came of age. He argues that the first noticeable group of African American intellectuals included those "priests and medicine men" who were brought to North America as enslaved people. Banks identifies numerous educated Blacks during the antebellum era who were ministers, teachers, newspaper editors, and members of the convention movement and literary societies. The period from 1865 until 1915, he logically contends, gave rise to the first "genuine black intellectual group" in large part because of African Americans' increased access to educational institutions. Although he discusses some of the movers and shakers from the Harlem Renaissance, Banks does not examine in detail the history of Black intellectuals from World War I through the modern civil rights movement. Beginning with the civil rights–Black Power movement, he surmises that Black intellectuals gained more visibility in US society and academia. During the Black Power era, he also posits, many Black activists adopted an anti-intellectual ethos, favoring hands-on activism instead. By the mid-1990s Banks seems to have suggested that Black intellectuals had, again logically at one level, reached the apex of their "respectability" in mainstream US culture. The latter part of his book consists of reflections on the ideologies of, as well as brief biographical sketches of, Black scholars whom he clearly admires. If we take Banks's generic definition of what it means to be an African American intellectual, then Black intellectual history is the sweeping history of potentially *all* African American "individuals who are reflective and critical, who act self-consciously to transmit, modify, and create ideas and culture."[38] In other words, Black intellectual history can indeed be conceptualized as a massive field with few, if any, boundaries. Such an approach does not appeal to those who wish to have Black intellectual history be construed as a specific subfield with its own methodologies and parameters.[39]

Since the 1990s many historians have produced scholarship that could be considered Black intellectual history. These publications could be grouped in many categories, including intellectual biographies; scholarship on Black leadership, social movements, and radicalism; studies on groups of professionally trained, PhD-holding scholars like Jonathan Holloway's work on Abram Harris Jr.,

E. Franklin Frazier, and Ralph Bunche, and Francille Rusan Wilson's examination of Black social scientists from 1890 until 1950; literary scholars' analyses of novelists, playwrights, and poets; anthologies on Black thinkers; studies on racial uplift thought during "the nadir" like Evelyn Brooks Higginbotham's and Kevin K. Gaines's brilliant, theory-embedded, pathbreaking books; and wide-reaching scholarship that attempts to canvass African Americans' ideas over time. Many works published during the last two decades could be justifiably discussed in this essay. Here, I touch upon Mia Bay's *White Image in the Black Mind: African-American Ideas about White People, 1830–1925* (2000), a study that broke new ground in Black intellectual history by examining what a wide array of African American thinkers fancied about White people for a century beginning during the antebellum era. According to one historian, Bay's study had the potential to spark the further development of "the new black intellectual history."[40]

In Bay's estimation, scholars of Black intellectual history had not carefully enough identified and analyzed the history of "black racial thought" (African American thinkers' views of White Americans, mainly, Black ethnology) as a specific body of thought and intellectual tradition. Bay stresses that because of the onslaught of racist thought that justified enslavement, Jim Crow segregation, and the continued oppression of Black people, Blacks' anti-White sentiments were almost inevitable and unsurprisingly widespread. Simply put, a prevailing, anti-White ideology was a central, albeit reactionary, feature of Black thought; "Black ideas about white people are inextricably entwined in the history of African-American intellectual resistance to racism."[41] Drawing upon countless illuminating examples—from David Walker's famous *Appeal* to the obscure works of Harvey Johnson to the musings of twentieth-century "religious racialists"—Bay convincingly demonstrates that "black racial thought" came in many forms and was more often than not "ambivalent" and "self-contradictory." Although Bay critically and quite brilliantly unpacks the ideas of Black abolitionists, amateur historians, ethnologists, theologians, and PhD holders, such as Locke and Du Bois, she also discusses the "intellectual weapons" of enslaved African Americans by creatively combing through Works Progress Administration (WPA) narratives and interpreting slave folklore. Bay excavates how bondspersons articulated and interpreted their mistreatment at the hands of their owners and White people, in general. Her discussion of the distinctions that bondspersons made between different classes of White oppressors as well as her argument that the enslaved likened their status to domesticated animals is fascinating.

Bay's study is important for several reasons. One, she demonstrates that expressions of race vindication were often couched in calculated "black ethnological defenses." Two, like Moses, among others, she recognizes that since the antebellum era, Black thinkers' ideas were often full of contradictions that were the byproduct of the complex times that shaped them. Three, she highlights the change-over-time factor when exploring the decline and refashioning of Black ethnological thought. Lastly, she effectively accomplished what historians like Earl E. Thorpe claim to be interested in attempting to pull off but did not: she examines the ideas of bondspersons and "ordinary" Blacks side-by-side with the ruminations of Black leaders, intellectuals, and spokespersons. More than any other historian of her generation, Bay took on the challenge of envisioning Black intellectual history as embodying the history of the thought of all Black people who, as Banks suggests, acted as intellectuals.

More recently, several scholars have directly sought to theorize Black intellectual history. Recent studies such as these tend to envision Black intellectual history as being the study of the ideas generated by a clearly defined group of Black thinkers: professional scholars, prolific writers, leaders, novelists, and public intellectuals. In 2010 *Renewing Black Intellectual History: The Ideological and Material Foundations of African American Thought* was published. Some readers may find the title a bit misleading because the vast majority of the chapters in this edited volume had been previously published. Editors political scientist Reed and literary scholar Warren do, however, call for a reinvigoration of African American intellectual history within the context of Black studies. They claim that Black studies practitioners have been preoccupied with the novelty of the African diaspora and, more so, a desire to represent the "Black community" and "get inside the minds and to read the vernacular and quotidian practices of 'everyday folk.'" According to Reed and Warren, Black studies scholars have all too often since the post–Black Power era passively accepted assumptions about the Black past and have overtheorized the lives of "nonelite" Black Americans. This social history–like approach reminiscent of the scholarship produced by "culture and community" slavery scholars during the 1970s and 1980s has become popular, they maintain, at the expense of abandoning and oversimplifying the challenging craft of Black intellectual history. Instead, Reed and Warren claim many scholars have adopted the "commonsense narrative for making claims about black collective *mentalité*."[42]

Reed and Warren do provide a thoughtful conceptualization of Black intellectual history, noting that the evolution of the field has been intimately linked to the times that shaped its various incarnations. The exercise of Black intellectual history, they note, "is itself an ideologically laden endeavor. . . . Scholars' accounts of the historical trajectory of black thought, therefore, frequently have been linked to extramural political agendas, or at least have been seen as having implications for them. Black studies consolidation as an institutionally recognized field of study only fortified those connections."[43]

In *From Du Bois to Obama: African Americans in the Public Forum* (2010), Charles Pete Banner-Haley contemplates what it meant to exist as a Black intellectual from the era of the Great Depression into the first decade of the twenty-first century. He was, perhaps, most interested in how Black intellectuals transitioned from "invisibility to visibility" in American society and academic culture. This process is, no doubt, complex, and Banner-Haley provides general turning points and explanations. If Banner-Haley has an overarching argument, it is that beginning during the late twentieth century, African American intellectuals with more "visibility" in the public sphere have lost their connections with the masses and fallen into a state of "moral lapse." In this sense he echoes dimensions of Banks's argument and Houston A. Baker Jr's dismissal of Black intellectuals in *Betrayal: How Black Intellectuals Have Abandoned the Ideals of the Civil Rights Era* (2008). The argument is understandable and common: since integration during the post–civil rights–Black Power movement, African American public intellectuals have increasingly wandered away from the ideals of their forerunners. Using Michel Foucault as a springboard, Banner-Haley maintains that Black intellectuals have historically told the masses of their people what to do and how to think while also serving as a "moral force" in the United States, especially pertaining to issues surrounding race.

In the late 1990s political scientist Joy James attested to the existence of Black male profeminists, such as Du Bois and Marable, but ultimately ratiocinated that Black male intellectuals and scholars often contributed to the production of Black male elitism by "the privileging of males in black intellectualism." In her estimation, male leadership has been "naturalized as universal and normative in the history of black thought and politics."[44] Black intellectual history has followed a similar trajectory. For most of the twentieth century, Black male intellectual historians have neglected the viewpoints of Black women leaders and thinkers. As a result, since the 1970s and 1980s a significant group of Black women historians generated much counteracting scholarship that could be considered intellectual history. Many of the field's practitioners have focused on the lives and thoughts of elite and middle-class Black female leaders, spokespersons, and icons. Despite such efforts, during the twenty-first century, scholars have corroborated James's observations. One of the first explicit anthologies on Black women's intellectual history was published recently.

The editors of *Toward an Intellectual History of Black Women* (2015), who are also the founders of the Black Women's Intellectual and Cultural History (BWICH) Collective—Bay, Farah J. Griffin, Martha S. Jones, and Barbara D. Savage—argue that Black women have all too often been examined as "the objects of intellectual activity" and not as "the producers of knowledge. . . . The field of intellectual history has until now resisted embracing the implications of the new work on African American women." In essence, they call for "the intellectual history of black women *writ large*" that recognizes its diversity in the United States and the African diaspora. Like their predecessors who researched dimensions of Black women's history three and a half decades earlier, they consider their scholarship to be "the work of recovery" because male African Americanists and authors of books on the history of ideas have been oblivious to Black women's presence. For the members of BWICH Collective, Black women's intellectual history constitutes a "new history of ideas" or "intellectual history 'black woman–style,'" an approach that understands ideas as necessarily produced in dialogue with lived experiences and always inflected by the social facts of race, class, and gender."[45] Because through much of the twentieth century, Black women have been systemically excluded from political spheres and academic spaces, the scholars of Black women's intellectual history must search for their female subjects' ideas in unconventional sources and spaces. The Black women's intellectual history described and called for in *Toward an Intellectual History of Black Women* can provide genuinely new directions in Black intellectual history. In *Beyond Respectability: The Intellectual Thought of Race Women* (2017), Cooper minces no words in calling upon scholars to theorize Black women's intellectual history and provides up-and-coming historians of Black women thinkers with important blueprints.

More scholarly production in the field of African American intellectual history—in its various incarnations—is warranted. I agree wholeheartedly with Byrd's assertion that African American intellectual history is "essential, not additive" and boundless. Moreover, as Cooper underscores, Black women must be viewed as producers of African American thought in all periods. This is something that Martha S. Jones accomplishes in her digestible and eloquently written narrative on Black women's political thought from the early nineteenth-century through the first half of the twentieth century, *Vanguard: How Black Women Broke Barriers, Won the Vote, and Insisted on Equality for All* (2020). Citing directly from Black women abolitionists, orators, preachers, clubwomen, and suffragists, Jones demonstrates the richness of Black women's political thought leading up to the passage of the Nineteenth Amendment. In her fascinating book *Wayward Lives, Beautiful Experiments: Intimate Histories of Social Upheaval* (2019), moreover, Saidiya Hartman portrays young "ordinary" Black women ("anonymous figures") between approximately 1890 and 1935 as "social visionaries," "innovators," and "radical thinkers" who "tirelessly imagined other ways to live and never failed to consider how the world might be imagined otherwise." By reading deeply into photographs, combing through archives, and unpacking the historical contexts and environments that shaped her "cast of characters," Hartman democratizes Black intellectual history. Assuming the role of an interdisciplinary intellectual historian, she strives to view her character's potential realities "through their eyes." Her approach is instructive to the field of African American history's practitioners.[46] While women scholars and historians (particularly, African American) have engaged in the enterprise of unraveling the thought of Black women historical figures for decades, Black men intellectual historians should also do so beyond gesturing token nods to the utterances of iconic Black women thinkers. Case and micro studies that make connections between the specific subjects under investigation and broader trends and contexts are also still important in the field, and the diversity of Black thought throughout the ages must be acknowledged. Returning to issues raised by scholars who have explicitly sought to define Black intellectual history, the field can be conceived as the analysis of *all* African Americans from various time periods who possessed and articulated ideas and/or the unpacking of the writings, musings, and speeches of Black scholars, leaders, spokespersons, and personalities who spent their lives thinking and sharing their ideas with a broader public. This latter group could be thought of as intellectuals by vocation or profession. In dealing with this group who more often than not tends to be the subject of conventional Black intellectual history, their documented thoughts should be carefully read and re-read by the practitioner as if they are the coveted primary documents that social historians often search day and night for.

As we continue in the new millennium and witness yet another new and invigorating phase of the study of African American history that challenges upcoming generations of historians to carve out niches for themselves by revisiting and contesting previous scholarship, discovering original topics, and formulating cutting-edge approaches, I am sure that I am not alone in encouraging younger scholars not to turn their backs on Black intellectual history as a viable subspecialty to pursue. Not only are there still golden opportunities to reinterpret the personal histories and ideas of many prominent Black thinkers and spokespersons but there are also many other African American historical personalities whose thoughts merit rigorous study, especially "radicals" from various time periods and a wide-range of contemporary Black historical intellectual personages active from the 1970s through as late as the 1990s. Equally important, the ideas of those often deemed "ordinary," everyday black people from the past, whose thoughts are often hard to pinpoint, decipher, and categorize, deserve historians' attention. I humbly suggest that it is the duty of the scholars of Black intellectual history to explore their subjects' thought within the particular historical contexts that shaped their identities, to determine the trends and diversity of thought during the historical moments that molded their subjects, to historicize their subjects' ideologies and worldviews, to adopt a transdisciplinary approach, to translate into a twenty-first-century language what their subjects were thinking, and in the tradition of pragmatic Black studies to strive to make the ideas of past thinkers, when relevant, useful to our understanding of the present.

Notes

1. See Wilson Jeremiah Moses, *Creation and Conflict in African American Thought* (New York: Cambridge University Press, 2004); Melissa Victoria Harris-Lacewell, *Barbershops, Bibles, and BET: Everyday Talk and Black Political Thought* (Princeton, NJ: Princeton University Press, 2006); Kimberly K. Smith, *African American Environmental Thought: Foundations* (Lawrence: University Press of Kansas, 2007); Nick Bromell, *The Time Is Always Now: Black Thought and the Transformation of Democracy* (New York: Oxford University Press, 2013). Although Patricia Hill Collins first published *Black Feminist Thought* in 1990, she published several revised editions of this "classic" in the twenty-first century. More than any other scholar, she popularized the phrase "black feminist thought."

2. "Constitution," *African American Intellectual History Society*, http://www.aaihs.org/constitution/, accessed March 10, 2017. See Len Gutkin, "New Black Intellectual Histories: The Scholar Brandon Byrd Discusses a Field That Has Been 'Marginalized for Too Long,'" *Chronicle of Higher Education*, September 1, 2020, https://www.chronicle.com/article/new-black-intellectual-histories, accessed October 27, 2020; Brandon R. Byrd, "The Rise of African American Intellectual History," *Modern Intellectual History* (August 7, 2020): 1–32, doi:10.1017/S1479244320000219. It is worth noting that Byrd's article is among the very few articles on African American history that appears in *Modern Intellectual History*.

3. In order to narrow down the focus of this essay, I decided to zero in on historians' contributions to Black intellectual history. Readers will notice that I have not incorporated the scholarship of literary critics. Their scholarship is important and vast. They have analyzed the ideas and minds of novelists, playwrights, and poets in great detail. Implicit and central to their approaches are close readings of their subjects' writings. Notwithstanding cross-disciplinary interactions, most historians have not been significantly influenced by literary criticism. At the same time, I acknowledge that a truly comprehensive study of African American intellectual history would include the works of leading literary critics.

4. Adolph Reed Jr. and Kenneth W. Warren, conclusion to *Renewing Black Intellectual History: The Ideological and Material Foundations of African American Thought*, ed. Reed and Warren (Boulder, CO: Paradigm, 2010), 304.

5. Thorpe is an important figure in Black intellectual history. He authored the first major studies on Black historians. See *Negro Historians in the United States* (Baton Rouge, LA: Fraternal, 1958); *Black Historians: A Critique* (New York: Morrow, 1971). *The Mind of the Negro* was not widely and positively reviewed. See, for instance, August Meier, review, *Journal of Negro Education* 30 (Autumn 1961): 410; Winthrop D. Jordan, review, *Journal of Southern History* 28 (November 1962): 496–498. Thorpe responded to Jordan's negative review in Thorpe, review, *Journal of Negro History* 78 (Spring 1993): 123–127.

6. Carter G. Woodson, ed., *The Mind of the Negro as Reflected in Letters Written during the Crisis, 1800–1860* (New York: New American Library, 1970), v. Even after Thorpe, scholars and historians continued to spotlight "the Negro mind." See, for instance, S. P. Fullinwider, *The Mind and Mood of Black America* (Belmont, CA: Dorsey, 1969).

7. See John Herman Randall Jr., *The Making of the Modern Mind* (Boston: Houghton Mifflin, 1926); Perry Miller, *The New England Mind: The Seventeenth Century* (Cam-

bridge, MA: Harvard University Press, 1939); Wilbur J. Cash, *The Mind of the South* (New York: Knopf, 1941); Henry Commager Steele, *The American Mind: An Interpretation of American Thought and Character since the 1880s* (New Haven, CT: Yale University Press, 1950). Widely praised during their times and re-released in subsequent editions, Randall's, Miller's, Cash's, and Steele's works have been credited with significantly shaping American intellectual history during its formative years and are considered by many to be classics.

8. For some examples of how leading White intellectual historians ignored and in some cases trivialized African American intellectuals for the last half century, see Johns Hopkins History of Ideas Club, *Studies in Intellectual History* (Baltimore: Johns Hopkins University Press, 1953); Harvey Wish, *The American Historian: A Social-Intellectual History of the Writing of the American Past* (New York: Oxford University Press, 1960); Robert Allen Skoptheim, *American Intellectual Histories and Historians* (Princeton, NJ: Princeton University Press, 1966); John Higham and Paul K. Conkin, eds., *New Directions in American Intellectual History* (Baltimore: Johns Hopkins University Press, 1979). First published in the late 1980s, David A. Hollinger and Charles Capper's popular two-volume *The American Intellectual Tradition: A Sourcebook* largely ignored African American intellectuals with the exception of Frederick Douglass, Du Bois, Martin Luther King Jr., Malcolm X, and Ralph Ellison. In *The American Intellectual Tradition* (2012), Hollinger did discuss the evolving place of Black intellectuals, reducing them to being "race theorists." See Hollinger, "What Is Our 'Canon'? How American Intellectual Historians Debate the Core of Their Field," *Modern Intellectual History* 9 (2012): 193–194. In his exhaustive, eight-hundred-plus–page *The Modern Mind: An Intellectual History of the 20th Century* (New York: HarperCollins, 2001)—a narrative of "the great ideas that have shaped the twentieth century" and "the achievement of twentieth-century thought"—historian Peter Watson mentions, in passing, a small cadre of Black intellectuals, mainly acclaimed twentieth-century novelists. He describes Du Bois, "one of the black minority," as being "a small, bearded, aloof academic from Fisk and Harvard Universities" (6, 109).

9. Two recently published essays in *Modern Intellectual History* focus on Black historical subject matter. See Andrew M. Fearnley, "When the Harlem Renaissance Became Vogue: Periodization and the Organization of Postwar American Historiography," *Modern Intellectual History* 11 (2014): 59–87; Edward J. Blum, "The Triumph of the Negro Intellectual," *Modern Intellectual History* 12 (2015): 253–263.

10. David A. Hollinger, "American Intellectual History, 1907–2007," *OAH Magazine of History* (April 2007): 14–17.

11. A bright spot is Ulrich Johannes Schneider's vision of the global intellectual history. Although heavily Eurocentric, he calls for the inclusion of some Black voices in an encyclopedic overview of global intellectual history. See Schneider, "Intellectual History in a Global Age: *The International Dictionary of Intellectual History*," *Journal of the History of Ideas* 66 (April 2005): 143–154.

12. Lewis R. Gordon, "Reasoning in Black: Africana Philosophy under the Weight of Misguided Reason," *Savannah Review* 1 (November 2012): 88.

13. Thorpe did not, however, totally ignore enslaved Blacks' consciousness. Not only

did he speculate on bondspersons' behavior patterns but he also cited enslaved persons' testimonies from Works Progress Administration (WPA) narratives.

14. Earl E. Thorpe, *The Mind of the Negro: An Intellectual History of Afro-Americans* (Westport, CT: Negro Universities Press, 1970), xi, xii.

15. Ibid., xviii, xiii.

16. Drew Maciag, "When Ideas Had Consequences—Or, Whatever Happened to Intellectual History?" *Reviews in American History* 39 (December 2011): 743–745.

17. Hollinger, "American Intellectual History," 14.

18. Russell Jacoby, "A New Intellectual History?" *American Historical Review* 97 (April 1992): 405–424; Dominick LaCarpa, "Intellectual History and Its Ways," *American Historical Review* 97 (April 1992): 425–439.

19. Editorial, *Modern Intellectual History* 1 (2004): 1–2.

20. See Pero Gaglo Dagbovie, *What Is African American History?* (Cambridge, UK: Polity Press, 2015).

21. The first mention of the term "Negro intellectual history" that I was able to locate is in the title of a dissertation that was announced in the *Chicago Defender* in 1935. See "Atlanta Adds Two French Teachers," *Chicago Defender*, November 23, 1935, 10. The column notes that G. B. Harris, professor at Atlanta University from Guadeloupe, was writing a dissertation, "Abbé Henri Grégoire: A Source of Negro Intellectual History." Given that Grégoire was a French Roman Catholic priest and outspoken abolitionist, Harris certainly did not conceptualize "Negro intellectual history" in ways future scholars would. Also see Ernest Kaiser, review, *Freedomways* 9 (Winter 1969): 24–41. During the 1960s the term was evoked without any real theorization. During the 1970s and 1980s, "Afro-American intellectual history" and "Black intellectual history" were used interchangeably.

22. In the mid-1990s, literary critic Hortense J. Spillers lamented that the twenty-fifth anniversary of *The Crisis* was not acknowledged, but during the new millennium, Cruse's legacy has certainly been reinvoked. In 2002 historian Jelani Cobb released *The Essential Cruse: A Reader*, and in 2004 *The Crisis of the Negro Intellectual Reconsidered: A Retrospective*, edited by Jerry G. Watts, was published. Several months after Cruse died in March 2005, the *New York Review Books* republished *The Crisis* with an introduction from music and cultural critic Stanley Crouch, who, perhaps inspired by the spirit of Cruse's iconoclasm, claimed that Black intellectual history or a Black intellectual tradition did not exist before and after *The Crisis*.

23. See, for instance, Howard Brotz, ed., *Negro Social and Political Thought, 1850–1920* (New York: Basic Books, 1966); August Meier and Francis Broderick, eds., *Negro Protest Thought in the Twentieth Century* (Indianapolis, IN: Bobbs-Merrill, 1966).

24. W. E. B. Du Bois, *The Souls of Black Folk: Essays and Sketches* (Chicago: McClurg, 1903), 50.

25. See Kelly Miller, *Race Adjustment: Essays on the Negro in America* (New York: Neale, 1908); Lelia Amos Pendleton, *A Narrative of the Negro* (Washington, DC: Pendleton, 1912).

26. Alain Locke, foreword to and "The New Negro" in *The New Negro*, ed. Locke (with an introduction by Arnold Rampersad) (New York: Touchstone, 1997), xxv–xxvii, 3–16.

27. Ralph J. Bunche, "The Programs of Organizations Devoted to the Improvement of the Status of the American Negro," *Journal of Negro Education* 8 (July 1939): 540.

28. Myrdal appropriated a great deal from Bunche's and other Black scholars' research. See Gunnar Myrdal, *An American Dilemma: The Negro Problem and Modern Democracy* (New York: Harper, 1944); David W. Southern, *Gunnar Myrdal and Black-White Relations: The Uses and Abuses of an American Dilemma, 1944–1969* (Baton Rouge: Louisiana State University Press, 1987).

29. Ralph J. Bunche, "Conceptions and Ideologies of the Negro Problem," *Contributions in Black Studies* 9, no. 1 (1992): art. 6, http://scholarworks.umass.edu/cibs/vol9/iss1/6, accessed April 13, 2015.

30. August Meier, *Negro Thought in America, 1880–1915: Racial Ideologies in the Age of Booker T. Washington* (Ann Arbor: University of Michigan Press, 1963), ix, 4, 16, 24, 208.

31. Hanes Walton Jr., "Black Political Thought: The Problem in Characterization," *Journal of Black Studies* 1 (December 1970): 213–218.

32. Judith Stein, "'Of Mr. Booker T. Washington and Others': The Political Economy of Racism in the United States," *Science & Society* 38, no. 4 (1974–1975): 423, 463.

33. Adolph Reed Jr., *Stirrings in the Jug: Black Politics in the Post-Segregation Era* (Minneapolis: University of Minnesota Press, 1999), 29.

34. Sterling Stuckey, *The Ideological Origins of Black Nationalism* (Boston: Beacon, 1972), 5, 6, 26.

35. Wilson Jeremiah Moses, *The Golden Age of Black Nationalism, 1850–1925* (New York: Oxford University Press, 1978), 11, 33, 270.

36. John W. Blassingame, "Ideas without Men," *Reviews in American History* 3 (June 1975): 218–221.

37. John Hope Franklin, foreword to *Black Intellectuals: Race and Responsibility in American Life*, by William Banks (New York: Norton, 1996), ix, ix–xi. During the 1990s other historians noted that Black intellectual history was underdeveloped. See, for instance, Charles Pete Banner-Haley, "Still the Long Journey: Thoughts concerning the State of Afro-American History," *Trotter Review* 5 (June 1991): 13–18. He claims that there was a "paucity of studies done on black intellectuals."

38. Banks, *Black Intellectuals*, xvi.

39. V. P. Franklin considered his study of the Black autobiographical tradition as constituting "an overview of African American intellectual history." See Franklin, *Living Our Stories, Telling Our Truths: Autobiography and the Meaning of the African-American Intellectual Tradition* (New York: Scribner, 1995), 9.

40. Patrick Rael, "The New Black Intellectual History," *Reviews in American History* 29 (September 2001): 357–367. Unclear about what this "new black intellectual history" specifically entailed, Rael suggests, among other things, that historians needed to more thoroughly engage with how "dominant discourses of race" influenced and manipulated antebellum-era Black thinkers.

41. Mia Bay, *The White Image in the Black Mind: African-American Ideas about White People, 1830–1925* (New York: Oxford University Press, 2000), 8.

42. Reed and Warren, introduction to *Renewing Black Intellectual History*, vii, viii, ix.

43. Ibid., 305.

44. Joy James, *Transcending the Talented Tenth: Black Leaders and American Intellectuals* (New York: Routledge, 1997), 56, 57.

45. Mia Bay, Farah J. Griffin, Martha S. Jones, and Barbara D. Savage, eds., *Toward an Intellectual History of Black Women* (Chapel Hill: University of North Carolina Press, 2015), 2, 4, 5. For further discussions of Black women's intellectual history, see Kristin Waters and Carol B. Conaway, eds., *Black Women's Intellectual Traditions: Speaking Their Minds* (Burlington: University of Vermont Press, 2007). Also see the extensive notes in *Toward an Intellectual History of Black Women*.

46. Martha S. Jones, *How Black Women Broke Barriers, Won the Vote, and Insisted on Equality for All* (New York: Basic Books, 2020); Saidiya Hartman, *Wayward Lives, Beautiful Experiments: Intimate Histories of Social Upheaval* (New York: Norton, 2019), xii–xv, 31.

CHAPTER 2

AFROCENTRICITY AND AUTOBIOGRAPHY

HISTORIOGRAPHICAL INTERVENTIONS INTO BLACK INTELLECTUAL TRADITIONS

AARON DAVID GRESSON III

We are not going to share modern civilization just by deserving recognition. We are going to
force ourselves in by organized far-seeing effort—by outthinking and outflanking the owners
of the world today who are too drunk with their own arrogance and power successfully to
oppose us, if we think and learn and do.
—W. E. B. Du Bois, "Education and Work"

I think it is important to say that Afrocentricity is in opposition to the imposition of
particularisms as if they are universal. There has to be cultural and intellectual opportunity in
the curriculum for cultures and people other than European. . . . Intellectual space must be
shared because all humans have contributed to human civilization.
—Molefi Asante, "Why Afrocentricity?"

Obama originally planned to write a book discussing Afrocentrism . . . but changed his mind
and ended up with the autobiography *Dreams of My Father: A Story of Race and Inheritance.*
Nonetheless, *Dreams of My Father* reveals some of his experiences with Afrocentrism and
many reasons why Afrocentrism would be problematic for him. Actually, we can gain insight
into Afrocentrism and into Obama by examining Afrocentrism through Obama's eyes and
Obama through Afrocentric eyes.
—Algernon Austin, "Barack Obama and the Ironies of Afrocentrism"

Black intellectual space—agency in thought, growth, and action—has not always been recognized by those "drunk on their own arrogance and power."
Indeed, it has been undermined in a variety of ways, including suppression
of African ancestry, cultures, languages, and religions. Nonetheless, since the
1960s, Black intellectual space has enlarged and evolved along several trajectories, including Black history, womanist theory, Black queer theory, radical

pragmatism, Black nihilism, Black existential theory or critical theory, Afrofuturism, and Afrocentricity. Together, these various intellectual trajectories have enhanced the place of *alterity*—lived experiences producing differing lens through which to think about and act on the human condition—in the Black Intellectual Tradition.[1]

Afrocentricity's contribution to alterity inheres in its centering the African continent—its diverse cultural traditions and possibilities—in discourses and actions affecting Blacks in diaspora. Its educational significance to the Black Intellectual Tradition is rooted in both its liberation agenda and the twofold strategy—Afrocentric education and Black and/or Africana Studies. The scholarship on Afrocentricity's interface with K–12 urban education and postsecondary Black and/or Africana Studies has been extensive and diverse in scope and frequently contested in terms of its intellectual significance.[2] These works constitute a vast and important addition to the scholarship on Black intellectual thought, but they are not the focus here. Rather, this chapter forefronts the *dialectics* that have both emerged from within and animated Afrocentric discourses, particularly with respect to knowledge and education.[3] The focus here is on the dialectic energizing Black education as an emancipatory project in dialogic praxis with Afrocentricity; and the chapter proposes how the dialectic has contributed to the cultural shift or (multi)cultural turn that helps define Black diasporian identities and intellectual traditions in the twenty-first century.[4] "Afrocentricity *in* Education" is the expression used here to designate the ideological exchanges and educational initiatives linking Black diasporian consciousnesses and activism to an African cultural matrix.

Afrocentricity in Education, I argue, emerged as a discourse out of the inevitable clash of *lived experience* and *visionary agency*, such as expressed in Afrocentrism broadly and Afrocentricity specifically. More precisely, (African) agency lived in the diasporian context not only birthed Afrocentrism but also its various iterations and the associated limitations of any one person's or group's vision of the real or imagined racial past and its relevance to the ongoing liberation project. This necessary alterity of vision has characterized both Afrocentricity—as a variant of Afrocentrism—but also those related visions that seek to affirm or delimit its visionary agency. It is this interplay of visions, expressed as intellectual activism, which has intensified the presence and power of autobiography in both historiography and Black Intellectual Traditions.

In this essay, my approach is autobiographical—thus, it belongs to this discursive turn. I use my own life and scholarly work, as well as that of other scholars, to highlight some of the major thrusts in Afrocentricity *in* Education. In thus privileging the role of autobiography in historiographical inquiry, I am inspired by V. P. Franklin's classic *Living Our Stories*;[5] but I am particularly guided by an emergent model, "historiographical intervention." Jaume Aurell has defined this as a strategy where "historians use their autobiographies, with a more or less deliberate authorial intention, to participate, mediate, and intervene in theoretical debates by using the story of their own intellectual and academic trajectory as the source of historiography."[6] This approach has not been undertaken without concern for "scholarly objectivity" on the part of historians, but they have persisted, convinced of the benefits since there is much in social reality that cannot be captured by the traditional analytic tools. The historian's use of autobiography as a component of truth seeking, moreover, joins it to the Black autobiographical tradition; both share an appreciation of the place of subjectivity in the construction of knowledge and the knowable. Further, both perspectives are related to the "Afrocentric idea" through the prominence it places on individual lived experience and understanding in the creation and/ or recovery of preferred African histories and futures.

Through a selective introduction to Afrocentric education, this chapter considers how autobiographical intervention in Afrocentric education illumines both the inevitability of contradiction in Afrocentric education and discourse. Then I consider how the dialectic essential to autobiographical subjectivity not only strengthened Afrocentric education but ushered in Afrocentricity *in* Education as a nuanced feature of Black Intellectual Traditions. The conclusion gives a prospective reflection on Afrocentricity *in* Education's *evolving* place in discourses of Black diasporian identities as a centering facet of future Black Intellectual Traditions.

Afrocentric Education and Autobiography: Possibilities and Pitfalls

The year is 1960: I am thirteen, living in one of the poorer sections—Berkeley— of Norfolk, Virginia. On this retrospectively special morning, I am hitchhiking a ride with a playmate to downtown Norfolk. Cars are passing, traveling mostly from the Portsmouth tunnel to the James River Bridge joining the two cities; most of the drivers are White, as usual. On this morning, I am "performing" for the drivers by loudly and flamboyantly telling my friend why I am not voting for John Kennedy as president. Most of the drivers pay us no attention; still, both my friend and I laugh, finding humor in the moment.

Back then, I was known as a "smart kid"—although I spoke "bad English," "hooked school" frequently, and was a notorious "classroom clown." Incidents like the above, moreover, would not have seemed unusual, if somewhat embarrassing to "proper Black folk" in my town. Still, despite the possible varied interpretations of this incident and my childhood persona, one idea held sway during the 1960s: *too many Black youths knew far too little about the larger world or their roles within it.* Furthermore, "miseducation" played a role in their deficits. More precisely, twin deficit perspectives—cultural and bioenvironmental—dominated the discourses of Black educational dysfunction. The cultural deficit model declares Blacks suffered from the deficits of poverty and "ethnic" practices that do not lead to school and societal success. Concepts like "low frustration tolerance," "restricted language codes," "bad English," and "inability to delay gratification" were part of this perspective. Closely related but more biologically based was the notion that a confluence of factors predisposed Blacks, in particular, to possible gross neurologically based deficits.

I first encountered these perspectives professionally when I returned to the United States in 1972 to practice school psychology in Philadelphia and Levittown, Pennsylvania: I was assigned to test poor, preschool minorities targeted for remediation due to possible minimal brain damage (PMBD).[7] During this period, I wrote my first articles criticizing the racist underpinnings of White educational and psychological scholarship and perspectives and challenging the strong cultural biases that defined dominant thinking about both Black achievement and genius. Although I had not yet heard of Asa Hilliard, I consider it deeply significant that he published a landmark report of Black giftedness in 1976, around the time I wrote one of the first essays claiming Blacks were potentially gifted and talented in ways not valued by Whites.[8] At the very least, we were two Black psychologists working with Black youth who saw not pathology but *cultural richness* permeating their cognitive behaviors. For my part, my claim for an "African cultural tradition" *and* African American continuity with it was rooted in both autobiography and my training; and it was but a short virtually unconscious move from this "arrogant" gesture to the Afrocentric idea in education: *the African past is both noteworthy and instructive.*[9]

Afrocentric schools were stimulated,[10] in part, by the failure of schools to deliver a range of goods to the minority child, notably with respect to the self-esteem, motivation, and material resources known to be pertinent to both high achievement and matriculation. But these schools had a larger agenda, as well. Influenced by emergent Africanists initiatives, such as Kwame Nkrumah's in Ghana, Afrocentric schools emphasized a concern for both the internal and external forces undermining Black liberation. Emphasis was on taking more control of the education of Black youth by recovering past African traditions and establishing new, more sustainable cultural nationalist traditions here in the United States. While these new Pan-African schools were fueled by the Black Power movement and related social movements, they were not wholly different from earlier Black school movements. Still, these newer initiatives, ranging from Black Muslim temple schools to local community schools, were guided by a rejection of the Eurocentric schooling model in favor of a *cultural* liberation education. Both what was known and knowable were the basis for this alternative vision of Black education.

Ironically, within mainstream (special) education at the time, "culture" was also being echoed in conversations about helping Blacks and the poor to get the right "cultural enrichment," the White middle-class language, values, and behaviors supposedly essential to public school success. This mainstream thinking paralleled, in a manner, the cultural reengagement model of Afrocentric education. While multicultural education represented an enlightened response to the significance of culture to the curriculum and pedagogy in public education, the Afrocentric goal, rather than pursuing greater engagement with "White culture," was recovering and centering traditional African-associated practices and perspectives. Specifically, the goal was to infuse the curriculum—science, history, math, literature, art, and other subjects—with relevant experiences, achievements, and cherished values of Blacks from Africa and elsewhere.

One underpinning assumption of Afrocentric education is that affect and cognition are related; identity, culture, and achievement are inextricably connected. This assumptive underpinning has been present throughout much of the history of Black education and achievement despite the failures prompting the 1960s upsurge in Black education activism. Realizing that not only curricular and pedagogical differences were contributors to the achievement differences among minority and White students, African American parents and community leaders had a long tradition of providing the affective components of a proper education.[11] Molefi Asante examines this issue in a 1991 essay, "An Afrocentric Idea in Education." There, he formally advocates for a strategic (re) turn to African beliefs, values, and traditions in challenging the "miseducation" of Blacks Carter G. Woodson described in his 1933 volume, *The Miseducation of the Negro*. For Asante, culture and ideology are intertwined in that both make a claim on the way a person will understand, relate to, and act on their lived experience. Among the various arguments put forth in this essay, one stood out as central: "place and space." For Asante, both a physical location (Africa) and a worldview (Afrocentrism) were central to *identity and achievement*. In his 1988 classic, *Afrocentricity*, he enlarged the "Afrocentric idea," stating that African cultural traditions could serve "as a critical corrective to a displaced agency among Africans."[12] And, as noted by Martell Teasley and Edgar Tyson, "[c]onsidering that efforts to promote African cultures and agency will continually be challenged by the relentless bombardment of Eurocentric discourse and epistemological assumptions, the Afrocentric project faces a monumental task. We refer to this task as the 'Afrocentric burden.'"[13]

Recognizing (African) agency has led to Afrocentric education's focus on specifying curricula and pedagogies that are pertinent to reversing the perceived detriments of traditional education: Black student alienation, discouragement, and failure. The creation of an alternative learning environment, one presumably infused with African artifacts, has been held as crucial toward this end. But this noble idea contains at least two contradictions, or dialectics: Blacks differ in their personal and familial (group) agencies—they have differential goals and successes within extant schooling forms; and successful implementation of an Afrocentric vision entails both recovery *and* "rebirth," which are, at best, difficult, given individual agency. Afrocentricity *in* Education as discourse—significantly as autobiography—has engaged both recovery and new-birth agenda and the critiques of these initiatives.

Afrocentricity *in* Education:
A Dialectic in Autobiography and Agency

Autobiographies, from the slave narratives to "Black diasporian autobiographies,"[14] have been chronicles of "the Black experience": they have described the daily lives, struggles, sorrows, joys, and hopes of Blacks in diaspora; they have also fueled a range of social movements—antislavery, civil rights, Black Power, Black Lives Matter. Autobiography, thus viewed, is contributory to Black consciousness, to the construction of a "Black experience" and the mobilization of collective agency. In this regard, Sudhi Rajiv, in *Forms of Black Consciousness*, explains the interplay of the rise of Black consciousness and autobiography—and the spirit underlying the Afrocentric idea:

> In Black autobiographies right from the earliest slave narratives down to Cleaver, Jackson and LeRoi Jones[,] . . . the dominant theme . . . has always been the same that of freeing themselves from the traps of the white world to a demand for freedom from the enslavement of the body, mind, and soul and the recovery of manhood. *The autobiographies of Malcolm X and Cleaver while expressing the need for a different identity also point out the inadequacy of the present system to provide the basis for such an identity. They go beyond the shores of white America to look for the basis for a new identity which will take into account the history of the Western World and the alternative being worked out by the new nations of the world.*[15]

The search for satisfactory identities, realized partly through lived experience and narrative representation of that experience, aided both individual and collective self-reflexivity and consciousness. Moreover, autobiographies from one era have influenced those of another. Thus, Frederick Douglass's *Narrative of the Life of Frederick Douglass, an American Slave* (1845) influenced Martinican psychiatrist Franz Fanon's *Black Skin, White Mask* and Angela Davis's *Autobiography*.[16] Additionally, as noted by Thompson, Conyers, and Dawson, Fanon, for example, "used a mixture of autobiographical and theoretical reflection to present a portrait of the struggle for freedom as one against a social world riddled with contradictions."[17]

The underpinnings of Afrocentricity *in* Education likewise have evolved from a blending of theory and autobiography, both individual and collective. And contradiction has been an important motivator, in a variety of ways. In his examination of Afrocentrism, *Afrotopia*, Wilson Moses begins with a potent proposition: "My contention is that black people are like all other people. They have been faced with the task of reconciling the ironies and contradictions that we all perceive in our minds and in the worlds that surround us. If black social thinkers have sometimes appeared to be tortured, inconsistent, and ambivalent, that is only evidence that they have reflected with honesty on the human condition."[18] In this passage, my old friend's authorial reflection exudes more than a bit of *autobiographical authority*: he recognizes that Afrocentrism is an agenda linked to the human condition, and, as such, it is heir to contradictions. Yes! Afrocentricism is dialectical, but more than this, it is self-reflexive. And, through *self-reflexivity* we may gain dynamic access to the character of this dialectic. This reflexivity is a central component of Afrocentric theory and method. It is also an interstitial part of the critiques prompted by Afrocentrism, generally, and Afrocentricity, in particular.

Some scholars engaged in self-reflexivity, often broadly, often drawing upon their own stories. V. P. Franklin, for instance, fused a moment of autobiographical recall to the Afrocentric idea in education as he grappled with retrieving African American cultural agency among Black Philadelphians:

> In the early 1970s as a student of urban educational history, completing my dissertation after the publication of *American Education: The Colonial Experience*, I must admit that I felt liberated by what Lawrence Cremin was doing. I had been studying African-American educational history, and the distinction, between "schooling" and the "educational configurations" that were constructed in ethnic communities over time, was extremely important. In fact, it allowed me to contrast the often inadequate, substandard, segregated schooling made available to Black Philadelphians at public expense, with the rich and varied, formal and informal educational programs and activities sponsored by the social, cultural, and political organizations in the African-American community.[19]

Franklin here, among other things, indicates the fact that Black family and/or community agency includes the capacity to differentiate and create the learning experiences that benefitted their children. In so doing, he is affirming Black awareness of the "schooling" versus "education" distinction and agentic engagement of the Afrocentric idea in education: the Black cultural creation of knowledge and practical action (praxis). Franklin also situates autobiography in the broader Afrocentric project: constructing a critical lens—cultural history—that enables a turning back on the "ethnic group"–and individual—as agentic.

Scholarly interest in Black *cultural* agency, as Franklin reflects, has been an important addition to the Black Intellectual Tradition, offering both instructive and evaluative feedback on the efficacy of self-reliance and culture building in the African American community. Of course, (Black) agency is at the heart of the Afrocentric idea in education. Mwalimu Shujaa comments regarding African American Independent Schools:

> African-American independent schools are products of the African-American social and cultural experience. They exist because of perceived needs for social change and reflect analyses of schooling's role in achieving individual and group goals in the absence of needed change. We find, for example, that African-Americans in the northern states founded and operated schools for their own upliftment as far back as the 1790s. We also find descriptions of how, following Reconstruction, African-Americans in the southern states combined their own resources to establish schools for themselves.

Shujaa, like Franklin, differentiates between schooling and education and affirms the ongoing presence of Black self-reliance and conscious culture-building agency. Also, he witnesses the role of personal lived experience or autobiography in framing the ideological integrity of the Afrocentric idea. In particular, Shujaa contextualizes his own Afrocentric identity with an autobiographical story of great moment:

> In concluding I want to share a personal recollection. . . . In 1957, when I was a second grader at Frederick Douglass School in Parsons, Kansas, my teacher, Miss Lacy Clark, taught a lesson that illustrates how African-Americans who understood the importance of doing so have always had to make strategic distinctions between education and schooling. One morning Miss Clark asked us to stop what we were doing and put everything on our desks away. She then distributed to each of us a copy of a drawing that looked as if it had come from a coloring book. The drawing showed an autumn scene in which a group of children were playing with leaves tumbling from their branches. The children were dressed warmly in caps, jackets, and scarves.
>
> Miss Clark collected our drawings when the bell for recess rang. When we returned after recess and took our seats, Miss Clark announced the winner of the prize. It turned out to be (*sic*) a boy who had colored the faces of the children in the picture brown to match his own. He was the only student among this class of 25 African-American children to do so. The rest of us had colored in every detail of that picture except the faces of the children.[20]

Shujaa's recollection might be that of millions of other Blacks in the diaspora. It poignantly affirms one ill effect of White domination, namely, "psychic dislocation." But it also exposes a dialectic—an important one for many: not all Blacks suffer from it as either individuals and groups; consider the self-aware student in Shujaa's class and among Franklin's Black Philadelphians.

As seen in the Franklin and Shujaa excerpts, Afrocentricity *in* Education has been inevitably influenced by autobiography. It is not at all surprising that scholar activists have framed their intellectual contributions within a narrative depicting both the neglects—scandals and interventions—and successes they have experienced. Both Afrocentricity *and* the existential condition require an authenticity grounded in lived experience, personal stories. And scholars grappling with the contemporary intellectual project invariable face this fact. For instance, George Dei begins his essay on Afrocentricity and pedagogy in this way:

> I focus on why and how I construct and legitimize Afrocentric knowledge, and I examine the pedagogical implications of Afrocentricity as an alternative way of knowing about the world. At the onset, it is important for me to locate myself as a continental African by birth, and as such I am speaking on Afrocentricity not from a disinterested perspective. It is also relevant that I acknowledge my "privileged" position as a man and a university professor. . . . The education I have received was, and still is, historically and socially constructed and fully interest-bound. . . . It has been an education that has, for the most part, not cultivated our self-esteem and pride as Africans. Even today, in many circles, Euramerican education continues to distort, misappropriate, and misinterpret many African peoples' lives and experiences.[21]

Dei both affirms and complicates the efficacy of the Afrocentric idea in education—and he illustrates Afrocentricity *in* Education. He echoes the traditional factors affecting Black school achievement in the diaspora: Eurocentric distortions, neglects, and sabotage. Yet, as an African, trained at McMaster University and University of Toronto and teaching outside of the continental United States, he recognizes the inability to speak on Afrocentricity from a *disinterested perspective*. The fact of interest, when applied to agency, generically, and across historical context, pushes us toward the inevitable clash of interests. Thus, there have been two notable tensions: one championed by those who see Afrocentricity as intellectually bankrupt and the other championed by those who recognize much of this criticism as itself illustrative of the need for the Afrocentric presence, which bears emphasis since it confronts both the matter of alterity and existence among Black diasporians.

Afrocentricity *in* Education, then, is a reaction to the challenge to address the need to survive against both the outside and the inside. In this respect, it rehearses the very dialectic in Black education history Ronald E. Butchart describes in his historiography: a dynamic embrace and/or nonembrace of statements and strategies for racial uplift in a racist yet unstable society.[22] Afrocentricity creates its own contradiction (dialectics) as it struggles with a metanarrative—"African essence"—that must ultimately resonate with the lived-experiences and standpoints of others. A distinction between the praxis of K–12 and the academy is notably located here: in schools, success and failure are central concerns, that is, how do Afrocentric principles and practices impact learning and success? Studies have been conducted to answer this basic question. They have generally yielded affirmative yet complicated outcomes with respect to the efficacy of an Afrocentric educational intervention. Clearly, curricula and pedagogies that center Blacks can positively impact self-esteem, motivation, and achievement—and this is generally approved of by educationalists. Yet, there is an overriding sense that this is not enough: there are the challenges of poverty and the social structural mechanisms that reproduce both material and cultural conditions of inequality.

The creation and survival of the Afrocentric idea in contemporary, primarily urban, Black public education are noteworthy both as a practical and intellectual matter. Pragmatically, the possibility of reversing the seemingly interminable academic difficulties of many Black youth is reason enough for the search for effective tools. Intellectually, the commitment to evaluate the proposed interventions reflect the logic within the pragmatist skepticism: that is, does it work? A profound dialectic is implicit here. And it is here that the proactive quality of Afrocentric interventions grates up against alterity or diverse agencies in a provocative, expansive manner. In *Black in School: Afrocentric Reform, Urban Youth, and the Promise of Hip-Hop Culture*, Shawn A. Ginwright cogently summarizes the dialectical tension:

> As an advocate for African-centered approaches to educating African American children, I have come to realize that many Afrocentric discussions and debates tend to be limited to scholars, students in the academy, educators. And some practitioners. Granted, there are groups of young self-educated members of black-nationalist organizations that subscribe to an Afrocentric philosophy, but for the most part, Afrocentric ideas have been confined primarily to the black, educated middle class.[23]

Ginwright's critique echoes—like Black Marxism—a critical strain in the Black Intellectual Tradition that remains alert to class effects of schooling. So many Blacks have not made it—and racism and White domination seem relevant, especially White control of knowledge and knowledge production.[24] In short, Blacks in different life circumstances enjoy different life chances and choices.

This aspect of *Black heterogeneity* (intersectionality) orients us to the ongoing centrality of difference in the Black experience. It also points to the dual tasks attending Afrocentric education: creation *and* assessment of the initiatives felt to be critical for addressing the failures associated with Eurocentric education of Blacks. In Ginwright's words, "Afrocentric reform must be closely tied to a critical understanding of racial and economic justice. From this perspective, black youth connect the cultural utility of Afrocentric education with the day-to-day reality of urban poverty."[25]

Afrocentricity *in* Education pertains to the range of discursive themes and activities evolving out of these dialectically rich agenda. It thus addresses the matter of liberation education—the goal of Afrocentric education—but incites many related discourses around "the Black experience," "African agency," and the possibilities and limits of "collective Black consciousness." Both the highly personal nature and reach of autobiography regarding Afrocentric agency have been nowhere more evident than in the work of Tunde Adeleke, a fierce critic of Afrocentricity. Adeleke argues in *The Case against Afrocentrism* against the explicit and implicit suggestion of a "consciousness of affinity for Africa, sustained by, among others, subscription to African cultural values, advocacy and invocation of African ideals and idiosyncrasies, and the conception of existential realities within an African cosmological framework."[26] Adeleke also argues that Afrocentricity offers little more than "a psychological and therapeutic feel-good-together philosophy."[27] The crucial dialectical and autobiographical factor is seen in his intellectual history of the perspective; one reviewer significantly renarrates the autobiographical keystone:

> *The Case against Afrocentrism* is intellectual history at its best. Adeleke critically analyzes Afrocentrism in five powerful chapters, and offers readers important personal and intellectual insights in his introduction and conclusion. He begins by recounting his personal encounters with Afrocentric scholars and the "intellectual intolerance" that these intellectuals have directed at him for critiquing Afrocentric ideas.[28]

In this excerpt, we glean both the highly personal nature of Adekele's engagement with the Afrocentric idea and the dialectics animating his challenges to it. It is noteworthy that often critics, as well as adherents to Afrocentricity, have fused their lived experiences and critical take on Afrocentricity. For instance, Moses embeds his grudging support of Afrocentricity in an autobiographical context:

> The strongest argument in favor of Afrocentrism is that it guides many of its adherents in the direction of increased cultural literacy. . . . The Afrocentrist dreams of appropriating the high culture of classical civilization, and disdains the low culture of gangsta rap. . . . In my personal experiences with black nationalists, including Black Muslims and many Afrocentrists, I have found that they insist, to their credit, that gangsta rap must be understood as social pathology. Unfortunately, many of these same black nationalist . . . [express] antiintellectualism . . . [in] their paranoid ravings about the ice man inheritance, Jewish conspiracies, and melanin theory.[29]

Moses here conveys precisely the ideological predilection that many of us jettisoned in the 1960s and 1970s. To be sure, there are legitimate aspects of Afrocentric-inspired scholarship that can and should be challenged. And a large body of work has taken this on. By joining with those Black nationalists who see Hip Hop as social pathology, Moses perhaps shows precisely the *dialectics of betrayal*—often cited as "Black contradictions"—of which he accuses W. E. B. Du Bois and others—which, in a moment of Afrocentric self-compassion, he recognizes as human.

Scholars like Mia Bay have also recognized contradictions in what Black people say, think, and do.[30] Bay, for instance, describes how many antebellum Black abolitionists and antiracists, nonetheless, drew problematic—contradictory—descriptions between Whites and Blacks in terms of ethnology: Blacks being superior to Whites, more Christlike, redeemers, and so forth. It is difficult to transcend this dialectical trap, although some have tried to imagine an escape for Afrocentricity, with some persuasiveness.[31] Perhaps, awareness and acknowledgment of the dialectic are critical links in the liberation process itself. Here I am reminded of a saying attributed to Booker T. Washington: "If you want to lift yourself up, lift up someone else."[32]

The significance of this struggle with one's own autobiography and the Afrocentric idea is worth thinking about a bit more. Consider Asante who has said, "I was never affected by the Du Boisian double-consciousness." Why? He recalls a past free of *othering* by the oppressor; he did not become torn by ambivalence or "twoness." Recalling his childhood in 1950s Georgia, Asante reflects:

> [The] tightly knit community of Africans who lived on the dirt roads of Valdosta never saw themselves as intellectually or physically inferior to whites. There existed no reference points outside of ourselves despite the economic and psychological poverty of our situation. . . . It might have been another matter if I had gone to school and to church with whites when I was younger. I might have suffered confusion, double-consciousness, but I did not.[33]

Millions of African Americans can probably tell a similar story of "escape" from the psychic damages of racial oppression; to be sure, many of us rejected the idea of massive, totalizing racial damage—"the mark of oppression"—popularized by Abram Kardiner and Lionel Ovesey in their book *The Mark of Oppression*.[34] Still, many of us did relate to the psychic tension Du Bois wrote about. This seems even true for Woodson; regarding Woodson's links to Afrocentricity, Greg Wiggan comments: "Although Woodson's early education was limited due to his commitment to supporting his family in the West Virginia coalfields, he completed high school and later earned a Ph.D. from Harvard. However, he argued that it took him almost twenty years to undo the miseducation and psychological and emotional trauma he endured at Harvard."[35]

While disclaiming psychic miseducation for himself, Asante recognizes we are vulnerable to these psychic wounds. His argument for both the need for and efficacy of the Afrocentric presence in Black education is grounded in his autobiographical awareness that so many fail to escape psychic displacement. Without exploring all aspects of Asante's self-reported escape of "twoness," we can, nonetheless, see that he is fusing autobiography—lived experience—to ideology, Afrocentricity. It is, thus, not surprising that his critics routinely allude to his autobiographical linkage to the ideology of Afrocentricity. Moses is merely one voice in this regard: "Since 1980 Asante has amended his definition [of Afrocentrism] several times, so that recent formulations are vastly more imaginative than his original statement."[36]

To be sure, Asante's narrative of self has evolved, and his engagement of the notion of Afrocentrism has as well. It is in autobiography that the Afrocentric idea must evolve and change; the implicit agency within the Afrocentric idea does not truncate itself. As we change, so must our ideas, if we are honest. Candidly, my own scholarship has been full of starts and stops, ideologically, and I have been challenged and chided more than once for my own contradictions in this regard. Of course, I ascribe this evolution to the inevitable and desirable intertextuality that marks the Black intellectual Tradition under conditions of alterity and Black diaspora.

Alterity and Afrocentricity in Education: Diasporian Identities

Afrocentricity *in* Education has hastened the inevitable return to the eternal struggle around existence and essence; and their seemingly shared embrace of something approaching an "essential" African cultural reality understandably concerns certain groups of scholars. Not surprising, perhaps, I titled my first book (in 1982) *The Dialectics of Betrayal: Sacrifice, Violation, and the Oppressed*,[37] largely because of both my own internal contradictions and the relational and ideological contradictions animating issues such as Black sexism, Black classism, and interracial duplicity. Only years later have I come to recognize that the focus on dialectics within my scholarship and self were inextricably linked and interstitial to Black emancipation—and the strong role of subjectivity and alterity in it.

Asante gave formal theoretical formulation to centrality of subjectivity to the Afrocentric spirit. But what is all too often missed is the deeply personal, existential basis for the eventual attraction to the idea of an African past prior to the arrival of the Whites and his claims. Asante describes in *Afrocentric Manifesto*: "I am a child of seven generations of the Africans who have lived in America. My entire life, including career, struggle against oppression, search for ways to overturn hegemony, political outlook, fortunes and misfortunes, friends and detractors, has been impacted by my Africanness. It is an essential reality of an African living in America."[38] This is important—it brings together lived experience, biohistory, and *resistance*.

Many do not share this memory of their past or an affiliation with Africa; anti-Afrocentrists often make this very point in affirming their nonessentialist manifesto. Still, Asante does, as do many who identify themselves as Afrocentrists. In so doing, he implicitly echoes Stokely Carmichael, who chided reporters' challenge of the notion "Black power" and paraphrased Oscar Wilde with his retort, "Criticism is autobiography." Popularly, this maxim has been understood to say that we often reach from deep within to gather the will and critical tools with which to offer an alternative view of what is what. The Afrocentric idea— the primacy of me as an African—took many of us into unfamiliar territory in the 1960s and 1970s. But we were individually and collectively grounded in autobiography—a story that differed from those told by others about us; as we gained a fuller appreciation both of their lives and their arrogance, we gained courage to both recover useable pasts and construct valid fictions. But even back then, some of us understood the complicated, though familiar, venture we were undertaking: I can recall as if it were just yesterday musing with the late Rhett Jones, in his Cranston, Rhode Island, home, over a bottle of local beer, that *someday only those would be Black who wanted to be Black*.

This attitude expressed our shared, co-constructed experiences and interpretations of the ever-changing nature of "Blackness" in the diaspora. Afrocentricity was an expression of this attitude as well. Asante has recently written: "Afrocentricity holds that all definitions are autobiographical."[39] Afrocentricity came forth as a way of refocusing the "Black" person in diaspora back upon his or her "Origins"—the cultures, traditions, and stories, real and imagined, that predate contact with aggressive, enslaving cultural contacts. With respect to Jones and me back then in the 1980s, such a belief reflects our different yet convergent biographies. It also points to the ironic in life; the uncertainties, the contradictions, the flip-flops, and ever-present possibility of "being bamboozled."

What did the enslaved Africans know, forget, intuit, and concede? This is an ontological and epistemological question. It is also the question of past facts and fictions, actual and hoped-for attainments both preceding and following the diasporian experience. At core, Afrocentric education and Afrocentricity in education are aspects of the Black Intellectual Tradition that have attempted to both chronicle and construct liberation education following the Black experience created by encounter and engagement with racialized realities within Euro-American oppression. A dialectical tension has been always operative within this context.

Ironically, perhaps, the essential African-ness of irony and its persistence into the African American diasporic experience was suggested by Henry Louis Gates Jr. in his important work *The Signifying Monkey*, where he links in kinship the

African American "icon" the Signifying Monkey to the African trickster god Esu Elegbara.[40] In this powerful book of literary theory and criticism, Gates attempts to enrich understanding of the Black tradition's verbal handling of the complexities of being both human and Black, especially when "Black" is not real. Asante, interestingly, shows sympathy for Gates's project here but goes on to note: "Blackness is more than a biological fact; indeed, it is more than color; it functions as a commitment to a historical project that places the African person back on center and, as such, it becomes an escape to sanity."[41] This is a profound statement: it does not reject the existential, the givenness of being, yet it recognizes that being, once historicized, that is, defined by another's agency (such as the racist's designation of African as Black, bad, and inhuman), invites, impels a counteragency that points us toward the autobiographical and the Afrocentric idea.

Not surprising, Gates himself took to the autobiographical when he attempted to establish an almost eerily affinity between his Esu and the Signifying Monkey: "In a curious way, which I was to realize only much later, my discovery of *Esu* was a rediscovery; for my supervisor at Cambridge, John Holloway, had forced me to read Frobenius's *The Voice of Africa*, a decade ago, and it was there that I first met *Esu-Elegbara*. But it was the Afro-American tradition that generated the concept of Signifyin(g)."[42] Here Gates joins his own autobiographical connection to the Afrocentric idea as he fuses an African persona of irony and the existential—Esu —to its Afro-American cousin—the Signifying Monkey. He thereby, also ironically, joins with Asante in a gesture of Afrocentric recovery.

The tension implicit in these differing remembrances and commitments to an "essential" Black cultural tradition is important to emergent Black Intellectual Traditions. At core, this is a matter of both the authenticity and efficacy of a Black experience. Taken up by scholars concerned with the ontological significance of racialization and the human condition,[43] this matter led me to respond in *The Recovery of Race in America* to the Asante-Gates dialectic:

> Let there be clarity regarding "the traditions of 'the race'": Black people came to this continent in chains and survived by becoming one family—a "Black Family." This has been mainly a fictional family, but a family nonetheless. As whites lost their myths, so did Blacks. This is the combined message of [Joseph] Campbell [in *Hero of a Thousand Faces*] and Wilson Moses [in *Black Messiahs and Uncle Toms*]. Individual Blacks have validated this message in their choices of mates, politics, sexuality, social lifestyles, and so forth. By exposing the language symbolically conveying the rituals and traditions constituting the traditional "Black family," Gates exposes the contradiction.[44]

In this passage, I was both critiquing and grieving the "Black" human condition. I was critiquing both Gates and Asante for their contradictions, each embracing the very "arrogance" each challenged, and I was grieving out shared fate—having to essentialize even as we try to finesse this human need.

The Afrocentric idea is a critical movement toward enlargement of the Black and/or African American experience and societal agency through recovery of presumably lost cultural imperatives from an African past that must be regained to further the global liberation project. At core, the Afrocentric idea is an affirmation: established societies throughout history have had their own cultures, including narratives of origin, accomplishment, and purpose; the enslavement of African identified peoples interrupted and corrupted these cultural trajectories. The varied initiatives directed at arguing for and rejecting this affirmation constitute a new chapter in the Black Intellectual Tradition.

There is, in short, the recognition of the need to deal with existential matters. This need exposes, perhaps, the fact that Afrocentric education as schooling is not enough; there must be a renewal of Black folk, in coalition with others suffering under the form of capitalism dominating this nation if critical changes are to be realized. This fact regarding the global social structural challenge flows into a particularly persistent line of critique: the inaccuracies and mythological underpinnings of Afrocentricity *in* Education. What is the "Black" presence and share in the past glories of African civilizations? Related to this, of necessity, is the matter of an African and/or Black essence. Although not necessarily a postmodernist critique, this stance pursues the matter of differences among Blacks; as Adeleke correctly observes: "There is no one African and black Diaspora experience."[45]

Concluding Thoughts

I returned to Morgan State University as an adjunct in sociology after retiring from Penn State in 2008. Among my teaching assignments is an introductory sociology course. Recently in this class of forty students from across the world—Baltimore, Africa, Caribbean and West Indies, Middle East—I had a now-common experience: during a lecture on the social construction of race, my Black diasporians were especially excited about and attuned to the idea that race is a social construction and that identities are largely shifting, negotiated, and highly dependent on social interaction for whatever stability they have. I found students asking me, "What am I?" They were truly open to being told whether they were West Indian or African if they had a parent from either place. This fluidity or comfort in shifting identities is familiar to those who have understood the cultural turn to mean a shift in understanding how meaning and knowledge are dependent on the interplay of identities and interactions.[46] In short, alterity, notably Black diasporian diversity, has complicated Afrocentricity and the Black-liberation agendas in promising ways. But alterity is a complicated reality to maneuver, especially for individual Blacks and scholars.

Lewis Gordon, in the chapter "A Problem of Biography in Africana Thought" from his *Existentia Africana*,[47] argues we Blacks are perceived as so vastly alienated from humanity in the sight of others that we are rushed headlong toward a kind of nothingness, described as "epistemic closure" (there is nothing novel to be known) or racial essence—I am wholly "Blackness." This is a heady, paradoxical, even contradictory proposition: we Blacks cannot escape "Black existence."[48] And yet, "Black existence" is not *being* until we construct and/or perform it.

In beginning his important study on Black existentialist thought with this philosophical, epistemological, and–need I say—existential matter, Gordon exposes the instructive irony within Afrocentricity *in* Education for the Black Intellectual Tradition: Afrocentricity, like the Black autobiography birthing it, can be liberating, but it must not escape into stasis, reductionism, and inauthenticity. In his words, "That black voices are already locked in the biographical and autobiographical moment transforms these moments from the contingent to the necessary." In Gordon's case, he clarifies that his own use of the autobiographical moment in his book affirms his appreciation of its relevance. However, he continues: "My concern is with the implications of the ongoing practice of locking black intellectuals and their productions in the biographical moment."[49]

It is, I believe, partially through rejecting entrapment in the "necessary" pursuit of a "universal subjectivity"—the "Black experience"—that scholars such as Gordon enlarged the discourses attending Afrocentricity *in* Education. Of course, to do so requires at least a partial engagement of the autobiographical moment as a dialectical project. Alterity has emerged as an increasingly significant aspect of this conversation, in particular, alternative lived experiences, subjectivities, interpretations, and preferred life choices. Implicit in the idea of an unlocked Black autobiography are the dialectical changes that occur within the individual her- or himself, as well as those interlocking but shifting identities between related folk.

A powerful illustration of this newer direction is found in an excellent essay by a young Black diasporian, Ryan Jobson. In an undergraduate study on the interface of Afrocentricity and its existential significance, he shares:

> For me, the tension between my inherited, ethnic identities and a racialized, black identity was reconciled through my engagement with various diasporic texts and cultural productions. . . . At the age of 14, I consumed Malcolm [X]'s narrative, strongly identifying with his bicultural heritage—of Grenadian and African American descent—which he reconciled through the diasporic philosophies of Garveyism and the Nation of Islam. The sense of rootedness proclaimed by both movements, centered in a physical and ideological return to Africa, respectively, was attractive for someone such as me. . . . Embracing the narrative of Alex Haley's renowned work Roots, another text I readily consumed, I viewed Africa as the source and object of my racial identity. The

philosophy of Afrocentricity, alongside that of other black nationalist movements such as Garveyism, the Nation of Islam, and its offshoot the Nation of Gods and Earths (a.k.a. the Five Percent Nation), was a useful heuristic in forging a narrative of racial subjectivity.

This young's man's autobiographical reflection is not only impressive and powerful; it is also suggestive and instructive. First, this essay is a student research project undertaken at the University of Pennsylvania, and we can readily detect the quality of his "schooling." But education and Afrocentric praxis are equally evident, for he states further: "Upon enrolling as an undergraduate at the University of Pennsylvania, I joined the staff of the Ase Academy, which as an African-centered educational program for middle and high school students in the surrounding Philadelphia area embraced the ideals of Pan-Africanism and Afrocentricity with which I personally identified."[50]

This young man's autobiographical reflection or manifesto points to several of the themes taken up in this essay. Namely, Afrocentric education will continue to claim a place in the lives of many Black families who experience benefit from its curricular and pedagogical enhancements of liberation education.[51] Afrocentricity *in* Education also participates in this process, especially among a new generation of scholars who engage the challenges of Black alterity. We see it, as well, among the broad array of Black diasporians who remain intrigued by the invitation within Afrocentricity and choose to fuse aspects of its claims—real and imagined—into their personal narratives, even as they reject others. In this context, the Black Intellectual Tradition promises to both impact and be, in its turn, influenced by the inevitable challenges and promise of diasporians oriented to the invitation of Africology and/or Black Studies and their alterities.[52] And Afrocentricity *in* Education has emerged as an important *liberating* contribution to the ever-emerging discourses within the various Black Intellectual Traditions.[53]

Notes

1. Alterity is a complex concept; here I am using it simply to signal that which can and does occur because of agency and difference. Further discussions of the notion, however, are worth noting; see Joyce E. King, *Afrocentric Praxis of Teaching* for *Freedom* (1947; New York: Routledge, 2016), 190; Michael Birenbaum Quintero, "Utterance, against Orality, beyond Textuality," in *The Caribbean Oral Tradition: Literature, Performance, and Practice*, ed. Hanétha Vété-Congolo (Springer, 2016), 126–166.

2. The wide range of criticism stimulated by Afrocentric scholars is not only vast, it is also highly important to the enlargement of both Black and Anglo intellectual historiography on agency and essentialism in historical discourse. I do not delve into this larger literature although it clearly bears greatly on the question of Afrocentricity's efficacy. Important works on this topic include Ketra L. Armstrong, "Black Students'

Responses to Afrocentric Communication Stimuli," *Journal of Black Psychology* 31 (February 2005): 67–86; Prince Brown Jr. "Educational Achievement in a Multiethnic Society: The Case for an Afrocentric Model," *Afrocentric Scholar* 4 (December 1996); B. Cooksey, "Afrocentricity: Will This New Approach to Education Provide the Answers to a System Plagued with Inequalities," *Journal of Law & Education* 22, no. 1 (1993): 127–133; Rachel M. Cohen, "The Afrocentric Education Crisis," *American Prospect*, September 2, 2016, http://prospect.org/; Rhett Jones, "One Africanity or Many? Researching the Structural Location of Blackness," *International Journal of Africana Studies* 8 (Fall 2002): 27–43, 116; Subira Kifano, "Afrocentric Education in Supplementary Schools: Paradigm and Practice at the Mary McLeod Bethune Institute," *Journal of Negro Education* 65, no. 2 (1996): 209–218; Kmt G. Shockley, "Literatures and Definitions: Toward Understanding Afrocentric Education," *Journal of Negro Education* (Spring 2007): 103–117.

3. As I use the term, "dialectics" refers to the creative tensions generic to agency and its alterities. From this perspective, any given moment or movement contains the seeds of its limitation or difference.

4. Paget Henry, "Sociology: After the Linguistic and Multicultural Turns," *Sociological Forum* 10, no. 4 (1995): 633–652.

5. V. P. Franklin, *Living Our Stories, Telling Our Truths: Autobiography and the Making of the African-American Intellectual Tradition* (New York: Scribner's, 1995).

6. J. Aurell, "Making History by Contextualizing Oneself: Autobiography as Historiographical," *History and Theory* 54 (2015): 244–268.

7. Barton D. Schmitt, "The Minimal Brain Dysfunction Myth," *American Journal of Diseases of Children* 129, no. 11 (1975): 1313–1318.

8. A. G. Hilliard III, *Alternatives to IQ Testing: An Approach to the Assessment of Gifted "Minority" Children (Final Report to the Special Education Support Unit)* (Sacramento: California State Department of Education, 1976), ERIC Document Reproduction Service No. ED 147 009; Aaron D. Gresson and David G. Carter Sr., "In Search of the Potentially Gifted: Suggestions for the School Administrator," *Clearing House* 50, no. 8 (1977): 369–371; Aaron D. Gresson and David G. Carter, "Equal Educational Opportunity for the Gifted: In Search of a Legal Standard," *NOLPE School Law Journal* 6, no. 2 (1978): 145–154. In recent decades, a fair bit of scholarship has been generated on Black giftedness, particularly, in the important work of Donna Ford. See Donna Ford, *Reversing Underachievement among Gifted Black Students: Theory, Research and Practice*, 2nd ed. (Waco, TX: Prufrock, 2010).

9. See Aaron D. Gresson, "The Sociology of Social Pathology: Focus on Black Education," *Black Sociologist* 6, no. 2 (1978): 25–39, and "The Black Special Educator as Educational Pathologist," *Journal of Negro Education*, 49, no. 1 (1980): 31–41.

10. Martell Teasley, Jandel Crutchfield, Sheara A. Williams Jennings, M. Annette Clayton, and Nathern S. A. Okilwa, "School Choice and Afrocentric Charter Schools: A Review and Critique of Evaluation Outcomes," *Journal of African American Studies* 20, no. 1 (2016): 99–119.

11. Janice Hale-Benson, *Black Children: Their Roots Culture and Learning Styles*, rev. ed. (Baltimore: Johns Hopkins University Press, 1986).

12. M. K. Asante, "Afrocentricity, Race, & Reason. Race and Reason," cited in Judith-

Ann Stewart, *Journal of Black Studies* 29, no. 2 (1998): 306–17, http://www.jstor.org/stable/2668095.

13. Martell Teasley and Edgar Tyson, "Cultural Wars and the Attack on Multiculturalism: An Afrocentric Critique," *Journal of Black Studies* 37, no. 3 (2007): 393.

14. Phyllis B. Bischof, "The Power and Place of Black Diasporan Autobiography: An Annotated Bibliography of Autobiographies," in *African Diasporas in the New and Old Worlds: Consciousness and Imagination*, ed. Genevieve Fabre and Klaus Benesch (Amsterdam: Rodopi, 2004), 322–353.

15. Sudhi Rajiv, *Forms of Black Consciousness* (New York: Advent, 1992), 42, emphasis added.

16. Angela Y. Davis, *Angela Davis: An Autobiography* (New York: Random, 1974).

17. Julius E. Thompson, James L. Conyers Jr., and Nancy J. Dawson, eds., *The Frederick Douglass Encyclopedia* (Santa Barbara, CA: Greenwood, 2010), 23.

18. Wilson Jeremiah Moses, *Afrotopia: The Roots of African American Popular History* (New York: Cambridge University Press, 1998), 95.

19. V. P. Franklin, "Education in Urban Communities in the United States: Exploring the Legacy of Lawrence A. Cremin," *Paedagogica Historica*, 39, no. 1–2 (2003): 160–161.

20. Mwalimu J. Shujaa, ed., *Too Much Schooling, Too Little Education: A Paradox of Black Life in White Societies* (Trenton, NJ: Africa World Press, 1994), 362–363, 362–363, 33.

21. George Dei, "Afrocentricity: A Cornerstone of Pedagogy," *Anthropology & Education Quarterly* 25, no. 1 (1994):3–28.

22. Ronald E. Butchart, "'Outthinking and Outflanking the Owners of the World': A Historiography of the African American Struggle for Education," *History of Education Quarterly* 28 (Fall 1988): 333–366.

23. Shawn A Ginwright, *Black in School: Afrocentric Reform, Urban Youth, and the Promise of Hip-Hop Culture* (New York: Teachers College Press, 2004), 2.

24. See Kamui Rashid, "Jacob H. Carruthers and the African Centered Discourse on Knowledge, Worldview, and Power," *Journal of Pan African Studies*, 5, no. 4 (2012): 24–45.

25. Ginwright, *Black in School*, 2–3.

26. Tunde Adeleke, *The Case against Afrocentrism* (Jackson: University Press of Mississippi, 2009), xi.

27. Ibid., 180.

28. Gregory D. Smithers, review of *The Case against Afrocentrism*, by Tunde Adeleke, *African Studies Review* 53, no. 22 (2010): 188–190.

29. Moses, *Afrotopia*, 34.

30. Mia Bay, *The White Image in the Black Mind: African-American Ideas about White People 1830–1925* (New York: Oxford University Press, 2000).

31. Mark Lawrence McPhail, "From Complicity to Coherence: Rereading the Rhetoric of Afrocentricity," *Western Journal of Communication* 62, no. 2 (1998): 14–40. The work of Joyce King has been especially important in addressing the dialectical challenge implied here; see, for example, Joyce Elaine King and Carolyn Ann Mitchell, *Black Mothers to Sons: Juxtaposing African American Literature with Social Practice*, 2nd ed. (New York: Lang, 1995), where King describes her rationale and methodology for a "dialectical research strategy" for the recovery of "cultural knowledge."

32. Booker T. Washington, "Quotes from *Up from Slavery*," https://www.goodreads.com/author/quotes/84278.Booker_T_Washington.

33. Molefi Kete Asante, "Racism, Consciousness, and Afrocentricity," in *Lure and Loathing: Essays on Race, Identity, and the Ambivalence of Assimilation*, ed. Gerald Early (New York: Penguin, 1993), 136, 133, 137.

34. Abram Kardiner and Lionel Ovesey, *The Mark of Oppression: A Psychological Study of the American* Negro (New York: Norton, 1951).

35. Greg Wiggan, "Afrocentricity and the Black Intellectual Tradition and Education: Carter G. Woodson, W. E. B. Du Bois, and E. Franklin Frazier," *Journal of Pan African Studies* 3, no. 9 (2010): 128–149, 140.

36. Moses, *Afrotopia*, 2.

37. Aaron D. Gresson III, *The Dialectics of Betrayal: Sacrifice, Violation, and the Oppressed* (Norwood, NJ: Ablex, 1982). Also see Bay, *White Image*.

38. M. K. Asante, *An Afrocentric Manifesto: Toward an African Renaissance* (Cambridge, UK: Polity, 2007), 2.

39. Molefi Kete Asante, "Afrocentricity," April 13, 2009, *Asante.net*, http://www.asante.net/articles/1/afrocentricity/.

40. Henry Louis Gates Jr., T*he Signifying Monkey: A Theory of African-American Literary Criticism* (New York: Oxford University Press, 1988).

41. Molefi Asante, *The Afrocentric Idea* (Philadelphia: Temple University Press, 1988), 125.

42. Gates, *Signifying Monkey*, ix, xx.

43. See Lewis Gordon, introduction to *Africana Philosophy* (New York: Cambridge University Press, 2008), and Molefi Kete Asante, "Lewis Gordon's Existential Cartography," *Asante.net*, January 26, 2015, http://www.asante.net/articles/55/afrocentricity/.

44. Aaron D. Gresson III, *The Recovery of Race in America* (Minneapolis: University of Minnesota Press, 1995), 203.

45. Tunde Adeleke, *The Case against Afrocentrism* (Jackson: University Press of Mississippi, 2009), 116.

46. See Mary Bucholtz and Kira Hall, "Identity and Interaction: A Sociocultural Linguistic Approach," *Discourse Studies* 7, no. 4–5 (2005): 585–614. See also Dexter B. Gordon, *Black Identity: Rhetoric, Ideology, and Nineteenth-Century Black Nationalism* (Carbondale: Southern Illinois University Press, 2006).

47. Lewis Gordon, *Existentia African: Understanding Africana Existential Thought* (New York, Routledge, 2000), 22–24.

48. See Gresson, *Recovery of Race*, 15–17.

49. Gordon, *Existentia African*, 26.

50. Ryan Jobson, "Afrocentricity and Commodity Fetishism : Cultural Objectification and the 'New' African Diaspora," *Penn McNair Research Journal* 2, no. 1 (2010): 3–4, 4.

51. Nadezhda Khokholkova, "Afrocentricity: The Evolution of the Theory in the Context of American History," *Social Evolution & History* 15, no. 1 (2016): 111–125.

52. Jobson, "Afrocentricity," 4.

53. Ibid.

PART II

ARTS AND LETTERS

Introduction

LEONARD HARRIS

Advocacy aesthetics is the leitmotif of African American artistry. Advocacy aesthetics creates and uses forms of beauty through art, music, autobiographies, novels, and all other forms of media to advance social justice. Advocacy is voiced by creative agents, but it is always inside and beside creative works. Advocacy aesthetics includes the meaning of the beautiful and appropriate symmetry, balance, rhythm, melodies, tempos, modes, pentameters, verses, and sayings that promote some form of social justice, whether tethered to conceptions of civil rights, abolition of prisons, Black nationalism, socialism, or civil rights. There is no one form of the aesthetic or entertainment media simply definable as "authentically" African American. There is, however, a legacy of advocacy within a vast differentiated world of aesthetic temperaments. The chapters of part 2 explore the advocacy modality that helps establish the outlines of the unique heritage within and outside the American heritage that especially resonates with the civil rights era; the too often neglected memories, leadership, and voices of Black women; and different artistic genres.

Jeffrey Lamar Coleman in "Singing *Is* Swinging: The Soul Force of Twentieth-Century Black Protest Music" contends that singing is itself an agent, an agent of swing when the songs are songs of socially conscious formation. Moreover, just as various methods of protest, for example, Martin Luther King Jr.'s moral pacifism and nonviolent direct action and Malcolm X's warrant for violent self-defense, are complementary forms of social action aimed to achieve a common goal, and music from sharecroppers to urban-based Public Enemy to the eclectic Prince are complementary forms of swinging. Singing helps engender a feeling of empowerment; it encourages and promotes moral fortitude and staves off despair. Opposition to racial oppression, whether from the voice of Billie Holiday or KRS-One, Sweet Honey in the Rock or Common. The civil rights movement, as Coleman describes, helps make possible songs such as "Uptown," and the entertainment modes of such singers as Marvin Gaye or Bob Dylan exist in tandem with social justice sounds.

The chapter by Venetria K. Patton, "The Post–Civil Rights Era and the Rise of Contemporary Novels of Slavery," reveals the similarities and changes in the character and focus of neo-slavery novels with a particular emphasis on the role of women. A significant majority of neo-slave novels are by Black women who make women, especially mothers, agents. The authors of neo-slave novels insist on the humanity of women, not as inane breeders but as persons with agency. Patton takes account of such works as Timothy A. Spaulding, *Re-Forming the Past: The Fantastic and the Postmodern Slave Narrative*; Vanessa F. Dickerson and Michael Bennett, editors, *Recovering the Black Female Body: Self-Representations by African American Women*; and Ashraf H. A. Rushdy, *Remembering Generations: Race and Family in Contemporary African American Fiction*, to tell the story of memory, regeneration, and the struggle for social justice made loud and clear by voices of Black women in a myriad of texts. Neo-slavery novels make as central features of stories the agency of women on behalf of their own liberation and their own creative recovery from brutality and silencing. In addition, Patton covers post–civil rights speculative science fiction, which allows more creativity than the confines of realist fiction, especially that fiction which uses slavery as a background. Thus, modern narratives of escape may encompass the remote past but encode that past as deeply connected to an imagined future. Images of a postracial future and heterogeneous form of gender are conveyed by stories with sheroes no longer pictured as subordinates.

Patton foregrounds the intersectional facets of race, class, and gender inside such works as Arna Bontemps, *Black Thunder*; Margaret Walker, *Jubilee*; Toni Morrison, *Beloved*; and Jewelle Gomez, *The Gilda Stories*. Intersectional facets are discussed in conjunction with the importance of memory as a conduit for sharing, recovery, and sustenance. The emphasis on memory is compatible with contemporary social movements that proclaim that we should "stay woke," that is, remain aware of social subjections. The author believes that stories of ghosts and vampires and other imagined scenes can have especially valuable roles, for example, as therapeutic and ways of imaging the nature of liberation because the protagonist has a lifespan that stretches from slavery to an imagined future. Fleeing south from the terrors of life in the north, rather than north from the terror of southern slavery, paradoxically, is the theme in some neo-slave narratives.

Stephanie Y. Evans in "Letters to Our Daughters: Black Women's Memoirs as Epistles of Human Rights, Healing, and Inner Peace" links written records of memories, which function as acts of personal and social defiance and ways of encouraging voices to promote democracy. Evans describes the geographies of texts, whether an autobiography or novel, emphasizing the way ideas of human rights in the United Nations Universal Declaration of Human Rights are expressed by the authors. Whether words by Anna Julia Cooper, Maya Angelou, Dionne Brand, or Mariama Ba, the common themes in their writings provide a map of the past. Their works are educational and inspirational but also futurist—taking the wounds of the past and creating imaginative futures.

CHAPTER 3

SINGING *IS* SWINGING

THE SOUL FORCE OF TWENTIETH-CENTURY BLACK PROTEST MUSIC

JEFFREY LAMAR COLEMAN

Malcolm X once proclaimed, "Anytime you live in the twentieth century, and you walking around here singing 'We Shall Overcome,' the government has failed us. This is part of what's wrong with you: You do too much singing. Today, it's time to stop singing and start swinging."[1] While Malcolm X acknowledges the rich history in the Black community of confronting oppression through artistic engagement, he dismisses musical expression as a less effective mode of retaliation than direct, physical self-defense. Malcolm's impatience with America and the civil rights movement in 1964 is understandable, even laudable, but he unintentionally constructs a faulty binary between orality and physicality with respect to oppositional efficacy. The two methods of social resistance, though by no means identical, are not mutually exclusive, as Malcolm X was well aware, and at times are complementary, as the rap group Public Enemy made clear nearly three decades later. "Swinging while I'm singing" is the group's rejoinder in 1989's "Fight the Power" to Malcolm's "stop singing and start swinging."[2] Furthermore, from an artistically centered perspective that privileges figurative or metaphorical over literal interpretations, singing and swinging are not only harmonious but indistinguishable and interchangeable. Rapping about fighting the "powers that be," for example, is fighting the powers that be. No fisticuffs are required for this act of defiance, but a blow against the dominant social order is delivered, nonetheless. This essay, informed by implicit rhetorical theory, analyzes representative socially conscious cultural productions by Black American musicians of the twentieth century, ranging from often overlooked protest songs about sharecropping in the early days of the century to the emergence of Hip-Hop in the century's closing moments, and concludes with a brief single-artist exploration. Altogether, this essay argues that artistic combativeness and performative resistance, not unlike physical, corporeal opposition, are historically vital components of the Black community's collective efforts to counter and resist aggressive, terroristic social forces.

Bernice Johnson Reagon, a founding member of the Freedom Singers and Sweet Honey in the Rock, alludes to the rhetorical potential of songs during the 1960s: "The civil rights movement . . . taught me that singing was not entertainment, it was something else."[3] Reagon's realization that singing could be utilized for something other than entertainment alone "occurred at the same time that [African Americans] were fighting racism in the United States."[4] Thus, the conflation of racialized social forces and the desire to confront and neutralize those forces led to Reagon's discovery that singing could be employed as an aesthetic and cultural weapon in the battle against Jim Crow and White supremacy in America. As Kerran L. Sanger makes clear, Reagon was not alone in terms of recognizing the force of song: "The activists of the civil rights movement developed a strong sense of their rhetorical needs and the ways singing operated to help them meet those needs."[5] Furthermore, Sanger identifies four characteristics shared by protest singers:

1. Song is not ordinary communication but rather a form of discourse that energizes those who engage in it and allows them to express themselves in ways not available in other forms of discourse.
2. Song is an especially powerful form of communication that achieves its power from the generation, expression, and venting of intense emotion.
3. The powerful rhetoric of song both derives from and enhances the spirituality of those who engage in it.
4. As discourse, the singing of freedom songs was inherently transformative. Those who sang not only expressed themselves but were changed— made new and better—in the singing.[6]

Sanger's observations about the transformative force of songs during the civil rights movement are applicable to most if not all African American performers who dared to confront White supremacy and other impediments to the social advancement of the Black community in the twentieth century.

Not surprising, the civil rights movement and Vietnam War of the 1960s and 1970s tend to dominate the public imagination when the subject of twentieth-century Black protest music arises and are usually followed by socially conscious rap and Hip-Hop songs of the 1980s and 1990s. For example, the civil rights anthem "We Shall Overcome" is one of the most recognizable and utilized protest songs around the globe, and Edwin Starr's "War," with its emphatic call-and-response chorus of "War! What is it good for? / Absolutely nothing!" has transcended its Vietnam War–era origins and is often shouted by present-day

American protesters in times of international conflict.[7] Likewise, many rap protest songs from the 1980s and 1990s are still readily identifiable, including "The Message" (1982) by Grand Master Flash and the Furious Five about the living conditions of inner-city America and "Fight the Power" (1989/1990) by Public Enemy, a song that protests systemic, institutionalized racism by demanding its listeners to stand up and "fight the powers that be." While those eras are essential to understanding the variety and depth of the protest tradition, numerous recordings produced in the first half of the century are also worthy of attention. Some of these recordings involve labor movements that usually fail to receive the recognition they deserve. Michael K. Honey attempts to place such oversights in perspective when he argues that "freedom music is too often slighted from the canon of African American music, while labor protest songs have been nearly excised from popular culture."[8] For example, Hungarian immigrant Lawrence Gellert, born Laslo Grunbaum,[9] recorded hundreds of folksongs by Black sharecroppers and musicians during his travels through portions of the American south from approximately 1920 to 1940, but those recordings have only recently received substantive attention. Gellert's collection, archived at Indiana University–Bloomington, "contains more than 600 songs and half of them can be called songs of protest."[10] Songs that challenged or opposed Jim Crow's systemic oppression, especially involving issues of labor, property, and housing, were of particular interest to Gellert. Although Gellert's recordings cover multiple folk themes, he was primarily concerned with recording songs that presented "clear and direct expressions of social protest."[11] Gellert, a member of the Communist Party, made it clear that he was not interested in exploring "Negro" life as racial or anthropological exotica or as folklore for folklore's sake. Instead, Gellert was intent on helping disprove the myth that poor, disenfranchised Blacks of the early twentieth century, much like slaves of the previous century, were content with their inhumane lot in life.[12] Songs with titles such as "White Folks Want Nigger Just for Work and Sweat," "Pickin' Off de Cotton," "Work Ox," "Stan' Boys Stand," "Cause I'm a Nigger," "I Ain't Nothin' but Wages Hand," and "White Folks Take Your Money" drew attention to issues of poverty, exploitative work conditions, and racism. Many of these protest songs can be found on three albums compiled from Gellert's fieldwork: *Negro Songs of Protest: Collected by Lawrence Gellert* (1973); *Cap'n You're So Mean: Negro Songs of Protest, Volume 2* (1982); and *Nobody Knows My Name: Blues from South Carolina and Georgia* (1984). As a result of the songs' incendiary content and the subsequent potential for economic retaliation and physical violence against the singers, Gellert never revealed the identities of his recorded artists.[13]

Gellert's fears may have been influenced by labor-related violence that occurred in other parts of the Deep South in the opening decades of the twentieth century. Elaine, Arkansas, for example, was the site of a 1919 massacre that, depending on which death toll one believes, could be considered "the most deadly racial conflict in the history of the United States."[14] At the heart of the violence was a basic disagreement between sharecroppers and tenants and plantation owners over profits from crops. Sharecroppers and tenants formed an organization akin to a modern-day union and decided to cut out the plantation owners and market their own crops.[15] As a result, the White community retaliated violently, resulting in a massacre that left at least 5 Whites and between 20 to 856 African Americans dead. The death-toll discrepancy is a result of conflicting documents written within six years of the conflict.[16] The following account sheds light on the history of the events that transpired in Elaine, Arkansas, in late September and early October 1919:

> There was gunfire at the sharecropper meeting, and when it ended, a deputy sheriff was wounded and a railroad security officer was dead. For days afterward mobs of whites roamed with guns and hunted blacks in the thickets. U.S. Army troops were called in and may also have done some killing. Whites called it a black insurrection; blacks called it a massacre by whites. No one agrees on the tallies. Perhaps five whites were killed. Estimates run from 20 into the hundreds of black men, women, and children dead. The bottom line: This is one of the largest race killings of blacks in U.S. history, but most people today have never heard of it.[17]

This account illustrates the degree to which threatened plantation owners and like-minded citizens desired to maintain fiscal and racial dominance over sharecroppers and tenants. The massacre, unfortunately, was not an isolated event in 1919, a year that produced what came to be known as Red Summer. Race riots exploded in every region of the country from May through September, most notably in Chicago and Washington, DC, but in Georgia, Mississippi, Connecticut, Tennessee, Maryland, Arizona, Texas, Illinois, and other states, as well.

Unlike the enraged singers Gellert chronicled, John L. Handcox, an Arkansas native, was not an anonymous Great Depression–era protest artist. He was visible and vocal and, as a result, vulnerable. His opposition to unfair labor practices and subsequent consciousness-raising efforts in the Arkansas Delta were unpopular among landowners and eventually resulted in threats of lynch-mob violence and death.[18] Handcox, an often overlooked African American poet and singer, was also an organizer for the Southern Tenant Farmers Union (STFU). As such, he is an example of an early twentieth-century socially conscious individual who embraced praxis and valued the union of orality, performance, and community organizing. Handcox utilized the full range of his cultural concerns in the pursuit of social justice. In this vein, he served as a model and trailblazer for artists of future generations, including the likes of Reagon and the Freedom Singers. The STFU, "founded by Socialist Party activists and linked to the Great

Depression and the turbulent era's mix of Communists, Socialists and independent labor radicals," was responsible for generating and energizing "a vibrant agricultural worker's movement in the midst of horrific conditions."[19]

Although Handcox was only a teenager when the Elaine massacre occurred approximately fifty miles from his hometown, he was undoubtedly aware of the tensions that helped fuel the historic confrontation and likely grew up deploring the brand of inhumanity that kept impoverished White and Black sharecroppers under the thumb of unscrupulous White landowners in the 1920s and 1930s. Much of his dismay would later be expressed in his creative works, including his poetry and blues and folk songs.

The following excerpt from "Planter and Sharecropper" is representative of Handcox's political and lyrical oeuvre:

> If you ask the planter for your right
> You might as well just spit in his face and ask for a fight.
> The planter says he inherited his wealth from birth,
> But it all comes from the poor man who tills the earth.

Handcox's dichotomization of planter and sharecropper mirrors the gulf that often existed between the two, with the planter or landowner using the system of sharecropping to expand his coffers at the expense of the worker. The social chasm between the two classes is made clear in the song, especially with lines such as:

> The planter's children dresses up and goes to school
> While the sharecropper's puts on rags and follow a mule.
> . . . .
> The planter says he inherited his wealth from birth,
> But it all comes from the poor man who tills the earth.[20]

Taken together, these plainspoken lines address the impact the labor system had on the "poor man" and his children. The latter appear attired in "rags" and are sent to the fields to help plow the land to ensure a better life for the planter, whose children are adorned in nicer clothing and permitted to leave the plantation for school and an education that will presumably provide them with the skills to one day perpetuate the current planter-laborer system or better themselves elsewhere. Conversely, there appears to be no hope of upward mobility for the sharecropper's children; they are mired in a cycle of labor and debt. Handcox's lines give no indication that the sharecropper's children will ever be anything other than sharecroppers themselves, whereas the planter's children have the potential to become part of the educated, ruling class.

While resentment and a strong note of protest are present in these lines, Handcox provides one of his most poignant messages near the end of the song:

"I do want to be something more than a planter's slave."[21] Not only is this line notable for its insistence that sharecropping is essentially slavery by another name but it also represents the first and only time in the song that Handcox employs the first-person perspective, or "I." This is significant because the first-person mode signifies an intimacy with the subject matter and repositions the artist from distanced narrator to active participant and protester, thus enhancing his connection to the music, audience, and cause.

Handcox, amid threats of being lynched for his activism, reluctantly left his home state of Arkansas in 1937 and became a traveling labor activist. During his travels, Handcox helped organize and raise funds for the STFU in states such as Tennessee, Mississippi, and Missouri and in various cities, including Chicago, Detroit, New York, and Washington, DC. (Interestingly enough, 1937 is also the year blues legend Lead Belly penned "The Bourgeois Blues," a song that protests the treatment he received in Washington, DC. In the fourth verse he sings, "Well, them white folks in Washington they know how / To call a colored man a nigger just to see him bow.")

Handcox's experiences coincide with Sanger's four observations about implicit rhetorical theory and social movements, chiefly her first and fourth findings. Handcox discovered that "song is not ordinary communication but rather a form of discourse that energizes those who engage it" and that "the singing of freedom songs [is] inherently transformative" and possesses the ability to change the singer-activist for the better.[22] The power of song undoubtedly contributed to Handcox's desire and ability to organize for social change. The same can be said of those who came after him. Activists who followed in his footsteps used rhetoric, performance, and grassroots organizational acumen. The civil rights movement, for example, utilized many of the same strategies in order to empower volunteers and strengthen their morale and moral fortitude. Reagon, while recalling the desegregation campaign Albany movement of 1961 and 1962, expands on the connection among music, Black organizing, and Black social change:

> A lot of the sit-in songs were out of the rhythm and blues idiom or the arranged spiritual idiom. Those songs, as they went through Albany, Georgia, got brought back to the root level of Black choral traditional music. . . . In addition to all [Albany] did in terms of a mass movement, [it] also became a place where the music was so powerful that people became conscious of it. People who came to write about the Movement began to write about the singing and not even understand why. They couldn't understand what the singing had to do with all the other but it was so powerful they knew it must have some connection.[23]

The seemingly incomprehensible "connection" Reagon speaks of can be better understood by viewing it through the lens of Sanger's second and third rhetorical observations: "Song is an especially powerful form of communication that achieves its power from the generation, expression, and venting of intense emotion," and "The powerful rhetoric of song both derives from and enhances the spirituality of those who engage in it."[24] Through these lenses, the connection that some observers could not understand about civil-rights-movement performative practices becomes clearer. Music and singing connected artists and organizers in a substantive spiritual manner that cannot necessarily be understood empirically. This connection is reminiscent of King's advice to remain vigilantly nonviolent yet effectively forceful. "Again and again," he insists in "I Have a Dream," "we must rise to the majestic heights of meeting physical force with soul force."[25] The spiritual connection made between performer-activists and shared with audiences illustrates the "soul force" King had in mind and undergirds the "swinging" force of soulful singing.

Two years after Handcox left Arkansas, Billie Holiday sang about men and women less fortunate than Handcox, those who were unable to escape the threat of lynching. Holiday debuted her now-famous rendition of "Strange Fruit" at New York's Café Society, the city's first integrated nightclub. Her memorable performance about a strange and bitter crop of Black bodies swinging in the southern breeze, hanging from poplar trees, helped usher in a long line of songs that protested violence and discrimination. As Angela Davis recalls,

> "Strange Fruit" evoked the horrors of lynching at a time when black people were still passionately calling for allies in the campaign to eradicate this murderous and terroristic manifestation of racism. While she never sang "Strange Fruit" exactly the same way twice, each time Holiday performed it she implicitly asked her audiences to imagine a dreadful lynching scene, and to endorse and identify with the song's antilynching sentiments. Yet her performance of this song did much more. It almost singlehandedly changed the politics of American popular culture and put the elements of protest and resistance back at the center of contemporary black musical culture.[26]

Whereas Handcox's and Gellert's artists focused primarily on issues pertaining to labor, Holiday and a host of others broadened the scope of the African American protest song. Although an in-depth analysis of Black protest artists and songs that followed Holiday's "Strange Fruit" for the remainder of the twentieth century is beyond the scope of this project, a chronological, representative, yet by no means exhaustive list of songs is in order and should prove beneficial for students and others conducting further research on the topic:

- "Original Faubus Fables," Charles Mingus (1960), protests the racist stance of Arkansas Governor Orval Faubus and Little Rock Central High School integration crisis

- "Triptych: Prayer, Protest, Peace," Max Roach (1960), an eight-minute jazz meditation on three stages of resistance, punctuated by the vocals of Abbey Lincoln
- "Alabama," John Coltrane (1963), instrumental elegy for the four girls murdered during the bombing of the Sixteenth Street Baptist Church in Birmingham, Alabama
- "Mississippi Goddam," Nina Simone (1964), damns the state of Mississippi for the assassination of Medgar Evers; also damns Alabama, Tennessee, and those who stand in the way of racial progress
- "Forty Acres and a Mule," Oscar Brown Jr. (1965), a humorous inquiry about the feasibility of acquiring reparations for slavery
- "A Change Is Gonna Come," Sam Cooke (1965), protests segregation and racism while expressing optimism for equality
- "Do Right Woman, Do Right Man," Aretha Franklin (1967), feminist song demanding respect and equality from men
- "We're a Winner," Curtis Mayfield and Impressions (1967), celebrates Black pride and rejects racist assumptions of Black community
- "Say It Loud—I'm Black and I'm Proud," James Brown (1968), rallying cry for Black pride and self-sufficiency
- "Why? (The King of Love Is Dead)," Nina Simone (1968), an elegy commemorating the life and death of Martin Luther King Jr.
- "Freedom," Jimi Hendrix (1971), protests restrictions, personal and social
- "Attica Blues," Archie Shepp (1972), protests conditions at the Attica Correctional Facility that led to a riot inside the prison
- "March to the Witch's Castle," Funkadelic (1973), a prayer for American soldiers returning from Vietnam, a protest against the country that sent them
- "Living for the City," Stevie Wonder (1973), protests inner-city turmoil and wrongful imprisonment
- "Winter in America," Gil Scott-Heron (1975), protests a hollow, decaying America
- "Chocolate City," Parliament (1975), classic Black pride tune about majority-Black cities
- "Ain't No Stopping Us Now," McFadden and Whitehead (1979), an anthem of perseverance in the presence of obstacles and struggle
- "The Message," Grandmaster Flash and the Furious Five (1982), addresses a wide range of social ills, especially conditions in America's inner cities; classic Hip-Hop
- "Talkin' Out the Side of Your Neck," Cameo (1984), protests the politics of Presidents Richard Nixon, Gerald Ford, Jimmy Carter, and Ronald Reagan
- "Fast Car" and "Talkin' bout a Revolution," Tracy Chapman (1988), protests socioeconomic issues that harm the underclass

- "Fuck Tha Police," N.W.A. (1988), protests police misconduct and corruption
- "U.N.I.T.Y.," Queen Latifah (1993), protests the mistreatment of women by men and calls for gender equality
- "Leviticus: Faggot," Me'Shell Ndegeochello (1996), protests homophobia and discrimination against same-sex couples
- "Video," India.Arie (2000) calls for female empowerment and self-assertion

In addition to the songs listed above, there are songs that played an essential role during the civil rights movement that were, more often than not, revived, revised, and constantly evolving traditional spirituals. Some of the songs that fall into this category are: "Oh, Freedom," "Ain't Gonna Let Nobody Turn Me 'Round," "Hold On (Keep Your Eyes on the Prize)," "I Love Everybody," "This Little Light of Mine," "I'm Gonna Sit at the Welcome Table," "I Woke Up This Mornin'," "Go Tell It on the Mountain," and, of course, "We Shall Overcome." These songs, as Reagon mentions earlier, were used in various ways during the movement, including recruitment, consciousness-raising, spiritual and emotional sustenance, and group unity.

Furthermore, post–civil rights era groups and/or collections deserve to be mentioned. For example, the vast majority of Public Enemy's twentieth-century discography consists of protest material. The same could be said of KRS-One, The Roots, Sweet Honey in the Rock, and Common. In short, the list of songs and artists that followed Holiday's "Strange Fruit," whether they were influenced by the jazz-and-blues singer or not, is impressive and still ongoing.

This exploration of musical artists concludes with a coda of sorts by focusing on a single artist's career, if only briefly. I selected Prince for this purpose because he was a prolific genre-bending artist who was influenced by or incorporated elements of folk to Hip-Hop into his corpus of work. To be clear, most of the musical styles covered in this essay found their way into Prince's catalog or served as influences. In addition, he is one of the few African American artists of the twentieth century who unapologetically subverted racist and sexist practices in the music industry and in American culture by problematizing his own racial and sexual identities and simultaneously leaving himself open to accusations of producing racist and sexist lyrics and images. Furthermore, he confronted the music industry on behalf of artists' rights and profit margins. He was a complex and conflicted artist who underwent several metamorphoses from 1978 until 2016, a period in which he released no fewer than forty-seven albums and ninety-eight singles, including his last album, 2015's *Hit n Run Phase Two*.

Prince was also a conscientious and often controversial artist who consistently produced socially conscious lyrics that were often overshadowed by the sonic textures and erotic nature of his music and by his various transformations and personae, all of which have concealed the fact that he was one of America's most significant protest artists of the post–civil rights era. As a post–civil rights movement musician, Prince was the beneficiary of a ground paved by artists such as Handcox, Reagon, and many of the other artists mentioned above. Consequently, by the time Prince emerged on the music scene, the social fabric had been altered. Although equality was not fully realized, he and his generation enjoyed an unprecedented amount of social freedom. In addition, he inherited a musical tradition of using one's oratorical prowess for the sake of social protest and advancements. The combination of newfound generational liberation and a wealth of socially conscious musical predecessors to draw inspiration from resulted in Prince's desire to become part of the continuum of artists who voiced dissent about various aspects of social inequality. These factors are essential to understanding Prince not only as an aesthetically adventurous virtuoso but as a socially cognizant artist as well. Whereas Handcox's and Reagon's generations found racial hindrances their primary concern, post–civil rights artists like Prince were still mindful of those constraints but liberated enough to discern the interconnectivity of other modes of social marginality and oppression. For example, Prince found connections among racism, sexism, homophobia, and xenophobia. This helps explain why his initial engagements with protest-oriented songs demonstrated a more expansive view of civil and human rights.

Prince's third album, *Dirty Mind*, released in 1980, contains his first overtly political songs, "Uptown" and "Partyup." "Uptown" is a literal reference to a section of southwestern Minneapolis, Prince's hometown, and a metaphorical reference to a state of liberation. The song's narrator is approached by a female stranger while walking down the street. The woman summons the narrator and boldly asks, "Are you gay?" Somewhat taken aback, our narrator says,

> Kinda took me by surprise
> I didn't know what to do
> I just looked her in her eyes
> And I said, "No, are you?"[27]

First of all, the inclusion of the word "gay" in 1980 was highly unusual to say the least; not many pop artists incorporate the term today, but it speaks to Prince's liberatory ethos in a post–civil rights era America. In "Uptown," listeners are not privy to what prompts the initial inquiry about the narrator's sexuality but can deduce that his manner of dress or behavior plays a role. Surely, something about his bearing marks him as ambiguous. In other words, the woman, upon seeing the narrator, immediately determines that some aspect of his being does not align with heteronormativity and, therefore, needs to be confronted and interrogated. The narrator immediately detects the stereotypes at play in this encounter and informs listeners, "She's just a crazy . . . / Little mixed up dame." Furthermore, the narrator empathizes with her and insists that the American socialization process is to blame: "She's just a victim of society / And all its games." Listeners soon discover that the narrator and his friends actively resist the standards and mores of American culture:

We don't let society
Tell us how it's supposed to be
Our clothes, our hair
We don't care
It's all about being there.[28]

"There" refers to the Uptown district of Minneapolis. "That's where I want to be," the narrator sings, "Uptown / Set your mind free." It is interesting to note how soon the lyrics shift from the personal to the communal, how soon the terms "we," "us," and "our" are invoked, as if to imply that such interactions are not uncommon and not limited to a single individual but are being experienced by a larger community. Not only is Uptown a place where sexual and psychological liberation occurs but it is also a place free of racial tension. Whites, Blacks, and Puerto Ricans are specifically mentioned in the song, but we can assume that Uptown welcomes anyone with a mind free of stereotypes and limitations. Further evidence of this can be found when he sings, "It's all about being free." In short, Uptown is utopia for the Other, a refuge for a subculture comprising the misunderstood and marginalized. An Uptown state of mind rejects restrictions and discrimination. As such, "Uptown" can be understood as Prince's civil rights movement–inspired post–civil rights anthem that recognizes the goals and objectives of the movement and a desire to broaden those objectives to meet the demands of a new generation of young Americans. Prince is operating in the same vein as Handcox, who sang about the ills of sharecroppers, and Reagon, who sang about the ills of Jim Crow America. In short, Prince is recognizing his lineage as a Black protest musician and simultaneously widening the parameters of the Black protest tradition. "Uptown" the song could not exist without the advancements owed to the civil rights movement, and Uptown as an ideal world acknowledges at once the limitations of the movement and its hope for what America can become. And as we discover three tracks later in the song "Partyup," Uptown as a physical entity is also a place where one can go to freely protest the American military or escape to after such a protest.

According to the song's lyrics, "Partyup" should be considered a "revolutionary rock and roll" song explicitly designed to help youth resist the draft and the war because "Fightin' war / Is such a fuckin' bore." Although these lines are not terribly sophisticated, they are succinct and poignant. Shortly afterwards, our youth are told,

It's all about what's in your mind
Goin' uptown, baby
I don't wanna die
I just wanna
have a bloody good time.[29]

Instead of the Beatles' mantra of "Love is all you need" in order to extricate one's self from and transcend social chaos, Prince's mantra in "Partyup" seems to be, "*Partying* is all you need." The song's opening lines of "We don't give a damn / We just wanna jam" affirms this idea; however, in the midst of all the partying, a deep level of anxiety about war and death exists, a juxtaposition that infuses the song with a potent combination of tension and release. The song asks, "How you gonna make me kill somebody / I don't even know?" as well as, "Is it fair to kill the youth?" All of this culminates in a seemingly polyvocal chant (although Prince performs all vocals and instruments on the song) that emphatically and defiantly proclaims, in three consecutive iterations, "You're gonna have to fight your own damn war / 'Cause we don't wanna fight no more!"[30] The forceful proclamation of these last lines recalls Sanger's observation that "song is an especially powerful form of communication that achieves its power from the generation, expression, and venting of intense emotion."[31] Few listeners of "Partyup," especially its declarative closing lines, would disagree with Sanger's argument.

While these lyrics are arguably among the most overtly antimilitary of the 1980s, they are also among the most perplexing because when the song was recorded in May and June of 1980, America did not have a draft and was not actively engaged in a war. A question that begs to be answered is, why would Prince release an audaciously anti-authoritarian antiwar song in the absence of a war? Of course, Prince could have been addressing youth the world over, perhaps, those in countries at war, but I think there is something else at play here. The song is Prince's way of linking himself to the long line of established American protest singers who came before him, especially those who addressed war in addition to social injustice, such as Marvin Gaye, Joan Baez, John Lennon, Jimi Hendrix, Edwin Starr, fellow Minnesotan Bob Dylan, and others. Prince was born in 1958, and so his formative years took place during the era of the Vietnam War and civil rights movement when protest music and demonstrations were inescapably ubiquitous, a fact that undoubtedly informed his musical and social sensibilities. Prince seems to be sending a clear message that he intends to be considered a protest artist. There is also the possibility that the presence of war in "Partyup" is richly metaphorical, especially considering the song references the Uptown district, and is intended to speak to the broader war on American youth, especially a war on anyone who has not traditionally fit neatly into mainstream American culture, as well as anyone who may be considered "a victim of society / And all its games." With this interpretation in mind, the line, "Is it fair to kill the youth?" takes on increased significance and interrogates America's war on the spiritual as well as corporeal essence of its marginalized youth. As a post–civil rights anthem in the thematic vein of "Uptown," the song's valorization of youth is in direct opposition to the value placed on Black youth by racists during the civil rights era, especially if one recalls the deaths of Emmett Till in 1955 and Addie Mae Collins, Carol Denise McNair, Carole Robertson, and Cynthia Wesley, the four young girls who perished in the Sixteenth Street Baptist Church in September 1963. "Partyup" desires a world that honors the current generation of young Americans and encourages a distancing from and destruction of the mentality that too often led to the sacrifices of youth in previous generations.

Although "Uptown" and "Partyup" represent Prince's maiden voyage into the world of protest music, they would soon be joined by similarly themed songs throughout the remainder of the twentieth century, including some of Prince's most popular and commercially successful songs, such as "1999," "Pop Life," and "Sign o' the Times," as well as lesser-known but no less politically charged tunes such as "Ronnie, Talk to Russia," "Controversy," "Annie Christian," "Sexuality," "Free," "Lady Cab Driver," "America," "Papa," "Race," "Uncle Sam," "We March," and "Undisputed." We should also keep in mind that although Prince was virtually a one-man band early in his career, when he finally formed an official band, he gave the group a moniker that connotes politics and protest—he named his band The Revolution. However, as the twentieth century began to draw to a close, Prince's most political and controversial material addressed the music industry's exploitation of artists.

Prince's public standoff with and ultimate separation from Warner Brothers in the 1990s has been well-documented, but it's probably prudent to rehash it here in abbreviated form. The wildly prolific Prince wanted to release more than one album per year, but Warner refused out of a fear that flooding the market with multiple releases would dampen revenue. Furthermore, although Prince was able to extricate himself from his contract with the record label, he was not permitted to own the master tapes of his catalog, or roughly nineteen albums worth of material. The relationship between both parties devolved, and Prince began to view the situation as a master-slave enterprise. This period of Prince's career is not unlike the struggle Handcox waged for sharecropper rights or the uprising of sharecroppers in Elaine, Arkansas. The common element in these situations is the worth of the human being in relation to the music industry or landowners. Prince would often appear in public with the word "slave" scrawled along his cheek and present slavery and civil-rights-movement imagery during his concerts. During this period he also wrote songs titled "Slave," "Slave to the System," and, later, "Emancipation." Prince also encouraged other artists to leave major record labels and distribute their music independently through the Internet, thus eliminating the exploitation of the middle man and the chains and shackles of the industry. Many musicians, including Natalie Merchant, Nine Inch Nails, Public Enemy, and Sonic Youth, eventually left their labels, although it is not clear if Prince's situation played a direct role in their decisions.[32]

Clearly, the Uptown state of mind that emerged early in Prince's career that fought against stereotypes, discrimination, and social restrictions informed his later cultural productions as well and continued until the end of his life. For example, during the 2015 Grammy awards, Prince presented the award for best album, but before he handed it over, he said, "Albums still matter. Like books and Black lives, albums still matter." In a world in which single downloads are now the norm, often at the expense of an artist's overall conceptual vision for an album, Prince reminds us that the whole is greater than its parts. Also, his comments connect him to the Black Lives Matter movement, a movement that grew out of the 2012 death of Trayvon Martin and a movement Prince would later support with the song "Baltimore," which was written to protest the injustice surrounding the death of Freddie Gray in 2015. Prince's statements and songs about Black lives also remind us that more than thirty-five years after his first protest song, he remained a committed artist and was one of America's most significant protest artists of the post–civil rights era. Lastly, he reminds us, like all of the artists mentioned in this paper, especially Handcox and Reagon, of the vital, soulful role musicians and performers have played in the Black community with respect to countering and resisting racism and oppression.

Notes

1. Malcolm X, "The Ballot or the Bullet," in *Say It Loud: Great Speeches on Civil Rights and African American Identity*, ed. Catherine Ellis and Stephen Drury Smith (New York: New Press, 2010), 8.

2. Public Enemy, "Fight the Power," in *It Takes a Nation of Millions of Millions to Hold Us Back*, Def Jam, 1988, LP.

3. Bernice Johnson Reagon, interview by Marvette Pérez, *Radical History Review* 68 (1997): 4–24, https://doi.org/10.1215/01636545-1997-68-4.

4. Ibid.

5. Kerran L. Sanger, "Functions of Freedom Singing in the Civil Rights Movement: The Activists' Implicit Rhetorical Theory," *Howard Journal of Communications* 8, no. 2 (1997): 192–193, https://doi.org/10.1080/10646179709361752.

6. Ibid., 193.

7. Edwin Starr, "War," "War," in *War & Peace*, Motown, 1970, LP.

8. Michael K. Honey, *Sharecropper's Troubadour: John L. Handcox, the Southern Tenant Farmers Union, and the African American Song Tradition* (New York: Palgrave, 2013), 3.

9. Bruce M. Conforth,. *African American Folksong and American Cultural Politics: The Lawrence Gellert Story* (Lanham, MD: Scarecrow, 2013), 11.

10. "Gellert Collection," Lawrence Gellert Collection, Archives of Traditional Music, Indiana University–Bloomington, indiana.edu, December 12, 2014.

11. Steven Garabedian, "Reds, Whites, and the Blues: Lawrence Gellert, 'Negro Songs of Protest,' and the Left-Wing Folk-Song Revival of the 1930 and 1940s," *American Quarterly* 57, no. 1 (2005): 186.

12. Ibid., 182.

13. Ibid., 200.

14. Grif Stockley, *Blood in Their Eyes: The Elaine Race Massacres of 1919* (Fayetteville: University of Arkansas Press, 2001), xiv.

15. Michael Honey, interview with Robin Lindley, *Against the Current* 29, no. 3 (2014): 21.

16. Stockley, *Blood*, xiv.

17. Charles Bowden, "Return to the Arkansas Delta," *National Geographic* 222, no. 5, November 2012, 124–131.

18. Robert Hunt Ferguson, "The Land, the Lord, and the Union: Earthly and Spiritual Salvation in the Protest Songs of John L. Handcox," *Arkansas Review: A Journal of Delta Studies* 43, no. 2 (2012): 78–79.

19. Robin Lindley, "An Interview with Historian Michael Honey, John Handcox, 'Sharecropper's Troubadour,'" *Against the Current* 29, no. 3, 2014, 19.

20. Ibid.

21. Ibid.

22. Sanger, "Functions," 193.

23. Bernice Johnson Reagon, interview by Dick Cluster, "The Borning Struggle: The Civil Rights Movement," *Radical America* 12, no. 6, 1978, 17.

24. Sanger, "Functions," 193.

25. Martin Luther King Jr., "I Have a Dream," in *I Have a Dream: Writings and Speeches that Changed the World*, ed. James M. Washington (New York: HarperCollinss, 1992), 103.

26. Angela Y. Davis, *Blues Legacies and Black Feminism: Gertrude "Ma" Rainey, Bessie Smith, and Billie Holiday* (New York: Pantheon, 1998), 183–184.

27. Prince, "Uptown," in *Dirty Mind*, Warner Brothers, 1980, LP.

28. Ibid.

29. Prince, "Partyup," in *Dirty Mind*, Warner Brothers, 1980, LP.

30. Ibid.

31. Sanger, "Functions," 193.

32. Zack Stiegler, "'Slave 2 the System': Prince and the Strategic Performance of Slavery," *Journal of Popular Music Studies* 21, no. 2 (2009): 213–239, https://doi.org/10.1111/j.1533-1598.2009.01193.x3.

CHAPTER 4

THE POST–CIVIL RIGHTS ERA AND THE RISE OF CONTEMPORARY NOVELS OF SLAVERY

VENETRIA K. PATTON

In *The Grasp That Reaches beyond the Grave: The Ancestral Call in Black Women's Texts*, I contend that the 1980s and 1990s served as "a significant sociohistorical moment as African Americans began to seriously assess the gains of the Civil Rights Movement."[1] The 1980s and 1990s gave rise to an increase in neo-slave narratives or contemporary novels of slavery as writers responded "to a conservative impetus to present a homogeneous view of U.S. history that tends to dismiss the residual effects of slavery and its legacy on our national history" by creating counternarratives.[2] Although one can point to earlier neo-slave narratives, the 1966 publication of Margaret Walker's *Jubilee* is often cited as a transitional moment ushering in the modern neo-slave narrative. Bernard Bell, who coined the term "neo-slave narrative," considers Walker's *Jubilee* the first major neo-slave narrative. Bell defines the neo-slave narrative as "residually oral, modern narratives of escape from bondage to freedom."[3] African American culture and history specialist Ashraf H. A. Rushdy offers a slightly different definition for his term "neo-slave narrative," which refers to texts that "assume the form, adopt the conventions, and take on the first-person voice of the ante-bellum slave narrative."[4] Thus, Rushdy's neo-slave narrative is one particular form of a broader category of contemporary African American narratives of slavery.[5]

Literary scholar Deborah McDowell describes the emergence of neo-slave narratives as "mainly a post-sixties phenomenon," as "novels about slavery have appeared at an unstoppable rate" since the publication of *Jubilee*.[6] However, there is also a gendered component to the rise of neo-slave narratives that some critics have linked to Alex Haley's *Roots* (1976). Angelyn Mitchell observes,

Although contemporary black men writers such as Ernest Gaines, Ishmael Reed, and Charles Johnson have also engaged the historical moment of chattel slavery in their novels and even though Alex Haley's *Roots* (1976), both the novel and the television series, made significant contributions to the discourse of slavery, contemporary Black women writers beginning with Margaret Walker and her historical novel *Jubilee* (1966), have been at the forefront of revisiting slavery.[7]

Women writers' interest in writing about slavery is a shift from the slave-narrative tradition, which was dominated by male authors. African American slavery historian John Blassingame estimates that "black women wrote less than 12 percent of the published slave narratives. From this statistic we can conclude, not surprisingly, that, as autobiography, the slave narratives are primarily expressions of male subjectivity, and, as history, they are narratives of his-story."[8] Thus in many ways, neo-slave narratives provide Black women writers the opportunity to set the record straight on a number of levels. I argue that neo-slave narratives are exemplars of a Black feminist tradition of talking back as a form of self-defense. In other words, neo-slave narratives allow Black women to articulate their own stories of slavery—those in which they are not merely victims but active agents asserting their humanity in the face of an institution that put them on par with animals. Like Black feminist Hazel Carby, I also assert Black women's literature "should be read not as passive representations of history but as active influence within history. . . . The novels of black women, like the slave and free narratives that preceded them, did not just reflect or 'mirror' a society; they attempted to change it."[9] I am linking literary production to the intellectual tradition much like Nellie McKay in "Black Women's Literary Scholarship: Reclaiming an Intellectual Tradition."[10] Black women's fiction like Black women's intellectual tradition calls attention to the multiple and mutually constitutive aspects of identity and the dynamic nature of oppression. Thus, Black women writers resist binary notions of oppression and insist on a both/and approach as they reveal the gendered nature of racism.

Although the landscape is constantly shifting as writers continue to publish contemporary novels of slavery, a number of critics, myself included, have noted the predominance of Black women writers returning to the site of slavery. According to McDowell, "it is significant that the majority of contemporary novels about slavery have been written by black women. Moreover, it might be argued that these novels posit a female-gendered subjectivity, more complex in dimension, that dramatizes not what was *done* to slave women, but what they *did* with what was done to them."[11] I have argued that Black women's interest in contemporary novels of slavery is directly related to the history of "natal alienation" inherent in the slavery institution, as female slaves were routinely denied the role of mother and viewed merely as breeders.[12] Thus, Black women writers' emphasis on survival in the face of horrifying atrocities is a gendered response to the racial and historical oppression of an entire people. By insisting upon the humanity of the enslaved mother, they, in turn, argue for the humanity of all Black people. Therefore, the enslaved mother's pain becomes the strength of her people. Contemporary Black women writers appear to be responding to both the invisibility of Black women's stories and the limited role Black women are given when they are depicted by male authors. In Black women's contemporary novels of slavery, the Black woman is no longer silent but instead serving as the backbone of future generations' responses to oppression.

Walker ushered in the modern neo-slave narrative era in 1966 as the country was transitioning from the civil rights movement to the era of Black Power, but the genre really gained momentum in the 1980s and 1990s as the United States moved further from the civil rights movement. In *Remembering Generations: Race and Family in Contemporary African American Fiction*, Rushdy explains the rise of palimpsest novels of slavery in the 1970s: "the metaphor and idea of slavery, the original form of policing African American life, proved apt for describing the resurgent forms of structural racism that survived and defied the civil rights acts of the mid-sixties."[13] African American writers were not so sure that African Americans had overcome the obstacles of Jim Crow, the legacy of slavery. As a nation, discussions were circulating about a color blind or postracial society, but contemporary novels of slavery call for rethinking the nature of freedom and the meaning of race.

The rise of contemporary novels of slavery at the same time that conversations about color blind and postracial societies were beginning points to a racial divide in the way in which the state of race relations are viewed. One need only look at the 2016 election and the divisive rhetoric exchanged by Hillary Clinton and Donald Trump supporters as well as the results that gave Trump an electoral victory despite the loss of the popular vote to see how deeply divided the United States is regarding just how far we have come with regard to race relations. Many pointed to Barack Obama's election as the first Black US president as a sign that the country had indeed achieved postracial status, but others point to Trump's Make America Great Again campaign as a resounding backlash to racial progress. The continued racial divide in the United States is also evident in the 2020 presidential election, which saw over seventy-three million voters cast their ballots for a president who espoused White supremacist ideologies. However, writers of contemporary novels of slavery had already recognized that we had not arrived as a country and that we must revisit our nation's history of racial injustice in order to address our current moment as well as to move beyond the pain of our past.

I contend that moving beyond the confines of realistic fiction through speculative fiction provides writers with more latitude to address concerns related to an allegedly postracial society. Thus, I am particularly interested in the intersection of the rise of neo-slave narratives and the Black speculative fiction watershed of the mid- to late 1990s. According to Sandra Govan, speculative fiction is an "umbrella genre that shelters the subgenres of fantasy, science fiction, utopian and dystopian fiction, supernatural fiction, and what has come to be called by some critics fabulative fiction or fabulation."[14] Each of the subgenres "shares in the basic premise underlying speculative fiction—the presentation of a changed, distorted, alternative reality from the reality readers know."[15] Although the rise of speculative fiction pushes conversations regarding race and gender to new dimensions, the Black women writers addressed in this chapter are part of a Black woman's intellectual tradition. According to Black feminist Patricia Hill Collins, "Black women intellectuals have laid a vital analytical foundation for a distinctive standpoint on self, community, and society and, in doing so, created a Black women's intellectual tradition."[16] One of the key components of this intellectual tradition is the insistence on the multiple and mutually constitutive aspects of identity. Thus, even before the coinage of intersectionality, Black women intellectuals have resisted binary articulations of oppression as they recognized the dynamic nature of oppression. Therefore, as contemporary Black women writers turn to speculative fiction to grapple with what it means to be a liberated woman, these concerns mean addressing race, class, and sexuality—not just gender.

Because speculative fiction is not confined by the bounds of realism, authors are able to imagine a world of possibilities, including those that trouble the current state of race relations. Author Walter Mosley observes:

> Science fiction and its relatives (fantasy, horror, speculative fiction, etc.) have been a main artery for recasting our imagination. . . . The genre speaks most clearly to those who are dissatisfied with the way things are: adolescents, post-adolescents, escapists, dreamers, and those who have been made to feel powerless. And this may explain the appeal that science fiction holds for a great many African-Americans. Black people have been cut off from their African ancestry by the scythe of slavery and from an American heritage by being excluded from history. For us, science fiction offers an alternative where that which deviates from the norm is the norm.

Mosley's comments reveal the attraction of speculative fiction for African Americans, who are often viewed as the ultimate alien: "Science fiction allows history to be rewritten or ignored. Science fiction promises a future full of possibility, alternative lives, and even regret."[17] This ability to rewrite history is also the attraction of the neo-slave narrative genre and other contemporary novels of slavery, so it is not surprising that writers might meld the two. Contemporary novels of slavery often serve as correctives exploring veiled aspects of the peculiar institution, while speculative fiction allows one to explore what could be.

Black women writing at the intersection of slavery and speculative fiction are able to probe the complexities of race and gender. In *Recovering the Black Female Body: Self-Representations by African American Women*, editors Michael Bennett and Vanessa D. Dickerson observe, "In slavery, the black female body served as one of the prime technologies of reproduction and commodification. It, more than any other body, politically belies the American declaration of democracy, equality, and freedom."[18] Thus, I argue that speculative novels of slavery offer a unique opportunity to expose the lie of Black inferiority through their representations of the Black female body. The protagonists of these novels are seeking to reclaim what was denied them—their bodies, but they are also re-presenting these bodies and asking their readers to see them differently—not as broodmares but as mothers—not as property but as fellow humans. By incorporating the techniques of the speculative, these writers are able to grapple with aspects of Black history often deemed "unspeakable."[19] Mitchell argues, "Contemporary African American writers who engage the theme of slavery do so in order to bear witness to the 'unspeakable,' to correct enduring misrepresentations and misinterpretations of Black Americans forged in slavery, and to present history from a racialized perspective."[20] Although I do not argue that one must enter the realm of the speculative to engage racial and gender concerns, I do share Ellen Morgan's views about the applicability of speculative fiction for writers who wish to question social norms. According to Morgan:

> The social reality in which the realistic novel is grounded has been, and is still, firmly patriarchal, and it still makes the realistic novel about a liberated woman very nearly a contradiction in terms. The fantasy is still the only forum for the depiction of women successfully breaching all the barriers of sexual caste, and it serves the important function of taking the reader where neither the realistic novel nor the real woman has yet been able to go. It expands our store of images of what is possible.[21]

Speculative contemporary novels of slavery, such as Toni Morrison's *Beloved* (1987) and Jewelle Gomez's *Gilda Stories* (1991), not only reflect on the history and legacy of slavery but also ponder the possibility of truly liberated women.

For Morrison, the speculative trope of the ghost is the ideal mechanism for broaching the painful history of slavery. In her 1994 interview with Angels Carabi, Morrison notes:

> With *Beloved*, I am trying to insert this memory that was unbearable and unspeakable into the literature. Not only to write about a woman who did what Sethe did, but to have the ghost of the daughter return as a remnant of a period that was unspoken. It was a silence within the race. So it's a kind of healing experience. There are certain things that are repressed because they are unthinkable, and the only way to come free of that is to go back and deal with them.[22]

A ghost, then, is a perfect image for addressing repressed or difficult memories. Beloved might be Sethe's personal ghost, but slavery is the nation's ghost. The appeal of the ghost metaphor is apparent when one thinks of the contemporary moment of Morrison's novel: "In *Beloved*, published in 1987, Morrison seems to be writing against forgetfulness when we consider the retreats and reversals in civil rights legislation alive in the 1980s."[23] This observation is reminiscent of Mosley's comments regarding what speculative fiction makes possible. Beloved the ghost and *Beloved* the novel call attention to the unfulfilled promises of liberty and justice—the United States still falls short of its pledge of life, liberty, and justice for all found in the Declaration of Independence and Pledge of Allegiance. Rather than write a political diatribe about the amnesia of the post–civil rights moment, Morrison can subtly point to what has been forgotten via a ghost who refuses to be disremembered. It is quite apropos that Morrison builds off of the slave-narrative tradition as those forebears to the African American literary tradition also called out the latent hypocrisy of slavery and asked our nation to live up to its Christian ideals.

Beloved is a rich novel with many themes: slavery, maternity, and spirituality among them; however, this essay focuses primarily on the text's concern with memory, which appears to undergird the novel from its opening dedication to "Sixty Million and more" to the ambiguous closing refrain: "This is not a story to pass on."[24] However, the concern with memory is not merely the insistence that one remember but that the memory is truly digested. Literary scholar Sharon Holland describes the process well: "Morrison wields memory so that it circumvents traditional ideas of past, present, and future. . . . Beloved/*Beloved* is about remembering, slowly, easily, and painfully."[25] I contend that the pain comes from the insistence that something must be done with the memories. The memories are not for display but for action. Sethe initially flounders because she is attempting to repress her past, but once she and Denver confront the past, they are positioned to be full members of their community. *Beloved* calls on its protagonists and readers to both remember and contend with our nation's past as the novel explores the nature of Black women's liberation.

Beloved's emphasis on memory resonates with contemporary social movements' injunctions to "stay woke." "Woke," an adjective, was included in the 2016 shortlist for words that captured the public imagination.[26] The word appeared on T-shirts and in various social-media streams to indicate being alert to social injustice, especially racism. While "woke" has been a part of African American vernacular for a long time, it became increasingly popular in 2014 following the fatal shooting of Michael Brown in Ferguson, Missouri, as the Black Lives Matter movement took up this catchphrase to indicate they were woke and they wanted others to stay woke. Thus, phrases such as "stay woke" and "woke af" (woke as fuck) became calls to action, similar to Morrison's usage of memory in *Beloved*.

Beloved opens with the ominous lines, "124 was spiteful. Full of a baby's venom."[27] It soon becomes clear that the home is haunted by the ghost of a dead baby, and its mother, Sethe, and sister, Denver, are the only family members left to feel its pain. However, when Paul D, the last of the Sweet Home men, finds Sethe, he inquires about the evil in the house. Although Sethe claims, "It's not evil, just sad," Denver contends that the ghost is not evil or sad but "[r]ebuked. Lonely and rebuked."[28] Marilyn Sanders Mobley maintains in "A Different Remembering: Memory, History, and Meaning in Toni Morrison's *Beloved*," "The obsolete meaning of rebuked—repressed—not only suggests that the ghost represents repressed memory, but that, as with anything that is repressed, it eventually resurfaces or returns in one form or another."[29] Thus, Denver's contention that the ghost is rebuked serves as a foreshadowing of Beloved's later incarnation. Sethe has repressed the memories of her enslavement and the killing of her child to prevent her enslavement under the Fugitive Slave Act of 1850.[30] However, this repression is futile because Sethe can only keep the past at bay for so long before it literally and figuratively comes crashing upon her when her deceased daughter returns.

Kathleen Brogan argues, "Haunting in *Beloved* signals the return of a past that can neither be properly remembered nor entirely forgotten."[31] This difficulty is reflected in the ambiguity surrounding Beloved's appearance. Paul D seems to have driven away the ghost in that the house has stopped rocking and the red light has disappeared, but shortly thereafter Beloved appears "as a fully dressed woman walking out of the water, her return is typically seen as a rebirth of sorts. While she is described as a woman, her actions seem more like a child—she has difficulty holding her head up and staying awake and even more intriguing—she 'had new skin, lineless and smooth.'"[32] The sense that Beloved is Sethe's child reborn is further confirmed by Sethe's reaction upon seeing Beloved—her bladder fills and she voids an excessive amount of fluid as though her water were breaking. Although it appears that Paul D has rescued Sethe from her memories by driving off the ghost, in reality the ghost has merely changed form. As a ghost, Beloved could not be forgotten, but when she returns as a grown woman, it also becomes clear that she could not be properly remembered. As Denver's namesake, Amy Denver remarked years before, "Anything dead coming back to life hurts."[33] Beloved profoundly demonstrates this truism.

The complicated nature of memory is revealed early in the text when Sethe tells Denver about her rememory, "Some things go. Pass on. Some things just stay. I used to think it was my rememory. You know. Some things you forget. Other things you never do. But it's not. Places, places are still there. If a house burns down, it's gone, but the place—the picture of it—stays, and not just in my rememory, but out there, in the world."[34] Speculative contemporary novels of slavery, such as *Beloved*, allow Black women writers to grapple with their contested history and to assert their own interpretations. I have commented previously, "As rememory made flesh, Beloved forces Sethe to confront painful memories she has repressed. While this is clearly a painful process, it is also a necessary one."[35] Sethe has sought to avoid her past, but Beloved forces her to reckon with her actions. Sethe's decision to slit her child's throat is born out of love as she cannot bear the thought of her child enslaved, but it is also enmeshed with the shame of her own mother's abandonment.

Sethe's action seems inexplicable. She tries to explain to Paul D how she felt after escaping slavery with her children only to be threatened with recapture: "I couldn't let her nor any of em live under schoolteacher. That was out." But even as Sethe explains, she realizes her attempt was futile. Morrison's goal is not to justify Sethe's actions but to help her readers understand her motivations. Sethe sought liberation for her child. After her few days of freedom, she could not imagine allowing herself and children to be remanded to slavery once again. For Sethe, death was freedom if the alternative was slavery. She tries to explain this to Paul D, who had also been at Sweet Home, and to Beloved, her daughter returned. While Paul D is repulsed by Sethe's actions, Beloved wants to be assured that Sethe will never leave her again. Beloved's fear of abandonment appears to resonate with Sethe's own shame regarding her mother's abandonment. According to Deborah Horvitz, Sethe's "memories of Ma'am are buried not only because their relationship was vague and their contact prohibited but also because those recollections are inextricably woven with feelings of painful abandonment. If Sethe remembers her mother, she must also remember that she believes her mother deserted her."[36] Thus for Sethe, her taking of Beloved's life must be seen in terms of liberation, not abandonment. Sethe believes her mother died while trying to escape without her, so she understands Beloved's feelings of abandonment, but she wants Beloved to see her actions in terms of liberation, not desertion. Thus, Morrison troubles our understanding of liberation by questioning maternal responsibility: Can mothers choose their notion of liberation for their children? Can mothers choose liberation for themselves without also abandoning their children?

For Sethe to make peace with what she has done, she must believe Beloved has returned. However, this return is not a blissful reunion but, instead, an opportunity for Beloved to torture her mother and make her pay for what she has done. As time passes, a sort of role reversal occurs in which Sethe is constantly at Beloved's beck and call and places her needs before her own. This change is reflected in the physical dimensions of the characters, "as Beloved expands, Sethe shrinks; as Beloved fills with vitality, Sethe drops listlessly."[37] Sethe and Denver are both in danger of starving now that Sethe has lost her job and become entranced with Beloved and her needs. Sethe has completely abdicated her role as mother and is utterly dominated by Beloved, who becomes enraged any time Sethe attempts to assert maternal authority.

It is at this critical moment that memory becomes essential. Denver recognizes that she needs to venture out into the community for assistance, but it is the memory of her grandmother Baby Suggs that finally emboldens her to act. Although Baby Suggs is deceased, Denver hears her clearly, "You don't remember nothing about how come I walk the way I do and about your mother's feet, not to speak of her back? I never told you all that? Is that why you can't walk down the steps?"[38] This speculative technique of ghostly communication provides Denver with another avenue to the past. Because of the pain associated with their slave past, Sethe and Baby Suggs had not shared much of this past with Denver. However, after her death, Baby Suggs comes to recognize the limitations of this approach. By shrouding the past from Denver, she and Sethe have also kept from her the memories that would inspire her:

> Baby Suggs realizes that in agreeing with Sethe that some things were unspeakable, she had deprived Denver of essential knowledge about her past that might empower her later. Thus in not talking about Sethe's feet, they protected Denver from the pain of slavery, but they also hid from her the power of self-determination. The women may have been ashamed of the beatings that led to Baby Suggs' misshapen hip and Sethe's scarred back, but Baby Suggs now recognizes that these are not necessarily badges of shame, but symbols of survival as she tells Denver to go on out the yard.[39]

Thus, Baby Suggs shows Denver that memory can be liberating as she urges Denver to tap into familial memories as sources of encouragement. Sethe's approach of burying one's memories does not work, as repressed memories will only surface much like Beloved returned. We must address our memories—good and bad—in order to move on and avoid stasis. By leaving the yard, Denver rejects Sethe's approach of repressing memory and, instead, uses the power of memory to sustain her and move toward liberation.

Denver's decision to leave the yard also sets the stage for Sethe's rescue and reintegration with the community. The neighboring women provide food for Denver's family and even help her find work, but they also ask questions about Beloved: "The news that Janey got hold of she spread among the other colored women. Sethe's dead daughter, the one whose throat she cut, had come back to fix her. Sethe was worn down, speckled, dying, spinning, changing shapes and generally bedeviled." Ella, a neighbor, convinces the other women that Sethe needs to be rescued: "Whatever Sethe had done, Ella didn't like the idea of past errors taking possession of the present."[40] Ella leads the other women in an exorcism that appears to lead to Beloved's disappearance, which critics tend to read as a sign that the past has been addressed. Ella appears to advocate for a healthy integration of past and present along the same lines as her openness to communication between the living and the dead. However, Beloved has gone too far in trying to hold Sethe accountable for her past, and Sethe has not gone far enough by ignoring and denying her past. A healthy future is only possible with a reasonable integration of past and present. Liberation is only possible for Denver and Sethe when they truly contend with the past. Thus, the past cannot be denied or ignored, but neither should it consume the present.

I argue that a similar belief undergirds the admonition to "stay woke." Staying woke does not imply despair in the face of past or current injustice. Rather, it suggests resilience and even a healthy anger in the more colloquial "woke as fuck" rendition. By acknowledging injustice, those who are woke are better prepared to fight that injustice because they are fully aware and willing to challenge power structures. The willingness to speak truth to power is also a reflection of hope for society to live up to its professed ideals.

Beloved ends with ambiguity as the reader is reminded again and again, "It was not a story to pass on."[41] Linda Krumholz comments, "This line recapitulates the tension between repression and rememory figured throughout the novel. In one reading, the story is not one to pass by or to pass over. At the same time, the more evident meaning is intensely ironic—'This is not a story to pass on,' and yet, as the novel shows us, it must be."[42] So the novel ends where it began with the tension between the need to remember and the pain of doing so. However, this fruitful tension reveals the essence of humanity. To be whole, one must feel, and to appreciate happiness, one must know sorrow. Moreover, as a nation, the United States must remember the past—the good, the bad, and the ugly. It is only through remembering and learning from the past that the country can mature as a nation.

The significance of memory is also evident in Gomez's *The Gilda Stories*, which traces its protagonist over a span of two hundred years from 1850 to 2050. In this rewriting of the traditional vampire novel, Gomez creates a Black woman vampire who troubles notions of gender, sexuality, and family. The storyline follows the life and travels of an escaped slave who is transformed into a vampire by the woman whose name she then assumes. Literary scholar Elyce Rae Helford views *The Gilda Stories* as part of a "recent trend in speculative fiction to simultaneously emphasize both utopian and dystopian elements." For Helford, this utopian writing "is permeated by cynicism yet retains the capacity to inspire positive cultural change."[43] She links this movement to the antifeminist backlash of the 1980s and the speculative literary response associated with the end of the Ronald Reagan–George H. W. Bush years. Like *Beloved*, *The Gilda Stories* is written in the context of retreats and reversals of gains regarding civil rights and women's rights. Thus, I am particularly interested in how the speculative form of the vampire novel allows Gomez to explore the intersections of race, gender, and sexuality in asking what it might mean to be a liberated woman.

In *Alien to Femininity: Speculative Fiction and Feminist Theory*, Marleen Barr argues, "Speculative Fiction has in recent years been enlivened by the contribution of new female (often feminist) voices. Because these writers are not hindered by the constraints of patriarchal social reality, they can imagine presently impossible possibilities for women. Their genre is ideally suited for exploring the potential of women's changing roles."[44] As a vampire, Gilda is given a long memory that allows her to make connections over two hundred years of her country's history. Yet, by revising the vampire trope and making her vampire Black and female, Gomez asks readers to reconsider their notion of the Other and in the process prods them to envision a liberated woman as an ideal to be sought rather than feared. This revisionist agenda is signaled by the opening epigraph from Audre Lorde's prologue:

> At night sleep locks me into an echoless coffin
> sometimes at noon I dream
> there is nothing to fear. . . . [45]

These lines call on the reader to rethink one's assumptions—the height of day, noon, is now a time for sleep and dreams, and it is the vampire who is in fear rather than feared. Through the vampire trope, Gomez asks whether a liberated woman is truly a source of fear.

The Gilda Stories is a hybrid text that bridges the slave narrative with the vampire tale in a way that encourages readers to question identity norms related to race, gender, and sexuality. In "The Feminist Dystopia of the 1990s: Record of Failure, Midwife of Hope," Jane Donawerth traces the use of the slave narrative within feminist dystopias. According to Donawerth, "1990s feminist dystopias incorporate the slave narrative as a myth of human intelligence and adaptability. The slave narrative, always set in a dystopian society, nevertheless tells a story of change. Science fiction writers of the 1990s turn to the slave narrative to find a way out of the failures and dead ends of stalled political reform."[46] For contemporary writers like Gomez, it is the aftermath of slavery that is at stake. Thus, an immortal vampire protagonist with a life span that encompasses her enslavement in 1850 Louisiana to the imagined future of 2050 is uniquely positioned to explore the nature of liberation.

The Gilda Stories, like other speculative fictions, has a fraught relation with history. In "Speculative Fictions of Slavery," Madhu Dubey argues, "Speculative fictions overtly situate themselves against history, suggesting that we can best comprehend the truth of slavery by abandoning historical modes of knowing." Thus for Dubey, the tension surrounding history may be resolved via narrative techniques: "Refusing to regard the past of slavery as history, speculative novels suggest that the truth of this past is more fully grasped by way of an antirealist literary imagination that can fluidly cross temporal boundaries and affectively immerse readers into the world of slavery."[47] Hence, Gomez can reach readers with a protagonist who travels between their remote past, immediate past, and potential future while showing the continued impact of racism and sexism across these various times.

As Gilda travels through the years and across the country, she often finds herself in fellowship with women who are negotiating gender boundaries and in essence determining the nature of women's liberation. She first arrives as the Girl to the first Gilda's brothel, Woodard's, but the women there were not like any the Girl had seen before:

> These women embodied the innocence of children the Girl had known back on the plantation, yet they were also hard, speaking of the act of sex casually, sometimes with humor. And even more puzzling was their debate of topics the Girl had heard spoken of only by men. The women eagerly expressed their views on politics and economics: what slavery was doing to the South, who was dominating politics, and the local agitation against the Galatain Street "houses."

Although these women work in a brothel, they carry themselves with a sense of self-assurance that allows them to discuss topics that were at the time deemed the purview of men. Gilda's reflection on these women who work for her is also telling, "They all had the manners of ladies, could read, write, and shoot." This final ability suggests that these are women who can take care of themselves and do not require the protecting shelter of men. However, this does not mean that the women are not challenged, such as when one of Gilda's customers persists in soliciting the Girl despite being told that she works only in the kitchen. Gilda is able to redirect the customer, but her ability to do so may be related to her blurring of gender identity as the Girl at one point mistakes her for a man. Gilda assures the Girl, "*I am a woman, you know that. And you know I am a woman as no other you have known, nor has your mother known, in life or death. I am a woman as you are, and more.*"[48] This response foreshadows her later revelation of being a vampire, but it also points to what is possible within the realms of speculative fiction.

One of the things that appears to be possible in *The Gilda Stories* is an intersectional analysis, which foregrounds race and gender; however, this is often lacking in our social movements. Even the Black Lives Matter movement, which was begun by three Black women, Alicia Garza, Patrisse Cullors, and Opal Tometi, has been plagued by the disappearance of women's voices and stories.

> [T]he deaths of Michael Brown, Eric Garner, Freddie Gray, and others have mobilized an unprecedented mass movement against police brutality and racism. [However,] black women—like Rekia Boyd, Michelle Cusseaux, Tanisha

Anderson, Shelly Frey, Yvette Smith, Eleanor Bumpurs, and others—have also been killed, assaulted, and victimized by the police. Often, women are targeted in exactly the same ways as men—shootings, police stops, racial profiling. They also experience police violence in distinctly gendered ways, such as sexual harassment and sexual assault. Yet such cases have failed to mold our analysis of the broader picture of police violence; nor have they drawn equal public attention or outrage.[49]

Mamie Locke argues in "Whose Lives Really Matter: The Invisibility of African American Women in the Political Discourse of the Black Lives Matter Campaign" that "African American women have played central roles in every social and political struggle and movement in the United States since its inception. Despite immersing themselves in these struggles and movements and being agents of change, African American women are often historical footnotes and afterthoughts, generally pushed to the periphery of discourse and policymaking in reality."[50] In response to the invisibility of Black women in the Black Lives Matter movement, the African American Policy Forum launched the Say Her Name social-media campaign to call attention to the increased risk of poverty, violence, and sexual assault facing Black women and girls. Say Her Name "documents and analyzes Black women's experiences of police violence and explains what we lose when we ignore them. We not only miss half the facts, we fundamentally fail to grasp how the laws, policies, and the culture that underpin gender inequalities are reinforced by America's racial divide."[51] Collins points to the historical importance of intersectionality to Black women's activism: "For African-American women, the knowledge gained at the intersection of race, gender, and class oppression provides the stimulus for crafting and passing on the subjugated knowledge of a Black women's culture of resistance."[52] Black women's intellectual tradition has long recognized that without an intersectional lens of analysis, gendered aspects of racism go unaccounted and unaddressed.

Barr contends, "Speculative fiction in the best cases makes the patriarchal structures which constrain women obvious and perceptible."[53] This is definitely the case in *The Gilda Stories*, in which both iterations of the Gilda character illustrate what women might be if they could reach their full potential and not be stunted by patriarchal expectations. It is her time at Woodard's with Gilda that prepares the Girl to probe the possibilities for true liberation as she travels the country and lives through significant changes over the decades. One particularly significant time is 1921 while living in Rosebud, Missouri. The Nineteenth Amendment giving women the right to vote had been passed the year before, so women had gained more rights but were still significantly restricted by social expectations. The chapter opens with an introduction to Aurelia, who has been widowed for a year. Although Aurelia endured bleak days during her first year of widowhood, "she had always thought of her life as satisfying, perhaps even more so in widowhood which had bestowed an unfamiliar independence."[54] In her portrayal of Aurelia, Gomez questions the lack of independence that preceded her widowhood. One has the sense that Aurelia lived in her husband's shadow before his death, so that only after his death did the sitting room feel like hers. It was as if she had no separate identity while married and could only claim one as a widow.

On the evening that the reader is introduced to Aurelia, she is hosting a women's church circle with Alice Dunbar as the invited speaker. Dunbar is certainly a reference to Alice Dunbar-Nelson, a writer and activist. Dunbar-Nelson wrote stories, poetry, and essays about racism, sexism, work, family, and sexuality and was involved in the woman's suffrage movement and antilynching campaigns. However, Gomez may have alluded to Dunbar-Nelson because of her multiple marriages and lesbian relationships, as her personal life appears to reflect the concerns that Gomez seeks to highlight, as well. For example, Gomez counters Aurelia's excitement over the evening with Edna Bright's discomfort due to her husband's impatience. Mr. Bright derogatorily refers to women's socials as "talk and twitter," causing Edna to war "against herself—her desire to stay and hear more, to say more, battled with the knowledge that he waited. The longer she lingered, the more the women's efforts would be belittled."[55] As a married woman, Edna lacks Aurelia's newfound independence. Gomez seems to imply that marriage encumbers women by limiting their ability to act freely.

Aurelia, with her husband and both of her parents deceased, is financially comfortable but without patriarchal supervision. Gomez uses Aurelia's friendship with Gilda to explore the possibility of women's true liberation. The possibility of a lesbian relationship is suggested by Dunbar's seductive gaze as well as Aurelia's desire to be alone again with her special friend, Gilda; yet, this isn't fully explored. However, it is suggested that in 1921 Rosebud, Missouri, lesbian relationships would not be accepted.

Gilda is able to live as a single woman in the town under the guise of being a widow, but she is seen as a bit of an eccentric for doing such things as driving a car—something of an oddity for a Black woman. It is as if the community recognizes that Gilda is not truly one of them. In "Women and Vampires: Nightmares or Utopia?" Judith Johnson argues, "The social position of the typical vampire is no accident. It tells us that part of the inherent metaphorical material in society's dreams of vampire narratives is social, and involves questions of social justice, power, exploitation, race, and class, as well as the more obvious gender conflict."[56] As a vampire, Gilda can broach social mores in a way mortal women cannot. She moves from community to community, and as time passes, Gilda encounters various women who are navigating gender norms in hopes of finding a path to true liberation.

In 1955 Gilda is established in the South End of Boston as a beautician with friends who include the working girls of the avenue. This community in many ways echoes that of Woodard's, but these women living nearly one hundred years later are even more determined to assert themselves. The chapter follows the stories of two different sex workers—Savannah and Toya. It is significant that both the "Louisiana: 1850" and "South End: 1955" chapters draw on women as sex workers to explore women's identity. While Nina K. Martin, in "Porn Empowerment: Negotiating Sex Work and Third Wave Feminism," acknowledges, "For some young feminists, sex work has become celebrated rather than contested ground." Gomez's depiction of sex work suggests that the potential of sex work for empowerment is not fully realized and, instead, suggests a queer alternative. The Girl's experience of being accosted while working in the kitchen at Woodard's shows the potential dangers of the sex industry, but Toya's episode with her pimp, Fox, explores the limitations and dangers of sex work in greater detail. On one hand, sex work at Woodard's is shown to provide women with greater autonomy. Readers see this initially at Woodard's where the women are free to discuss politics and economic, topics generally reserved for men. Economic freedom is also suggested by Savannah's use of her trade to acquire additional income when necessary. Savannah certainly does not see herself as coerced or sexually exploited; however, Martin warns, "For every empowering aspect of sexual labor, there exists an equally negative consequence that constrains the possibility of feminist support." This possibility is at play in the very different circumstances of Savannah and Toya. While Savannah can tap into "sex work's transgressive force" by making men pay for her services, Toya is a victim "of coercion and sexual exploitation."[57] However, I contend that Gomez provides a queer alternative, which disrupts the heterosexual social order and its associated gender conventions.

Although Savannah is depicted as a strong, assertive woman who is empowered as a sex worker, a story from her past suggests that this empowerment comes in part from her encounter with Fancy Danny. In her younger days, Savannah was pursued by Franklin, who scared off her customers by hanging over her and claiming she was not going to leave him. As a last resort, Savannah turns to Danny, "this woman who had a rep as big as Franklin's." Danny agrees to Savannah staying at her place, and Savannah agrees "to be one of her girls." After this arrangement is made, Franklin confronts Savannah in front of Danny, which leads to a fight outside between Danny and Franklin: "Danny come back in the bar ten minutes later, put her rings back on, and ordered a martini. I never forgot it. Cool as a cuke. And that was that." Franklin never bothers Savannah again, even a year later when she leaves Danny's. However, that she remained at Danny's even after the threat to her safety was gone suggests that there was more for Savannah at Danny's than protection. As Savannah tells the story, Skip inquires what took her so long to leave. "Savannah laughed, 'Well, she was right. She never had to chain nobody.'"[58] This is an understated but telling response that suggests there was more to their relationship.

Gomez uses silences and gaps to suggest queer possibilities for Black women's sexuality. This turn to silence is emblematic of what women and gender studies scholar Evelynn Hammonds finds in dominant discourses: "The sexualities of black women have been shaped by silence, erasure, and invisibility." Thus, readers are not told that Fancy Danny is a butch lesbian, but the description of her reputation, sharp threads, solid build, cool persona, and pulled-back hair are all suggestive. That Savannah remains even after she is safe from Franklin is further evidence that her desire to be with Danny is not just about being away from Franklin. That Savannah laughs as she acknowledges that Danny "never had to chain nobody" also suggests pleasure in the relationship. Hammonds argues, "[B]lack queer female sexualities should be seen as one of the sites where black female desire is expressed."[59] For Savannah, this desire appears to be expressed with Danny and even later with her younger boyfriend, Skip, whose masculinity is questioned.

Throughout *The Gilda Stories*, Gomez depicts homosocial bonding, but as the novel progresses, the queer possibilities multiply, suggesting that Gilda's liberation is in part due to her queer identity. Homosocial bonding is evident among the women at Woodard's, the women on the avenue, and the women at the club. Lesbian desire is suggested to different degrees in Gilda's relationships with Aurelia, Eleanor, and Effie. However, Gilda's relationships with Julius, Bird, Sorel, and Anthony further trouble our notions of gender, sexuality, and family. I maintain that Gilda's status as a vampire is particularly advantageous in rethinking these arenas. Ingrid Thaler, author of *Black Atlantic Speculative Fictions*, observes, "Since the 1970s, the vampire has been reclaimed as a trope that presents a dramatic change in cultural attitudes toward marginalized groups, primarily in terms of sexuality and gender."[60] As a creature who takes or shares blood, the vampire is well positioned to penetrate social barriers.

This breaking down of social barriers is also sought by the Black Lives Matter movement, which Marcia Chatelain, creator of the #FergusonSyllabus, describes as "feminist in its interrogation of state power and its critique of structural inequality." She further observes, "It is also forcing a conversation about gender and racial politics that we need to have—women at the forefront of this movement are articulating that 'black lives' does not only mean men's lives or cisgender lives or respectable lives or the lives that are legitimated by state power or privilege."[61] Like Locke, Chatelain comments on the initial focus of the Black Lives Matter movement on the deaths of Black men, but she also notes the refocused attention on Black women and others on the margins of society, such as poor, elderly, gay, and transgender people. While she concedes that gendered police violence and the criminalization of poor, Black women have not been adequately represented in the protests, she points to the movement's attention to intersectionality.[62] However, Locke entreats the movement to take an intersectional perspective, as "race, gender and class overlap intricately, impacting the social, political, and economic lives of African American women."[63] These divergent assessments of the degree of intersectionality evident in the Black Lives Matter movement suggests the difficulty of enacting an intersectional frame of analysis.

This difficulty is also reflected in *The Gilda Stories*. Intersectionality may be imagined by Gomez, but Gilda finds it challenging to live at the intersection of her race, gender, and sexuality. The novel both opens and closes with Gilda fleeing for her life. Timothy A. Spaulding remarks, "Gomez forces us to reconceptualize the threat of violence and the source of evil in the text. As both an escaped slave and a vampire, the protagonist of *The Gilda Stories* . . . is the hunted rather than the hunter, constantly in danger of discovery and re-enslavement."[64] The first and final chapters feature bounty hunters pursuing the Gilda. While the last chapter focuses on Gilda's flight, the final line is hopeful, "Gilda was no longer fleeing for her life" as she and Ermis turned southward to meet Julius and Effie.[65] This is an interesting reversal of the slave narrative, which typically involves a flight north. By heading south, Gomez signifies on the cycle of history and the relationship of speculative fiction to history.

Speculative contemporary novels of slavery have a fraught relationship with history in that the speculative form suggests an attempt to break away from history, while the subject of slavery insists on recognition of the impact of history. In many ways, the texts enact contemporary society's desire to be postracial while revealing our inability to cut the ties of race. According to Dubey,

> With the legal termination of Jim Crow and the formal achievement of equal rights for African Americans, the nation supposedly passed into a postracial era, and in this sense the Civil Rights movement was believed to mark the end of a very long period of racial inequality spanning from slavery to the 1960s. The suspicion of history in speculative novels of slavery bespeaks a sharp sense of incredulity toward this historical narrative of racial emancipation.

Speculative fiction is the ideal genre in order to exhume the legacy of slavery that continues to haunt us. Dubey comments, "Because current manifestations of racism take more insidious forms than they did in the past, often going by names other than racism, the memory of slavery becomes a way of making them legible in terms of the familiar scripts of the past."[66] I suspect writers will continue writing contemporary novels of slavery at least until we are truly postracial, just as we will continue to have social movements until nations live up to their professed ideals.

Notes

1. Venetria K. Patton, *The Grasp That Reaches beyond the Grave: The Ancestral Call in Black Women's Texts* (Albany: State University of New York Press, 2013), 3.

2. Ibid., 4.

3. Bernard Bell, *The Afro-American Novel and Its Tradition* (Amherst: University of Massachusetts Press, 1987), 289.

4. Ashraf H. A. Rushdy, *Neo-slave Narratives: Studies in the Social Logic of a Literary Form* (New York: Oxford University Press, 1993), 3.

5. See Ashraf H. A. Rushdy, "The Neo-slave Narrative," in *The Cambridge Companion to the African American Novel*, ed. Maryemma Graham (Cambridge, UK: Cambridge University Press, 2004), 87–105.

6. Deborah E. McDowell, "Negotiating between Tenses: Witnessing Slavery after Freedom—*Dessa Rose*," in *Slavery and the Literary Imagination*, ed. McDowell and Arnold Rampersad (Baltimore: John Hopkins University Press, 1989), 146.

7. Angelyn Mitchell, *The Freedom to Remember: Narrative, Slavery, and Gender in Contemporary Black Women's Fiction* (New Brunswick, NJ: Rutgers University Press, 2002), 5.

8. McDowell, "Negotiating," 146.

9. Hazel Carby, *Reconstructing Womanhood: The Emergence of the Afro-American Woman Novelist* (New York: Oxford University Press, 1987).

10. Nellie McKay, "Black Women's Literary Scholarship: Reclaiming an Intellectual Tradition," *Sage* 6, no. 1 (1989): 89–91.

11. McDowell, "Negotiating," 146.

12. See Orlando Patterson, *Slavery and Social Death: A Comparative Study* (Cambridge, MA: Harvard University Press, 1982).

13. Ashraf H. A. Rushdy, *Remembering Generations: Race and Family in Contemporary African American Fiction* (Chapel Hill: University of North Carolina Press, 2001), 14.

14. Sandra Y. Govan, "Speculative Fiction," in *The Oxford Companion to African American Literature*, ed. William L. Andrews, Frances Smith Foster, and Trudier Harris (New York: Oxford University Press, 1997), 683.

15. Ibid.

16. Patricia Hill Collins, *Black Feminist Thought* (New York: Routledge, 1991), 5.

17. Walter Mosley. "Black to the Future," in *Dark Matter: A Century of Speculative Fiction from the African Diaspora*, ed. Sheree R. Thomas (New York: Warner, 2000), 405.

18. Michael Bennett and Vanessa D. Dickerson, introduction to *Recovering the Black Female Body: Self-Representations by African American Women*, ed. Bennett and Dickerson (New Brunswick, NJ: Rutgers University Press, 2001), 13.

19. In "Unspeakable Things Unspoken: The Afro-American Presence in American Literature," first presented as the Tanner Lecture on Human Values at the University of Michigan, Toni Morrison discusses African Americans as subjects of their own narratives.

20. Mitchell, *Freedom to Remember*, 5.

21. Ellen Morgan, "Human Becoming: Form and Focus in the Neo-feminist Novel," in *Feminist Criticism: Essays on Theory, Poetry, and Prose*, ed. Cheryl Brown and Karen Olson (Metuchen, NJ: Scarecrow, 1978), 237.

22. Angels Carabi, "Interview with Toni Morrison," *Belles Lettres: A Review of Books by Women* 9, no. 3 (1994): 38.

23. Mitchell, *Freedom to Remember*, 106.

24. Toni Morrison, *Beloved* (1987; New York: Vintage International, 2004), xii, 324.

25. Sharon Patricia Holland, *Raising the Dead: Readings of Death and (Black) Subjectivity* (Durham, NC: Duke University Press, 2000), 50.

26. "Stay Woke . . . We're in a Post-Truth World," *Sun*, November 17, 2016.

27. Morrison, *Beloved*, 3.

28. Ibid., 10, 16.

29. Marilyn Sanders Mobley, "A Different Remembering: Memory, History and Meaning in Toni Morrison's *Beloved*," in *Modern Critical Interpretations: Toni Morrison's* Beloved, ed. Harold Bloom (Philadelphia: Chelsea, 1999), 23.

30. Patton, *Grasp*, 125.

31. Kathleen Brogan, *Cultural Haunting: Ghosts and Ethnicity in Recent American Literature* (Charlottesville: University Press of Virginia, 1998), 63.

32. Patton, *Grasp*, 126.

33. Morrison, *Beloved*, 42.

34. Ibid., 43.

35. Patton, *Grasp*, 139.

36. Deborah Horvitz, "Nameless Ghosts: Possession and Dispossession in *Beloved*," in *Critical Essays on Toni Morrison's* Beloved, ed. Barbara H. Solomon (New York: Hall, 1998), 95.

37. Rachel Adams, "The Black Look and 'the Spectacle of Whitefolks': Wildness in Toni Morrison's *Beloved*," in *Skin Deep, Spirit Strong: The Black Female Body in American Culture*, ed. Kimberly Wallace-Sanders (Ann Arbor: U of Michigan P, 2002), 171–172.

38. Morrison, *Beloved*, 288.

39. Patton, *Grasp*, 140.

40. Morrison, *Beloved*, 300, 302.

41. Ibid., 323, 324.

42. Linda Krumholz, "The Ghosts of Slavery: Historical Recovery in Toni Morrison's *Beloved*," in Bloom, *Modern Critical Interpretations*, 95.

43. Elyce Rae Helford, "The Future of Political Community: Race, Ethnicity, and Class Privilege in Novels by Piercy, Gomez, and Misha," *Utopian Studies* 12, no. 2 (2001): 125.

44. Marleen S. Barr, preface to *Alien to Femininity: Speculative Fiction and Feminist Theory*, ed. Barr (New York: Greenwood, 1987), xi.

45. Audre Lorde, acknowledgments to *The Gilda Stories*, by Jewelle Gomez (Ithaca, NY: Firebrand, 2005), 8.

46. Jane Donawerth, "The Feminist Dystopia of the 1990s: Record of Failure, Midwife of Hope," in *Future Females, the Next Generation: New Voices and Velocities in Feminist Science Fiction Criticism*, ed. Marlene S. Barr (Lanham, MD: Rowman, 2000), 54.

47. Madhu Dubey, "Speculative Fictions of Slavery," *American Literature* 82, no. 4 (2010): 784, 785.

48. Jewelle Gomez, *The Gilda Stories* (Ithaca, NY: Firebrand, 2005), 20, 25, 16, original emphasis.

49. Kaavya Asoka, "Women and Black Lives Matter: An Interview with Marcia Chatelain," *Dissent* 62, no. 3 (2015): 54.

50. Mamie Locke, "Whose Lives Really Matter: The Invisibility of African American Women in the Political Discourse of the Black Lives Matter Campaign," *Virginia Social Science Journal* 51 (2016): 17.

51. Asoka, "Women," 54.

52. Collins, *Black Feminist Thought*, 10.

53. Barr, preface to *Alien*, xx.

54. Gomez, *Gilda*, 103.

55. Ibid.

56. Judith E. Johnson, "Women and Vampires: Nightmares or Utopia?" *Kenyon Review* 15, no. 1 (1993): 75.

57. Nina K. Martin, "Porn Empowerment: Negotiating Sex Work and Third Wave Feminism," *Atlantis: Critical Studies in Gender, Culture, and Social Justice* 31, no. 2 (2007): 36, 36, 35.

58. Gomez, *Gilda*, 153, 153, 154, 154.

59. Evelynn Hammonds, "Black (W)holes and the Geometry of Black Female Sexuality," *Differences* 6, no. 2–3 (1994): 130, 136.

60. Ingrid Thaler, *Black Atlantic Speculative Fictions: Octavia Butler, Jewelle Gomez, and Nalo Hopkinson* (New York: Routledge, 2010), 53.

61. Asoka, "Women," 57.

62. See ibid., 58–59.

63. Locke, "Whose Lives," 21.

64. Timothy A. Spaulding, *Re-forming the Past: History, the Fantastic, and the Postmodern Slave Narrative* (Columbus: Ohio State University Press, 2005), 105.

65. Gomez, *Gilda*, 252.

66. Dubey, "Speculative Fictions," 793, 795.

CHAPTER 5

LETTERS TO OUR DAUGHTERS

BLACK WOMEN'S MEMOIRS AS EPISTLES OF HUMAN RIGHTS, HEALING, AND INNER PEACE

STEPHANIE Y. EVANS

Black women have written life stories to teach their intellectual daughters critical lessons, particularly lessons pertaining to rights, justice, and peace. Through life narratives, Black women have encouraged readers to look back for wisdom, look inward for strength, and look forward for courage. Recognizing memoirs as a vital part of Black women's intellectual history allows readers to learn from reflections of historical experiences for several purposes: to re-create effective practices of personal and collective peace activism (retrospection), to define identity in ways that promote health and healing (introspection), and to engender a politics of resistance that allows for a model of sustainable well-being (prospection). This chapter builds on foundational scholars of Black women's intellectual history to advance the supposition that reading Black women authors teaches contemporary peace activists and social justice educators how to sustain our work and avoid burn-out.[1]

Black women's memoirs are narratives of healing and offer clues about how to repair pain caused from violence. Consequently, these memoirs constitute an act of not only personal but social defiance, often encouraging progressive action toward liberation, espoused in Toni Cade Bambara's groundbreaking 1970 collection *The Black Woman*. African American intellectual history is steeped in spiritual and social consciousness that undergirds Black women's pursuit of rights and justice. Thus, a collective of scholars, including Martha S. Jones, who penned an introduction for the book *Toward an Intellectual History of Black Women* (2015), are correct to identify "race, gender, and justice" as the main thrusts of Black women's public intellectual history. Recently, LaRonda Manigault-Bryant's contribution "I Had a Praying Grandmother: Religion, Prophetic

Witness, and Black Women's Herstories" in *New Perspectives on the Black Intellectual Tradition*, expands on the concept of intergenerational epistemologies of "well-being and survival" despite enduring inequalities, connecting identity and justice to foremother wisdom.

Like Manigault-Bryant's "grandmaternal knowledge" as an archival source, this chapter demonstrates how the study of memoir as epistolary writing expands how we identify and interpret primary source material on Black women's knowledge production. While narratives have always been considered one important source of historical analysis, explicitly looking at the expansive library of memoir and autobiography (rather than a select few of the more popular publications) broadens the scholarly landscape. Considering memoir as epistolary expression offers an extensive bibliography that outlines initial phases of autobiography, including survival narratives by authors such as Harriet Jacobs (writing under the pseudonym Linda Brent) and cornerstone storytellers such as Maya Angelou, while contextualizing well-known authors with lesser-known writers from Africa, India, Australia, the Caribbean, Europe, and Latin America.

With a focus mainly on eras of the civil rights and Black Power movements, this chapter introduces a chorus of women authors who wrote to find their liberatory voices in ways that encourage future generations to do so, as well. By highlighting the quality of "letters," this essay emphasizes the relationship of author to reader as part of a necessary critical discussion.

Seeking a central location for life-writing resources, I created the AfricanaMemoirs.net online database in 2013; there, over five hundred Black women's published life stories are identified from around the globe. This broad temporal, geographic, and cultural spectrum shows unexpected areas of divergence and convergence. For example, readers who investigate diaspora narratives will discover divergent reactions of African American travelers—like Fanny Jackson Coppin, Era Bell Thompson, and Katherine Dunham—who visited countries in Africa and recorded variant feelings of connection. At the same time, readers can learn about women memoirists who have created convergence and community—exemplified by Maya Angelou writing the preface to Celia Cruz's autobiography or a collective of powerful activists, including Byllye Avery, Shirley Chisholm, Donna Brazile, Dorothy Height, Julianne Malveaux, Eleanor Holmes Norton, and Faye Wattleton, who collaborated on a 1989 document demanding reproductive freedom. This narrative library exponentially increases future research possibilities.[2]

Black women life writers form a dynamic, living network—one that depicts diverse experience and shared knowledge creation. National and international voices are central to a deepened study of civil rights, human rights, social justice, and peace studies. This chapter identifies literary tones, theoretical frames, historical themes, and practical applications in the field of autobiography and biography studies. Readers can gain inspiration and insight from Black women's writing because essay, memoir, and autobiographical forms are penned as epistles, purposefully designed to guide future generations. This is feminist-womanist scholarship in that it follows anthology and analysis scholarship by Beverly Guy-Sheftall and Patricia Hill Collins but also reflects Layli Maparyan's spiritually grounded notion of self-development as justice work: "change yourself, change the world." Certainly, the world needs changing.[3]

The United Nations Universal Declaration of Human Rights (UDHR) set a benchmark in world history. Drafted by a representative leadership team from nine nations, the United Nations General Assembly formalized the UDHR in Paris on December 10, 1948.[4] World War II created conditions of unprecedented destruction, and the declaration became a pact to ensure the devastation would not be repeated.[5] Eventually, however, the United Nations realized rights were not sufficient to ensure peace, and a document in 2006 acknowledges the need to actively advocate social justice as supplemental to human rights language.[6] The committee conceded:

> The concept of *social justice* and its relevance and application within the present context require a more detailed explanation. . . . The concept first surfaced in Western thought and political language in the wake of the industrial revolution and the parallel development of the socialist doctrine. It emerged as an expression of protest against what was perceived as the capitalist exploitation of labour and as a focal point for the development of measures to improve the human condition. It was born as a revolutionary slogan embodying the ideals of progress and fraternity. Following the revolutions that shook Europe in the mid-1800s, social justice became a rallying cry for progressive thinkers and political activists.[7]

A decade before this pairing of social justice with human rights in the United Nations, *Teaching for Diversity and Social Justice* (1997) was published, grounding a pioneer program in social justice and higher education. All of these resources are important to facilitate a full understanding of the breadth of contribution that Black women's narratives can bring to human rights and social justice literature and to reinforce foundational concepts, such as diversity, inclusion, oppression, antiracism, privilege, and power. Authors of Black women's memoirs show that all human beings have a "right to grow," and a close reading of the genre reveals legacies, lessons, and guides for social regeneration espoused by scholar activists, such as Anna Julia Cooper.[8] "This RIGHT TO GROW is sacred and inviolable," Cooper stated in 1925, "based on the solidarity and undeniable value of humanity itself."[9]

In addition to the term "social justice," the term "social regeneration" also originated in the Progressive Era, and W. E. B. Du Bois argued the concept was a fundamental goal of Black education. Black women's historical examination and literary criticism reflect the genre of memoir as dynamic, intergenerational, and timeless. To use Anna Julia Cooper's and Du Bois's term, I define this body of work as "regenerative."[10]

Like regenerative medicine, Black women's life writing can be used to restore, repair, and replace failing or unhealthy aspects of society. Regenerative writing combines the past, present, and future tense to facilitate growth. Growth can include spiritual, individual, communal, social, political, or global health. Medical doctors are now pushing boundaries of exploration in order to repair cells, tissues, and organs and restore functionality to bodies.[11] Similarly, I argue Black women's regenerative writing serves to repair, replace, restore, and regenerate health in individual lives, communities, societies, and nations. Specifically, Black women authors write to instruct their intellectual daughters on pathways to wellness. Given the increase in mental and physical duress since the political turmoil of the 2016 US presidential election, followed by epic stressors of the pandemic of 2020 amid intense ongoing Black protest, this guidance is sorely needed.[12]

Ancient Letters

Autobiography and memoir sit at the crossroads of literature and history. There are rich traditions of authors who pen personal stories and a growing number of analysts who extract or ascribe meaning to those stories. This is not new. Epistle is one of the most ancient, recognizable, and popular forms of life writing. As Sharon Harley has commented,

> Fortunately for me, and undoubtedly for many of the readers of this current volume, personal narratives, memory, and reflections are now viewed as critical and, indeed inseparable from one's intellectual perspectives and pursuits.[13]

And Nell Irvin Painter remarks,

> Like all my writing, it sounds like me. Themes, diction, narrative story line all original, all phrased in my own voice.[14]

Epistolary writing is widely recognized to mean letters or documents written as correspondence. These letters may be published or not, but epistles are, in an ancient form, prose of communication, as can be seen in some biblical verse. Moreover, spiritual writing beyond mainstream Western religion can be viewed in the epistolary tradition. For example, *The Teaching of Ptahhotep* was written as proverbs by an elder to instruct his son on "good speech." Lao Tzu's *Tao Te Ching* was reportedly delivered by a prophet heading out of China when war was on the horizon; he left instructions behind for anyone who cared to live a life of peace and balance. Similarly, Makeda, commonly known as the Queen of Sheba, should be acknowledged as a philosopher—literally, lover of wisdom, who operated in the epistolary tradition. Though she did not pen stories herself, accounts of her journey to quiz Solomon are recorded in the Talmud, Bible, the Quran, and Ethiopia's *Glory of Kings: The Kebra Nagast*. Most notably, in the European Middle Ages, Italian Renaissance poet Francesco "Petrarch" Petrarca (1304–1374) penned 638 letters, establishing his place in history as a forerunner of the move out of the Dark Ages. He addressed his prose to a future audience, identifying early on both humanist and futurist consciousness. Epistolary writing can take many forms but often reflects a desire of the author to convey a sense of information, inspiration, or instruction to the reader.[15]

Modern epistolary publications have most often taken the form of narrative fiction with a story told through letters or documents, such as Bram Stoker's 1897 *Dracula*, or a novel written in letter form, such as Stephen King's 1974 novel *Carrie* or Alice Walker's 1982 *The Color Purple*. In 1995 Blake Morrison penned *What My Mother Never Told Me*, billed as an "epistolary memoir," and in 2008, the undisputed icon of Black women's autobiography, Maya Angelou, offered *Letter to My Daughters* as the epitome and apex of this form. In 2015 Ta-Nehisi Coates wrote *Between the World and Me*, a letter to his son. The book was his second publication—both memoirs—and garnered critical acclaim from Toni Morrison and the *New York Times*, as well as winning the National Book Award and recognition as a Pulitzer Prize finalist. Like all cultural traditions, Africana life writing has taken numerous forms. Epistle is very popular, though understudied as a specific contribution to Black intellectual history.[16]

In *Toward an Intellectual History*, Arlette Frund rightly identifies Phillis Wheatley as a "public intellectual" as a result of her public letters and private correspondence. My use of the term "epistle" incorporates this lineage and moves beyond a strict interpretation of "composition in the form of letter" to encompass the genre in its broadest sense: a collection of letters, essays, documents, poems, or prose gathered to tell a public story in whole or in part. Thus, I present memoir as epistle not to argue life writing is monolithic but to highlight the ways in which individual collections such as Cooper's essays and speeches compiled for *A Voice from the South* (1892) and W. E. B. Du Bois's *Souls of Black Folk* (1903), present a format rich with possibilities for exploration as letters to future generations, much like Ptahhotep, Lao Tzu, Makeda, and Petrarch.[17]

A cursory look at the descriptions of several contemporary Black women's memoirs substantiates this analysis of memoir as public letters:

- Dionne Brand, *A Map to the Door of No Return: Notes to Belonging* (2001). [Brand draws] on cartography, travels, narratives of childhood in the Caribbean, journeys across the Canadian landscape, African ancestry, histories, politics, philosophies, and literature.[18]

- Carroll Parrott Blue, *The Dawn at My Back: Memoir of a Black Texas Up-bringing* (2003). Filmmaker Carroll Parrot Blue extends the boundaries of memoirs with this engrossing look at her life and the life of the nation. Using text, photographs, letters, and periodicals, Blue focuses on her own experiences and those of her mother as black women struggling beyond the constraints of the segregated South. [A companion DVD includes a broader array of media, including film, interviews, e-mails, and other].[19]
- Hilda Jarman Muir, *Very Big Journey: My Life As I Remember It* (2004). Hilda Muir was born on the very frontier of modern Australia, near the outback town of Borroloola in the Northern Territory in about 1920. She was known to many in the Northern Territory as "Aunty Hilda," and her life story was told during the federal apology to the Stolen Generations in Australia.[20]
- Zetta Elliott, *Stranger in the Family* (2011). *Stranger in the Family* is a mixed-media memoir that examines the shifting terrain upon which we negotiate race, kinship, and identity. . . . [The book] uses essays, photography, short stories, and poetry to trace the author's evolution as a black feminist, a writer, a daughter, and a Canadian.[21]
- Mariama Ba, *So Long a Letter* (2012). The book itself takes the form of a long letter written by a widow, Ramatoulaye, to her friend, over the mandatory forty-day mourning period following the death of a husband. This semi-autobiographical account is a perceptive testimony to the plight of educated and articulate Muslim women.[22]
- Tanisha C. Ford, *Dressed in Dreams: A Black Girl's Love Letter to the Power of Fashion* (2019). From sneakers to leather jackets, a bold, witty, and deeply personal dive into Black America's closet. In this highly engaging book, fashionista and pop culture expert Tanisha C. Ford investigates Afros and dashikis, go-go boots, and hotpants of the sixties, hip hop's baggy jeans and bamboo earrings, and the #BlackLivesMatter-inspired hoodies of today. The history of these garments is deeply intertwined with Ford's story as a black girl coming of age in a midwestern rust-belt city.[23]

Ba's work is a semi-autobiographical novel, further recognizing the literary quality of life writing so readily present in Angelou's work. Both Blue's and Elliot's works are mixed media, Muir's story is part of federal record collected during a national inquiry into social injustices of removed children, and Brand's memoir maps her life journey and family story from the Continent and Caribbean to Canada. Ford's work traces the evolution of her personal identity within the broader context of American fashion. The topics of these memoirs point to Black women's human rights issues, including fallout from the transatlantic slave trade, African women's rights and polygamy, Pan-African identity, racial segregation and poverty in the southern United States, as well as lives of the Stolen Generation of Aboriginal Australians, and the politics of fashion, including the black leather jacket and beret of the Black Power movement and the hoodie reflecting racist violence and police brutality.

Numerous Black women scholars have used memoir as a form. Groundbreaking scholars who have long studied the genre include the authors in Patricia Bell-Scott and Juanita Johnson-Bailey's coedited *Flat Footed Truths: Telling Black Women's Lives* in 1998. Bell-Scott also recently published *The Firebrand and the First Lady: Portrait of a Friendship: Pauli Murray, Eleanor Roosevelt, and the Struggle for Social Justice* (2016), which explores letters between Pauli Murray and Eleanor Roosevelt and establishes Bell-Scott's expertise in the form of epistle and on the subject of social justice. Johnson-Bailey is also a pioneer scholar of the genre, beginning with her dissertation in 1994 on Black women's educational narratives. Tellingly, she identifies herself as a "narrativist."[24]

Other highly visible scholarship on memoir includes Joanne Braxton (1989), bell hooks (1998), Nellie McKay (1998), Margo V. Perkins (2000), Rosetta R. Haynes (2011), Layli Maparyan (2012), and Angela A. Ards (2016). Collectively, these works cover a broad scope of analysis but can be interpreted as clearly defining three ways memoirs speak to audiences: the past (Haynes's historical spiritual motherhood; bell hooks's memory), present (Braxton's self-creation; Maparyan's vitality), or the future (McKay's resistance; Perkins's and Ards's activism). Narrative continues to play a central role in Black women's scholarly imagination as can be seen in Ytasha Womack's personal reflections in her definitive work *Afrofuturism: The World of Black Sci-Fi and Fantasy Culture* (2013). These ideas are grounded in Black women's narratives but also influenced by arcs of critical scholarship.[25]

Though the focus of this chapter lies mainly on memory and activism, relevant insight for healing is also present: "self-creation," the look inside, is a temporal bridge between the past and future. Memoirs are mentors. Books about life lessons show readers how to foster what Maparyan calls "vibrant health." Many contemporary Black women, particularly survivors of violence, struggle with mental health and wellness; studying these narratives can offer useful resources of how those who have come before have effectively dealt with social injustice and still kept presence of mind to record their voice for the benefit of others. This moves beyond the discussion of the "strong Black woman" and reveals a gallery of women who struggle for peace and balance in tangible ways that can be identified, celebrated, and emulated. This part of reading letters is important so today's social justice workers can understand a life-saving lesson that activists like Pauli Murray, Marian Wright Edelman, Rosa Parks, and Angela Davis teach: struggle is necessary, but suffering is not.[26]

Empowerment through literature can be a multigenerational experience. For example, legendary basketball player Kareem Abdul Jabar recalls being profoundly impacted by *The Autobiography of Malcolm X*, after which he converted from Roman Catholicism to Islam. In the same vein, media mogul Oprah Winfrey gained inspiration and insight from reading Angelou's first autobiography, *I Know Why the Caged Bird Sings*. After finding encouragement in Angelou's voice, Winfrey not only shared her own story of surviving sexual violence but then repeatedly encouraged singer Tina Turner to publicly share her testimony of surviving domestic violence. Turner relates,

> Whatever I felt about Ike and our past, and as much as I wanted to put it behind me, I was moved that my sad story had the power to help others. Oprah, who has interviewed me many times, had a habit of asking me the same tough question: "Do you remember the first time Ike hit you?" Sensing that I was tired of reliving these memories, she said privately, "Tina, you know why I keep asking." Oprah saw a higher purpose in our discussion. She helped me understand how important it was for me to keep talking, that I was offering a lesson. It was an opportunity to reach out to abused women and bring the difficult subject into the light. If they heard me talking honestly about my experiences, they might find the courage to do something about their own situations. I'm told over and over again by fans, those who approach me in person, others who write very emotional letters, that some aspect of my story—my escape from Ike, my determination to survive on my own, my dedication, my resilience, and yes, my optimism—actually did help them.[27]

Readers of all ages can learn from books about how to create visible, mobile, and active lives. I call this practice "narrative mentoring," which means using memoirs as a path to self-empowerment, particularly empowerment that enables us to move more freely within global contexts.

I read Africana memoirs as collected letters, documents, and missives written to pass on wisdom. Even when narratives are not explicit about the audiences they address, many readers are clear about how they read life stories for more than comprehension; they read for evaluation and application. They read and can be changed. I do not assert that this process is guaranteed; just as Angelou framed her "letters" as an offering of lessons, she did not assume that all readers would take away the same message.

Telling Histories: Black Women Historians in the Ivory Tower (2008) presents personal experiences of seventeen professional historians. Stressors recorded in the edited volume include miscarriage, death of colleagues, death of loved ones, charges that their work was of little or no academic value, illness in the midst of tenure review, policies not conducive to allow adequate time for healing, and hostile administrators who exacerbate poor health conditions. The professional memoirs are "both primary and secondary sources" that offer a microscopic view of how and why scholars choose a certain profession, topic, location, and career track. The volume also places in the spotlight experiences of the two first women to earn doctoral degrees in the field of history: Anna Julia Cooper and Marian Wright. Deborah Gray White, editor of the collection, states clearly her intent on collecting narratives:

> It is my hope that [*Telling Histories*] does not just chronicle the recent past but that it serves as a sort of "how-to" survival manual for those who are currently struggling against entrenched historical methods, historiographies, and faculties.[28]

Black women regularly write in community and envision a community that traverses time and place. Part of the community building includes consciousness raising on how to overcome violence, exclusion, and discrimination uniquely experienced by intersectional oppression. Reading Angelou, Hill-Scott, and White together, we find that Black women's memoirs offer lessons of healing and guidance toward wellness.

Often, historians and philosophers have presented time as a line, a hierarchy, a cycle, a braid, or a continuum. I contend Black women writers present time as a living network—a braided continuum with open lines of communication between past and future. Black women write time as "retrospection, introspection, and prospection," as Cooper acknowledged.[29] Theorists like hooks, Braxton, and Perkins discuss narrative themes that outline a tripart framework that defies linear representation of time. These concepts of writing through a dynamic concept of time (for the explicit purpose of addressing personal and social problems) also can advance understanding of the relationship between authors and audience. As Manigault-Bryant brings to light, authors and readers often share a feeling of familial knowledge exchange.[30]

In her essay "Womanhood: The Vital Element of Regeneration and Progress of the Race," Cooper describes women's central role in race progress and social regeneration:

> It is well enough to pause a moment for retrospection, introspection, and prospection. We look back . . . that we may learn wisdom from experience. We look within that we may gather together once more our forces, and . . . address ourselves to the tasks before us. We look forward with hope and trust.[31]

Black women have long insisted on, as the centenarian sister-authors Sadie Delany and Bessie Delany would write, "having our say." Cooper's reflections on race and gender are addressed to Americans in order to claim her voice (self-creation), eradicate American injustice (activism), and edit the historical record to include Black women's experience and perspectives (memory). Like Cooper, Black women authors have not been passive recorders of chronology. A look at the collection of narratives that make up the Africana Memoirs database reveals how authors moved beyond a two-dimensional, linear concept of events; many Black women authors were active elements interacting with historical figures and *creating* history, even as they were writing it.

Social Justice, Human Rights, and Civil Rights

As stated earlier, scholars of Black women's intellectual history identify a tradition of writing about race, gender, and justice. So, how do Black women articulate ideals of social justice in their lives, work, and writing? Ards, in *Words of Witness*, comments,

> A major objective of *Words of Witness* is to help build the burgeoning field of black women's intellectual history by moving beyond rote gender politics to put black feminist thought in conversation with broader political thought. In capturing how select black women's autobiographies published in the last two decades act as counternarratives to official and often nostalgic representations of the civil rights and Black Power movements, . . . the study has sought to outline critical interventions black women intellectuals are making to shape a progressive post-*Brown* politic.[32]

A close look at narratives reveals a complex level of contributions best understood by studying how Black women theorists situate race and gender within sociopolitical experience. Thus, a contribution by Angela Davis's *Race, Gender, and Politics* reveals the value of narrative to interpret experience. In 1987 at Bennett College, Davis delivered a speech, "Sick and Tired of Being Sick and Tired: The Politics of Black Women's Health"—its title from Mississippi civil rights movement activist Fannie Lou Hamer—detailing health disparities, such as heart disease, arthritis, hypertension, diabetes, cancer, and AIDS, and how they are exacerbated by poverty and political disenfranchisement. In the speech, published in Evelyn C. White's 1990 *The Black Women's Health Book: Speaking for Ourselves*, Davis offers a clear and straightforward look at six fundamental elements of Black women's experience: body, mind, and spirit (personal peace) and social, economic, and political (collective peace). These levels of how Black women experience health are parallel to how human rights are defined on national (civil rights) and international (human rights and social justice) levels. Looking closely at how Black women reflect on their lives illuminates the nuances of how human beings experience and conceptualize basic rights.

To some extent, we are familiar with narratives that discuss human rights abuses of lynching, segregation, suffrage, and reproductive justice, but a more comprehensive study is necessary to more fully examine the depths of issues authors address in their reflections. Black women's narratives are irreplaceable primary sources for this endeavor. Septima Poinsette Clark offers a prime example of an educator who bridges the personal and political.

Like several Black women educators, Clark insists on the need for students' active participation in their own educational process. Clark penned two autobiographies about her life in the civil rights movement and chronicled her struggle to improve conditions through citizenship education, *Echo in My Soul* (1962) and *Ready from Within* (1990). As with Cooper, social justice is the desired outcome of education and action. Further, Clark contends, "Social justice is not a matter of money, but of will, not a problem for the economist as much as a task for the patriot; to me its accomplishment requires leadership and community action rather than monetary investment." She asserts that democracy is an issue for educators, and educators are to teach and learn in communities in order to demand access to all aspects of the democratic political process. Pedagogy, curriculum, and administration of schools are to be tools for participatory democracy. Education is a social affair.[33]

Searching a comprehensive library of autobiography exposes numerous possibilities to connect Black women's intellectual history to social justice education. This encourages a deeper consideration of both form and function.[34] Over 118 Black women's narratives in the Africana Memoirs database mention social justice. Within this group is significant overlap of terms; outside of this larger set of social justice narratives, 25 solely reference human rights, and 18 mention civil rights. Neither "human rights" nor "civil rights" as terms were referenced as often as "social justice," which is most likely a function of the timing of the terms: "social justice" was used in the early twentieth century, human rights came into popular use after World War II, and civil rights surfaced most notably in the 1950s and 1960s. Further, the term "human rights" was found in more international settings, while the term "civil rights" was largely in reference to a movement in the United States. Search terms for this survey of memoirs are included from all three areas, with a total of 161 Black women's memoirs that reference "social justice, human rights, and civil rights."[35]

Below, a listing by state of the locations of civil-rights-movement narratives and their authors is followed by an outline of social justice and human rights themes. The civil rights era is identified by location and topics, while the larger picture of rights and justice is situated within a framework of the most comprehensive articulation of rights, the United Nations' UDHR. National and international narratives are classified by the six categories outlined in the document: natural rights, individual rights, communal rights, political rights, social rights, and democratic rights. Author locations can be mapped to track the convergence and divergence of themes in states, regions, and countries.

Readers who access the database might study the civil rights movement by doing a search by states. Not surprising, the southern part of the United States as a region is most prevalent in narratives; Alabama offers a comparatively rich collection of voices:

- Alabama: Jo Ann Gibson Robinson, Margaret Charles Smith, Carolyn Maull McKinstry, Coretta Scott King, Rosa Parks, Sheyann Webb-Christburg, Janet Harmon Bragg, Martha Hawkins, Jan Willis, Eartha Kitt
- Arkansas: Melba Pattillo Beals
- California: Deborah Santana
- Florida: Tananariva Due and Patricia Stephens Due
- Georgia: King Farris, Ann Nixon Cooper
- Kentucky: Georgia Davis Powers
- Mississippi: Winson Hudson, Endesha Ida Mae Holland, Bertha M. Davis
- North Carolina: Bernadette Gregory Watts and Nina Simone
- South Carolina: Essie Mae Washington Williams
- Texas: Ella Mae Cheeks Johnson

These stories may be contrasted with accounts of the movement authors outside of the traditional southern conceptualization have chronicled, for example, Frankie Muse Freeman and Ada Lois Sipuel Fisher in Missouri; Mary Church Terrell and Constance Baker Motley in Washington, DC; Memphis Tennessee Garrison in West Virginia; and Angela Davis, Florence Kennedy, Judy Scales-Trent, Patricia Williams, and Ruby Dee in New York.

As an example of the ways in which memoir can expand extant scholarship, thematic and periodic events can be studied. For example, topical approaches of the civil rights movement would include general tactics, as well as specific organizations and events:

- nonviolent direct action: organizing, demonstrations, voter registration, sit-ins: universal
- tributes to local leaders of the movement, such as Martin Luther King Jr. as a symbol of struggle: universal
- Sixteenth Street Church bombing: Carolyn Maull McKinstry, Angela Davis, Condoleezza Rice
- Montgomery, Alabama, bus boycott: Jo Ann Robinson, Rosa Parks
- National Association for the Advancement of Colored People work: Winson Hudson, Constance Baker Motley, Memphis Tennessee Garrison, Tananarive Due and Patricia Stephens Due, Ada Sipuel Fisher, Daisy Bates, Janet Cheatham Bell
- Student Nonviolent Coordinating Committee work: Endesha Ida Mae Holland
- Atlanta University statement on human rights: Ann Nixon Cooper
- Little Rock High School desegregation: Melba Pattillo Beals, Daisy Bates

Although oral histories and scholarship about the civil rights movement abound, there is ample room to expand research in this area, particularly given the millennial rollback in rights gained during the 1950s and 1960s social struggles. The struggle for progressive rights—and the fight against conservative backlash—are certainly simultaneously local, national, and global issues.

Human Rights and International Social Justice

The UN UDHR lists six levels of guarantees, ranging from Divine rights of each individual to rights concerned with participation in a civil and democratic society. Within this range of rights of self and other exist familial, social, and political safeguards. Essentially, rights are defined as relationships to God and nature, to one's self, community, and nation and to the world. Nellie Y. McKay, in "The Narrative Self," makes this observation:

> Whatever their strategies of self-construction, active resistance to oppression of all kinds has been at the center of the history of Black women's lives in this country from slavery to the present time. These narratives are as politically significant as more overt modes of protest.[36]

Given this framework, Black women's writing becomes more easily recognizable as a tapestry of epistles about basic guarantees needed for each human being to thrive and live a full life. The thirty articles of the UDHR are prefaced by a set of resolutions that state the moral and political imperative of each human's basic needs. When life writing is placed in this historical context, it becomes clear that Black women writers have addressed human rights in all forms. The Africana Memoirs database shows how primary sources can be engaged to better understand the six levels of human rights guarantees.

Natural Rights

SPIRITUALITY

- spiritual education and development: Alice Walker and Edith Hudley
- spiritual activism: Layli Maparyan, Donna Brazile, and Winson Hudson
- conversion: Ahuvah Gray, Emily Robateau

IDENTITY AND BELONGING

- interracial identity: Rebecca Walker, Essie Williams Washington, Bliss Broyard, Pauline Black, June Cross

- adoption: Rita Simon
- mental health: Katherine Dunham, Anne Moody
- lesbian and transgender identities: Shamara Shantu Riley, Janet Mock, Jala A. McKenzie-Burns
- deaf identity: Maxine Childress Brown
- colorism and self-hatred: Carroll Parrott Blue
- nationality and travel: Anita Reynolds, Zetta Elliott, Paule Marshall, Colleen McElroy

Individual Rights

SLAVERY AND INCARCERATION

- enslavement: Harriet Jacobs, Ellen Craft, Saidiya Hartman
- incarceration: Asha Bandele, Dolores E. Cross, Angela Davis
- judge on criminal-justice policies impacting Black women: Paula C. Johnson
- American Civil War family history: Adele Logan Alexander, Thulani Davis
- Aboriginal removal: Ruth Hegarty, Hilda Jarman Muir

LYNCHING, POLICE BRUTALITY, AND POLITICAL PRISONERS

- lynching: Ida B. Wells
- Black Panther Party political prisoner: Assata Shakur, Safiya Bukhari
- police brutality: Kadiatou Diallo, June Jordan

Communal Rights

FAMILY AND HEALTHCARE

- rural healthcare: Margaret Charles Smith, Billie Jean Young
- mothering role: Kesho Yvonne Scott
- South African women teachers fired for pregnancy: Sindiwe Magona
- family history: Yelena Khanga, Shirlee Taylor Haizlip, Carole Ione
- abortion and reproductive rights and family planning: Faye Wattleton, Joan Morgan, Star Jones

DOMESTIC AND SEXUAL VIOLENCE

- domestic violence: Alice Swafford, Meri Nana-Ama Danquah, Gaiutra Bahadur
- polygamy and gender oppression: Mariama Ba

- foster child abuse: Debraha Watson
- female genital mutilation: Fauziya Kassindja, Soraya Mire, Waris Dirie

Political Rights

JOURNALISM, PRESS, MEDIA RESEARCH

- Black press: Gail Lumet Buckley, Belva Davis
- race and social attitudes: Dionne Brand, Ethel Smith
- media treatment of Black women: Jill Nelson, Anita Hill

LAWYERS, POLITICAL OFFICE, AND MILITARY SERVICE

- elected officials: Shirley Chisholm, Barbara Jordan, Ellen Johnson Sirleaf, Benedita Da Silva, Avel Louise Gordly, Billie Jean Young, Unita Blackwell
- appointed officials: Condoleezza Rice, Star Parker, Lani Guinier
- lawyers: Flo Kennedy, Constance Baker Motley, Judy Scales-Trent, Evelyn Williams, Patricia Williams, Dovey Johnson Roundtree, Marian Wright Edelman, Cornelia Sorabji
- military service: Gail Harris

Social Rights

SCHOOL DESEGREGATION, EDUCATIONAL ACCESS, AND YOUTH

- school segregation: Shirley Robinson Sprinkles, Daisy Bates, Ada Sipuel, Charlayne Hunter-Gault
- programs for educational equity: Maxine Childress Brown, Stephanie Y. Evans, Betty Brown-Chappell, Sara Lawrence-Lightfoot, Ruby Berkley Goodwin, Anna L. Green
- discrimination and harassment: Vivian Stringer

BUSINESS, LABOR, AND ORGANIZATIONS

- business owner: Madam C. J. Walker, Lillian Lincoln Lambert, Dorothy Pitman Hughes
- empowerment organization: Mary Church Terrell, Dorothy Height, Jane Edna Hunter, Frankie Muse Freeman
- social organization: Martha Stephens Wilson Rappaport
- business boycott: Rosa Parks

WRITING AND ENTERTAINMENT

- creative writing: Ellen Tarry, Ann Petry, Margaret Walker, Sonia Sanchez, Vertamae Smart-Grosvenor, Nikki Giovanni, Toni Morrison
- theater, film, music, and television: Norma Miller, Ruby Dee, Carolyn Marie Wilkins, Shirley Verrett, Celia Cruz, Nina Simone, Darlene Love, Dionne Warwick, Diahann Carroll, Shonda Rhimes
- archival research: Jennifer Morgan, Lorene Cary

Democratic Rights

BLACK POWER, ANTI-APARTHEID, AFRICAN CIVIL WAR

- Community meetings and centers: Janet Cheatham Bell, Peggy Wood
- Black Power activism: Elaine Brown
- South African anti-apartheid: Adrina Abrahamse, Maphele Ramphele, Winnie Madikizela Mandela, Lynne Duke

CARIBBEAN, AFRO-LATINA, DALIT

- Afro-Latina and Puerto Rican activism: Marta Moreno Vega, Maria Beuno
- Caribbean: Audre Lorde, Edwidge Danticat, Susan Fales-Hill
- Dalit activism: Bama Faustina Soosairaj

ABORIGINAL ACTIVISM

- Indigenous activism: Roberta Sykes, Doreen Kartinyeri

The thirty UDHR articles clarify dimensions of human rights; these rights—and how diverse populations define and pursue them—are essential for all who seek to more clearly study and advocate for social regeneration. Civil rights narratives have been explored by several scholars, particularly Vicki Crawford, V. P. Franklin, and Bettye Collier-Thomas. Human rights and social justice narratives have much to offer future generations who want to more clearly define what it means to have a "right to grow," as Anna Julia Cooper states.

This comparative search also brings to the fore contrasts and complexities in Black women's ideas. For example, Condoleezza Rice mentioned the civil rights movement and the bombing of the Sixteenth Street Baptist Church in Alabama but also spoke disparagingly about social justice—in derisive tones about South American leaders. Similarly, Star Jones echoed conservative stances and often takes a regressive social position, not a progressive one.

This collection of letters offers a clear focus for study, particularly when the lens is broadened from the US civil rights movement to global struggles. Further, the deep historical, thematic, and geographic connections become visible when considering the larger data set. Lastly, these narratives open the door for a deeper analysis of human rights as they are connected to peace studies.[37]

Maps to Inner Peace and Sustainable Struggle

Recently, self-care has become an increasingly visible focus in public discourse—especially as a reaction to fatigue in activist circles. However, Black women activists have engaged meditation, yoga, and prayer to strengthen their individual and collective efforts in social justice movements for generations. This, too, is a valuable inheritance recorded in memoir. In order to connect divine peace with larger quests for democratic principles of global human rights, we must discuss reflections like yoga and meditation by activists. As recorded in Anne Moody's 1968 memoir, *Coming of Age in Mississippi*, civil rights work is traumatic. This notion is also famously captured in Bambara's 1980 novel, *The Salt Eaters*, which explores themes of Black women's civil-rights-movement activism, generational trauma, and healing traditions. As such, several activist memoirs advise that activist self-care is not a self-indulgent distraction but, as Audre Lorde describes, a necessary act of self-preservation and political resistance.

Many women who meditate, practice yoga, and pray do so as a means to bolster their capacity to change the world. Writers like Alice Walker have dedicated several volumes to self-care reflections. Searching extant memoirs, two activists with the most prolific use of the term "meditation," Murray and Edelman, provide alternate views of civil-rights-movement work. In addition, Parks and Angela Davis suggest wellness as a useful tool for future generation of leaders and offer practical advice about how Black women move internally to change the world externally.

Murray provides a fascinating perspective of connection of one's spiritual path to work in the world:

> Jesus was not an ascetic; he enjoyed good food and drink and convivial company. But he was a free human being, refusing to become enslaved to material desires. He could eat raw corn plucked from the fields as well as feast at a rich man's table. And while he occasionally withdrew from crowds for meditation and prayer, it is in the community of faith that we see him carrying out his ministry and performing his mighty works.[38]

As an ordained Episcopal priest, Murray intertwined their academic, activist, legal, and spiritual work to change many injustices that they and their family experienced. This integration of health, purpose, and vocation is seen widely by women involved in the Black women's club movement and civil rights movement.[39] This insight is echoed in the work of many movement activists.

Edelman founded the Children's Legal Defense fund, an organization committed to the health and well-being of children; her activism largely stemmed from the civil-rights-movement legacy she joined as a young adult. Edelman notes that movement meetings—which were most often held in churches— were steeped in a collective understanding of purpose: "Each day our meetings began with a meditation and joyful rendition." Very much in the tradition of Black abolitionists and women in the early twentieth-century club movement, collective reflection and pausing to pray and steady the mind bolstered the resolve and physical capacity of individual to fight for change. Edelman's work on behalf of children makes use of meditation and prayer as a main means to discuss her work. In her book *Guide My Feet: Prayers and Meditations on Loving and Working for Children*, she explains:

> I cannot recreate the same small-town childhood of my past for my children, but I can teach and try to live the same enduring God-given and life-giving values of faith, integrity, and service. These prayers and meditations reflect my ongoing struggle to do so.[40]

Edelman's work with children and her several reflective works allow activists to witness a sustained body of advocacy that is not based in fear or anxiety.

The ultimate example of sustainable struggle is Parks, who (like Harriet Tubman) lived to be a nonagenarian, despite lifelong struggles with health, chronic stress, and surviving several types of violence. Parks (1913–2005) practiced yoga for four decades and offered yoga lessons in her community. According to published family narratives, papers, and pictures held at the Library of Congress, as early as 1965, at age fifty-two, Parks learned yoga with her nieces and nephews. By 1973, right after her sixtieth birthday, she was demonstrating yoga at community events in Detroit. Parks, most widely known for political resistance that led to the 1955 Montgomery bus boycott, lived to be ninety-two years old, and her "quiet strength" lifework developed to include public health advocacy throughout her lifetime. When I recently discovered the previously unpublished 1973 picture described as "Rosa Parks practicing yoga at an event" in the library's digital archive, I recognized it is a poignant illustration of how Black women's healing traditions are historical, spiritual, creative, and political. Her niece and nephew bring to light her practice in early years, and Parks reveals in her memoir, *My Story* (1992), that she learned "daily stretching" from her mother, who incorporated it into her teaching practices.

Accounts by Angela Davis offer the salient examples of wellness practice and sustainable social justice work in the Black Power era. Davis notes in her

1974 autobiography that in order to relieve her migraine headaches, she began doing various exercises while imprisoned—a recommendation from a doctor working with the Black Panther Party. She used yoga and meditation as forms of resistance in the otherwise violently controlled prison environment:

> The fact that this cell was to be the area where I worked on my case, they pushed to the absurdity: because I was supposed to be working there, I could not also eat there; I could not do my daily exercises there. But they could do nothing to prevent me from doing calisthenics, katas, or headstands when I felt like it in the work cell. Often, I exercised precisely at the moment when I knew they were peeping in on me.[41]

Decades after her release, Davis continues her yoga and meditation practice alongside her prison-abolition activism, engaging in many conversations about defining sustainable struggle. Conversations about wellness as resistance include with her sister, Fania Davis, a restorative justice lawyer and wellness advocate, and John Kabat-Zinn, founder of mindfulness-based stress-reduction (MBSR) and intersect with demands for Black women's health and wellness. Peace activism, particularly for survivors of personal, social, or structural violence often exacerbates traumatic stress. Although post-traumatic stress disorder (PTSD) is often referenced regarding Black women's mental health experiences, a more accurate assessment would be continuous traumatic stress (CTS). Too often, social injustices mean that there are no "post" chronic stressors, just repeated and compound stressors. Thus, increasing knowledge of how elders in past generations not only survived but sustained their spirit is an essential contribution.

Activist narratives from the civil rights and Black Power movements and writers like Parks and Angela Davis can also be read as letters of longevity. The Africana Memoirs database is filled with similar stories of struggle and guides for healing, balance, well-being, and inner-peace practices.[42]

Conclusion

In *Toward an Intellectual History*, Jones affirms the concept of Black women's multidirectional historiography in a vignette about a conversation between Sojourner Truth and Michelle Obama. Jones asserts we are accountable to history and ancestors who look over our shoulders. I agree and add that Black women memoirists move beyond looking over our shoulders in observation. They have actively written directly to us. I believe they not only expect us to write back, they expect us to write forward. In short, these authors inspire contemporary writers to contribute to the narrative of civil rights workers, social justice educators, and human rights scholar-activists. In her 1989 *Black Women Writing Autobiography*, Joanne Braxton comments,

As black American women . . . we have been as invisible to the dominant culture as rain; we have been knowers, but we have not been known. . . . Aframerican autobiographical tradition encompasses survival, search for public voice, personal fulfillment, and self-creation.[43]

Black women's intellectual history is inextricably linked to peace studies. As outlined in *Black Women in the Ivory Tower, 1850–1954: An Intellectual History* (2007), Black women's scholarship exemplifies empowerment education and advances four central characteristics: applied research, cultural standpoint, critical epistemology, and moral existentialism. In the 1800s women such as Maria Stewart, Frances E. W. Harper, Nannie Helen Burroughs, and Anna Julia Cooper wrote that the disadvantaged position of Black women based on race and sex was one that allowed for and required Black women activists to lead the country into the true possibilities inherent in both progressive and radical ideals of democracy. An intellectual history of Black women's wellness deepens understanding of known scholars like Anna Julia Cooper by encouraging a deeper reading of practices in which she and others engaged that enabled her to live to age 105.[44]

Clearly, Black women academics have been doing intellectual social justice work for several generations. Pedagogies and curricula reveal solutions to problems and offer a range of ideologies and philosophies about the role of education in society and effective means for African Americans to overcome barriers to educational, economic, and political access.[45] Notably, approximately thirty contemporary educators have penned memoirs featured in the Africana Memoirs database. Of this group, fourteen mention social justice in their book titles or as their main theme: Lani Guinier, Angela Davis, Carole Boyce, Yvonne Bobb-Smith, Jan Willis, Judy Scales-Trent, Layli Maparyan, Sara Lawrence-Lightfoot, Betty Brown-Chappell, Janet Cheatham Bell, Adele Logan Alexander, Yvonne Shorter Brown, Endesha Ida Mae Holland, and Paula C. Johnson.

These memoirs reflect retrospection, introspection, and prospection. For example, Trudier Harris in *Summer Snow: Reflections from a Black Daughter of the South*, Jamaica Kincaid in *A Small Place*, and Hartman in *Lose Your Mother: A Journey along the Atlantic Slave Route* look back to explore regional, national, and continental family histories as grounding for their work. Maparyan looks inside to identify "vital health" in *The Womanist Idea*, Toi Derricotte creates her racial identity in *The Black Notebooks: An Interior Journey*, and Willis goes inside herself to imagine her multifaceted spirituality in *Dreaming Me: Black, Baptist, and Buddhist*. And Guinier uses her own struggle to shine the light on "zero sum" politics and advocate for a more equitable future in *Lift Every Voice: Turning a Civil Rights Setback into a New Vision of Social Justice*.

In addition to memoirs serving as mentors to Black women in an array of professions, educators of all levels can benefit from this body of work. Regenerative writing can directly contribute to conceptions of regenerative education recently established in many K–12 schools. In her 2008 dissertation, Ashley Nielson pioneers the philosophy of regenerative education and uses terms such as "living schools" and "holistic education" to outline parameters of educative practice dedicated to developing "self and systems."[46] Theoretical approaches such as these provide a frame for the substance of narratives to be read as valuable curricular guides.

Memoir can fuel new research, as evidenced by books that I have already published from the Africana Memoirs database: *Black Passports: Travel Memoirs as Tools for Youth Empowerment* (2014), *Black Women's Mental Health: Balancing Strength and Vulnerability* (2017), and *Black Women and Social Justice Education: Legacies and Lessons* (2019). Further, this research advances work in digital humanities and lends itself to mapping and other practices that make use of innovative teaching technologies. These works also highlight the potential for practical application in community agencies, counseling centers, and organizations dedicated to expanding human rights for Black girls and women. As seen in my book *Black Women's Yoga History: Memoirs of Inner Peace* (2021), researchers, students, and mental health practitioners can use this paradigm of narrative humanities to discover ways to improve their own quality of life as they pick up the baton from past activists.[47]

As intimated in Angelou's collected works and India Arie's lyrics, Black women's memoirs can be read as letters to future generations about how to find strength, courage, and wisdom. We need all possible encouragement in the Black women's struggles against erasure of memory, distortion of identity, and violent subjugation (whether personal or political). In order to claim rights and justice, we must first be able to define them. Black women's intellectual history offers a foundation of memory needed to build a healthier self and society.

Memoirs and autobiographies are inherently reflective forms of writing. Choosing to focus on how Black women reflect on their meditative processes and innermost feelings adds an additional layer of the view inside one's life. In Willis's writing, healing and inner peace are integral parts of appreciating the value of meditation in practice as well as contemplative forms of writing:

> When I first began doing family history research in the South, I began having a series of recurrent dreams about lions. I believe these lions are me, myself. Perhaps they are my deepest African self. . . . I have begun to make peace with my own inner lions. . . . In Buddhism, the lion's roar is the mark of eloquence and power of the Buddha's speech. . . . Every now and then, a lion must roar. It is part of her nature. If my life's story is of some benefit to others, that will be *a fine roar.*[48]

Willis reflects on her journey to enlightenment in terms of making a conscious choice against violence. Although she had been a part of the Black Power movement at Cornell University, she chose nonviolence as her contribution to social movements: "I had made a conscious decision to turn away from violence and to seek a way of bringing healing and peace into my life. Although I didn't yet know exactly how this would be accomplished, I hoped that on our journey I would find the answers I sought." Willis's phrasing mirrors Black women theorists framing of mindfulness as consciousness and is part of the narrative tradition. Willis's reflection also underscores the notion that reflective writing is often done with hopes of mentoring or assisting readers in some way.[49]

Morrison articulates that one main purpose of human existence is to pass on knowledge—but she underscores that knowledge is not merely information but wisdom that is information congealed through values. In her essay "How Can Values Be Taught in the University," Morrison challenges the myth of objectivity in higher education. She argues that, essentially, all education is values-based education. She outlines four steps in the process of education: to examine, evaluate, posit, and reinforce. As a university professor who researches Black women's intellectual history through memoirs, my work centers on teaching values of inner peace (health and wellness) and outer peace (human rights and social justice). Working in the #MeToo era as a survivor of sexual violence myself, I am conscious of the complex layers of struggle and the impact of traumatic stress on chronic stress. If "passing on human knowledge" ignores Black women's life writing, we miss a vital opportunity to ensure values of social justice are passed on to future generations, and we also miss out on how to have the wherewithal to not let the freedom struggle kill us all the time.

Sanchez has said, "Peace is a human right." Though a paucity of literature exists, the topic of inner peace has been selectively addressed for well over a decade. Research on inner peace appears in several scholarly publications in various disciplines, including the *American Journal of Health Behavior* (2003), *Et Cetera: A Quarterly Journal of Artistic Essays and Art Criticism* (2011), *Global Review of Ethnopolitics* (2002), *International Journal of Humanities and Peace* (2005), *International Journal of Information and Education Technology* (2015), *Journal of Business Ethics* (2012), *Journal of Peace Education* (2005), *Journal of Social Sciences* (2012), *Justitia: Justice Studies Association Newsletter* (2004), *Library Journal* (2002), and *National Catholic Reporter* (2011). Scholars have also penned dissertations on the topics of inner peace in areas of social work (1999) and American literature (1973). However, relatively little connects intersectional causes of exploitation to Africana women's quests for peace. Certainly, as argued by actress Taraji P. Henson in her June 2019 address to the US Congress about youth suicide, African American mental health is a human rights issue for the twenty-first century.[50]

Hundreds of authors have taken the time to collect their life stories and share reflections from their minds, bodies, and souls. Only a small number are represented in this essay, but this collection clearly demonstrates we have only begun to tap available resources in this area. By connecting to Black women's intellectual history, we can more effectively expand conceptions and practices of human rights, civil rights, and global social justice. Like Anna Julia Cooper, we must engage in progressive peace, restorative justice, and regenerative education. Like Sanchez, we must continue to find creative ways to sustain a healthy struggle for peace. *A luta continua.*

Notes

1. The author thanks the following persons and groups for feedback: Paul Gorski and Cher Chen, "'Frayed All Over': The Causes and Consequences of Activist Burnout among Social Justice Education Activists," *Educational Studies* 51, no. 5 (2015): 385–405; the panel members of "Space and Place," at the Africana/Black Studies—An NEH Institute on Spatial Humanities conference, June 11, 2016, Purdue University; the panel members of "The Role of Explicit and Embedded Narrative," University of Georgia Graduate Scholars Leadership, Engagement, and Development LEADS Summer Institute, 2017; and the presenters of "Souls of Black Folk and the Human Rights Legacy of W. E. B. Du Bois," a program of Humanity in Action and Center for Civil and Human Rights John Lewis Fellowship, 2015.

2. See AfricanaMemoirs.net database of Black Women's Autobiography, Dr. Stephanie Y. Evans, (2013), www.africanamemoirs.net.

3. Radhika Mohanram, *Black Body: Women, Colonialism, and Space,* (Minneapolis: University of Minnesota Press, 1999); Layli Maparyan, *The Womanist Idea* (New York: Routledge, 2012).

4. UN, Universal Declaration of Human Rights, 1948, *United Nations,* http://www.un .org/en/universal-declaration-human-rights/.

5. UN, Universal Declaration of Human Rights, "History of the Document," *United Nations,* 2020, http://www.un.org/en/sections/universal-declaration/history-document/ index.html.

6. International Forum for Social Development, *Social Justice in an Open World: The Role of the United Nations* (New York: United Nations, 2006), *United Nations,* 2020, http://www.un.org/esa/socdev/documents/ifsd/SocialJustice.pdf.

7. Ibid., 11–12, original emphasis.

8. Maurianne Adams and Lee Anne Bell, *Teaching for Diversity and Social Justice: A Sourcebook* (New York: Routledge, 1997).

9. Anna Julia Cooper, "Souvenir," in *The Voice of Anna Julia Cooper: Including a Voice from the South and Other Important Essays, Papers, and Letters,* ed. Charles Lemert and Esme Bhan (Lanham, MD: Rowman, 1998), 339.

10. W. E. B. Du Bois, "Of the Training of Black Men," in *The Souls of Black Folk* (1903). Du Bois said, "The function of the Negro college, then, is clear: it must maintain the standards of popular education, it must seek the social regeneration of the Negro, and it must help in the solution of problems of race contact and cooperation. And finally, beyond all this, it must develop men." W. E. B. Du Bois, *The Souls of Black Folk* (Boston: Bedford, 1997), 101.

11. Dario Coletti, Laura Teodori, Zhenlin Lin, Jean Francois Beranudin, and Sergio Adamo, "Regenerative Medicine," *Research* 1, no. 4 (2013): 1–11; Steve Bauer, "Stem Cell Therapy: FDA Regulatory Science Aims to Facilitate Development of Safe and Effective Regenerative Medicine Products," *FDA Voice*, August 12, 2014, *US Food and Drug Administration*, 2020, https://www.massdevice.com/stem-cell-therapy-fda-regulatory-science-aims-facilitate-development-safe-and-effec/https://www.massdevice.com/stem-cell-therapy-fda-regulatory-science-aims-facilitate-development-safe-and-effec/.

12. "Stress in America: The State of Our Nation," *American Psychological Association*, November 1, 2017, 2–5, https://www.apa.org/news/press/releases/stress/2017/state-nation.pdf.

13. Sharon Harley, "The Politics of Memory and Place," in *Telling Histories: Black Women Historians in the Ivory Tower*, ed. Deborah Gray White (Chapel Hill: University of North Carolina Press, 2008), 101–134.

14. Nell Irvin Painter, "Un Essai d'ego-histoire," in White, *Telling Histories*, 28–41.

15. "The Epistolary Petrarch," in *The Cambridge Companion to Petrarch*, ed. Albert Russell Ascoli and Unn Falkeid (Cambridge: Cambridge University Press, 2015), 120–121.

16. Rob Nixon, "Mother of Invention," *New York Times*, April 13, 2003, http://www.nytimes.com/.

17. Suzanne Marie Ondrus, "Writing about Writing: African Women's Epistolary Narratives," PhD diss., University of Connecticut, 2014; Heather Treseler, "Epistolary Memoir," *Notre Dame Review* 24 (Summer/Fall 2007): 260; Jonathan Russell Clark, "7 Variations of the Epistolary Novel," Read It Forward, *Penguin Random House*, 1995–2020, http://www.readitforward.com/essay/7-variations-epistolary-novel/.

18. Dionne Brand, *A Map to the Door of No Return: Notes to Belonging* (Toronto: Doubleday, 2001), back cover.

19. Carroll Parrott Blue, *The Dawn at My Back: Memoir of a Black Texas Upbringing* (Austin: University of Texas Press, 2003), back cover.

20. Hilda Jarman Muir, *Very Big Journey: My Life as I Remember It* (Canberra, Australia: Acton: Aboriginal Studies Press, 2004), back cover.

21. Zetta Elliott, *Stranger in the Family* (Scotts Valley, CA: CreatesSpace, 2011), back cover.

22. Mariama Ba, *So Long a Letter* (Long Grove, IL: Waveland, 2012), back cover.

23. Tanisha C. Ford, *Dressed in Dreams: A Black Girl's Love Letter to the Power of Fashion* (New York: St. Martin's, 2019), back cover.

24. Juanita Johnson-Bailey, "Making a Way Out of No Way: An Analysis of the Educational Narratives of Reentry Black Women with Emphasis on Issues of Race, Gender, Class, and Color," PhD diss., University of Georgia, 1994; Patricia Bell-Scott and Juanita Johnson-Bailey, *Flat Footed Truths: Telling Black Women's Lives* (New York: Holt, 1998); Patricia Bell-Scott, *The Firebrand and the First Lady: Portrait of a Friendship: Pauli Murray, Eleanor Roosevelt, and the Struggle for Social Justice* (New York: Knopf, 2016).

25. Joanne Braxton, *Black Women Writing Autobiography: A Tradition within a Tradition* (Philadelphia: Temple University Press, 1989); bell hooks, "Writing Autobiography," in *Women, Autobiography, Theory: A Reader*, ed. Sidonie Smith and Julia Watson (Madison: University of Wisconsin Press, 1998), 429–432; Nellie Y. McKay, "The Narrative Self: Race, Politics, and Culture in Black American Women's Autobiography," in Smith

and Watson, *Women, Autobiography, Theory*, 96–107; Margo V. Perkins, *Autobiography as Activism: Three Black Women of the Sixties* (Jackson: University Press of Mississippi, 2000); Rosetta R. Haynes, *Radical Spiritual Motherhood: Autobiography and Empowerment in Nineteenth-Century African American Women* (Baton Rouge: Louisiana State University Press, 2011); Layli Maparyan, *The Womanist Idea* (New York: Routledge, 2012); Angela A. Ards, *Words of Witness: Black Women's Autobiography in the Post-Brown Era* (Madison: University of Wisconsin Press, 2016).

26. See Chanequa Walker-Barnes, "When the Bough Breaks: The StrongBlackWoman and the Embodiment of Stress," in *Black Women's Mental Health: Balancing Strength and Vulnerability*, ed. Stephanie Y. Evans, Kanika Bell, and Nsenga K. Burton (Albany: State University of New York, 2017), 43–56.

27. Tina Turner, *My Love Story* (Kindle 2018) (New York: Atria Books, 2019), citations are to the Kindle edition.

28. Gray White, introduction to *Telling Histories*, 21.

29. Cooper, *Voice*, 61.

30. For discussion on historiography and philosophies of history, see "Philosophy of History," *Stanford Encyclopedia*, http://plato.stanford.edu/entries/history/; "Philosophy of History," *New World Encyclopedia*, http://www.newworldencyclopedia.org/entry/Philosophy_of_history. History has been represented as a line (positivist/progressive Stephen Hawking), hierarchy (Friedrich Hegel), cycle (Confucius), tug-of-war (Michel Foucault, Karl Marx), braid (Penelope Corfield), and continuum (Joseph Adjaye).

31. Anna Julia Cooper, "Womanhood: A Vital Element in the Regeneration and Progress of a Race," in *Voice*, 53–71.

32. Ards, *Words of Witness*, 153.

33. For more, see Stephanie Y. Evans, *Living Legacies, Black Women, Educational Philosophy, and Community Service, 1865–1965*, PhD diss., University of Massachusetts, 2003, https://scholarworks.umass.edu/dissertations_1/915/.

34. V. P. Franklin, *Living Our Stories, Telling Our Truths: Autobiography and the Making of the African-American Intellectual Tradition* (New York: Scribner, 1995); Henry Louis Gates Jr. and Evelyn Higginbotham, *African American Lives* (New York: Oxford University Press, 2004); Stephanie Evans, *Black Passports: Travel Memoirs as a Tool for Youth Empowerment* (Albany: State University of New York Press, 2014).

35. For a full bibliography, see the online library of the database of www.africanamemoir.net. The sample includes only those persons whose names are searchable in this database.

36. McKay, "Narrative Self," 105.

37. In *Eyes Off the Prize*, Carol Anderson convincingly argues that scholars must grant attention to the importance of human rights, even as we honor civil rights activists.

38. Pauli Murray, *Pauli Murray: Selected Sermons and Writings* (Mary Knoll, NY: Orbis, 2006), 151.

39. Sources surveyed include encyclopedias, books, articles, dissertations, and blogs.

40. Marian Wright Edelman, *Guide My Feet: Prayers and Meditations on Loving and Working for Children* (New York: Harper, 2013), 41, 207–210.

41. Angela Davis, *Angela Davis: An Autobiography* (New York: Random, 1974), 300.

42. Stephanie Y. Evans, "Black Women's Historical Wellness: History as a Tool in Culturally Competent Mental Health Services," *Association of Black Women Historians*, June 21, 2019, http://abwh.org/2019/06/21/black-womens-historical-wellness-history-as -a-tool-in-culturally-competent-mental-health-services/.

43. Joanne Braxton, *Black Women Writing Autobiography* (1989), 379.

44. Stephanie Y. Evans, *Black Women in the Ivory Tower, 1850–1965: An Intellectual History* (Gainesville: University Press of Florida, 2007).

45. Ibid.

46. Ashley Nielson, "The Philosophy of Regenerative Education and Living Schools," PhD diss., Saybrook University, 2008. In the abstract to her dissertation, Nielson states: "Building from this foundational review of the holistic education movement, the philosophy of regenerative education was developed, comprising four types of education: understanding-based, self-revealing, systems, and spiritual education. . . . In a regenerative education learning environment, students engage in self-actualization, self-realization, system-actualization, and system-realization growth processes. This dissertation also provides a framework for bringing the philosophy of regenerative education to life: the living school."

47. Evans, *Black Passports*, 14–15, and *Black Women's Yoga History*.

48. Jan Willis, *Dreaming Me: Black, Baptist, and Buddhist—One Woman's Spiritual Journey* (Somerville, MA: Wisdom, 2008), 345, original emphasis. See also Jan Willis, "Zen Peacemakers Symposium for Western Socially Engaged Buddhism," Wesleyan University, Middletown, CT, September 27, 2010, https://www.youtube.com/watch?v=3LoC5GtiChY, accessed July 1, 2014.

49. Willis, *Dreaming Me*, 153.

50. "Actress Taraji P. Henson to Testify at Second CBC Youth Suicide Forum on June 7," press release, *Congressional Black Caucus*, June 9, 2019, https://cbc.house.gov/, accessed July 30, 2019.

PART III

SOCIAL ACTIVISM AND INSTITUTIONS

Introduction

NIKKI M. TAYLOR

This section illuminates the strong Black intellectual tradition at the heart of Black religious, social, cultural, and political institutions. These authors demonstrate that the Black intellectual tradition in the twentieth century is nurtured and sharpened in institutions such as Black Greek-lettered sororities and fraternities, historically Black colleges and universities, Black religious institutions, civil rights organizations, the Black press, and women's spiritual and social organizations in West Africa. The discourses in these institutions have influenced how Black people understand racial, gender, and class oppression while also informing their activist strategies and perception of progress. The three following essays categorically affirm that the Black intellectual tradition is primarily purposed to find concrete solutions to the problems facing people of African descent. Hence, Black thought is most effective when it is actualized to advance and uplift Black humanity.

Layli Maparyan, in the first essay, "Into the *Kpanguima*: Questing for the Roots of Womanism in West African Women's Social and Spiritual Formations," makes a compelling case for why the Black intellectual tradition must include womanist theory. Maparyan uses Sande cultural and social practices as a lens to illuminate womanist praxis in action in West Africa. Although womanism was first articulated by Alice Walker in the United States in 1979, Maparyan contends that the core principles of womanism embody age-old African cosmologies, worldviews, values, and cultural practices. Womanism values women and their experiences, human diversity, the collective, nature, and the spiritual; it mobilizes all of these assets to combat oppression of all stripes. Womanism, then, is distinctive from Western feminisms, social movement philosophies, and even other types of Black thought. Maparyan emphasizes that, ironically, womanism, as a form of Black thought, is not ideological, theoretical, or dependent on highly educated people to uncover its essence: it focuses less on ideas and more on everyday people and everyday actions that embrace, unite, inspire, and mobilize people to solve social problems and elevate humanity. Certainly, womanism summons the more organic, inclusive, holistic, spiritual, and communal aspects of the Black intellectual tradition.

"New Negro Messengers in Dixie: James Ivy, Thomas Dabney, and Black Cultural Criticism in the Postwar US South, 1919–1930," by Claudrena N. Harold, illuminates the intellectual contributions of two Black thinkers in the post–World War I era, Thomas Lewis Dabney and James Waldo Ivy. The thinking of these two men married the theories of the New Negro and the New South movements, with the goal of forging a more egalitarian and racially and economically just society in the south. That aside, one of the biggest contributions of Harold's essay is that it uses Dabney's and Ivy's intellectual biographies to demonstrate how historically Black colleges and universities served as incubators and training grounds for Black intellectuals. Black professors at these institutions believed teaching and training of students to be a form of activism. "Master teachers" inspired and molded younger generations of intellectuals and advanced strategies for pursuing social and economic justice. Extracurricular student organizations, such as campus chapters of the National Association for the Advancement of Colored People (NAACP) and campus newspapers, provided these young scholars with forums to disseminate their ideas and a lab in which to enact them. Without a doubt then, the Black intellectual tradition owes a great debt to historically Black colleges and universities and their master teachers for building an intellectual legacy that has withstood the challenges of time and progress.

Finally, Maurice J. Hobson, in "Tackling the Talented Tenth: Black Greek-Lettered Organizations and the Black New South," examines Black Greek-lettered organizations—the Divine Nine—as the embodiment of W. E. B. Du Bois's Talented Tenth concept, especially its emphasis on education, racial uplift, and mutual obligation. Hobson demonstrates that each one of the Divine Nine organizations was founded on a guiding philosophy of racial uplift, community service, and self-help, although they each had different visions about how to achieve them. These organizations and their individual members actualized these philosophies to improve the condition of the masses of African Americans. Hobson charts the myriad and sustained contributions that members of these organizations have made to advance civil rights, integration, equality, and racial, economic, and social justice across the twentieth century. By outlining the historic contributions of members of these organizations, Hobson underscores the staying power of the racial uplift philosophy and its efficacy as a strategy and goal for long-term Black activism.

In the final analysis, Maparyan, Harold, and Hobson underscore how vital Black institutions have been to developing Black thought and mobilizing it in real ways to improve the condition of people of African descent.

CHAPTER 6

INTO THE *KPANGUIMA*

QUESTING FOR THE ROOTS OF WOMANISM IN WEST AFRICAN WOMEN'S SOCIAL AND SPIRITUAL FORMATIONS

LAYLI MAPARYAN

Womanism has emerged as a culturally situated social and ecological change perspective devised and named by—but not limited to—Africana women. While some scholars have struggled to define the uniqueness of womanism relative to feminism and humanism, others have authored decidedly womanist scholarship with great exuberance and little concern for how womanism relates to any other perspective. For many decades, it has been my scholarly quest to identify and name the defining attributes of womanism and to articulate what makes womanism a distinctive and potent worldview and praxis. This chapter attempts to situate womanism within the Black intellectual tradition in the United States in the twentieth century by illuminating ways in which womanism is informed, if not constituted, by various aspects of African metaphysics and cultural practice. The emphasis is on the ways in which Africanity is gendered and how this gendered Africanity refigures our thinking about contemporary social and ecological problem solving, particularly in light of the complex problems already beginning to define the twenty-first century.

This essay unpacks the ontological and epistemological underpinnings of womanism by linking contemporary womanism to the metaphysical and cultural foundations of West African women's social and spiritual formations, most notably the Sande society. In this analysis, I make an argument for how this makes womanism qualitatively different from feminism, particularly Western forms of feminism, because they evince from a European philosophical tradition that is liberal, secular, and colonizing in its orientation. Properly identifying the metaphysical and cultural foundations of womanism helps to illuminate not only what makes womanism distinct from feminism but also what makes it distinctive as a form of Black thought that is uniquely potent in terms of social and ecological problem solving on a global scale. The analysis also helps explain why such a vital and comprehensive system of thought and action as womanism has, for so long, largely flown under the radar of those in the academy while animating so many everyday women, men, and people of all genders around the world, especially in the Africana world.

A single text that transformed my thinking stands at the center of this analysis: Sylvia Ardyn Boone's 1986 *Radiance from the Waters: Ideals of Feminine Beauty in Mende Art*.[1] This highly ethnographic art-history treatise, written by the first woman ever to teach a Black Women's Studies course at Yale University (and subsequently the first Black woman to be tenured at Yale), focuses on the West African Sande society, a woman's sodality that has, in eras past, frequently been referred to as a secret society. Based on insights gained from Boone's text, I devised three theses about womanism: First, the African roots of womanism can be seen in African women's social and spiritual formations, such as the West African Sande society. Second, womanism is a New World vehicle for many of the ideas and dispositions that have historically been preserved by these African women's social and spiritual formations. Third, inherent in the organization and spirit of these ideas and dispositions is a unique orientation to social and ecological problem solving, rooted in a gendered form of Africanity. This unique orientation toward problem solving has manifested under many guises in many sites, despite not being named as womanism until 1979 by Alice Walker.[2] Yet, even in the United States, within the named and studied Black intellectual tradition, this highly gendered form of Black thought—womanism—has also flown beneath the radar. To name it and see it, we must, figuratively, go into the *kpanguima*, or secret lodge.

Womanism, I argue, has been a significant development within the Black intellectual tradition in the United States, both in general and in terms of Black women specifically. With reference to the latter, Mia Bay, Farah J. Griffin, Martha S. Jones, and Barbara D. Savage have offered an expansive account in their groundbreaking volume, *Toward an Intellectual History of Black Women*,[3] which surveys and analyzes the intellectual contributions of notable Black women from 1619 to 2015. In this text, womanism is mentioned only a few times, largely in connection with Walker, the progenitor of womanist terminology in its current usage. Thus, there is room for a wider-ranging exploration of womanism and its contributions to the Black intellectual tradition, which is offered here.

What Is Womanism?

I have written previously, "Womanism is a social change perspective rooted in Black women's and other women of color's everyday experiences and everyday methods of problem solving in everyday spaces, extended to the problem of ending all forms of oppression for all people, restoring the balance between people and the environment/nature, and reconciling human life with the spiritual dimension."[4] Womanism presents a view on the entire world and all its problems through a women-centered lens informed by culture—a view that includes perspectives on gender and sexism but does not privilege them as sole or even primary concerns. Womanism creates a vehicle through which the genius of everyday women from around the world, particularly those whose cultural perspectives have been historically sidelined, can be brought to the table of discourse and contemporary global problem solving.

Five core concepts animate womanism: First, womanism is *anti-oppressionist*, with the aim of ending all forms of oppression and violence, named or unnamed, for all people. Second, womanism is *vernacular*, meaning it is identified with everyday people and everyday life, acknowledging the power of change in everyday spaces and practices by people whose social and transformational power may or may not be institutionally validated or acknowledged within dominant power structures. Third, womanism is *nonideological*, with a methodological gradient toward bringing people together rather than creating lines of separation and with an ultimate aspiration of recognizing that all human beings are deeply and richly cultured while also constitutive of an emerging global human transculture. Fourth, womanism is *communitarian*, recognizing and balancing the integrity and rights of both individuals and collectives, particularly cultures and other identity-based groups. Fifth, and perhaps most distinctively, womanism is *spiritualized*, meaning that it acknowledges and takes as axiomatic the existence of a metaphysical realm, however named, which interpenetrates the visible, material realm, connects humans with all livingkind, and is a source of energy and power for social and environmental change work.

Methodologically, womanists are inclined toward activities that promote healing, restoration, well-being, harmony, and balance among and between humans, between humans and the environmental or ecological realm, and between humans and the spiritual realm. Womanists place great value on dialogue, particularly of the kitchen-table variety, and view arbitration and mediation as effective forms of transforming conflict. Womanists assume an unbreakable family relation among and between all humans, within which differences of opinion can and must be reconciled, as no members of the human family can be written off or ejected from the whole. Many activities that are often reckoned as unimportant because they fall within the private sphere of reproductive labor—such as mothering, hospitality, and everyday caretaking—are considered by womanists to be deeply transformative of society at large. Mutual aid and self-help, as methods that have historically mobilized low-resource communities for well-being outside supportive institutional structures, are valued and validated by womanists. Additionally, womanists view the promotion of physical and mental health, including self-care, as essential to social and ecological transformation.

The bottom line is this: Womanism works to transform hearts and minds, that is, emotions and cognitions, because they underpin our material and institutional structures as well as our political and economic processes. Each of these things grows out of a cosmological worldview and a set of beliefs about human beings. From a womanist perspective, structural change—social, political, or economic—is impossible without consciousness change, and womanism works on consciousness, performing what Gloria E. Anzaldúa calls "the inner work," while also attending to societal change, known as "the outer work."[5] Often, the inner work occurs through seemingly small "everyday" practices in seemingly minor "everyday" spaces, and the outer work becomes a cumulative total or outgrowth of these "small and minor" events.

Womanism is defined by the *politics of invitation* rather than the politics of opposition. The foundation of the politics of invitation is the view that all human beings are indissolubly bonded by a universal family relationship, as well as the view that sustainable change occurs when people engage in it voluntarily. The friendly presentation of a new and better reality often inspires people to become a part of it, particularly when people perceive that their basic goodness is being assumed up front. This womanist social-movement philosophy is quite different from those social-movement philosophies that trace their roots back to Marxism, socialism, the New Left, or even the European Enlightenment, because all of these divide human beings into classes, pit the classes against each other, and posit social change in terms of conflicts (or processes of colonization) that yield distinct winners and losers. Womanism's carrying capacity for human diversity—of culture or of political thought—is much greater than these more "ideological" positions because womanism simply invites people to move forward together in a more humanizing direction, regardless of their starting point.

A Brief History of Womanism

Womanism was first named by Walker in 1979: "A womanist is a feminist, only more common."[6] In 1983 she expanded this definition to mean "a black feminist or feminist of color."[7] The term "womanist" was given additional depth and dimensionality by two additional early scholars. Chikwenye Okonjo Ogunyemi coined the term "Black womanism" in 1985 to refer to forms of womanism characteristic of Black women of the African continent as distinct from African American women;[8] in 1996 she renamed her concept "African womanism" in a greatly expanded discussion of the topic.[9] In 1988 Clenora Hudson-Weems introduced the term "Africana womanism" to refer to a positionality emerging from and consonant with Pan-Africanism and Black nationalism, which she elaborated in 1989 and 1993.[10]

One point of agreement among all of these authors was that they were not creating something new, but, rather, they were naming something that had long been in existence: a worldview and a methodology characteristic of women from Africana cultures around the world. All of these authors advanced the notion that womanism has its own cultural genealogy that makes it independent of feminism and not a version of feminism. Despite this, from the 1980s onward, Women's Studies scholars and others persisted in attempting to define womanism as a branch or subtype of feminism, often equating it with Black feminism, or failing to see it altogether.[11] From a womanist perspective that uses a family metaphor, womanism and feminism are cousins, and womanism and Black feminism are sisters—in both cases, distinct but related. In terms of identity or praxis, people can be womanist, feminist, womanist and feminist, or none of the above—and, regardless, can contribute to moving the world in a positive direction. From a womanist perspective, all are welcome.

Womanism has continued to be a generative point of view inside and outside the academy, taking distinct forms in popular culture as well as scholarly discourse. The Internet explosion and advances in social media over the last two decades have propelled womanism globally, further cementing its democratic center of gravity as more and more women outside the academy are empowered to develop and share womanist ideas online. This greater exposure has linked Black womanists and other people of color claiming their own culturally or religiously centered ethnogendered intellectual traditions. Womanism has also taken up new areas of concern, such as mental health, and generated new areas of inquiry, such as transwomanism, or womanism inflected by a transgender perspective.[12]

Womanist Praxis in Action

Womanist social- and ecological-change activity is evident in the life and work of numerous figures from history, both well known and lesser known. Additionally, there are organizational examples, most notably Black women's mutual-aid and self-help societies. For an example that blends both, Elsa Barkley Brown has written about the womanist social change praxis of Maggie Lena Walker, founder of the Saint Luke Penny Savings Bank and first woman bank president in the United States.[13] This bank was established in 1903 to serve low-income African American women and other similarly situated stakeholders in Richmond, Virginia. It was part of a larger community-building effort maintained by the Independent Order of Saint Luke, led by Walker for many years, which also ran a large department store called the Emporium (at one time the largest employer of Black women in Richmond, providing a better-paid alternative to domestic service), an educational loan fund for young people, and a weekly newspaper. The Independent Order of Saint Luke was women-led but not exclusively women, involving men in community building along the lines of arguably womanist blueprints for development.

Iris Carlton-LaNey has described the womanist consciousness-raising work of Elizabeth Ross Haynes, a Progressive-Era social work pioneer, "race woman," and community activist who authored the first comprehensive research study of African American domestic workers in the United States. Born in Alabama, she gained prominence through leadership work in the Young Women's Christian Association (YWCA), organizing and expanding the "colored branches." A traditionalist in some respects, she resigned paid work when her husband, George Edward Haynes, became the first executive director of the National Urban League, which he also cofounded. However, she continued to work in unpaid capacities as a volunteer and researcher. For example, when her husband became the director of Negro economics for the US Department of Labor, she became a "dollar-a-year" worker for the division that would later become the Women's Bureau, under whose auspices she completed the massive study on domestic workers, and she became an acknowledged expert on women in industry. Later, she served in local politics in Harlem, over time developing a web of affiliations that included, in addition to the YWCA, the National Association of Colored Women (NACW), the Alpha Kappa Alpha sorority, the Abyssinian Baptist Church, and a variety of other influential organizations. Meanwhile, she tutored schoolchildren and engaged in both research and educational advocacy on her vacation trips back to Alabama. As LaNey points out, the hallmark of Haynes's womanist praxis was her "holistic organizing"—an ability to interweave diverse networks of people while advocating for and influencing systems change, aided by a humble and graceful persona that brought people to the table of shared work.[14]

We see examples of womanist praxis even in accounts of historical figures who have not been characterized as womanist. For example, Mary Frances Berry's account of Callie House as the mother of the US reparations movement demonstrates many womanist features.[15] From the "start where you are" praxis that, despite her limited personal means, compelled her, as a Nashville, Tennessee, washerwoman, to launch a national movement for burial pensions for ex-slaves, to the way that she built support for this movement "in the hood," to her cross-racial organizing tactics vis-à-vis White male members of the US Congress, to the national organization with town chapters that she built, we see the womanist "can-do" attitude that puts large-scale visions into action despite the lack of formal institutional resources or backing. We can observe House's dedication to the dignity, health, and well-being of formerly enslaved people and her creative thinking about how to fund the reparations (in this case, drawing from the taxes on seized rebel cotton). House's brilliant strategizing and self-less organizing work were, ultimately, stopped in their tracks by the US Justice Department, which concocted a mail-fraud scheme to criminalize her direct mail–marketing techniques, but her womanist genius has been unequivocally documented by historian Berry.

Moving beyond the United States, Cheryl Johnson Odim and Nina Emma Mba (but see also Judith A. Byfield) have documented the remarkable life work of Funmilayo Ransome-Kuti of Nigeria, the leading female nationalist of Nigeria's independence movement and a prominent women's organizer who stood for election as Nigeria's first woman candidate even before Nigerian women had attained suffrage.[16] Born in Abeokuta, Nigeria, and fluent in both Yoruba and English, her movement strategies included conducting political rallies in Yoruba instead of English to deflect and mystify British colonial officials and wearing Yoruba traditional dress (and also refusing to bow) at official functions where Western dress and cultural deference were expected. She held organizing meetings in her home, at the neighborhood school where she and her husband were teachers and administrators, and at picnics and festivals, breaking down the walls between domestic and political spheres and demonstrating the power of both hospitality and everyday space to advance the self-determination of her community and nation. Additionally, she and her husband worked side by side as "passionate comrades" in the movement for national independence, exhibiting a diarchic orientation to political labor. She turned a local "ladies club" into a national women's empowerment organization, radicalizing others as she herself became radicalized. In these organizations, she brought Christian, Muslim, and Yoruba women together for the common causes of women's empowerment and national independence. She organized and led a massive market women's action against taxation without representation, aided by the long-standing organizational structures of market women in Nigeria, which allowed them to mobilize quickly and effectively. Later, she became active in the international peace movement, joining the Women's International League for Peace and Freedom and traveling and speaking internationally. In her work, she stood for the simultaneous integration of women's, nationalist, and international concerns, truly demonstrating how an activist can support their own gender, their own ethnic group, and their own religion and still be a genuine global citizen with a humanitarian orientation.

In *The Womanist Idea*, I present case studies of five women from around the world (of Africana and other heritages) who embody the concept of womanist spiritual activism in particular.[17] To conclude the illustration of womanist praxis in action, one woman is mentioned briefly here, Wangari Maathai. A Kenyan of mixed Kikuyu and Maasai ancestry, she grew up in a traditional community living close to the earth at the base of Mount Kirinyaga. Eventually, she attended Catholic school and converted to Christianity, incorporating rather than abandoning her traditional cultural beliefs and values. Inspired by Kikuyu ecological values of sustainability and deep respect for the environment, along with Christian injunctions to care for creation, she became a biologist and developed the green belt movement, for which she received the Nobel Prize in 2006. Her goal was to restore the ecological vitality of Kenya's natural landscape, which had been devastated by colonial monoculture agricultural practices. In the process, she also lifted up and economically empowered "everyday women" whose agricultural and horticultural genius was being overlooked by largely male agricultural authorities, whether British or Kenyan. Together with these women, she reforested Kenya. Along the way, she and the women of the green belt movement shaped Kenya's prodemocracy movement and contributed to the expansion of freedoms and legal equality. Her frequent invocation of spiritual concepts or practices—whether traditional and/or cultural, Christian, or ecofeminist or ecowomanist—in the doing of this work was notable from a womanist perspective as well as from a perspective of spiritual activism.

Examples of womanist praxis in action, in the United States and around the world, could fill volumes. Yet, these few examples are, hopefully, sufficient to set the stage for examining the connections between womanism and women-gendered Africanity as embodied in women's sodalities like the West African Sande Society.

The Cosmological Roots of Womanism

Arguably, womanism is not truly cognizable unless one goes inside an African cosmological worldview. Seeing African worldviews in their wholeness is not easy when one is working within Western and/or Eurocentric cosmological frames, which dominate the Western academy and its offshoots. Western and/or Eurocentric cosmology has become hegemonic to the point of invisibility, which is one reason why womanism is so important in the West: Womanism provides a window into intact African cosmologies in action in the contemporary world, and it contributes to the equalization of Western and African worldviews and problem-solving methodologies in the global context. Historian Jon Sensbach acknowledges the role of African women's spiritual cosmology in the making of African America: "They played important roles as priestesses, diviners, healers, and spiritual leaders in West African societies, capabilities they brought across the Atlantic to deploy in similar functions in the Americas. . . . If the fundamental basis of intellectual history is the history of the creation and transmission of ideas, then women's spiritual epistemology must be placed at the center of any African American religious history, even if their ideas were not always written down."[18]

This West-South cosmological distinction can be illustrated in an examination of womanism alongside feminism. Western feminism, as has been repeatedly recorded, grew out of European "Enlightenment" philosophical and political foundations, especially liberalism.[19] This worldview is founded on a materialist ontology and a rationalist-empiricist epistemology with a bent toward nomotheticism and universalism. Its logic is taxonomic and hierarchical, and its philosophy of science (like its politics) is oriented toward prediction and control. This nexus of axioms yielded a liberal and secular political philosophy focused on individual rights and freedoms, particularly for men. Historically, this position also yielded a subsumptive colonizing tendency toward the non-White peoples of the world and a tendency toward oppositional (conflict-based) methods of change.[20] Western feminism, despite its objective to dismantle patriarchy, enable women's empowerment, realize gender equality, and undo other structures of oppression, has not been entirely able to escape the clutches of this worldview, despite ongoing valiant and authentic attempts. One evidence of this failure to escape has been the ongoing tendency to attempt to "place" womanism within the Western feminist history of consciousness, despite certain kinds of differences that make it a bad fit.[21]

This question of bad fit puzzled me for many years until it occurred to me to think through the implications of cosmology—not just epistemology, as is more commonly considered—for social change–oriented critical theories and social-movement philosophies and methodologies. Cosmology is, among other things, the branch of philosophical inquiry that deals with origin stories, or accounts of what exists, how it came into being, and how the various elements are arranged or interrelate. My "Aha!" moment came when I realized that womanism has an African cosmological foundation. That is, womanism is based on a different understanding about what exists, how it all came into being, how all of the parts interrelate, and what creation tends toward than is feminism.

The African cosmology I am talking about is vitalist in nature, highly spiritualized, beginning with an understanding that the universe, including people, animals, plants, the Earth, and all that exists in the cosmos (including star stuff and even, potentially, other kinds of beings, visible or invisible) is spiritually alive and infused, dynamically and holistically interconnected, personological, and oriented toward integration and the promotion of vitality. This worldview emphasizes the collective over the individual, with family as a central metaphor, attaching rights and responsibilities to collectives and individuals in interaction. In many versions, this worldview is also diarchic, placing women and men in complementary yet equal positions of power, influence, importance, authority, and responsibility—although it also has hierarchical features, such as the hierarchical relations between elders and younger people, parents and children, and initiated over uninitiated people. All told, this is a qualitatively different universe of ideas and expectations than that produced by the European Enlightenment and its derivatives (for example, Marxism and neo-Marxism), and it is a form, if not a wellspring, of Black thought—womanism being just one example. These African cosmological roots of womanism can be seen in African women's social and spiritual formations, such as the West African Sande society.

Although internal variations are underneath the umbrella of African cosmology and although there continue to be debates about whether these varying cosmologies have a unifying principle and/or ethos or not, I have long taken and continue to endorse the cultural unity of Africa thesis at the level of cosmology and ethos, and doing so informs my approach to thinking and talking about Africanity and, especially, women-gendered Africanity.[22] Some texts that have informed this thinking include Kola Abimbola, *Yoruba Culture: A Philosophical Account*; Fu-Kiau Bunseki, *African Cosmology of the Bantu-Kongo*; Hassimi Oumarou Maïga, *Balancing Written History with Oral Tradition: The Legacy of the Songhoy People*; John S. Mbiti, *African Religions and Philosophy*; Ifeanyi Menkiti, "Person and Community in African Traditional Thought"; and Linda James Myers, "Understanding an Afrocentric Worldview: Introduction to Optimal Psychology," in addition to Sylvia Ardyn Boone's *Radiance from the Waters*, among others.[23] Each of these texts has presented a window into African worldview that has enabled me to gaze outside the Western frame that has dominated my Western education and into a frame with which I am not only ancestrally connected but also one that makes new ways of being in the world and ways of problem solving possible. It is in this spirit that I link womanism with not only African cosmology in general but also with gender-inflected African-centered perspectives and with the twentieth-century Black intellectual tradition.

Sylvia Ardyn Boone and Making the Connection

Art historian Sylvia Ardyn Boone (1940–1993) examined the social, cultural, and spiritual dimensions of the Sande society in her classic book, *Radiance from the Waters: Ideals of Feminine Beauty in Mende Art* (1986), published well before the womanist idea was in wide circulation. Yet, the Sande-originated ideas, orientations, and practices Boone's text presents help elucidate the elusive core dimensions of womanism and demonstrate why womanism is the fruit of a distinctly African intellectual genealogy, born of African cosmology. Inherent in the organization and spirit of these ideas and dispositions is a unique orientation to social and ecological problem solving, rooted in woman-gendered Africanity. This section explores not only the connections between the Sande worldview or praxis and womanism but also the life and work of Boone as a unique Black intellectual who made these connections possible.

As mentioned, Boone was the first Black woman to be tenured at Yale University.[24] In 1970 she was recruited to Yale by one of its first Black female students, Vera Wells, to serve as a visiting lecturer for Yale's first Black Women's Studies course, "The Black Woman" (one account calls the course "On Black Women"; another offers "from Nefertiti to Rosa Parks"), in the Afro-American Studies program. At this time, she held a master's degree from Columbia University and a bachelor's from Brooklyn College. She had also studied briefly in the 1960s at the University of Ghana, where she met and formed friendships with W. E. B. Du Bois, Malcolm X, Maya Angelou, Rosa Guy, Tom Feelings, and Julian Mayfield. Later, she conducted fieldwork in Sierra Leone. This time on the African continent resulted in her first book, the comprehensive and insightful *West African Travels: A Guide to People and Places* (1974), produced for popular audiences.[25] While at Yale, she pursued and obtained an additional master's as well as a PhD from the Yale Graduate School under the direction of Robert Farris Johnson, an influential historian of African art. Her prize-winning dissertation is titled *Sowo Art in Sierra Leone: The Mind and Power of Woman on the Plane of the Aesthetic Disciplines*. She joined Yale's art history faculty in 1979, being promoted to associate professor in 1985 and receiving tenure in 1988 and also serving on the Women's Studies program executive committee in the early 1980s. In the middle of all this, she published the book for which she is best known, the scholarly *Radiance from the Waters*.

Other of her accomplishments include organizing the Chubb Conference on Black Women at Yale, one of the first of its kind in the United States; helping establish Yale's Black Film Festival; and, in 1989, helping organize the nationwide commemoration of the 150th anniversary of the Amistad Affair, which became an annual event in New Haven, Connecticut. She also consulted with the Smithsonian Institution's National Museum of African Art and served on the United Nations International Children's Emergency Fund (UNICEF) committee that selects annual greeting cards. Sadly, Boone experienced an untimely death at the age of fifty-two (some accounts say fifty-four), succumbing inside her faculty residence to heart failure. She is buried in New Haven's Grove Street Cemetery, and since her passing, portraits and monuments have been erected in her memory, graduate and undergraduate writing prizes have been named after her, and in 2001 Yale held a major commemorative event, sponsored by the Prince Hall Masons, celebrating her life and work and recognizing her legacy.

Radiance from the Waters might have escaped my attention were it not for the recommendation of the philomathic and polymathic Ako Mutota, owner-operator of the highly-regarded Oasis Bookstore, a Black and metaphysical bookstore in South DeKalb Mall in suburban Atlanta, Georgia, who said, over a decade-and-a-half ago, "You should read this." It sat on my shelf for some time—until, in fact, I traveled to Liberia, West Africa, and first met women belonging to the West African Sande Society. One of these women, Mama Tormah, was the head *zoe*, or top traditional leader, in Liberia and performed a naming ceremony for me, in which she named me after Gormalon P. Walker, an important female paramount chief in Liberia, known for bringing women and men into agreement. Over time and across many visits to Liberia, I had many opportunities to interact with Mama Tormah and to discuss many matters with her.

My interest in the Sande society had been building because, as a professor of Women's Studies and a womanist scholar engaged with the works of Alice Walker, I had had many occasions to think deeply about the practice of female genital cutting (FGC) and its representation in scholarly and political discourse. FGC has historically been practiced by the Sande society, among others, as an initiation ritual. I paid close attention to arguments for and against FGC, made by Western feminist critics as well as African women practitioners or defenders, and, in particular, to controversies around the film *Warrior Marks*, produced by Alice Walker and Pratibha Parmar.[26] *Warrior Marks* takes an unequivocal stance against FGC but has been accused of oversimplifying the issues associated with FGC and even reinscribing a Western colonial gaze, despite the fact that both Walker and Parmar are women of color. My interest, however, was less about who was right or which side I should take and more about how Black African women were, once again, being rhetorically collapsed into unidimensional figures lacking subjectivity or culture, in this case, as uncomplicated victims of cutting. My curiosity about the context surrounding this initiation ritual, and my irritation with others' seeming indifference or obliviousness to this context, grew steadily. Enter *Radiance from the Waters*.

Boone's study involved many years of building relationships and trust with the leaders of the Sande society in Sierra Leone, as well as other local spokespersons, during the mid- to late 1970s, and she was granted limited access to the Sande society and its realm of activities. As an art historian, her ultimate goal was to understand the iconic Sowo mask, one of the few recognizably female-centered artistic traditions of Africa. She was not the only scholar studying the Sande society and its masks and masquerades during the 1970s, but her positionality as a woman of African descent was unique within this cohort.[27] Laced throughout her text are intimations of her sense of spiritual and cultural connection with the subject matter. In addition to being situated within mainline art history, her scholarship also stood in relation to developments in the field of Black studies during the 1970s, including Black Aesthetics, Black women's artistic production, and Black Women's Studies.[28] On this scholarly journey (which could also, arguably, be described as a journey of self-discovery and/or a journey of going "back to her roots"), Boone gathered a wealth of information that has subsequently provided her readers with a rare window into the Sande society and its cultural wealth and currently provides a foundation for looking at the links between womanism and Sande.

When I refer to Sande or the Sande society, I am not viewing Sande as a "relic," as a formation from the past that is "fixed in tradition," or as some romanticized and pristine African cultural "artifact" from "over there." Sande is a living, breathing tradition and a powerful organization with many members today, inside Africa and throughout the diaspora. I know many people who belong to it, but I am not one of them. In some respects, I am ancestrally and culturally connected to it, but I am also an outsider for all practical purposes. Making these scholarly links between womanism and Sande is, in fact, risky for all the reasons I have named and more. Yet, I am driven by a sense of responsibility as a "Black intellectual" to counter the negation of Africanity that occurs through the erasure of Black thought forms and to advance scholarship that highlights the intellectual integrity of African people and cultures, diasporically considered. Additionally, I feel a special responsibility to the women's themes within the African cultural arc, and I seek the blessing of the women of Sande, past and present. These commitments animate this essay and my research more broadly.

Also important are the contributions of scholars other than Boone who have done significant research on the Sande society. The work of Filomina Chioma Steady is singularly informative, particularly with regard to the status of Sande in recent times.[29] Her accounts of Sande society activity in urban areas, such as Freetown, Sierra Leone, add great dimensionality to Boone's much-older account situated within a traditional, rural context. Additionally, Steady has recorded in great detail African women's responses—inside and outside Sande, from leaders and "everyday women" alike—to the debates about FGC, showcasing the diversity of opinion as well as a host of uniquely African-centered suggestions about how to shift this practice. My focus on Boone's text in this chapter does not reflect a lack of familiarity with or regard for other scholars who have written on Sande but, rather, it simply reflects the transformative effect that Boone's book had on my own thinking about womanism at a particular point in time, and the way that reading influenced the direction of my scholarship on womanism.

What Is Sande?

The Sande society is a women's *hale*, or sodality. Diarchic social structures, such as prevail in Mendeland and throughout much of West Africa, require, at minimum, a women's hale and a men's hale. In this way, women's power qua women and men's power qua men is preserved without interference from the other, particularly in light of the fact social institutions also bring women and men together. The Sande society is a powerful social organization. It is international and multiethnic, crossing geographic and linguistic boundaries all over West Africa, and numerically immense. It is normative for women who live in communities where Sande is resident to belong to Sande; thus, it can be described as a ubiquitous condition of womanhood in many places. Unlike initiatic societies in the West, to which typically only a minority of people in a given community belong, Sande (and its male counterpart, Poro) are grand in scale and scope. Through Sande, women acquire political expertise, authority, organization, mobilizing skills, and a power base. Leadership in Sande can be a pathway to paramount chiefdom, as well as other political offices, traditional or state-based. As Boone relays, Sande *is* the government for women where it exists; however, it also gives women political authority among men. As is evident, the Sande notion of womanhood resounds with notions of women as powerful, empowered, agentive, and authoritative beings who are existentially equal to men.

To quote Boone, "[t]he Sande Society is a concept, an ideal, and organization, a body of knowledge, a collection of objects, a fellowship of women."[30] Within Sande and by Sande, women's physical, moral, and spiritual beauty is cultivated as a way of protecting, preserving, and elevating the community as a whole. Implicit in Sande is a modality of social and ecological transformation based on women shaping women, women shaping the community, and women shaping the world. In the world of Sande, beauty is at the center of the universe, and women personify beauty. Beauty attracts and holds relationships together. Beauty is sublime and, hence, spiritual. Beauty is a force of social cohesion. Beauty is also sexual, pleasurable, fecund, and generative. Beauty, morality, and practicality go hand in hand, and beauty is an attractor force. Within Sande, beauty is a universal characteristic of women and also a public good delivered by women collectively. Sande cultivates and refines beauty, maximizing its power for good.

At the heart of Sande is *Sowo*. Sowo is the spirit of women, women's togetherness, and women's beingness. *Sowei*, the human personification of sowo, is the head of women and of the Sande society. In the society, women are arranged hierarchically for educational purposes by age, status, and ability. Women are held to standards that are enforced and adjudicated by sowei and her assistants. Sowei also adjudicates on behalf of the whole community (women and men). Women and men alike fear and love sowei. Sowei mobilizes, harmonizes, and coordinates the women of the community. Sowei exists to benefit the community, to keep it cohesive and functioning. Sowei ensures the power and desirability of older women. Sowei also teaches the healing arts, the domestic arts, the sexual arts, and the visual and performing arts, including singing and dance.

Soweisia are the "arbiters and creators of beauty and morality in Mende (Sande) society"—the teachers, judges, and healers of women.[31] A sowei is responsible for all of the women of the community, and it is her job to promote the well-being of every woman. The spirit of sowo and sowei are enshrined within the iconic sowo mask, as elaborated in Boone's text.

Into the *Kpanguima*

The *kpanguima* is the secret lodge (or sacred grove) of the Sande society, specifically, Mendeland in Sierra Leone. Historically housed deep in the forest, or "bush," this is the inviolable world where women initiate other women into womanhood and where women can be fully themselves, sharing information and wisdom, including spiritual and domestic arts, healing practices and medicinal formulas, music and dance, cultural history, market economics, political leadership, and self-comportment. Boone refigures the kpanguima as "the world of beauty that Sande makes."[32] Effectively, the kpanguima is "women's space," both materially and spiritually; it is made anywhere women come together and bring their cosmological womanness. It is animated by *tingoi*, the divine essence of beauty, who occupies the river and presides over Sande. From the river, sowei draw *hojo*, a cool white clay, with which Sande initiates are covered, symbolizing their special status and their connection with tingoi. This world of the kpanguima is detailed in *Radiance from the Waters*.

As stated earlier, global feminist debates around FGC as an initiatic practice have obscured the role of the Sande society in transmitting deep cultural knowledge intergenerationally and training women in practices that are useful to themselves as well as society as a whole. Because of the way in which FGC has been spotlighted by Western feminists and others, it has been nearly impossible to see the Sande society as anything other than the agent of a troubling form of woman-on-woman violence. It has been one more way of Black female erasure within neocolonizing narratives by dominant-culture protagonists claiming good intentions and innocence to make this view of Sande normative and exclusive. Critics have seemed to be speaking from a positionality that failed to recognize or even see the existence and operation of another, completely distinct worldview in which different logics operate, and the critics have seemed equally unable to acknowledge parallelisms between FGC as an "unacceptable" form of body alteration and other forms of bodily alteration more commonplace or popular in the West and/or North viewed as "acceptable," such as the circumcision of male infants, breast augmentation, or vaginoplasty. These concerns have made it impossible to recover or explore the liberatory aspects of formations like Sande within a feminist frame; yet, a womanist frame makes this form of seeing and recovery possible.

To extricate ourselves from this predicament, we must construct something that I call the "negative space of FGC." This metaphor of "negative space" comes from the art world and refers to learning to see everything that falls beyond the borders of a focal object. Western feminism has made FGC the focal object of African women's social and spiritual formations ("secret societies") in a way that has prevented the seeing of other perspectives on these sodalities and, in fact, the seeing of the perspectives of the women of those sodalities themselves. This focus on FGC has also limited those looking through this particular feminist lens from seeing African women as organized and effective social and/or political thinkers, unless they take a "feminist" stance and necessarily reject FGC outright. But how many women and their genius does this leave out? Womanism includes these women, while remaining in dialogue about FGC, and allowing African women to lead the dialogue.

A womanist reading of Boone's text that utilizes the negative-space metaphor helps to clarify the uniqueness of womanism by homing in on the richness of Sande worldview and praxis and the transformational genius of the women who belong. It allows us to highlight the methodological implications of the Sande perspective with regard to social and ecological problem solving from within an African-centered instead of a Western hegemonic frame. This cosmological distinction is at the heart of why womanism cannot be effectively subsumed into feminism or simply viewed as a version of it. Womanism is, in part, a move to recover, preserve, and nurture the genius of African and African-descent women as social and/or political thinkers and problem solvers, with or without certain culturally specific initiation rituals. To complete this recovery, we must intrepidly enter the figurative kpanguima and experience it through the lens of Africanity from a women's perspective. Regardless of our own opinions, we must cast off our preformed ideas and emotions about FGC so that we can see other things. Returning to our metaphor, the old negative space becomes the new positive space, and the former focal point becomes just one more thing embedded in a larger, richer context and ecology, with value for all humanity.

The range of arts and sciences that women learn in Sande, inside the kpanguima, is vast. It encompasses homecraft and domestic arts; child care; beauty, comportment, and self-refinement; proper social relations; arts, song, and dance; health, hygiene, and healing arts (including herbalism); ethics and morality; history and myth; political and economic skills; literacy; and mystical and/or metaphysical knowledge.[33] The list of virtues actively inculcated includes *nema-hulengo* (cleverness, intelligence, use of the mind); *kahungo* (physical strength, endurance, stamina); *kpayango* (authority and power, social strength, command over a social unit); *ndilongo* (bravery, courage, and the ability to press on to victory despite difficulties and pain); *fulo-fulongo* (ability to finish in no time and to get things done sharply and smartly); *dingo* (continuing until a job is done, even when tedious); *malondo* (silence, quietness, and the ability to endure without complaint); *tonyango* (the ability to fearlessly declare truth in a dispute and to serve as a good judge); *ponango* (being accountable for one's actions and to one's point of view); and *hindawandango* (virtually infinite generosity).[34]

Sande and Womanism: Parallelisms

Like a women's sodality, womanism has functioned beneath the radar as a vessel for preserving and a vehicle for transmitting a certain view of the world, particular practices, and specific knowledges. As this vessel or vehicle made (and continues to make) the transcultural and transhistorical journey, it has changed and adapted yet retained key understandings, orientations, and methodologies, based on African women's cosmology. This cosmology establishes the foundational equality of women and men; articulates and affirms women's power, authority, genius, and bond; establishes the caretaking roles of both women and men with respect to the family, the community, the nation, and humanity; and affirms the fundamental interrelationship between humans, the natural environment, and the spiritual realm.

The Sande society translates this worldview into an educational experience for girls and women. The focus of this education is to shape girls and women into people who will foster optimal community life, whether local, regional, national, or international. They are trained to cultivate beauty as a means of inviting people to goodness through both pleasure and divinity. They are provided with practical instruction that will make sure that food is plentiful and well-prepared, contributing to the health and happiness of their families and communities; that they are able to heal the sick and ailing of their communities through herbs and other methods, thus contributing to wellness; and that they will be able to both perform and appreciate the arts, whether singing, dancing, or visual forms, including the beautification of everyday objects. They are trained and tested with regard to virtues and noble attributes that will make them effective family members, friends, workers, leaders, teachers, businesspeople, and judges. They are given an understanding of the mystical and metaphysical dimensions of life and how to "work the energy." They inherit an intergenerational sisterhood and support system that will carry them through life.

This educational system is, in itself, a powerful social-change methodology. It is holistic and comprehensive, encompassing body, mind, spirit, relationships, and the environment. It shapes consciousness and behavior, teaching girls and women to be changemakers on scales both small and large, using methods that are largely invitational rather than oppositional. It connects women both within and across communities, and it also contributes to gender balance and gender equality.

This educational system–qua–social change methodology reflects several things: First, it reflects a qualitatively different set of expectations for girls and women than is generally inculcated in the West, particularly outside Black communities, reflecting a specifically West African worldview about the female gender. Second, it offers a network (or package) of expectations and attributes that work together as a carefully curated and cultivated system of girls' and women's empowerment. Third, it embodies a set of attributes believed to produce "the good society" through women's moral leadership, which is made attractive through their physical and spiritual beauty.

The Sande system of education in arts and sciences similarly reflects a very distinctive educational perspective—one that is holistic, ecological in orientation, and, like womanism, embracing of the tripartite realms of human society, the natural environment, and the spiritual world. We can think of the kpanguima as part finishing school, part mystery school, and part "university of the forest." Stated differently, Sande is an African-centered form of formal schooling, designed to mold human beings in the direction of the social good, and that social good is conceived as highly relational, industrious, collaborative, and mystical and engaged with nature and suffused with beauty. It connects with other culturally rooted, African-centered, liberationist perspectives on education, such as those of Joyce E. King, Asa G. Hilliard III, and Hassimi O. Maïga of Mali, all of whom analyze the role of African worldview and epistemology on the development of systems of education for Black children and youth and in the educational outcomes of Black children and youth.[35] These perspectives on education stand in contrast to the Western and/or Eurocentric notion of the good society as individualistic, competitive, materialistic, and secular (characterized by the separation of religion and government), and education as purely intellectual, leaving aside bodily, emotional, social, or spiritual concerns. One is reminded of Walker's 1983 definition of womanist, that a womanist is "not a separatist, except periodically, for health," and that the womanist is "committed to survival and wholeness of entire people, male *and* female."[36]

Conclusion: What We Could Learn

Some of the most intractable problems that humanity faces today are a result of the unchecked fractionation of human beings—whether as individuals, communities, or cultures—and of the environment, once a dynamically self-regulating network of ecosystems and, now, seemingly a runaway train or ticking time bomb of chaos and unsustainability. Both Sande and womanism are holism makers, healers of injury, repairers of disorder, and restorers of beauty, goodness, joy, and well-being. In this global scenario, all kinds of problem solvers are needed at the table. Because everyday Black women have seen sidelined within the halls of power and mainline discursive arenas, valuable perspectives have gone unnoticed and underutilized within the world community. Womanism and Sande both deliver new and badly needed insights and strategies to a world community that can never have enough good ideas.

Notes

1. Sylvia Ardyn Boone, *Radiance from the Waters: Ideals of Feminine Beauty in Mende Art* (New Haven, CT: Yale University Press, 1986).

2. Alice Walker, "Coming Apart," in *The Womanist Reader*, ed. Layli Phillips (New York: Routledge, 2006), 3–11.

3. Mia Bay, Farah J. Griffin, Martha S. Jones, and Barbara D. Savage, eds., *Toward an Intellectual History of Black Women* (Chapel Hill: University of North Carolina Press, 2015).

4. Layli Phillips, ed., *The Womanist Reader* (New York: Routledge, 2006), xx.

5. Gloria E. Anzaldúa, "now let us shift . . . the path of conocimiento . . . inner work, public acts," in *This Bridge We Call Home: Radical Visions for Transformation*, ed. Anzaldúa and AnaLouise Keating (New York: Routledge, 2002), 540–578.

6. Walker, "Coming Apart," 7.

7. Alice Walker, preface to *In Search of Our Mothers' Gardens: Womanist Prose* (San Diego, CA: Harcourt, 1983), n.p.

8. Chikwenye Okonjo Ogunyemi, "Womanism: The Dynamics of the Contemporary Black Female Novel in English," *Signs: Journal of Women in Culture and Society* 11 (1985): 63–80.

9. Chikwenye Okonjo Ogunyemi, *Africa Wo/Man Palava: The Nigerian Novel by Women* (Chicago: University of Chicago Press, 1996), 15–127.

10. Clenora Hudson-Weems, *Africana Womanism: Reclaiming Ourselves* (Troy, MI: Bedford, 1993).

11. For a treatment of this topic, see Chela Sandoval, *Methodology of the Oppressed* (Minneapolis: University of Minnesota Press, 2000), 41–64, 192–198.

12. Layli Maparyan, ed., *Womanism Rising* (Champaign: University of Illinois Press, forthcoming).

13. Elsa Barkley Brown, "Womanist Consciousness: Maggie Lena Walker and the Independent Order of Saint Luke," in *Womanist Reader*, ed. Layli Phillips, 173–192.

14. Iris Carlton-LaNey, "Elizabeth Ross Haynes: An African American Reformer of Womanist Consciousness, 1908–1940," in *Womanist Reader*, ed. Layli Phillips, 309.

15. Mary Frances Berry, *My Face Is Black Is True: Callie House and the Struggle for Ex-slave Reparations* (New York: Knopf, 2005).

16. Cheryl Johnson-Odim and Nina Emma Mba, *For Women and the Nation: Funmilayo Ransome-Kuti of Nigeria* (Urbana: University of Illinois Press, 1997); Judith A. Byfield, "From Ladies to Women: Funmilayo Ransome-Kuti and Women's Political Activism in Post–World War II Nigeria," in *Toward an Intellectual History*, ed. Bay, Griffin, Jones, and Savage, 197–213.

17. Layli Maparyan, *The Womanist Idea* (New York: Routledge, 2012). See esp. chap.

11, "Spiritualized Sustainability: Wangari Maathai, *Unbowed*, and *The Green Belt Movement*," 254–287.

18. Jon Sensbach, "Born on the Sea from Guinea: Women's Spiritual Middle Passages in the Early Black Atlantic," in *Toward an Intellectual History*, ed. Bay, Griffin, Jones, and Savage, 18, 19.

19. Rosemarie Tong, *Feminist Thought: A Comprehensive Introduction* (Boulder, CO: Westview, 1989), but see also Tong, *Feminist Thought: A More Comprehensive Introduction* (Boulder, CO: Westview, 2013).

20. Kum-Kum Bhavnani, ed., *Feminism and "Race"* (Oxford: Oxford University Press, 2001).

21. Sandoval, *Methodology*, 41–64, 192–198.

22. Cheikh Anta Diop, *The Cultural Unity of Black Africa: The Domains of Matriarchy and of Patriarchy in Classical Antiquity* (London: Karnak, 1989).

23. The list of texts that have informed my perspective on African cosmology and epistemology include: John S. Mbiti, *African Religions and Philosophy* (Oxford: Heinemann, 1969); Ifeanyi A. Menkiti, "Person and Community in African Traditional Thought," in *African Philosophy: An Introduction*, ed. Richard Wright (Lanham MD: University Press of America, 1984), 171–182; Linda James Myers, *Understanding an Afrocentric Worldview: Introduction to an Optimal Psychology* (Dubuque, IA: Kendall/Hunt, 1987); Asa G. Hilliard III, *SBA: The Reawakening of the African Mind* (Gainesville, FL: Makare, 1998); Edward Bruce Bynum, *The African Unconscious: Roots of Ancient Mysticism and Modern Psychology* (New York: Teachers College Press, 1999); Kimbwandende Kia Bunseki Fu-Kiau, *African Cosmology of the Bântu-Kôngo: Tying the Spiritual Knot: Principles of Life and Living* (Brooklyn, NY: Athelia Henrietta, 2001); Charles S. Finch III, *The Star of Deep Beginnings: The Genesis of African Science and Technology* (Decatur, GA: Khenti, 2001); Kólá Abímbólá, *Yorùbá Culture: A Philosophical Account* (Birmingham, UK: Iroko Academic, 2005); Hassimi Oumarou Maïga, *Balancing Written History with Oral Tradition: The Legacy of the Songhoy People* (New York: Routledge, 2010), as well as Boone, *Radiance*.

24. Biographical information on Sylvia Ardyn Boone was obtained from the following sources, all with a Google search, October 31, 2015: Bruce Lambert, "Sylvia A. Boone, 52, First Black Woman Given Tenure at Yale," *New York Times*, May 1, 1993; "Sylvia Ardyn Boone Prize" Department of African American Studies, and "Program Recalls Contributions of Late Art Historian," *Yale University* website; "Timothy Dwight College: Sylvia Ardyn Boone," *Yale Visitor Center* website; Elise Jordan, "Yale Pays Tribute to Professor," *Yale Daily News*, February 16, 2001, and Charlotte Martin, "Speakers Reflect on Eli Women," November 8, 2005, *Yale Daily News* website. However, see also a brief entry on Boone in Farah J. Griffin and Cheryl Fish, eds., *A Stranger in the Village: Two Centuries of African-American Travel Writing* (Boston: Beacon, 1998).

25. Sylvia Ardyn Boone, *West African Travels: A Guide to People and Places* (New York: Random, 1974).

26. *Warrior Marks: Female Genital Mutilation and the Sexual Blinding of Women*, directed by Alice Walker and Pratibha Parmar (New York: Women Make Movies, 1994), DVD. For a critical treatment, see Inderpal Grewal and Caren Kaplan, "Warrior Marks:

Global Womanism's Neo-colonial Discourse in a Multicultural Context," in *Womanist Reader*, ed. Layli Phillips, 379–401. For another Western treatment of FGM in Sierra Leone, see Aimee Molloy, *However Long the Night: Molly Melching's Journey to Help Millions of African Women and Girls Triumph* (New York: HarperOne, 2013).

27. See also Carol MacCormack, "Sande Women and Political Power," *West African Journal of Sociology and Political Science* 1 (1975): 42–50; Ruth B. Phillips, *Representing Woman: Sande Masquerades of the Mende of Sierra Leone* (Berkeley: University of California, 1995); Frederick Lamp, "Women's Helmet Masks of the Sande/Bondo Association of Sierra Leone and Liberia," exhibition, Yale Van Rijn Archive of African Art, Yale University, 2011; Gavin H. Imperato and Pascal James Imperato, *Bundu: Sowei Headpieces of the Sande Society of West Africa* (Bayside, NY: Kilima, 2012).

28. Toni Cade, *The Black Woman: An Anthology* (New York: New American Library, 1970). See also Hannah Foster, "The Black Arts Movement (1965–1975)," *BlackPast.org*, March 21, 2014, www.blackpast.org/aah/black-arts-movement-1965–1975, accessed November 15, 2015.

29. Filomina Chioma Steady, *Women and Collective Action in Africa* (New York: Palgrave, 2006), 95–109.

30. Boone, *Radiance*, 153.

31. Ibid., 34.

32. Ibid., 45.

33. Ibid., 16–17.

34. Ibid., 34–37.

35. Joyce E. King, "A Transformative Vision of Black Education for Human Freedom," in *Black Education: A Transformative Research and Action Agenda for the New Century*, ed. King (Washington, DC: American Educational Research Association, 2005), 3–17. See also Joyce E. King, "A Declaration of Intellectual Independence for Human Freedom," in *Black Education*, ed. King, 19–42, and Hassimi Oumarou Maïga, "When the Language of Education Is Not the Language of Culture: The Epistemology of Systems of Knowledge and Pedagogy," in *Black Education*, ed. King, 159–181. Finally, see Hilliard, *SBA*.

36. Alice Walker, preface to *In Search of Our Mothers' Gardens*, n.p.

CHAPTER 7

NEW NEGRO MESSENGERS IN DIXIE

JAMES IVY, THOMAS DABNEY, AND BLACK CULTURAL CRITICISM IN THE POSTWAR US SOUTH, 1919-1930

CLAUDRENA N. HAROLD

On the morning of February 12, 1965, the noted educator Horace Mann Bond delivered a moving address at the centennial celebration of the founding of Virginia Union University. Before an enthusiastic crowd of students, faculty, and administrators assembled at Barco-Stevens auditorium, Bond detailed the school's many contributions to African American social and political thought during the first half of the twentieth century. Taking special note of Union's "distinguished production of academic scholars," Bond reminded the audience of the university's importance to the maturation and development of the African American intelligentsia: "I do not believe that there is another institution in the United States that produced, between 1910 and 1930, so many scholars of rare distinction when the size of the institution is considered."[1] To substantiate his claim, Bond enumerated a few of Union's most celebrated graduates: Charles Spurgeon Johnson, a pioneering sociologist and former president of Fisk University; Charles Henry Thompson, founding editor of the *Journal of Negro Education* and dean of the graduate school at Howard University; the noted economist Abram Lincoln Harris, a longtime professor at Howard University and later the University of Chicago; religious scholar Vattel Elbert Daniel of Wiley College; and John Malchus Ellison, the first African American president of Virginia Union. Not mentioned in Bond's address but certainly contributing to Union's rich intellectual legacy were those graduates whose intellectual pursuits existed largely outside the confines of the academy. Counted among this distinguished group of thinkers were two of the most astute cultural critics of the New Negro era: Thomas Lewis Dabney and James Waldo Ivy. Each man, in his own decisive fashion, posed bold challenges to both conventional and emerging paradigms for studying the so-called Negro problem. By the onset of the Great Depression, the intellectual contributions of Dabney and Ivy, along with those of their fellow Union alum Abram Harris, provided a theoretical preview to what political scientist Charles P. Henry refers to as the Howard school of thought.[2] Moreover, Ivy and Dabney stood out among a rare group of New Negro intellectuals willing to expose the political limitations of the much-celebrated school of New South modernists. Thus, their intellectual endeavors provide a unique perspective on the New Negro intelligentsia and its complex engagement with matters related to race, class, culture, and region.

Their endeavors also underscore the importance of the American south as a vibrant intellectual space during the New Negro era. Although scholarly examinations of Black intellectual life during this period focus primarily on developments taking place in Harlem and Chicago, we must also be attentive to activities and initiatives below the Mason-Dixon Line. Southern institutions like Richmond's Virginia Union and Hampton Institute's *Southern Workman* were critical spaces in which Black thinkers and activists developed new and provocative ideas around questions related to the trustworthiness of White liberals, the political strengths and limitations of biracial labor organizing, the problem of authoritarianism within the labor movement, and the limits of culture as a tool for Black liberation. Few individuals provide better entry into this dynamic world than one of this chapter's principal subjects, Dabney.

Initially plugged into the New Negro intellectual circuit as a student at Virginia Union, Dabney garnered national attention during the postwar period for his astute political commentary in the *Modern Quarterly*, *Socialist Review*, *Norfolk Journal and Guide*, Urban League's *Opportunity*, and Hampton Institute's *Southern Workman*. His writings dissected the inner workings of organized labor, countered myopic representations of African American workers as "anti-union," and exposed the theoretical shortcomings of both "race-first" and "class-first" perspectives within postwar Black political thought. Two interrelated objectives guided Dabney's journalistic endeavors: the democratization of the US labor movement and the increased presence of African Americans in trade-union and left-wing politics. Though cognizant of the entrenched racism within the world of organized labor, particularly the American Federation of Labor, Dabney championed trade-union politics as the most viable vehicle through which Black workers could improve their material condition and empower themselves politically. "Unionism," Dabney routinely asserted, "adds dignity to labor and imparts self-respect to the workers. . . . It forms the economic basis for a wholesome psychology toward both work and leisure."[3]

Not alone in his political convictions, Dabney found support among several of his Virginia Union classmates, most notably Ivy. Although scholarly references to Ivy focus almost exclusively on his work as literary critic and book editor for *The Crisis* during the 1940s and 1950s, public recognition of his intellect reaches as far back as the New Negro era, when the Danville, Virginia, native gained national attention for his literary contributions to the socialist monthly *The Messenger*. As the editor of *The Messenger*'s book-review section, Ivy captured the respect of such noted writers as W. E. B. Du Bois, Claude McKay, Harris, and George Schuyler. To the delight of his faithful readers, Ivy covered a wide range of topics, from gender relations to the utility of college fraternities.

Consistent with the leftist impulse of *The Messenger*, he also engaged the struggles of African American laborers. Ivy's solidarity with Black workers, particularly those involved in trade-union politics, surfaced in his challenges to the uplift ideology of the Black elite, his denunciation of racist White labor leaders, and his celebration of Black social scientists who devoted their attention to the lives of African American laborers. To advance the interests of Black workers, Ivy also leveled strong critiques against liberal Whites who promoted themselves as "friends of the Negro" yet endorsed a system of racial exclusion and discrimination in the labor arena: "Negrophiles are today quite willing to contribute their thousands, and even their millions, to teach the Negro how to work; but none of them is willing as far as I know, to give these able recipients of their munificent educational bounties a chance to put their knowledge to good use by giving them ordinary decent jobs and a living wage."[4]

A similar disposition characterized Ivy's assessment of the southern literary renaissance, a movement anchored by the nonfiction of DuBose Heyward, Julia Harris, Emily Clark, Paul Green, and Julia Peterkin. These writers, along with Howard W. Odum and Gerald Johnson, sparked a great deal of conversation among New Negro critics, particularly Alain Locke, Benjamin Brawley, and James Weldon Johnson. Locke, in particular, envisioned "New Southerners" and New Negroes as potential collaborators in a larger struggle to bring into existence a more democratic and racially integrated society. To achieve this end, Locke pushed African American writers to reach out to their "cultural cousins" living south of the Potomac: "Let the New Negro therefore welcome the New South in the confident hope that the New South will welcome the New Negro."[5] No writers of the era challenged this position with more consistency than Ivy and Dabney. Indeed, both men acknowledged the emergence of a new generation of White southern intellectuals willing to cast a critical eye toward the region. "There is a resolute minority in the South," Ivy readily admitted, "that is intelligent and above all, realistic; they are certainly not afraid of facing the facts, which the old type Southerner would never do."[6] At the same time, he demanded that his readers understand the complex nature and limitations of the south's shifting intellectual terrain. This message reverberated in several of Ivy's writings, most notably his review of Edwin Mims's *The Advancing South*, a book that generated tremendous debate among White and Black liberals. "In recent years," Ivy conceded, "the rapid industrialization of the South has been responsible for the infiltration of capitalist ideas to the detriment of Confederate ideology. But do not for a moment believe that the South has suffered a change of heart, for she has not, despite Professor Mims' discovery that some Southerners are actually civilized."[7] A similar position echoed in the writings of Dabney, who viewed the south's "trend toward liberalism" as "the result of the economic orientation of Southern life." The rise of liberal voices was to be expected, he reasoned, but would not lead to an improvement in the material lives of the south's Black laboring majority.[8]

To better understand how Dabney and Ivy came to their respective positions on a variety of issues related to region, race, class, and politics, one must begin with the institution that had the greatest impact on their intellectual trajectory during the postwar era: Virginia Union. Located on the west end of Richmond, Virginia Union traces its roots back to 1865, when the American Baptist Home Mission Society founded National Theological Institutes in Richmond and Washington, DC. Later known as Wayland Seminary, the DC-based institute had a much smoother beginning than its Richmond counterpart, which for three years housed its classes in a former slaveholding pen called Lumpkin's Jail. The two schools eventually merged in 1899 to become Virginia Union. Over the next fifty years, Union gained a reputation as not only a fine liberal arts college but also an important institutional center of Black intellectual life in Richmond and the larger African diaspora. No small factor in Union's intellectual vibrancy was its impressive roster of professors who placed tremendous emphasis on developing effective pedagogical techniques to better facilitate the intergenerational transmission of knowledge between themselves and their students. The names that loomed the largest among this distinguished group of faculty were the master teacher–philosopher Joshua Baker Simpkins, whose list of students included Abram Harris and Charles Johnson; literary critic Arthur Paul Davis, who chaired Union's English Department from 1934 to 1944; Gordon Blaine Hancock, the founder of Union's School of Race Relations; the historian Rayford Logan, whose legendary battles with Hancock and the university's president, William J. Clark, remained a topic of conversation long after his departure from the school; and the noted theologian Samuel D. Proctor, whose theological writings and teachings influenced a long line of African American ministers and religious scholars.

Of Union's constellation of stellar professors, no one received greater praise than Joshua Simpson. A professor of the classics and theology, Simpson elicited praise from Union's most accomplished alums, including Charles Johnson,

Charles Thompson, and Abram Harris.[9] Nearly two decades after graduating from Union, Harris remained indebted to the teachings of Simpson, to whom he credited with introducing him to the study of economics: "In spite of the fact that he often antagonized people, no student ever went into Simpson's classroom and came out without a burning desire to know, and that in my judgment is the essence of good teaching. For him teaching was a great art and he knew that whereas the methods of others were an aid the true artist must often create his own methods. He had no patience with the educational theory that the way to teach men was to make every answer simple and easy. Learning for him was a severe discipline."[10]

Leaving an indelible mark on the women and men who enrolled in his courses, Simpson belonged to a distinguished group of "master teachers" whose pedagogical endeavors had a profound influence on New Negro–era college students. Counted among this distinguished group were Simpson, Benjamin Mays and Samuel Archer of Morehouse, and Benjamin Brawley of Shaw University. These master teachers defined their intellectual worth and legacy not simply by the scholarship they produced but also by the students they trained. To borrow from the historian Vincent Harding, their pedagogical agenda entailed not simply providing students with "factual information" but tapping "the magnificent but underdeveloped faculties of their imagination."[11] This important aspect of the Black professor's vocation was eloquently articulated in Brawley's fascinating 1926 article, "The Profession of the Teacher":

> To Take our boys and girls, our young men and women and to lead them into the knowledge of truth; to acquaint them with the master-minds of the ages; to help them to be clean of heart and pure of spirit; to teach them to have self-respect without arrogance and chivalry without pride; to help them to have faith even if they see wrong all around them. This is no mere business, no simple matter of office routine. It is the highest task that God can give a mortal.[12]

As was the case for Brawley, Joshua Simpson viewed his teaching as an integral component of his life's vocation. Therefore, he pushed his Union students beyond their intellectual comfort zone, demanded their absolute best, exposed them to a wide range of literature, and treated them with the upmost respect. A similar commitment guided the pedagogical work of another stellar Union professor, John W. Barco. Another one of Union's beloved professors who specialized in the ancient languages, Barco served as a mentor for students like Ivy and Dabney. Upon Barco's death, one of his former students and a classmate of Dabney, John Ellison, remembered him as a master teacher whose selflessness enriched the intellectual culture of the university: "With stern purpose, keen insight and uncompromising method, he sought to inspire the student to discover his powers and develop them to the fullest extent. His friendship was not the kind that encouraged or tolerated weakness and questionable indulgences. His purpose and efforts were always to spur the student to live at his best in study and in work."[13] To a degree not always recognized in the scholarly literature (but definitely pointed out in the memoirs of noted Black thinkers), professors like Barco and Simpson factored significantly in molding the Black intellectual tradition. Their intellectual rigor within and beyond the classroom provided a model for students who sought to transform the world through their political and scholarly engagements.

Fortunately for students, Union's extracurricular activities both affirmed and complemented many of the intellectual values and lessons Simpson, Barco, and other professors upheld in their classrooms. Take as a case in point the intellectual work of the Gamma Chi Literary and Debating Society. Every Saturday evening, the Gamma Chi featured stimulating exchanges and orations on subjects ranging from woman suffrage and birth control to government ownership of railroads. An intellectual anchor at Union, the group amassed a distinguished group of participants, including Charles Johnson and Chandler Owen.

Immediately upon his entry into Union in the fall semester of 1915, Dabney immersed himself in this vibrant intellectual culture. His encounters with such respected professors as Simpson, religious scholar Miles Mark Fisher, and Barco opened him to new ways of imagining his place not just at Union but the larger world. Dabney also benefitted from his friendships with a small yet tightly knit group of students committed to pushing their peers and Black Richmond to a higher level of political consciousness and civic engagement. The first step in these students' political agenda involved "radicalizing" the university. Toward this end, campus activists formed a college chapter of the National Association for the Advancement of Colored People (NAACP). Chartered in June 1914, the Virginia Union NAACP garnered support from accomplished students like John Malchus Ellison, William Colson, and George William Clement Brown. Much more than a local extension of the national NAACP, the Union branch developed into an important incubator of New Negro thought and political expression for many students. Its major initiatives stressed the importance of race pride and Black cultural awareness, group unity, cross-regional collaboration among young African Americans, and the necessity of consistent political engagement. In its formative period, the Union chapter protested local screenings of the controversial film *The Birth of the Nation,* raised funds for the NAACP's antilynching work, implemented cultural programming to enrich the educational experiences of their fellow students, and sought to raise the consciousness of African Americans beyond Union's campus.

Intimately involved in these student-led initiatives, Dabney sharpened his political skills within the institutional matrix of the NAACP. His leadership responsibilities as vice president of Union's chapter and sales agent for *The Crisis* proved crucial to his political maturation, as well as his emotional well-being. As was the case for many Black collegians across the country, Dabney idolized James Weldon Johnson and Du Bois for both their literary achievements and their political work. As Dabney later confided to Du Bois, "When I was a poor struggling student at Virginia Union, I sold the *Crisis* and supported the NAACP, without which I would have died in despair. I owed my spiritual existence to the *Crisis* under your editorship and the NAACP under the guidance of the late James Weldon Johnson."[14]

Viewing himself as the disciple of both Johnson and Du Bois, Dabney vowed to transform the Union chapter into a powerful force in local and national politics. Unfortunately, the United States' entry into World War I forced him to put his lofty plans on hold. On June 5, 1917, Dabney walked into a registration office in Mechanicsville, Virginia, and added his name to the list of able-bodied men eligible and liable for military service.[15] Not too long thereafter, the twenty-three-year-old departed for France, where he along with thousands of African Americans fought for the Allied Powers.

As was the case with other soldiers, Dabney's participation in the war affected him emotionally, socially, and politically. By the time he returned stateside in 1919, he was a proud socialist committed to improving the material lives of America's laboring classes, particularly those of African descent. Though many Black leftists used New York and Chicago as their organizing base, Dabney remained committed to completing his degree at Virginia Union. Much to his frustration however, financial difficulties delayed his reentry for two years.

Upon his return to Union in 1921, Dabney wasted no time in forging a bond with the small sect of students who embraced a leftist perspective in their approach to contemporary politics. Two students in particular, Abram Harris and James Ivy, encouraged his growing interest in Marxian political analysis and iconoclastic literature. Although fond of Harris, Dabney developed an especially close relationship with Ivy, who was not just his intellectual comrade but also his roommate. The two men participated in a variety of intellectual endeavors, including the formation of the Club for the Study of Socialism, an affiliate of the Intercollegiate Society. The club's formation in 1921 coincided with two other important developments on campus: Abram Harris's launching of the independent student newspaper, the *Union Gazette*, and the creation of the Open Forum, celebrated in some circles as the "most liberal and advanced organization ever formed by the students."[16] The *Gazette*, along with the Open Forum, provided safe spaces where young women and men could showcase their intellectual acumen, debate domestic and foreign policy, enumerate the many wrongs of the current economic system, or simply gain exposure to new and exciting ideas.

To further radicalize the student body, Ivy and Dabney launched their own newspaper in 1923: *The Critic*. *The Critic* was the third in a series of student-run newspapers that appeared on campus in the early 1920s.[17] As Ivy later recalled, the paper's irreverent approach to student life and university politics rather than its high literary value contributed to its popularity among students: "We gave everything going on around campus hell. Whenever we posted a new edition of the *Critic* students would cluster around reading it."[18] Ivy and Dabney found literary inspiration in periodicals like the *Sunday Call*, *Iconoclast*, *Messenger*, and *Appeal to Reason*. "Anything that was iconoclastic," Ivy later noted, "I became interested in. [Anyone who] helped to tear down or criticize . . . the supposed sanctified institution of the United States of America" drew his immediate attention, if not respect.[19]

The literary endeavors of Ivy and Dabney would not go unnoticed among Union professors and graduates. The two men eventually piqued the interest of one Union alumnus who visited the campus quite often: Chandler Owen. Although Bureau of Investigation agents closely monitored Owen's Richmond visits, Union officials welcomed his presence on campus.[20] As Ivy explains: "Union was proud of its alumni if it made any sort of achievement. So a famous preacher would be welcomed if he came back, and also a radical like Owen if he came back."[21] On one particular visit to the campus, Owen spoke in one of Ivy's classes and encouraged students to write for *The Messenger*, already a favorite among Dabney, Ivy, and their socialist friends.

Enmeshed in this vibrant network of Union alumni whose connections extended from Richmond to various cities in the Northeast and the Midwest, Ivy and Dabney had options outside the south upon their graduation from Union. Surely, they could have taken the path of other Union graduates that had launched their careers in New York, Chicago, or Pittsburgh. Indeed, migration north posed its own challenges, but Dabney and especially Ivy had important contacts that could help them navigate their transition to the urban north. On his travels to New York during summer breaks from Union, Ivy had socialized with some of the leading figures in the New Negro renaissance, most notably McKay. As mentioned earlier, Owen had encouraged the budding writer to consider relocating to New York and contributing to *The Messenger*. The vibrant intellectual world of Harlem and the Village intrigued Ivy, but like Dabney, he remained in Virginia. On the heels of his college graduation in 1925, Ivy accepted a teaching position at Union High School in Hampton Roads, where he taught Greek, English, and French. One of his students included the noted anthropologist Hylan Lewis, who later praised Ivy as a first-rate teacher.[22] Though opting for the security of a teaching position, Ivy still welcomed the chance to contribute to *The Messenger*, a monthly whose irreverent approach meshed perfectly with his literary style.

To the respected monthly, Ivy brought brilliant prose, a sparkling intellectual curiosity, and an unwavering confidence in the singularity of his literary voice. Taking advantage of the freedom provided by the magazine's editors, Ivy touched on an array of topics, ranging from sex and marriage to the future of global capitalism. His broad intellectual palette and biting wit ensured that *The Messenger*'s book-review section was never predictable or dull. However, one constant in Ivy's writings was his treatment of the African American working class. His unflappable resolve to expose *Messenger* readers to the deep layers of emotional depth and beauty that animated the quotidian struggles of African American workers surfaced in his musings on politics, labor, and even aesthetics. Due in no small part to his interactions with African American workers in Hampton Roads, Ivy demonstrated a great deal of interest in Black workers: "The future of Negro labor is in some ways quite encouraging, yet there are many obstacles to be overcome; many fallacies to be exploded; prejudices to live down. Yet Negro labor is forging ahead, this is significant." If Negro labor was to continue its forward march, Ivy deemed it necessary for the African American leadership class to deal with the race's proletarian character. As he explains in his glowing review of Charles Wesley's seminal study, *Negro Labor in the United States, 1850–1925*, "Ninety-nine percent of the Negroes in this country are laboring people. Yet the majority of our Negro leaders proceed upon the assumption that we are a race of bourgeois: comfortable, middle-class shopkeepers. It is this notion which is at the back of our so-called leaders' aloofness to the black worker and his problems; it, too, is responsible for the exasperating aping of the upper-class by our so-called rich."[23]

Coupled with his criticism of Black leaders for not devoting enough attention to the concerns of Black workers, he also lashed out at the White labor movement for its entrenched racism. On numerous occasions, he attributes the failures of the American labor movement to the provincialism of White workers: "It is the American laborer's selfishness, coupled with his extravagant sense of Nordic superiority, that makes him resist attempts at the organization of Negroes into unions, or even their admission into existing white unions. He doesn't see beyond his eyelashes that the little material benefit which accrues to the Negroes as a result of organization is nothing in comparison with the larger benefits coming to labor as a whole."[24]

An even more sophisticated analysis of the labor movement comes from Dabney, who put forth a more expansive reading of the undemocratic structures of organized labor. Upon his graduation from Union in 1925, Dabney worked intermittently as a teacher, a journalist, and a labor organizer. Notwithstanding his socialist engagements in college, Dabney secured a position as principal of the newly formed Buckingham Training School in 1924. Located in Dillwyn, Virginia, the school embodied African Americans' unwavering commitment to expanding their children's educational, economic, and political opportunities within a rural context.[25] Dabney's interactions with schoolchildren and their parents, fellow teachers, and the local county deepened his understanding of the unique challenges and opportunities facing the rural south. The spirit of self-determination that engulfed African American communities in New York, Chicago, Norfolk, New Orleans, and other urban centers also existed in small-town America and certain parts of the countryside. Although deeply appreciative of the learning experiences in rural Virginia, Dabney's mounting interest in labor politics quickly pulled him in another direction.

Within months of accepting the position at Buckingham, Dabney departed central Virginia for upstate New York. Thanks to scholarships from the American Fund for Public Service and the NAACP, Dabney enrolled at Brookwood Labor College in the fall of 1925. Located on the outskirts of Katonah, New York, Brookwood was the brainchild of socialist A. J. Muste, who opened the school immediately after World War I. Initially conceived as a community school for local residents, Brookwood transformed into a labor college specifically designed to train workers for trade-union leadership. "Well to the left" of adult educational institutions like New York City's School for Social Research, Brookwood developed into "one of the most important sites of cooperation between organized labor, pacifism, and progressive intellectuals during the 1920s."[26] The school admitted native-born Whites, a few African Americans, and immigrants from Europe, Latin America, and Asia. Its pedagogical agenda was largely shaped by one question: "What can a resident school do to enable American workers to work more effectively in the American labor movement?"[27] With the goal of assisting organized labor in its pursuit of social and economic justice, Brookwood professors and administrators implemented a rigorous curriculum with the stated purpose of producing activists skilled in the art of public speaking, labor journalism, media relations, and labor and community organizing. In Dabney's first year at Brookwood, he studied a wide range of topics, including American and international labor history, English, economics, public speaking, social psychology, labor journalism, trade-union organizing and administration, and parliamentary law.[28] Unafraid to immerse himself in the cultural activities of the student body, Dabney even participated in a student-produced play centered on the social and labor lives of a fictive coal-mining family. These cultural experiences, along with his coursework, solidified in his mind Brookwood's potential as "a potent factor in the labor movement for the social betterment of the working class in America."[29]

If Brookwood officials viewed Dabney as someone who would spread the school's message to the larger world, then they would not be disappointed with his postgraduation activities. Not long after his departure from Brookwood, he placed articles in the *Southern Workman*, *Messenger*, and *Opportunity*. His broad intellectual interests found a welcoming home in the *Southern Workman*, where he explored modernizing efforts in the rural south, labor relations, global youth activism, foreign affairs, and American race relations.[30] Since its inception at Hampton Institute in 1872, the *Southern Workman* had espoused a political philosophy that emphasized interracial cooperation and capitalist accumulation within the context of the existing Jim Crow system. It routinely ran features on Black landownership, the progress of Black businesses, the state of African American education in the rural south, and the organizational endeavors of the Commission on Interracial Cooperation. The monthly's political tone was decidedly moderate, but increasingly during the interwar years, it welcomed writers and scholars who hardly fit the category of "racial accommodationists." These writers include but are not limited to Howard Thurman, E. Franklin Frazier, Locke, Rayford Logan, and Allison Davis.

Consistent with larger intellectual developments in the world of southern reform and North Atlantic thought, Dabney focused his attention on the rural hinterlands in his first two pieces for the *Southern Workman*. Using central Virginia as his case study, he challenges the idea of the rural south as isolated from and disconnected to the monumental transformations taking place in the larger world. As if writing a rural analogue to Locke's urban-centered account of New Negro life, Dabney identifies the proliferation of rural conferences, the establishment of county training schools for Black youth, and educators' growing attention to the "careful and scientific study of rural problems" as evidence of "a new awakening" in the south's countryside.[31]

Taking advantage of the insight gleaned from his brief tenure at Buckingham, Dabney duly notes the progress of Black education in locales like Buckingham County, where through private and state support, two schools had been built for African Americans. The growing number of rural conferences and fairs also caught his attention: "Through these conferences a sort of social consciousness is being developed among rural people which is indispensable for group cooperation and advancement. This is a great accomplishment for any rural community, for farmers are by occupation very individualistic."[32] Although careful to point out instances of social progress, Dabney recognizes the vast problems still facing Black rural communities. Social isolation, poor farming techniques, and inadequate social services constituted major obstacles for those searching to build strong and vibrant communities. So, too, did the gross imbalances in educational opportunities among Black and White children in rural Virginia. "Poorly equipped one- and two-room schools taught by inefficient teachers," Dabney complains, handicapped too many Black children.[33] Through his early writings on education and other issues, Dabney sought to draw attention to the challenges facing rural people, as well as their collective and individual efforts to remedy them. His quest for a deeper understanding of the rural hinterlands eventually led him to Europe, a magnet for many Americans studying the US countryside. As the historian Daniel Rodgers notes, "the problem of the folk" along the edges of modernity had been a focus of intellectuals and reformers in both the United States and Europe during the Progressive and interwar eras.[34] Moreover, many US-based intellectuals turned to Europe for additional insight into solving the social and political dilemmas of rural life. Dabney was no exception. Early in the summer of 1925, he traveled with a delegation of American students, which included Glenn Carrington, to Soviet Russia in order to study problems and solutions pertaining to education, health, gender relations, and the like. On the basis of those travels, he produced a fascinating account of the improvements in Russia's social-welfare services in the postwar period. Although circumspect in his language, Dabney judged the health care and welfare services provided under the Soviet regime as superior to those existing in the rural sections of the Jim Crow south.

A freelance journalist whose intellectual contributions extended beyond the *Southern Workman*, Dabney also wrote for *The Messenger* between 1926 and 1928. Comparatively speaking, Dabney's articles in *The Messenger* were geared more toward organized labor than those he published in the *Southern Workman*. His meticulous detailing of trade-union politics provided a nice addition to the monthly's labor coverage, which during the 1920s increasingly focused on the political struggles of A. Philip Randolph's Brotherhood of Sleeping Car Porters. Much of Dabney's writings for *The Messenger* centered on the governing structures of trade-union politics: "One of the vital questions of the trade union movement, is that of democratic government. At present practically all power rests in the hands of officials of national and international unions. Some of these officials are dictatorial and indifferent to the interests of workers. Many are dishonest and spend much of their time making themselves and their friends secure in office. . . . [T]hey need an intelligent following to hold them in check." On the important matter of the governing structures and social relations shaping trade-union politics, Dabney spared neither workers nor labor leaders from serious critique. The undemocratic arrangements of the labor movement, he argues, "is not due merely to the kind of officials in the trade unions but it is due in part to the inclination among the masses to worship leaders. It is a product of group psychology. The average worker is well nigh helpless before both his boss and his union leader. As peculiar as this situation may seem, it is the very thing that the trade union movement is supposed to remedy for this relation between leaders and the workers must be changed."[35]

In hopes of remedying the situation, Dabney called for the creation of institutional structures and pedagogical platforms centrally concerned with empowering workers. His advocacy of a labor-oriented educational movement, dedicated to advancing the material interests of the working-class majority, reflects his growing commitment to challenging the institutions that legitimized, politically and ideologically, the prevailing social order. Such work was of critical necessity,

Dabney believed, precisely because opposition to the collectivist principles and democratic vision of the labor left existed in every facet of public life. To prove this important point, he took special notice of the school system's active role in serving the nation's "business interests." Perhaps in anticipation of criticism from liberal progressives anxious to point out current reform endeavors in the south, Dabney portrays recent changes in the educational system as consistent with the political agenda of the ruling elite: "From time to time, we have found it necessary to reorganize our educational system. We have had to make certain changes to meet the demands of a rapidly developing social system. Moreover, our broader knowledge of psychology has enabled us to fashion our educational agencies to meet the needs of the individual. Despite these changes, however, one idea has remained the same. That idea was and is that workers should be educated to respect and serve the business interests. No changes, whether in content, pedagogy or otherwise, ever [a]ffected the main idea of education." Now more than ever before, a growing number of workers recognized the need to "establish and control their own educational institutions." As he explains, "They do not expect the beneficiaries of a system to favor a type of education against that system."[36]

In laying out his vision of a more robust pedagogical agenda for the labor movement, Dabney distinguishes his goals from those of various reform agencies: "Workers' education does not mean merely educating the workers. It means providing a definite kind of education for the workers, for the tremendous social responsibility, which rests upon them as a group. This type of education transcends race, creed, nationality and sex. It has but one limitation and that is class. It is class education in that it is for workers only or those who have the workers' viewpoint."[37] Although appreciative of his educational experiences at Brookwood, Dabney believed strongly that the pedagogical work of labor must extend beyond labor schools:

> Workers' education is not by any means limited to the schools. It is fostered by labor publications, lecturers, pictures, libraries and open forums. The Workers' Education Bureau and the League for Industrial Democracy are doing much work in the field of education for the workers. In the schools the workers are kept in touch with the labor movement at home and abroad by lectures given by leaders and distinguished persons in the movement. On the other hand workers not directly in touch with school facilities have the opportunity occasionally to listen to lectures from instructors in the schools and leaders in the labor movement. In these ways workers' education is becoming a real vital part of the labor movement.[38]

Although the labor left definitely faced an uphill climb in its quest to democratize the bureaucratic structure of trade-union politics, Dabney remained hopeful in the possibility of building an expansive labor movement, particularly in the south. An important source of his optimism was his encounters with Black trade unionists when he was a lead researcher for the National Urban League. Landing a position with the league in the summer of 1926, Dabney conducted most of the interviews for the league's national survey of Blacks in the labor movement. Eager to learn more about labor politics, Dabney crisscrossed the country, interviewing both Black and White trade unionists on the state of organized labor in their communities, the level of interracial cooperation among workers, and the general morale among skilled and unskilled laborers. On the southern portion of his tour, he encountered determined Black trade unionists dedicated to the principles of class solidarity and collective action. These encounters had a noticeable impact on Dabney's journalistic endeavors, particularly his writings for *Labor Age*, the *Socialist Review*, and the *Locomotive Engineers Journal*, an important leftist publication whose contributors included Charles Beard and Mary Beard, George Soule, and Paul Douglas.[39]

Much like Ivy, Dabney was drawn to Black workers whose behavior challenged stereotypical images of African American laborers as politically apathetic and hostile to unions. He embraced the task of highlighting the deep political commitments of Black workers, a group frequently maligned by White labor unions. As he explains in an article for *Labor Age*, "Many of the leaders and members of trade unions do not understand the psychology of Negro workers with respect to the Labor Movement. In principal and theory Negro workers to a considerable extent favor trade unionism. The philosophy of the Labor Movement has a tremendous appeal for them; but they have learned by bitter experience that the theory of trade unions is one thing and their practice is another." Sounding markedly similar to the African American trade unionists that frequented the American Federation of Labor's annual conventions during and immediately after the war years, Dabney pulled no punches in addressing the entrenched racism of the labor movement. "There are cases where Negro trade union members were loyal and faithful to the organization, going out on strikes and supporting the campaigns for higher wages and better working conditions only to lose their jobs when the settlement was made with the employees."[40] Even amid these betrayals, thousands of African Americans still belonged to local and national trade unions.

Dabney's travels as a researcher and labor organizer provided him with a particular perspective on how the south might be pushed in a more progressive direction. For one, he envisioned Black workers as principal agents of change in the region. On this important issue, Dabney, along with Ivy, diverged from other New Negro writers who increasingly pointed to southern White liberals as the region's most likely redeemers. No small factor in their divergent opinions was their rootedness in the south. Unlike many of their New Negro contemporaries who judged Dixie from afar, Ivy and Dabney remained residents of Virginia for much of the 1920s. As such, they accessed the region from a different vantage point than their northern counterparts. Perhaps nowhere was this more apparent than in their provocative assessments of the southern literary renaissance.

Simultaneous with the increased production and dissemination of African American literature, music, and visual arts during the 1920s was the heightened visibility of a new generation of White writers and artists who challenged the "old assumptions and old gods" of the mythic south. This group included novelist Peterkin, sociologist Odum, journalist Gerald Johnson, and dramatist Green. Their literary and scholarly achievements signaled, for some, the beginning of a new day in the south's intellectual culture and by extension its political landscape.[41] Turning his attention away from his own community's unfolding renaissance, New Negro luminary Charles Johnson duly noted the shifting intellectual terrain of the New South. "Simultaneously with the appearance of the 'New Negro,'" Johnson editorialized in the summer of 1926, "comes 'The Awakening South' with its emancipated liberals, its intellectual revolution and its industrial prosperity." Insisting that the south no longer be treated as a bastion of intellectual conservatism, Johnson alerts his readers to the emergence of "splendid journals like the *Southwest Review*, the New Orleans *Double Dealer*, the *Reviewer*, [and] *Social Forces*." The latter journal, which the mercurial writer H. L. Mencken praised as "full of dynamite," had Odum as its editor. It also featured regular contributions from one of the region's most insightful journalists, Gerald Johnson. Although cognizant of the dangers involved in criticizing the region from within, Johnson and Odum defended their work as critical to the south's rebirth. As Odum wrote in 1924, "The South needs criticism, and severe criticism."[42] The new critical spirit found in *Social Forces* was not the only magnet drawing Charles Johnson and other New Negroes to White New Southerners. "Most interesting of all," Johnson opined in 1926, "is the queer turn of fortune, which reveals in such superb examples as Peterkin's *Green Thursday*, Heyward's *Porgy*, T. S. Stribling's *Birthright*, and Odum's *The Negro and His Songs*."[43] To this list of the south's most impressive, creative achievements, Johnson would soon add the "movingly human plays of Paul Green."[44]

Over the next few months, Johnson and other *Opportunity* contributors published a series of reviews that assessed the larger implications of the southern renaissance. One of the more intriguing assessments came from Locke, who in his review of Edwin Mims's *The Advancing South*, issues a call for members of the Black intelligentsia to incorporate into their writings "the progressive South" of George Gordon Crawford, Odum, Green, Gerald Johnson, John Eagan, Ashby Jones, Will Alexander, and Julian Harris. In justifying his stance, Locke insisted on the shared cultural and political sensibilities of New Southerners and New Negroes:

The New Negro and the New South have more than interesting parallelisms, they have many ideals, loyalties and objectives in common. Each seeks an emancipation from the old obsessions of the Southern traditions—a revolution of mind and social attitude sought as a necessary preliminary to any really vital reform; each demands a change of leadership based on concrete, constructive programs and a philosophy and policy of class cooperation and mass education; each is economically and not politically pointed; each strives to raise a stagnated but richly endowed folk tradition to the level of free-flowing and creative expression; each hopes to freshen and purify brackish group emotions through new, dynamic processes of cultural and spiritual release. Art for the minority, education for the masses, self-direction, self-criticism, self-determination in both, are the common creed and common spirit of these two movements; which only the most enlightened on either side will be able for a half generation or so to see and recognize. These movements and the constructive efforts they represent should therefore have not only the moral support of our intelligent sympathy but the practical help of our active participation. It should be one of the articles of faith of the young Negro movement to believe in the New South.[45]

On the question of whether the young Negro movement should believe in the New South, Ivy and Dabney had a different take than Locke. Like their northern counterparts, the two men closely monitored the intellectual endeavors of White women and men who positioned themselves as the region's new voices. Their respective contributions to the *Southern Workman* and *Opportunity* document not just the literary transformations taking place in the south but also such institutional developments as the introduction of race relations courses at all-White colleges like the University of North Carolina–Chapel Hill, Vanderbilt, and the University of Florida.

Though never positioning himself as a regional expert, Ivy devoted more attention to southern literature than any other writer for *The Messenger*. His first foray into the world of southern literature is a detailed analysis of the literary contributions of James Cabell. One of the most celebrated writers of the post–World War I period, Cabell sparked a great deal of controversy with the publication of his eighth novel, *Jurgen: A Comedy of Justice*. Published in 1919, *Jurgen* became a topic of national discussion when the New York Society for the Suppression of Vice pushed to have the book banned for what its members deemed "lewd, lascivious, indecent" material. The controversy did wonders for Cabell's book sales, which increased astronomically during the first half of the 1920s. In Ivy's view however, the controversy blinded critics and some supporters to the most important attribute of *Jurgen*: Cabell's literary genius. "The true, authentic, the flesh and blood Cabell is not known"; instead, he had been misinterpreted as a "ribald and smutty writer" who "concocts phrases of

perfumed and esoteric smut." Such a view, in Ivy's words, was especially prevalent "among the Ku Kluxers, Rotarians, and one hundred percent Americans."[46]
Here, Ivy echoes his literary hero Mencken, who identified Cabell as the writer
"around whom the revival of literature in the South, if it is ever to come, must
revolve."[47] Like Mencken, Ivy judged Cabell to be a "great romantic writer with
a wonderful command of English phrase and diction." Most important, Cabell
avoided falling into the trap of sentimentalism and seasoned "his romanticism
with the salt of irony, wit, and skepticism."[48] His unique style, Ivy explains, "is
not understood by the *vulgus*; and since they get no joy out of it and can perceive
no beauty therein, they proceed to slander, to hurl vile epithets, and to even
succeed in suppressing 'Jurgen.'" And yet, despite the fierce opposition to his
work, Cabell, according to Ivy, continues "writing beautiful, polished sentences,
and paragraphs and inventing romances of supreme charm and beauty."[49]

In the next few issues of *The Messenger*, Ivy applauded the literary accomplishments of other New Southerners, most notably Peterkin, Emily Clark, and
Green. When Peterkin released *Black April*, Ivy added his name to her growing
legion of admirers. "In *Green Thursday*," he reflects, "there was a magic of loving
comprehension which appealed to the deepest humanity in us. Now in *Black
April*, she again reveals her astounding talent in a sympathetic study of a certain
class of South Carolina Negroes." Ivy also approves the work of Richmond's own
Clark, whose *Stuffed Peacock* he declares a "must read" for Negroes.[50] Although
impressed by the literary talents of Clark, Peterkin, and others in the New
Southerner crowd, Ivy is not always as sanguine about these writers' intentions
as New Negro critics like James Weldon Johnson or Locke. His caution came
out in a rather tepid review of Edward C. L. Adams's *Congaree Sketches*. This
collection of folklore and tales had received quite a bit of attention because
of Green's provocative introduction, which praises it as "one of the finest approaches by the written word to interracial understanding and good will ever
made."[51] Sharing Johnson's verdict on the high quality and emotional depth of
Green's insights, Ivy found much to admire in the book's introduction, which
he praised as "the best preface to any book by or about Negroes."[52] To prove his
point, Ivy excerpted for his readers one of the introduction's most discussed
paragraphs: "Here at the end of this century's first quarter the United States is
awakening to the fact that the destiny of the Negroes is its destiny, that black
and white are inextricably mingled in blood and bone and intention, and that as
the white man fails the Negro fails and as the Negro rises the white man rises."[53]

In Ivy's judgment, Green's vivid imagery of White and Black Americans'
mutual destiny constitutes a fine (and brave) piece of writing, but he found it
difficult to invest much more in the book. Ivy offers the very book to which
Green wrote his fine introduction as evidence of White southerners' staunch
racism. Although not at all opposed to portraits of working-class life, Ivy takes

umbrage with Whites' singular obsession with "the folk." Even more, he finds deeply disturbing White southerners' tendency to look down on the Black elite: "Whites make caricatures of our elite because of their superiority complex and the insidious nonsense, engrained in them from childhood that 'there aint no such animal' as an intelligent Negro."[54]

Though recognizing the need to acknowledge the emergence of New South modernists like Odum and Green, Ivy hardly sees these individuals as coalition-building material. Here, he disagrees with the Howard University professor Locke, who envisions the liberals of the "new intellectual South" as ideal political allies. To understand the difference of opinion between Ivy and Locke, one has to go beyond the world of literature and also consider their opposing views on an institutional center for many White southern liberals: the Commission on Interracial Cooperation. Characterized by the historian Patricia Sullivan as a "bold departure in the field of southern race relations," the Commission on Interracial Cooperation was founded in late December 1918. Under the leadership of its first director, Will Alexander, the commission endeavored to "promote dialogue and interaction among black and white community leaders as the essential first step to constructive race relations."[55] Their endeavors would be celebrated in Locke's essay "Welcome to the New South," which was published in *Opportunity* in 1927. "The inter-racial movement, halting and cautious as it has been, is nevertheless full of fine future possibilities," Locke describes. Then, without any hesitancy, he promotes the interracial movement as "the only possible constructive basis of practical reform."[56]

Feeling as if Black folk had better options in terms of political allies, Ivy had little patience or respect for the Commission on Interracial Cooperation. As he quips in the summer of 1927,

> I, for one, have little faith in these so-called inter-racial committees, for their Negro members are in so many cases hand picked "darkies" who know their master's voice when they hear it, and who, consequently exercise much more of their energy in placating their white overlords than in stating and defending the real grievances of the Negro. . . . According to the report of the committee for the year 1926, it has done some very commendable things for the Negro and the cause of racial justice in education, health and housing, institutional care and legal aid. I notice, however, that in the vital field of economic opportunity the committee has done nothing other than getting fifty Negroes jobs in a weaving plant in Newport News.[57]

Skepticism also marks Dabney's commentary on white southern progressives. Fully aware of the literary endeavors and political doings of New South modernists like Odum, Green, Alexander, and Guy Johnson, Dabney explores the political implications of their work in several articles published between

1926 and 1928. As was the case with Ivy, Dabney closely monitors the activities of the commission. He was especially interested in its role in implementing race-relations courses at over twenty-five southern white colleges, most notably the University of North Carolina, the University of Florida, and Vanderbilt. His *Southern Workman* essay on the growing popularity of race-relations courses among white college students reveals Dabney's complex relationship with the publication. On the one hand, Dabney's commitment to capturing the changing dynamics of southern society meshed perfectly with the *Workman*'s editorial policy of presenting a more progressive south. On the other hand, Dabney strongly believes that many of the individuals, institutions, and organizations that the *Workman* upheld as sources of progressive change deserved a more critical appraisal. With this in mind, he cautions his readers against placing too much faith in the Negro's popularity as a subject of critical inquiry on white college campuses: "The writer does not regard the present movement in the South to study the race problem as any radical change. It is promising and encouraging but the South is still conservative."[58] An important factor in Dabney's assessment is what he views as these race-relations experts' limited attention to political economy. "The friend of the South," he later asserts in an article for the *Modern Quarterly*, "is he who studies present-day Southern life critically and objectively and who supports interracial co-operation on the basis of the immediate *material interests* of the two races."[59]

In his essays for *The Messenger* and especially the *Southern Workman*, Dabney treads carefully when engaging white liberals and their race-relations work. However, in his private correspondence with V. F. Calverton, the editor of the *Modern Quarterly*, Dabney condemns liberals as "a positive menace of the revolutionary movement."[60]

Not one to plunge recklessly into public disputes, Dabney prefers to limit his critiques of southern liberals to the private realm. Furthermore, as depression-like conditions gripped the Black south in the late 1920s, Dabney confronted the much-bigger problem of supporting himself financially. His intermittent work as a freelance journalist, a labor organizer for the American Negro Labor Congress, and a paid researcher for the National Urban League gave him great flexibility in terms of his political endeavors but hardly covered his personal expenses. "I have no money to travel," he complained to his friend Calverton, "only enough to eat from day to day."[61] Lacking financial stability, Dabney grew increasingly frustrated with his intellectual progress. A combination of factors, ranging from his financial difficulties to his inability to place his more radical articles in mainstream publications, left him with reams of unpublished, misplaced, and incomplete manuscripts. In desperate need of more steady income, Dabney returned to Buckingham Training School in 1929 in the dual role of teacher and principal. Though his work in the classroom consumed a great deal of his time, he continued to write for a variety of publications, most notably the *Norfolk Journal and Guide*.

The equally active Ivy also balanced his work as an educator and first-rate journalist. Possessed with the rare ability to write on a wide range of subjects with great depth and intelligence, Ivy gained a national following for his brilliant essays on race, labor relations, literature, and global politics. As the New Negro renaissance gathered steam, he tracked the historical contributions coming out of Carter G. Woodson's Association for the Study of Negro Life and History, as well as the literary works of celebrated writers like Claude McKay. In the spring of 1928, Ivy weighed in on the literary merits of McKay's recently published and controversial novel *Home to Harlem*. Ivy had first come into contact with McKay during the summer of 1922. On one of his visits to New York, Ivy had a chance encounter with Countee Cullen's partner Donald Duff, at the Rand Bookstore. Over the course of their conversation, Duff asked him if he knew McKay. Upon learning that Ivy had never met the famous poet, Duff volunteered to escort him to McKay's apartment on East Fourteenth Street. As was the case for many young writers who fashioned themselves as New Negroes, Ivy held the author of the searing poem "If We Must Die" in high regard. On the journey to McKay's apartment, Ivy struggled to remain calm. "I was racking my brain wondering what to do. I wanted to make an impression. . . . [W]hat we talked about that night I don't remember, but we immediately became friends."[62]

Their friendship undoubtedly rendered Ivy somewhat protective of McKay, who genuinely appreciated his comrade's enthusiastic approach to his work. Ivy's deep appreciation for McKay's literary talents was particularly apparent in his review of the controversial novel *Home to Harlem*. "Now comes Claude McKay," Ivy enthusiastically proclaims, ready to "dissect the ulcer of brothels of Harlem for our eyes to see and our mind to grasp."[63] Here and in other assessments of *Home*, Ivy diverges from others who dismiss *Home* as an embarrassment to the race. Du Bois relates that after consuming the "dirtier parts" of the novel's "filth," he felt "distinctly like taking a bath."[64] Conversely, Ivy applauded McKay's creative foray into the world of "pimps, bulldykers, faggots, snoweaters, wild parties, razor fights, and sluttish women." Insisting that *Home* was not a comprehensive portrait of Harlem life but a slice of it, he categorizes McKay's work as "beautiful but frank to the verge of cruelty."[65] A year later, Ivy also heaps favorable praise on McKay's subsequent novel, *Banjo*, which he also judges to be a fine piece of literature.

Even though McKay appreciated and respected Ivy's literary taste, he never fully understood the Virginia native's rootedness in the south. "Couldn't you get a job up North," he queries in 1928. A year later, during his sojourn in Paris, McKay hints again at Ivy's need for a change of scenery: "Don't you make enough to take a trip abroad? So many of the Negro teachers and professors do Europe every summer."[66] This line of questioning would have been understandable if Ivy's journalistic endeavors had been subpar in quality or sporadic in output. But his monthly writings for *The Messenger*, along with his regular contributions to the *Afro-American*, wielded a great deal of influence among the New Negro crowd. Schuyler once noted, "So far as knowing about the black world, he is so superior to the other people around."[67] Until 1943, when Ivy and four other African American educators were fired in the wake of a successful lawsuit demanding equal pay for White and Black teachers, the brilliant social critic wrote primarily from his home base of Virginia.

The rigor with which both Ivy and Dabney approached their intellectual endeavors reminds us that deep thinking about the modern condition and its relation to the future of Black people globally was not confined to Black intellectuals in the urban north. Indeed, above the Mason-Dixon Line, existed a vibrant intellectual culture that owed a great deal of its dynamism to independent thinkers like Dabney and Ivy, regional-based monthlies like the *Southern Workman*, and intellectual training grounds like Virginia Union.

The diverse intellectual world that nurtured the talents of Ivy and Dabney experienced significant changes in the late 1920s. The economic challenges, as well as the political shifts, brought about by the Great Depression put a strain on many New Negro institutions and movements. One such institution was *The Messenger*, which in the late spring of 1928 went out of business. The New York–based monthly had been a critical outlet for Dabney and Ivy in the years following their graduation from Union. Though disappointed by the monthly's collapse, they were well aware of the hardships facing Black institutions as African Americans struggled under the weight of a weakened economy. "No living group," Dabney writes in 1928, "is facing a more acute situation in the matter of employment than the American Negro." Noting the "new work psychology" of White laborers, Dabney is particularly concerned about the status of Black southerners: "While employment is a grave problem for the Negro, both North and South, the present shift in the economic status of the Southern Negro has by far greater social implications." Dabney was clearly referring to the growing number of Whites willing to perform jobs previously dismissed as "beneath the dignity of a gentleman."[68] No different than the men and women they studied, Dabney and Ivy had to acclimate themselves to the changing times. In doing so, they relied heavily on the political networks and relationships forged during the vibrant 1920s.

Notes

1. John Malchus Ellison, "Some Achievements: Distinguished Scholars," John Malchus Ellison Papers, Virginia Union University, Richmond.

2. Charles P. Henry, "Abram Harris, E. Franklin Frazier, and Ralph Bunche: The How-

ard School of Thought on the Problem of Race," in *The Changing Racial Regime*, ed. Matthew Holden Jr. (Piscataway, NJ: Transaction, 1985), 36–56.

3. Thomas Dabney, "Negro Workers at the Crossroads," *Labor Age,* February 16, 1927, 9.

4. James Ivy, "Book Bits," *Messenger,* June 1927, 195.

5. Alain Locke, "Welcome the South," *Opportunity*, April 1926, 375.

6. James Ivy, "Book Bits," *Messenger*, March 1928.

7. James Ivy, "Book Bits," *Messenger,* May 1927, 167.

8. Thomas Dabney, "Dominant Forces in Race Relations," *Modern Quarterly* 4 (November 1927–February 1928): 271.

9. Patrick J. Gilpin and Marybeth Gasman, *Charles S. Johnson: Leadership beyond the Veil In the Age of Jim Crow* (Albany: State University of New York Press, 2003), 65.

10. Henry Jared McGuinn, "Phylon Profile V: Joshua Baker Simpson," *Phylon* 6, no. 3, (1945): 221.

11. Vincent Harding, "Is American Possible?" (2007), repr., *The On Being Project*, November 7, 2016, https://onbeing.org/blog/is-america-possible/.

12. Benjamin Brawley, "The Profession of the Teacher," *Southern Workman*, December 1928, 486.

13. John Malchus Ellison, "Some Achievements: Distinguished Scholars." John Malchus Ellison Papers, L. Douglas Wilder Library and Learning Resource Center, Virginia Union University, Richmond.

14. Herbert Aptheker, *The Correspondence of W. E. B. Du Bois* (Amherst: University of Massachusetts Press, 1973), 3:279.

15. Thomas L. Dabney, Voter Registration Card, June 5, 1917, ancestry.com.

16. Miles Mark Fisher, *Virginia Union University and Some of Her Achievements: Twenty-Fifth Anniversary, 1899–1924* (Richmond, VA: Brown, 1924).

17. Ibid., 64.

18. James Ivy, interview by Theodore Kornweibel, "No Crystal Star: Black Life and the Messenger Interviews," Theodore Kornweibel Collection, Schomburg Center for Research in Black Culture, New York Public Library, New York.

19. Ibid.

20. Theodore Kornweibel, *Seeing Red: Federal Campaigns against Black Militancy, 1919–1925* (Bloomington: Indiana University Press, 1998), 76–99.

21. James Ivy, interview, "No Crystal Star."

22. Hylan Lewis, "Pursuing Fieldwork in African American Communities: Some Personal Reflections of *Against the Odds: Scholars Who Challenged Racism in the Twentieth Century*," in *Against the Odds: Scholars Who Challenged Racism in the Twentieth Century*, ed. Benjamin P. Bowser and Louis Kushnick (Amherst: University of Massachusetts Press, 2004), 124.

23. James Ivy, "Book Bits," *Messenger*, June 1927, 195. Here, Ivy echoes many of the sentiments articulated in the writings of Abram Harris. Insistent that only a minority of Black intellectuals took class and labor issues seriously, Harris detests what he perceived as "the Negro's apathy toward economic reform and progressive political action." As he explains in a 1925 article: "So absorbed is the Negro intellectual with the race problem that problems of labor, housing, taxation, judicial reform and war, all of which affect

him, [are] relegated to the limits of minor significance." Especially vexing for Harris was the resurgence of racialist thinking, which found expression in a variety of political and artistic arenas. "Race psychology," Harris hisses, "thwarts comprehensive progressive political action and the growth of liberalism in America." Abram Harris, "A White and Black World in American Labor and Politics," *Social Forces* 4, no. 2 (1925): 381.

24. James Ivy, "Book Bits," *Messenger*, December 1927, 355.

25. The founding of the Buckingham Training School demonstrates how and to what extent the enterprising spirit of the New Negro extended beyond the urban terrain. In 1919 a group of African Americans, led by the Reverend Stephen J. Ellis, initiated fund-raising efforts for a training school in Buckingham. Small personal contributions, coupled with donations from various churches and social groups, provided the seed money for the Black community's purchase of nearly ten acres of land along with building material for the proposed school. The state refused Ellis's request for financial assistance; however, the General Education Board and the John F. Slater Fund supplied him with the necessary funds to ensure the school's completion in 1924. Thomas Dabney, "Rural Education in Buckingham County, Virginia," *Southern Workman*, February 1926, 79–82.

26. Joseph Kip Kosef, *Acts of Conscience: Christian Nonviolence and Modern American Democracy* (New York: Columbia University Press, 2009), 70.

27. Susan Kates, *Activist Rhetorics and American Higher Education, 1885–1937* (Carbondale: Southern Illinois University Press, 2001), 81.

28. Thomas L. Dabney, "Brookwood Labor College," *Messenger*, December 1926, 377.

29. Ibid.

30. These articles include Dabney, "Rural Education"; "Southern Students Study Race Relations," *Southern Workman*, September 1926, 398–400; and "Health and Welfare Work in Soviet Russia," *Southern Workman*, December 1926, 541–544.

31. Thomas Dabney, "Colored Rural Life Conference of Central Virginia," *Southern Workman*, May 1926, 224.

32. Ibid.

33. Dabney, "Rural Education," 79.

34. Daniel Rodgers, *Atlantic Crossing: Social Politics in a Progressive Age* (Cambridge, MA: Harvard University Press, 1998), 318.

35. Thomas Dabney, "Trade Union Movements," *Messenger*, November 1926, 327.

36. Thomas Dabney, "Workers Education," *Opportunity*, March 1926, 91.

37. Ibid. 92.

38. Ibid.

39. Howard Brick, *Transcending Capitalism: Visions of a New Society in Modern American Thought* (Ithaca, NY: Cornell University Press, 2006), 62.

40. Thomas Dabney, "Negro Workers," 10.

41. This view was expounded in the writings of the mercurial critic H. L. Mencken. In 1920 Mencken published his damning essay "Sahara of the Bozart," in which he condemned the south as an intellectual and cultural wasteland: "For all its size and all its wealth and all the 'progress' it babbles of, it is almost as sterile, artistically, intellectually, culturally, as the Sahara Desert. If the whole of the late Confederacy were to be engulfed by a tidal wave tomorrow, the effect upon the civilized minority of men in the

world would be but little greater than that of a flood on the Yang-tse-kiang. It would be impossible in all history to match so complete a drying-up of a civilization." He would not maintain this position as he became attracted to the work of several artists and writers in places like Chapel Hill, North Carolina, and Richmond, Virginia. Late in the fall of 1925, he alerted his readers to the south's shifting intellectual terrain: "Just what has happened down there, I don't know, but there has been an immense change of late. The old sentimental snuffling and gurgling seem to have gone out of fashion; the new southern writers are reexamining the civilization they live under, and striking out boldly." To those who may not have been paying attention to Mencken's evolving views on the region, his celebratory portrait of the group he affectionately referred to as the "New Southerners" probably came as a shock. Fred Hobson, *Serpent in Eden: H. L. Mencken and the South* (Chapel Hill: University of North Carolina Press, 1974).

42. Howard Odum, "Editorial Notes," *Journal of Social Forces* 2, no. 5 (1924): 730.

43. Charles Johnson, *Opportunity*, June 1926, 176.

44. Charles Johnson, "Our Book Shelf," *Opportunity*, October 1926, 324.

45. Alain Locke, "Welcome the New South: A Review," *Opportunity*, December 1926, 374–375.

46. James Ivy, "Book Bits," Messenger, October 1926, 318.

47. H. L. Mencken, "The South Begins to Mutter," *Smart Set*, August 1921, 140.

48. Ivy, "Book Bits," 318.

49. Ibid.

50. James Ivy, "Book Bits," *Messenger*, January 1928, 35.

51. Daniel Joseph Singal, *The War Within: From Victorian to Modernist Thought in the South, 1919–1945* (Chapel Hill: University of North Carolina Press, 1982), 267.

52. James Ivy, "Book Bits," *Messenger*, September 1927, 287.

53. Ibid.

54. James Ivy, "Book Bits," *Messenger*, May 1927, 168.

55. Patricia Sullivan, *Days of Hope: Race and Democracy in the New Deal Era* (Chapel Hill: University of North Carolina Press, 1996), 32.

56. Locke, "Welcome to the New South," 375.

57. James Ivy, "Book Bits," *Messenger*, June 1927, 196.

58. Dabney, "Southern Students," 400.

59. Dabney, "Dominant Forces," 271.

60. Thomas Dabney to V. F. Calverton, undated, V. F. Calverton Papers, Manuscript and Archives Division, New York Public Library.

61. Ibid., May 7, 1927.

62. Ivy, interview with Theodore Kornweibel, "No Crystal Star."

63. James Ivy, "Book Chat," *Baltimore Afro-American*, March 17, 1928.

64. W. E. B. Du Bois, "The Browsing Reader: Two Novels," *The Crisis*, June 1928, 202.

65. James Ivy, "Book Bits," *Messenger*, May–June 1928, 116.

66. Claude McKay to James Ivy, 1929, in *The Passion of Claude McKay Selected Poetry and Prose, 1912–1948*, ed. Wayne F. Cooper (New York: Schocken, 1973), 148.

67. Richard Long, "An Interview with George Schuyler," *Black World* 25, February 1976, 73.

68. Thomas Dabney, "The Conquest of Bread," *Southern Workman*, October 1928, 418.

CHAPTER 8

TACKLING THE TALENTED TENTH

BLACK GREEK-LETTERED ORGANIZATIONS AND THE BLACK NEW SOUTH

MAURICE J. HOBSON

In recent years, questions over the salience of Black Greek-lettered organizations have emerged as organizations have been ridiculed and received negative publicity. These images stem from unfair and purported links to White Greek-lettered organizations' activities that have long lauded boyish pranks, mean-spirited-girlness, binge drinking, drugs, and hazing. For Black Greeks, Spike Lee's motion picture *School Daze*, Bill Cosby's sit-com *A Different World*, along with the *Stomp the Yard* franchise, VH-1's *Sorority Sisters*, and most recently Netflix's *Burning Sands*, have projected themes of Black Greek-lettered organizations in both positive and negative, and realistic and unrealistic, lights.

However, inasmuch as we understand twentieth-century African American history as a field of research and scholarship, one would have failed to understand its full influence without considering the histories and contexts of Black Greek-lettered organizations. This is not to negate the prevalence of a violent hazing culture promoted by some of its members. But the histories of these organizations greatly outweigh any negative depictions. These organizations, which emerged between fifty and seventy-five years after the American Civil War and Emancipation, represent the highest educational, political, and economic aspirations and achievements of Black folk over the past century, amidst the most discontented and deprived circumstances for Blacks during the nadir of the Black experience. Thus, Black Greek-lettered organizations represent various interconnections and interactions between diverse Black populations within Black America, a development that is critical to better understanding the discourse and ethos of twentieth-century African American history.

The emergence of Black Greek-lettered organizations is inextricably linked to the emergence of Black higher education and is partially credited to the Freedmen's Bureau and liberal attitudes of Whites in the north and New England. Black Greek-lettered organizations grew in the tradition of the American Negro Academy of Washington, DC, where the role of research and scholarship pursued Black arts and science, as well as higher education, and were central to the historical arc of Black struggle in America. The liberal arts curricula introduced to private historically Black colleges and universities (HBCU) by White New England missionaries took on new meanings to Black folk pursuing a college education at the turn of the century. Although liberal arts education had a purpose to "discipline and furnish the mind, develop character, and enrich life by encouraging future learning" as historian Christie Farnham details, the implications of classical liberal arts education suggest that this curricula and the subsequent organizations that grew from Black institutions of higher learning served a larger purpose for the Black masses: the creation and pursuit autonomous Black communities.[1] A signature component of the American Negro Academy is that scholars published research that engaged Black experiences in the face of American racism. An example of this can be seen in Atlanta, Georgia. In the early part of the twentieth century, Atlanta was home to four Black colleges, one Black university, and one Black seminary center. This unique cluster of higher educational institutions played a pivotal role in the production of the city's Black caste and class system and helped situate W. E. B. Du Bois's establishment of the sociology department at Atlanta University. It is here where the strength of American Negro Academy demonstrated theory in practice.

At their beginning, Black Greek-lettered organizations were often portrayed as social junkets for affluent Blacks steeped in racial uplift theory, and the elites within Black Greek-lettered organizations held significant influence on negotiating with the White power structure on behalf of working and poor Blacks, which is problematic at best. This story is rarely explicated and analyzed but is a worthy and necessary discussion for any comprehensive and balanced treatment of Black America's social development in the field of twentieth-century African American history, in general, and in the tradition of Black intellectual history, in particular.

Although Black Greek-lettered organizations were linked to self-help, they provide a lens for understanding the early development and evolution of the Black intellectual tradition in the United States. This essay has several goals. The first focuses on the impact of such organizations by exploring the larger narrative of African American history experienced by the masses, helping make clear how Black Greek life served as a microcosm of larger Black society, regardless of class identification: that is, class demarcation is, at some points, trumped by race and racism. What is also prevalent here is that Black Greek-lettered organizations were more present in the day-to-day struggle to ensure the political, educational, social, and economic equality of Black people than other self-help organizations that emerged at the turn of the twentieth century. Secondly, this chapter utilizes historical themes from Reconstruction to the nadir, from Jim Crow to the era of self-help and racial uplift, from World War I to the Progressive Era, from the New Negro and Harlem Renaissance to the economic depression and on through the New Deal, and from World War II to Black liberation to demonstrate how Black Greek-lettered organizations asserted their might, which is worthy of considerable attention and treatment. Lastly, this essay seeks to engage trends and tensions surrounding Black Greek-lettered organizations and the intellectual shift from racial uplift as a tool of civilization to that of civic and social equality through Black political empowerment and electoral politics. This shift emerged as a result of what I call the Black New South. Here, the purview of Black politics and intraracial class tensions demonstrates the adjustment in Black intellectual history's development with national and international implications as seen in a post-1965 context. Grounded in primary and secondary sources, this essay seeks to create a better understanding of Black intellectual history by engaging numerous historiographies within the larger field of African American history—historiographies such as the new African American urban history, African American class formation and stratification, African American political history, civil rights or Black Power or the Black freedom movement, and literature on Black educational history—charting various manifestations as seen through the activities of Black Greek-lettered organizations. This essay examines and champions for the necessity and prominence of Black Greek-lettered organizations in the midst of unflattering publicity as a result of incidents of hazing or some criminal activity. This is not to suggest that hazing or other crimes are the prevailing notions of these organizations, and in no way is this essay meant to dismiss or exclude Blacks that do not partake in Black Greek life or with grassroots activity engaged by the Black masses.

Racial Uplift, Self-Help, and Black Education

At the dawning of the twentieth century, a movement concerning dignity and imagery emerged among the Black elite and middle classes. This movement grounded itself in self-help as service to the Black masses. In this the Black elite and middle classes attempted to distinguish themselves from the Black masses as agents of civilization by cultivating "positive" images of Blacks to challenge perceptions of pathology and contempt held by Whites. A central assumption of racial uplift was that Black material and moral progress would diminish White racism. However, the shortcoming was that the emphasis on class distinctions and patriarchal authority, as racial uplift, was inextricably linked to the same pejorative notions of racial pathology that Whites held against Blacks. Through this framework, scholars and deemed leaders squared off publicly to debate self-help and racial uplift. Scholar–intellectual activist Du Bois deemed it necessary to promote liberal arts and professional education that, he believed, trained a broadly defined Black intelligentsia. To Du Bois, liberal arts education was necessary for building autonomous Black communities as it disciplined and furnished the mind, developed character, and enriched life by fostering learning as conditions in America changed. Du Bois coined the concept of the "Talented Tenth," a byproduct of racial uplift and self-help.[2]

As such, some Blacks embraced the concept of self-help with aspirations of reaffirming personal dignity and hope for a better future. Others adopted the idea in more practical terms, "to pull themselves up by their bootstraps and be of service to the race."[3] However, a major theme in self-help was the acquisition of college education for Blacks. Indicative of this were trends such as the dramatic rise in literacy of Blacks, new and emerging literature on Black achievement, and college education for Blacks. College education was supported by both White and Black donations and by religious organizations. Yet, Black education, in general, and college education, in particular, became a political football in the post-Reconstruction South, as southern institutions of Black higher education received funding from large educational foundations, such as the General Education Board and Rosenwald Fund, and from White industrial tycoons, such as Andrew Carnegie, Robert Ogden, and John D. Rockefeller. Tuskegee Institute's principal Booker T. Washington rose as the most powerful Black man in America as a result of the aforementioned White philanthropy. However, a condition of receiving this kind of endorsement was predicated on the misperception by Whites that the industrial-education curriculum was disinterested in promoting racial equality.[4]

As the "redeemed" American south moved to disfranchise Blacks in every southern state, there was little done for the equal distribution of public educational funds. Blacks "double taxed" themselves in support of Black education and took on the onus of maintaining Black schools. Thus, as the number of college-educated Blacks rose, questions surrounding what the best type of education was: industrial training promoted by Hampton and Tuskegee Institutes or classical liberal arts learning promoted at Howard and Fisk Universities. With this, a contentious debate arose over what education was best suited for Black success. History has often pitted Du Bois, the champion for classical liberal arts education, against Washington, the deemed Wizard of Tuskegee, and its industrial machine. However, history shows that this conversation was greatly debated throughout Black communities.

On September 18, 1895, Booker Taliaferro Washington was the only "negro" to speak at the Cotton States and International Exhibition held in Piedmont Park in Atlanta, Georgia. In this speech, Washington asserted,

> Cast down your buckets where you are . . . making friends in every manly way of the people of all races. Cast down your buckets among these people who have . . . tilled your fields, cleared your forests, built your railroads and cities. . . . As we have proved our loyalty to you in the past, in nursing your children, watching by the sick bed of your mothers and fathers, and often following them with tear dimmed eyes to the graves. . . . In all things that are purely social we can be as separate as the fingers, yet, one as the hand in all things essential to mutual progress.[5]

Of the Black people that inhabited the crowd were two men of future prominence, Du Bois and John Hope. At the time of Washington's speech, neither Du Bois nor Hope were the intellectual and influential juggernauts that they would become. When Du Bois came to Atlanta University and built the Department of Sociology with a national reputation, he critiqued the elder Washington and detailed the growing tensions in Black communities between the perceived accommodationist attitude of Washington and the more radical demand the American Negro Academy presented for immediate equal rights that grounded the Black intellectual tradition.

To the abstracted eye, the advent of industrial education, as seen through Tuskegee, was deemed acceptable, as it was perceived as nonantagonizing to Whites, in America, in general, and in the south, in particular. This concept, in theory, was purportedly less threatening than a liberal arts education, which, in many instances, encouraged Blacks, in the New South, to seek social equality. White America believed that industrial education counseled Blacks to obey segregation laws and cooperate with White authorities. Much of this notion was laid, whether accurate or not, when Washington gave his Cotton States speech, which Du Bois later deemed the "Atlanta Compromise." As evidence of White America's narrow interpretation of Washington, it was his words delivered in Atlanta that gave the US Supreme Court the "separate but equal" strapline that codified segregation into American law as a result of the *Plessy v. Ferguson* (1896) decision.

To be fair, Du Bois's vision for Black education has often been debated and depicted to support notions associated with historian William Archibald Dunning's "school of civilization."[6] To Du Bois, some Blacks believed that morality and materialism ensured White validation, which were often lost on the Black masses because of their indifference toward Whites, accessibility, or affordability. Although some within Black America took to and benefitted from Washington's program in various ways, it was Washington's plan of industrial education that was most practical because it promoted the entrepreneurial spirit of production instead of consumerism. In this, the architects of Black Greekdom found sanctuary on liberal arts campuses when the programs of Du Bois and Washington were juxtaposed in this context. Thus, the perspective of White America positioned shareholders of Black Greek life as acceptable leaders—race men and women—agreeable enough to negotiate on behalf of the larger Black masses. However, outside of the lines of class formation and uplift, this issue would play out in the courts, which would later push Black Greek-lettered organizations to shift their emphasis toward the Black masses.

Black Greek-lettered organizations stood at the fore of diverse Black communities that met Washington's endorsement of industrial education with vehement opposition. Black recalcitrance emerged from Black women's suffragette Ida B. Wells, who in Black newspapers, such as the *Memphis (TN) Free Speech* and the *Chicago Defender*, protested lynchings and urged boycotts in and of the south. Her activities were the precursor to Delta Sigma Theta sorority's involvement with the franchisement of women. When Blacks were further terrorized, the Black press encouraged them to move to industrial centers for work, protest racism, and lead the fight for equality. This resulted in several Black mass exoduses known as the Great Migrations, when millions of Blacks moved from the south to northern cities for both better economic and perceived better social conditions. Migration gave Blacks new opportunities for industrial employment, and the subsequent Black middle class–led National Urban League helped to apprise newly arrived Blacks of the politics of Black respectability, a signature component of Black-Greek-lettered organizations. Other Black intellectuals, such as William Monroe Trotter, criticized Washington's emphasis on industrial education and political conciliation. Delta women Jessie Redmon Fauset and Mary Church Terrell, along with *New York Age* editor T. Thomas Fortune, wrote against Washington in numerous publications, Fortune using his platform to rail against the loss of Black civil and political rights. Organizations such as the Afro-American League and the National Afro-American Council grappled with Washington's notion of separate but equal. However, the most-scathing public critique came from the Fisk and Harvard University–produced scholar and member of Alpha Phi Alpha William Edward Burghardt Du Bois. In his timeless 1903 classic, *The Souls of Black Folk*, Du Bois critiqued Washington's philosophy by claiming that Whites, not Blacks, saw Washington as a leader of Black people. Du Bois rejected Washington's submission to racial inequality. It was in this vein that Black Greek-lettered organizations worked for Black communities through racial uplift.

Powerful and with powerful friends, Washington exacted revenge against Blacks that challenged his platform. However, one of Washington's most notable acts of retribution came against Du Bois, as he suggested that Washington's refusal to condemn segregation, lynching, and disenfranchisement won Tuskegee White financial backing and allowed him to punish his enemies. Thus, protest organizations formed in response to Washington's pervasive influence. Of these, the Niagara Movement met in 1905 in Niagara Falls, Ontario, Canada, and drafted a declaration of principles, a list of grievances, and a set of demands. This fifty-five-member group, including Du Bois and Trotter, promoted a thoughtful attack on White supremacy. The Niagara Movement and the subsequent interracial National Association for the Advancement of Colored People (NAACP) were built from the purported "Talented Tenth" that would later be fortified through Black Greek-lettered organizations. A showdown commenced within Black communities between those that aligned with Washington and those that preferred Du Bois's method. Thus, the push for Black Greek-lettered organizations was due in part to biracial coalitions—educated Blacks and liberal Whites—that sought to strike down White supremacy in the United States.[7]

The second meeting of the Niagara Movement was held at Harper's Ferry, West Virginia, the hallowed ground where struggle for Black freedom had emerged in the mid-nineteenth century and served as a dress rehearsal for the American Civil War. At this meeting, Du Bois laid the infrastructure of this movement and began to mobilize against Jim Crow. Distinct classes formed for Blacks, and the split was clear: the Black elite and middle classes and the Black masses. During this nadir period, the majority of Blacks in the south continued to be locked into forms of debt peonage and tenancy through sharecropping.[8] In this and Henry W. Grady's advocacy of the New South, Blacks hoped to make some economic gains through the New South industrial revolution. They embarked on programs of business enterprises within the segregated market. Black banks emerged. Blacks charted their own strategies for economic progress. The role of Black churches as multiservice institutions developed. Newspapers, schools, and libraries emerged and were maintained. As Blacks in the south made some strivings, the Black upper and middle classes worked to combat some of the preceding Old South images that reinforced Black stereotypes and promoted ideas of Black inferiority.

Black mutual aid or benefit societies, through the auspices of fraternal orders and benefit associations, also came to fruition during this period. Organizations such as the Odd Fellows, the Comus Social Club, Sigma Pi Phi (the Boulé), Reveille Club, Hellians, Chesterfield Club, and a host of others emerged for elite and middle-class Blacks.[9] Many of these organizations worked to care for the sick, to feed the poor, and to bury the dead. Some were chartered through churches, while others through other means, such as Black women's clubs, that not only promoted the aforementioned goals but also gave voice to gender-conscious civic activism also. Such organizations as the National Association of Colored

Women and other mothers' clubs are examples of these where activists, such as Terrell, used the strategy of racial uplift and the politics of Black respectability.

Also throughout this period, Blacks participated in intellectual and cultural endeavors pertaining to issues that were present amongst the Black elite and middle classes. The concept of Pan-Africanism emerged, and the American Negro Academy began to promote and exchange ideas among Black intellectuals to perpetuate Black protest tradition.[10] Discourse surrounding the duality of being Black and American emerged. Du Bois's concept of double consciousness gained traction as the complicated balance of Black identity shifted as Blacks slowly gained full citizenship amidst anti-Black resistance. Sports heroes became racial champions, striking literal and symbolic blows against racism in the fields of horse racing, boxing, and baseball. The prizefighter Jack Johnson is an example of this.

As the United States entered World War I, the Selective Service Act drafted Black men disproportionately, at the behest of American racism, as fewer Blacks received exemptions based on marriage or children. Moreover, Black women suffered from both racism and sexism, serving as nurses in the American Red Cross with hopes of gaining access to the Army and Navy Corps. Yet Black men and women fought valiantly for love of country. The blatant discrimination in the armed forces was undeniable. Black men were rejected for officer's commissions, and Black women were met with hostility where anti-Black resistance deemed them unfit for nursing. The NAACP, responding to the "Whites only" policies of the Army Officer Training Camps and taking military service on as a part of the organization's civil rights agenda, then pushed for the establishment of Black officer training camps. Eventually Blacks started Fort Des Moines, in Des Moines, Iowa, in October 1917 when the all-Black 25th Infantry Regiment began training.[11] Simultaneously Black women faced gender discrimination, and though they served as staffing canteens, nurses, seamstresses, and cookers and provided entertainment and educational activities for the soldiers—jobs restricted by paternalism and the era's expectations of women—they made a way for themselves in contributing to the efforts of World War I.

As Black college life was interrupted due to World War I, some Black young men and women were forced to serve in Jim Crow military camps and subjected to White recalcitrant racism within communities in which they were based. Blacks were subjected to larger community racism outside of military camps in Texas, South Carolina, and other hotbeds throughout the American south. These episodes shook these servicemen's faith in the federal government, yet they fought in numerous combat units, including the 369th, also known as the Harlem Hell-Fighters, the 370th of Chicago, the 371st, and the 372nd.

Perhaps the most significant moment in the creation of Black Greek-lettered organizations was seen through legal victories the NAACP attained from 1910 to 1920. The decisions of *Guinn v. United States* (1915) and *Buchanan v. Warley* (1917) suggested that any gains for Blacks would be won in the courts.[12] However, the period garnered the resurgence of the Ku Klux Klan, which grew as a result of postwar "superpatriotism." With this, anti-Black racism rose, and White terror toward Blacks and other ethnic and religious communities targeted Black soldiers upon their return stateside. Much of this was set on course by D. W. Griffith's *Birth of a Nation* (1915), a silent film that portrays Black men as unintelligent and sexually aggressive toward White women and paraded the Klan as a heroic force. Blacks were wrongfully depicted as rapists, and the arrogant depiction of racist Whites as heroes culminated when the Ku Klux Klan gained national notoriety by 1920.

It was in this context that Black Greek-lettered organizations emerged. America was mired in a domestic and international identity crisis. Fighting in World War I provided the conditions in which Blacks strived to proceed as they embodied self-help and racial uplift, looking to the future. At the dawning of the twentieth century, Du Bois's idea of the "Talented Tenth" was quixotic, to say the least. Thomas Jesse Jones's *Negro Education: A Study of the Private and Higher Schools for Colored People in the United States* (1917), commissioned by the US Bureau of Education and the Phelps-Stokes Fund, gave us the statistical data. In 1917, with six of the Divine Nine organizations, the original historically Black Greek-lettered organizations, now chartered, of the 100 million US citizens, 10 million were identified as Black. Of that 10 million, 1,789 attained or were attaining a college-level education. Of that 1,789, 1,001 of them attended Howard University. Thus, the Talented Tenth, in Du Bois's terms, was a myth, equating to .0001789 percent of the total Black population, or a little over one ten thousandth of 1 percent. However, of that small number, 56 percent of all Blacks having or seeking a college-level education attended Howard University, hence, the moniker "the hallowed grounds of Howard, the Mecca for Black education."[13]

The Organizations

Before the 1960s, there were eight intercollegiate Black Greek-lettered organizations. The first of the intercollegiate Greek-lettered fraternities was Alpha Phi Alpha (AΦA), founded on December 4, 1906, at Cornell University, Ithaca, New York. Seven men began Alpha, which was meant to serve as a study and support group for minority students in the midst of racial prejudice at Cornell. These "Jewels" recognized the need for a strong bond of brotherhood among men of African descent in the United States.[14] Alpha Phi Alpha holds fast to the principles of scholarship, fellowship, good character, and the uplifting of humanity. Their colors are black and old gold; their motto is "First of all, servant of all, we shall transcend all"; their mission "develops leaders, promotes brotherhood and academic excellence, while providing service and advocacy for our [Black] communities."[15]

On the hallowed grounds of Howard University, nine college women, during segregation and on a male-dominated college campus, founded Alpha Kappa Alpha (AKA) sorority in 1908, the first Black Greek-lettered organization to emerge at a Black institution of higher learning. It grew out of the need for support and networking for like-minded women who came together for mutual uplift, and they coalesced their talents and strengths for the benefit of others. They doted the promotion of Black culture and encouraged social action through presentation of Black artists and social advocates; worked to dispel notions that Blacks were unfit for certain professions; pushed antilynching legislation; established the nation's first mobile health clinic, providing relief to fifteen thousand Blacks plagued by famine and disease in the Mississippi Delta; promoted the establishment of the American Council of Human Rights to empower racial uplift and economic development and observer status from the United Nations; challenged the absence of people of color from pictorial images the government used to portray Americans; promoted Black businesses by depositing the initial $38,000 of the AKA Investment Fund with the first firm on Wall Street; promoted sickle cell disease research and education grants to Howard Hospital and publication of *The Sickle Cell Story* (1958); launched a heritage series about Black achievers; and pledged $500,000 to the United Negro College Fund. They were also the only sorority to be named an inaugural member of Operation Big Vote. Their colors are salmon pink and apple green; their motto is, "by culture and by merit"; their principles are "sisterhood, scholarship, and service to all mankind."[16]

On January 5, 1911, on the campus of Indiana University at Bloomington, ten Black college men founded Kappa Alpha Psi fraternity, originally founded as Kappa Alpha Nu and changed to Kappa Alpha Psi (KAΨ) in December 1914. At its founding, the few Black students at Indiana University enjoyed little to no social life as Jim Crow laws and pressure from White administrators and organizations discouraged Blacks from participating on the campus's White social events. Blacks were denied membership on most athletic teams with the exception of track and field. The fraternity's colors are crimson and cream, as are Indiana University's school colors; their motto is, "achievement in every field of human endeavor." A unique condition at the founding of Kappa Alpha Psi is that its constitution has no clause that excludes or suggests the exclusion of a man from membership because of his color, creed, or national origin.[17]

On November 17, 1911, a cold and rainy Friday, Omega Psi Phi fraternity was founded in the Science Hall (Thirkield Hall) on the hallowed grounds of Howard University. Three college members and world-renowned faculty member and scientist Ernest E. Just founded Omega Psi Phi. Unlike the other aforementioned fraternities, Omega Psi Phi (ΩΨΦ) came about during a series of unprecedented lynchings in the Maryland, District of Columbia, and Virginia area. These hate crimes were not the result of trumped-up charges of Black men sexually assaulting White women, as was the usual bogus suspicion used by racist Whites to justify lynching, but were brought on because Blacks, in this area, were deemed "uppity." Thus, Omega Psi Phi, begun as a mechanism for college men against lynching, is the first Black Greek-lettered fraternity founded on a Black college campus. The fraternity's colors are royal purple and old gold; its motto is, "Friendship is essential to the soul"; and its cardinal principles are manhood, scholarship, perseverance, and uplift.[18]

Once more on the hallowed grounds of Howard, twenty-two collegiate women aiming to use their collective strength to promote academic excellence and to provide service founded Delta Sigma Theta ($\Delta\Sigma\Theta$) sorority on January 13, 1913. Delta women not only promoted equal rights for Blacks but put women's rights at the fore, as well. One of their first acts of agency was the women's suffrage march held on March 13, 1913, in Washington, DC. Throughout the years, Delta Sigma Theta has worked to improve the political, educational, social, and economic conditions of Blacks and for international communities, providing scholarships and support to the underserved, and worked to educate and stimulate participation in the establishment of positive public policy. Its colors are crimson and cream; its motto is, "Intelligence is the torch of wisdom."[19]

Time again, at Howard, three Black college men organized Phi Beta Sigma ($\Phi B\Sigma$) fraternity on January 9, 1914, a Black Greek-lettered fraternity that "truly exemplified the ideals of brotherhood, scholarship, and service."[20] The founders wished to create an organization that viewed itself as "a part of" the general community rather than "apart from" the general community: "They believed that each potential member should be judged by his own merit, rather than his family background or affluence . . . without regard to race, nationality, skin tone or texture of hair. They desired for their fraternity to exist as part of an even greater brotherhood, which would be devoted to the 'inclusive we' rather than the 'exclusive we.'" From the onset, the Phi Beta Sigma founders perceived their fraternity as a vehicle to deliver services to the general community. Its colors are royal blue and white; the motto is "culture for service and service for humanity."[21]

Again at Howard, Zeta Phi Beta (ZΦB) sorority was founded on January 16, 1920. Five college women envisioned a sorority that would directly affect positive change, raise the consciousness of Black people, encourage the highest standards of scholastic achievement, and foster a greater sense of unity among its members. Much like their Sigma brothers, they believed that sorority elitism and socializing overshadowed the real mission for progressive organizations and failed to address societal mores, ills, prejudice, and poverty affecting humanity, in general, and the Black community, in particular. Zeta Phi Beta is the first sorority to be constitutionally bound to a fraternity, Phi Beta Sigma. The sorority is known by its colors of royal blue and white; its motto is "a community-conscious, action-oriented organization"; and its founding principles are scholarship, sisterhood, service, and finer womanhood.[22]

On November 12, 1922, seven educators founded Sigma Gamma Rho (ΣΓΡ) sorority in Indianapolis, Indiana. Unlike other Black Greek-lettered sororities, Sigma Gamma Rho was started by professionals instead of collegiate women. These women wanted an organization to offer members opportunities to develop their unique talents through leadership training. Sigma Gamma Rho's mission is to enhance the quality of life within the community where public service, leadership development, and the education of youth are the hallmarks of the organization's programs and activities. It became a collegiate sorority on December 30, 1929, when a charter was granted to its Alpha chapter on the campus of Butler University in Indianapolis. Its colors are royal blue and gold; its motto is "greater service, greater progress."[23]

Twelve college men founded Iota Phi Theta (ΙΦΘ) fraternity during the modern civil rights movement at Morgan State College (now University) in Baltimore, Maryland. Unlike the previous eight Black Greek-lettered organizations, which were started just before or after World War I, Iota was founded in 1963 by what are now referred to as nontraditional students, three to five years older than the average college students. All twelve of the founders held full-time jobs while maintaining full-time student status. The unique circumstances of this founding were shaped by their responsibilities and maturity, slightly different than college-aged men. Iota's purpose was "the development and perpetuation of Scholarship, Leadership, Citizenship, Fidelity, and Brotherhood among Men"; its colors are charcoal brown and gilded gold; their motto is, "building a tradition, not resting upon one."[24]

The collaborative organization for all Black Greek-lettered organizations is the National Pan-Hellenic Council (NPHC). Formed on May 10, 1930, at Howard University, it was created to promote "interactions through forums, meetings, and other mediums for the exchange of information and [to engage] in cooperative initiatives through various activities and functions."[25] The purpose and mission of the organization, on the onset, were "to foster cooperative actions of its members in dealing with matters of mutual concern." The founding members include Kappa Alpha Psi, Omega Psi Phi, Alpha Kappa Alpha, Delta Sigma Theta, and Zeta Phi Beta. Alpha Phi Alpha and Phi Beta Sigma joined the NPHC in 1931, Sigma Gamma Rho in 1937, and Iota Phi Theta in 1997.[26] These organizations, with the exception of Phi Beta Sigma and Zeta Phi Beta, which are constitutionally bound, were founded on their own terms. It was not until much later that they acknowledged the common threads of self-help and racial uplift that the NPHC galvanized.

The New Negroes

As more Blacks moved toward higher education and Black Greek-lettered organizations incorporated and expanded to other campuses at the national level, developments in technology allowed for Americans, in general, and Blacks, in particular, to connect. Electronic innovation, corporate publishing, and mass advertising and distribution made the nation ripe for the emergence of the New Negro movement coupled with the jazz age. The New Negro movement marked a period where Blacks avowed their dignity and refused to be treated as second-class citizens. The movement had its roots at Howard and in Harlem, where Howard professor Alain Locke made the term "New Negro" popular. The movement was grounded in the notion of race building and overall equality for Blacks.

Simultaneously, during this period, Black communities contemplated the role of art in the struggle for racial equality. Once again, the politics of Black respectability emerged and grappled over whether art should serve as propaganda to promote positive images of Blacks or whether art was for art's sake. An example of this was seen as the recorded music market developed, and White audiences had access to Black art without engaging Black people. With this market shift, recorded Black art shifted and catered to White audiences, indelibly changing the nature of the art when presented for Blacks. It was in this vein that Black elites and middle classes pushed Black artists to promote more-sophisticated images of Black life, rather than the more primitive forms seen in blues and jazz art forms. Black Greek-lettered organizations were at the fore of this movement. As such, as the New Negro movement gained traction, the Harlem Renaissance, the movement's expressive arm, was fully engaged.

To push the agenda of Black art as propaganda, Black entrepreneur Harry Pace created Black Swan Records, a music-production company that worked to promote Black art for racial advancement. Black Swan touted Black middle-class respectability and racial responsibility as key, and with national and live broadcast radio, Pace felt that Black respectability would be spewed and assessed critically by Black Swan. However, White recording companies eventually put Black Swan out of business, as White audiences were interested in the more primitive typifications of Blacks. Moreover, the New Negro movement and its expressive Harlem Renaissance became a battleground for the discussion over the politics of Black respectability, of which Black Greeks emerged on both sides of the argument. Omega's Langston Hughes obliged society with his poetic virtuosity. Zeta's Zora Neale Hurston and Delta women Gwendolyn B. Bennett and Fauset offered widely read novels. Alpha Phi Alpha's Du Bois brought his intellectual prowess, and Alpha's Noble Sissle served as one of the movements most sought-after entertainers.[27] Thus, the New Negro and Harlem Renaissance served another chapter of the modern American civil rights movement, debunking the myth of the classical phase of civil rights.

Roosevelt, the New Deal, and the Black Cabinet

With the emergence of the New Negro and the seriousness of Black dignity and self-respect, Black folk organized to protect their own interests when the stock market crashed in 1929. When Franklin D. Roosevelt was elected as the thirty-second president of the United States, his New Deal platform, promoting relief, recovery, and reform, had little impact on Black life. Roosevelt was seen as a quasi-ally to Blacks. His policies, such as the Agricultural Adjustment Act (1933), worsened conditions for the overwhelmingly Black tenant farmers and sharecroppers, coupled with overproduction, falling prices, and the boll weevil. In this the Black middle classes suffered due to the loss of commerce with Black workers. Thus, Black folk organized a campaign that championed the slogan, "Don't buy where you can't work." These boycotts were buttressed by the 1937 US Supreme Court decision for strikes against establishments that racially discriminated against workers.[28] Roosevelt's real connection to the Black community came at the behest of his wife and first lady, Eleanor Roosevelt, who received honorary membership to Alpha Kappa Alpha, and the fact that Roosevelt cabinet member and Delta woman Mary McLeod Bethune noted that Blacks could address injustices to an American president without fear of retribution.[29]

However, through Roosevelt's New Deal, Blacks witnessed a rebirth in the realm of politics. Blacks had become disaffected with the election of Herbert Hoover, the president prior to Roosevelt. Hoover's election suggested the Republican Party's capacity to court and win the vote of racist White southerners and alienate Blacks. As such, Black Greek-lettered organizations worked at the fore of the political resurgence by registering Blacks to vote. The most significant election was that of Oscar S. De Priest, who was elected to the US House of Representatives from Illinois in 1928. De Priest, a Republican, was the first northern Black representative in the US Congress as a result of galvanizing the Black vote in and around Black Chicago, comprising a large constituency of Black southern migrants.[30]

When Black Democrat Arthur Mitchell later defeated De Priest in 1934, Mitchell's election demonstrated Black political empowerment coupled with Republicans taking Black voters for granted. The Roosevelt presidency and the subsequent Mitchell election came in part with Black disenchantment with the Republican Party. Thus, Black voters became influential in crucial states and garnered great success at the state and local levels where greater concentrations of Blacks in urban centers increased the political consciousness and literacy for Blacks on local levels.

It was widely believed that Roosevelt established the Federal Council of Negro Affairs, commonly known as the Black Cabinet, at the urging of his wife, Eleanor. This cadre of "respectable" Black advisers met with Roosevelt on issues of race and gave Blacks hope. The Black Cabinet showcased Blacks working in national government and demonstrated Roosevelt's understanding of his image to Black voters. Also, it yielded jobs for Blacks in government, where Whites in the Roosevelt administration began to hire Blacks as racial advisers and as staff members. The Black Cabinet was never a formal entity but recognized Bethune as its chair. Here, the Black Cabinet comprised numerous members of Black Greek-lettered organizations: Bethune was a woman of Delta; Eugene Kinckle Jones was an Alpha man; Roscoe Brown, Robert C. Weaver, William Hastie Jr., and Lawrence A. Oxley championed Omega Psi Phi. It was evident that members of Black Greek-lettered organizations were seen as leaders by powerful Whites. Although the Black Cabinet expanded job opportunities in the federal government and increased a Black presence, the Black masses faced bigger problems.[31] Within the federal government, most Blacks worked low, unskilled, and semi-skilled jobs. The Black Cabinet was mere window-dressing for the Black community and had very little if no influence in larger Black communities. That Bethune was the only woman in the cabinet signals the glaring gender discrimination women endured. Finally, it was under the New Deal that the horrors of the Tuskegee Experiment emerged. Here, the study charted the progression of untreated syphilis in Black men without their informed consent. The results yielded the possibility of using syphilis as a biomedical weapon in war.

Through the issue of labor, Blacks fought for civil rights long before the purported classical phase of the modern civil rights movement. Blacks utilized the Congress of Industrial Organizations (CIO), a federation of unions whose membership was open to all races and genders. Working on behalf of marginalized groups, specifically Blacks and poor Whites, the CIO launched its first southern organizing drive in 1937 in support of civil rights unionism as a show of support among Black activist-workers in the labor movement. Sigma man A. Philip Randolph was the organizer of the Brotherhood of Sleeping Car Porters, the first Black union. Black Greek-lettered organizations rallied behind the International Labor Defense to help defend the Scottsboro Boys, nine Black boys falsely accused of raping two White women in Alabama. Here, Black Greeks were among those working with the National Negro Congress, the Popular Front, and the Southern Conference for Human Welfare.[32] Thus, Black Greek-lettered organizations united with the Black masses around the issue of labor. This demonstrates how race trumps class demarcation in America, where the Black elite and middle classes and the Black working classes and poor put aside their class differences for the advancement of the race. Subsequently, to supplement the labor–civil rights activities, Black expressive art emerged and grappled with the political climate as artists identified with the Black masses and championed on their behalf. Alpha's Paul Robeson and Omega's Hughes drew applause and ire with their connection to communism while Alpha Kappa

Alpha members Ella Fitzgerald and Marian Anderson and Omega's Count Basie provided uplift through the gift of music.

World War II, the GI Bill, and the New Black Middle Class

The threat of and subsequent entrance into World War II for the United States segued into ways in which Black Americans reframed democracy through the armed forces. Before the bombing of Pearl Harbor in 1941, Black leaders submitted a seven-point program that outlined the minimum essentials for the treatment of Blacks in the military. Leading this charge was the newly appointed general and Omega man Benjamin O. Davis Jr., who appointed other Blacks to significant positions in the US Air Force.[33] Yet, racism was still the prevailing practice of America, so much so that it prompted organizers and Sigma man Randolph and Omega's Bayard Rustin to plan an all-Black march on Washington, DC, to take place on the Washington Mall. Randolph emphasized a new style of activism, one that embodied large-scale direct action, demanding defense jobs and an integrated military. This new style of activism set a course that later changed the world forever. The original march-on-Washington demonstration did not happen in 1941 as government officials, alarmed at the demonstration's growing momentum, brokered with Randolph. Randolph agreed to call off the demonstration after Roosevelt issued Executive Order 8802, which prohibited discrimination in employment in the defense industry and government. Executive Order 8802 created the Fair Employment Practices Committee (FEPC) to receive and investigate complaints, yet held no power to impose punishment.[34]

Attorney and Omega's William Hastie led the charge that uncovered discrimination in the armed forces. His reports reveal the ways Blacks were underutilized and were discriminated against, detailing the overwhelming assignment of Blacks to unskilled and menial jobs. After the Selective Training and Service Act of 1940, more than three million Blacks registered for potential service, and during the 1940s, they served valiantly. While the navy and marines refused to train Black officers until 1942, when discriminatory policies were loosened, Blacks steadily agitated for opportunities to become commissioned officers. The passage of the federal bill to draft nurses ended the US Army Corps' discriminatory policy against women, and more than four thousand Black women enlisted. Working as nurses, Black women gained respect. The 1940s also yielded trained Black pilots, known as the Red Tails or, more commonly, the Tuskegee Airmen of the US Army Air Corps. Once the United States entered World War II after the Pearl Harbor attack, more than a half million Blacks in twenty-two Black combat units participated in European ground operations, and in 1945, American troops integrated to fight on German soil. However, troops remained segregated in the Mediterranean theater. Blacks also served in the Pacific and East Asia theaters.[35]

Moreover, the biggest gain for Black servicemen and servicewomen was the opportunity to participate in the Servicemen's Readjustment Act of 1944—better known as the GI Bill—which was a social mobilizer that "helped returning veterans go to college or train for vocations, support young families, and purchase homes, farms, and businesses. [Those Blacks who benefitted from the GI Bill] became more engaged citizens. Compared to veterans who did not use the education or training benefits, recipients reported involvements in 50 percent more civic associations and became significantly more politically active."[36] Many Blacks that seized this opportunity joined the modern civil rights movement. Prior to the 1940s, college for Blacks and Whites alike was in the large for those with money. The GI Bill opened the floodgates for Black servicemen and servicewomen to become first-generation college students and graduates and allowed for the poor or working classes to move to a new and emerging Black middle class. Thus, the GI Bill not only allowed for social mobility amongst Blacks due to professionalization, it also allowed for greater access to Black Greek-lettered organizations, as college enrollment was a mandate for membership eligibility. Black Greek-lettered organizations now endured the greatest shift in their focus. With the influx of first-generation college students, Black Greek-lettered organizations went from serving as mainstays of racial uplift and self-help that reinforced anti-Black stereotypes to grappling with the real issues faced by the Black masses. These real issues were articulated through the quest for full citizenship, and it was clear to Black Greek-lettered organizations that the most effective way of gaining full citizenship in the United States was to challenge the racist policies of this nation. A new chapter of the modern civil rights movements was spawned, where the most significant commitment of Black Greek-lettered organizations was to champion on behalf of full citizenship.

Modern Civil Rights and
Worldwide Blackness

Both graduate and college members of Black Greek-lettered organizations understood that the fight for full citizenship best took place in the courts. The NAACP shifted its legal strategy from equalization arguments to attacks on the basis behind segregation itself. In the courts, when the US Supreme Court sided with the NAACP in *McLaurin v. Oklahoma State Regents* and ended segregation at the University of Oklahoma in 1950, an onslaught of legal victories that buttressed full citizenship ensued. Simultaneously, the *Sweatt v. Painter* case detailed that the "separate but equal" doctrine of racial segregation used in maintaining a separate Black law school would not be equal because no access to all-White school's alums, reputation, and "relevant intangibles" would not offer an equal education. Both college and graduate members of Black Greek-lettered organizations understood that the battle waged against separate-but-equal would change the influence of their organizations. Thus, members took the cause to the masses and stood as lawyers, activists, and strategists in courts, on campuses, on city streets, and on rural roads. Separate-and-unequal education, particularly, in the American south, had immeasurable effects as seen through the differences in per-pupil expenditures and school property. An example of this is seen as the south's Black schools were funded so inadequately that it would take years of funding to achieve equality. In 1952 the NAACP took five school-segregation cases to the US Supreme Court: *Briggs v. Elliott* (filed in South Carolina), *Davis v. County School Board of Prince Edward County* (filed in Virginia), *Gebhart v. Belton* (filed in Delaware), *Bolling v. Sharpe* (filed in Washington, DC), and the most notable *Brown v. Board of Education of Topeka* (filed in Kansas). The lawyers in the cases were Alpha Phi Alpha's Charles Hamilton Houston and Thurgood Marshall and Alpha Kappa Alpha's Constance Baker Motley. Omega's Roy Wilkins led the NAACP; members Spottswood William Robinson III, Wiley A. Branton, and James M. Nabrit Jr. fought in the courtroom. When the US Supreme Court struck separate-but-equal rhetoric with the *Brown* case, it marked a watershed that started the de jure unraveling of American White supremacy.

A host of conversations in the discourse of the modern civil rights movement have emerged in similar fashion throughout this essay. By and large, the modern American civil rights movement has received its fair share of critique, as it has been described as a movement hinged on the politics of Black respectability, thus situating itself as a movement for the Black middle classes while ignoring the conditions of the Black masses. Currently, some historians debate whether 1966 is also a watershed moment when Black Power emerged, and the classical phase of the modern civil rights movement waned. This ongoing debate is centered on the "long" civil rights movement versus the classical phase; the change represented by Black Power; or whether or not all of these movements should be collapsed into one Black freedom movement. Also, new histories speak to the development of social histories within the American civil rights context, which removes the focus from charismatic male leaders, such as Martin Luther King Jr., and focuses more on grassroots organizing, women, and working-class Blacks with significant leadership roles in the movement.[37] Here, it is not my place to further this discourse. However, it is worthy of considerable research and attention. Lastly, new histories promote the modern movement for Black freedom as an international one. In charting the similarities of oppression in Africa, Asia, the Caribbean, and South America, one sees that White-supremacy strongholds employed both nonviolent and aggressive approaches toward racist governments as seen in these corners of the world. The common thread between the United States, Africa, Asia, the Caribbean, and South America is White supremacy. In all of them, it was clear that White oppression was prevalent, and through this we understand that the movement was an international one with the common denominator of oppressed people fighting for dignity and human rights. Yet, for the sake of this essay, we have focused on the influence of Black Greeks in the modern Civil Rights movement.

Perhaps, the most notable Black Greek of civil rights and "public intellectual" of the twentieth century was Martin Luther King Jr., a member of Alpha Phi Alpha and Sigma Pi Phi Boulé.[38] During his seminary and doctoral studies, the works of philosophers Leo Tolstoy and Mahatma Gandhi inspired King. Both King and Gandhi appropriated Tolstoy's work and employed the satyagraha, a philosophy loosely translated as nonviolent resistance. Seeing similarities with oppression, citizens of White supremacists' strongholds utilized nonviolent resistance toward racist governments, mainly South Africa and the United States, the only two nations with state-supported systems of apartheid. The common thread between India and South Africa was European colonization, and for the United States, White supremacy.[39] In 1954 King became the pastor of the Dexter Avenue Baptist Church in Montgomery, Alabama. In Montgomery, racial segregation on the public transit system disallowed Blacks to go to work with any dignity. Claudette Colvin, fifteen years old, was handcuffed, arrested, and forcibly removed from the bus when she refused to give up her seat to a White person. Colvin was a part of the NAACP's Youth Council but did not fit the build of Black respectability— educated and/or professional. Thus, local NAACP secretary and seamstress Rosa Parks was chosen to serve as the face of Black respectability and the start of the Montgomery bus boycott.[40] Because King was new to Montgomery and had not been steeped in the politics of the city's Black clergy, he was chosen to organize the bus boycott, which lasted from December 1, 1955, until December 20, 1956, when the US Supreme Court upheld *Browder v. Gayle*, which declared Montgomery's laws requiring segregated buses as unconstitutional. Parks, a woman of Alpha Kappa Alpha, was able to galvanize professional Black Greeks and students on the campuses of Alabama State College and Tuskegee Institute. Alabama State College English professor Joann Robinson created more than fifty thousand handbills calling for a boycott of this system.

All of the Black Greek-lettered organizations were at the forefront of the civil rights movement. Birmingham's Alpha man Arthur Shores organized for civil rights in the *Lucy v. Adams* case. Marshall and Houston served as lawyers for the NAACP Legal Defense Fund. Whitney Young became the executive director of the National Urban League.[41] Alpha Kappa Alpha women were freedom fighters and participated in voter-registration drives; served on boards; worked as major organizers with the NAACP, American Council of Human Rights, Congress of Racial Equality, and Student Nonviolent Coordinating Committee;

raised money to help pay fines, bail, and defense fees; and generally provided leadership for nonviolent, direct action.[42] Kappa men engaged in the civil rights movement and were inspired by members Reverend Ralph Abernathy and Tom Bradley. They were credited with taking a leadership role in President Lyndon B. Johnson's passage of the War on Poverty programs, including the Economic Opportunity Act.[43] The men of Omega Psi Phi, inspired by member and historian Carter G. Woodson, embraced Negro Achievement Week in 1927, which evolved into Black History Month. In 1945 the fraternity undertook a national social action program to meet the needs of Blacks in the areas of health, housing, civil rights, and education. Omega men participated in sit-ins and other peaceful demonstrations and promoted Operation Big Vote.[44] Delta women cosponsored the National Organization of Women for Equality in Education conference in 1960 and in 1963, the latter while celebrating its fiftieth anniversary; Delta women participated in the 1963 March on Washington and established their social action commission.[45] Sigma men held positions of leadership among various civil rights groups, organized protests, and proposed the March on Washington. Randolph helped with the establishment of the Southern Christian Leadership Conference; John Lewis was an organizer of the Student Nonviolent Coordinating Committee, and he and Hosea Williams were at the fore of the Selma, Alabama, campaign—the campaign that led to the Voting Rights Act of 1965; Huey P. Newton helped to establish the Black Panther Party of Oakland, California.[46] Zeta woman Autherine Lucy was the plaintiff in the US Supreme Court case *Lucy v. Adams* (1955), which prevented the University of Alabama from denying admission solely based on race or color.[47] Sigma Gamma Rho women not only became members of the American Coalition for Human Rights but the sorority also continued its avid support of the NAACP's legal defense and educational funds.[48]

However, the most significant policy changes that worked on behalf of Black folks were the Civil Rights Act of 1964, which followed the Birmingham campaign, and the Voting Rights Act of 1965, which came after the struggle in Selma and gave Blacks access to voting and political power. Although the Civil Rights Act of 1964 changed traditions and customs, it did little to challenge the political power relationships in the south and, in this regard, was far less consequential than the voting-rights passage, the watershed moment when social change prevailed and made the south ripe for change—and it was Black Greek-lettered organizations' participation with the Voter Education Project that effected that change.

The Voter Education Project was an Atlanta-based organization dedicated to the funding of voter-education programs and registration drives, as well as conducting research on voting and elections in the eleven southern states. Formed in 1962 as a program of the Southern Regional Council (SRC), the program only granted funds to civil rights organizations to support their voter registration drives and any voting-related research. The first executive director was attorney and Omega man Branton.[49] It was through the Voter Education Project that Black Greek-lettered organizations were able to leave their greatest impact, the election of Black politicians, that did the most the change this nation's most racist policies by striking down old laws and creating new ones. The best example of this is a new and emerging term, "the Black New South."[50]

The Black New South

The 1970s ushered in a new era for Black political empowerment and electoral politics in the American south. These changing demographics were evident with a nationwide trend that affected the former US Confederacy through the return migration of Blacks from the urban north, Midwest, and West back to a Black New South.[51] Black migration from the south to the north started after the Civil War and heightened during World War I as floods and the boll weevil devastated southern farming, and the northern industrialization attracted Blacks seeking employment. Indeed, the greatest out-migration of Blacks from the south to the north occurred in the early 1960s. Yet, by the 1970s, cities such as Atlanta had become symbolic of a Black New South, a land of opportunity for Blacks, where entrepreneurship and political ambitions flourished. In a 1971 US Census projection, 108,999 Blacks left other parts of the country to settle in the Black New South, up from 97,000 in 1970. Studies show that between 1970 and 1973, 247,000 Blacks moved to the south, and 166,000 moved out. The indicators here chart that the major shift was Blacks returning to their American ancestral homeland. However, about one-third of them had never lived in the south prior.[52]

By and large, most of the Blacks returning to the Black New South were young professionals moving to larger urban areas, with sizeable HBCU communities and a sunbelt-based economy, which included Atlanta; Birmingham; Charlotte and Raleigh-Durham, North Carolina; and Memphis and Nashville, Tennessee. For the most part, Black return-migrators understood that the region was not an idyllic promised land, free of racial strife, crime, and other social ills, even though some of the cities, such as Atlanta and Raleigh-Durham, boasted moderate race relations. Two major factors contributed to the south's new appeal: growing disenchantment with the north's racism and changes in the south's social climate as civil rights legislation knocked down the rigid racial policies that marked the racial subordination of the Old South. Despite the south's sordid issue of racism, Black folk still regarded it as a "last frontier," a place of hope contrasted to the gloomy despair of the urban north. To many northern Blacks, a Black New South offered more in terms of private entrepreneurship and the possibility of equal government services.[53] Thus, underneath the alluring image of the Black New South lay concrete evidence of changes in civil and political rights, much of it at the hands of Black Greek-lettered organizations.

For southern-born or -educated Black intellectuals, the primary reason for returning south was to reverse a trend known as the "Black brain drain" that occurred as a result of segregation. Before Blacks were able to attend or be employed at traditionally White institutions of higher learning, large northern universities hired away top faculty from southern historically Black colleges. For many, teaching in the north, Midwest, and West was in theory, and many wanted to teach Black students in practice. When southern traditionally White institutions integrated, they poached HBCUs of some of their highest-performing students. Because good Black professors attracted good Black students, a move to preserve the tradition of HBCUs was on the way.[54] Thus, during the early 1970s, the widespread belief suggested that the south was changing more rapidly than any other region of the nation. The integration of southern traditionally White institutions brought forth a new shift in Black Greek-lettered organizations, where chapters emerged on these campuses and doubled the numbers of Black Greeks and institutions and communities that accommodated them.

Clearly, a Black New South was the best place for Black economic development. The frustrating truth about politics and economics in the north was that the formation of Black political power was mostly symbolic because economic power was not its foundation. In the north, there were structured constraints on the creativity and opportunities of Black business owners. They were usually allowed to enter service kinds of operations relative to what was already established. It was difficult to attain land, the foundation to economic development in the north, because there was very little of it available. With Black land ownership in the south and the opportunities to broaden it, Atlanta seemed a place where Blacks could get in at the ground level in business and economic development, which was next to impossible to do in New York and Chicago. In 1950 Blacks owned or partly owned more than 12 million acres of land in the south, but by 1964 this was down to 7.2 million acres, a 40 percent decline. The Emergency Land Fund—a public–private sector program—was organized for the specific purpose of addressing the problem of declining Black land ownership and for providing assistance to those who wanted to remain on their land.[55] Cities such as Atlanta, Raleigh-Durham, and Nashville had their share of college students from the north and West, many the children of alumni, but the number of northern-born Black students steadily increased. Many stayed in these cities after finishing college, which added to Black return-migration movement to the south. Of these transplants, many found it comforting that they were able to operate in Black institutions, not only colleges but also other kinds of Black-owned and -affiliated ventures.

Thus, the American south was ripe and emerged as a stronghold where the influence of Black Greek life thrived. Evidence suggests that approximately of the 105 HBCUs, 100, or 95 percent of them, were located in states and the District of Columbia with large Black populations that are the result of American slavery; and 91 of the 105, or 87 percent, of all HBCUs are located in the former confederate states.[56] According to the 2010 US Census, Alabama has a Black population of 27 percent; Arkansas, 15.5; Florida, 17; Georgia, 31.5; Louisiana, 32.5; Mississippi, 37.5; North Carolina, 22; South Carolina, 28; Tennessee, 17; Texas, 12.5 and Virginia, 20.[57] Black Greek-lettered organizations, whether graduate or collegiate chapters, and their participation in voter-registration service projects yielded useful results.

In 1968 the United States had 1,469 Black elected officials. As of 2011 there were 10,500, an increase of more than 700 percent.[58] As a result of the Black New South, this growth was especially impressive at the state level. In five southern states—Georgia, Louisiana, Mississippi, South Carolina, and Texas—the total increase of Black elected officials between 1970 and 2015 was over tenfold. At the dawn of the twenty-first century, Mississippi and Alabama, states noted for racism and injustices, had more Black elected officials, 1,628, than the entire nation had in 1970s; in 1970 the ten states with the highest number of Black elected officials collectively had 821, proving the impact of Black political empowerment and electoral politics. In 1970 there were nine Black members of the US House of Representatives. The pioneers of that cohort were William Dawson (first elected in 1942), Adam Clayton Powell Jr. (1944), and Robert Nix (1958), with Charles Diggs, Augustus Hawkins, John Conyers Jr., William Clay, Louis Stokes, and Shirley Chisholm all entering office between 1962 and 1968. There was one Black US senator in 1970, Edward W. Brooke.[59]

Many of the Black elected officials holding offices in 1970 went on to be elected to higher offices, a cohort that included Yvonne Brathwaite (Burke), Harold Washington, and Charles Rangel, as well as then state senators Mervyn Dymally and Barbara Jordan and city councilperson Ron Dellums. The only Black big-city mayors in 1970 were Carl Stokes in Cleveland, Ohio, and Richard Hatcher in Gary, Indiana. Again, many future big-city mayors were to come, such as David Dinkins of New York City; Tom Bradley of Los Angeles; Willie Brown of San Francisco; Harold Washington of Chicago; Ernest "Dutch" Morial of New Orleans; Coleman Young of Detroit; Maynard Jackson, Andy Young, Bill Campbell, Shirley Franklin, and Kasim Reed and Kesha Lance-Bottoms, all of Atlanta; and Marion Berry of Washington, DC.[60]

As evidence of a Black New South, the ten states with the largest number of Black elected officials at the beginning of the twenty-first century were: Mississippi, 897; Alabama, 731; Louisiana, 701; Illinois, 621; Georgia, 582; South Carolina, 540; Arkansas, 520; North Carolina, 498; Texas, 475; and Michigan,

340.[61] These numbers in all but two of the top ten states are the result of the passage of the Civil Rights Act of 1964 and the Voting Rights Act of 1965 and the subsequent Black political empowerment and electoral politics. Illinois and Michigan held sizeable Black political empowerment and electoral politics as a result of Chicago and Detroit, areas deemed by some historians as the Up South.

Through the realm of Black political empowerment and electoral politics and the emergence of the Black New South, the Black masses experienced the most inclusion seen in their experience in the United States. This essay has examined the intellectual history and the numerous shifts in platform while interweaving the narrative of African American history to chart the nascence of Black Greek-lettered organizations. At the onset, it seemed that Black Greek-lettered organizations were created to serve as arbitrators between the Black masses and Whites, under the pretense that the existence of these organizations could change the antiracist attitudes of Whites. However, the Black elite and middle classes never achieved that feat and, thus, understood that the most effective methods of changing the conditions of Black folk were to push for full citizenship through civil and human rights and then to vote in their own interests. Hence, the most significant role of Black Greek-lettered organizations at the dawning of the twenty-first century is their push toward full citizenship through Black political empowerment and electoral politics. In the current century, new causes will arise in the arenas of equality and citizenship. This requires Black fraternities and sororities to reexamine themselves and how they define their approaches by looking to the past to chart out patterns that will assail Black America the coming decades. For if Black Greek-lettered organizations are to survive for another hundred years as champions of equality and uplift, it will require them to reinvent themselves and to open their minds to new challenges that await them.

Notes

1. Christie Anne Farnham, *The Education of the Southern Belle: Higher Education and Student Socialization in the Antebellum South* (New York: New York University Press, 1995), 69.

2. Maurice J. Hobson, *The Legend of the Black Mecca: Politics and Class in the Making of Atlanta* (Chapel Hill: University of North Carolina Press, 2017).

3. "To pull oneself up by one's boot straps" is conservative rhetoric used in American political discourse that means to succeed or elevate oneself without any outside help. Though this concept has its flaws, in the context of the era of self-help, racial uplife, and the American Negro Academy, this was the best vehicle in place to move Black America forward during the nadir period of the Black experience in this country.

4. Hobson, *Legend*.

5. Booker T. Washington, *Up from Slavery*, ed. W. Fitzhugh Brundage (New York: Bedford, 2003), 142–143.

6. The Dunning School believed that slavery was necessary to provide civilization and religion for people they portrayed as African savages. According to Du Bois's *Black Reconstruction*, which made Black Americans ordinary human beings, the Dunning School argued that Reconstruction was the most calamitous and corrupt period in the nation's history because imperialistic Radical Republicans empowered "riotous, sub-human blacks" to rule over a "respectable white South." This racist interpretation was popularized in *Birth of a Nation*, the 1915 slient film that served as a recruiting tool for the Ku Klux Klan.

7. "N. M. [Niagara Movement] First Annual Meeting," July 11, 12, and 15, 1905, Erie Beach Hotel, Fort Erie, Ontario, and 521 Michigan Avenue, Buffalo, New York, pdf, Photographic Image Database, W. E. B. Du Bois Library, University of Massachusetts–Amherst, http://scua.library.umass.edu/digital/dubois/312.2.839–01–03.pdf, accessed November 17, 2015.

8. David T. Gilbert, *The Niagara Movement at Harpers Ferry, National Park Service*, August 11, 2006, http://www.elegantbrain.com/academic/department/AandL/AAS/ANNOUNCE/niagaramovement/harpers/niagaraharpers.html, accessed November 30, 2020.

9. Lawrence Graham, *Our Kind of People: Inside Black America's Upper Class* (New York: Harper), 128.

10. The term "Pan-Africanism" originally was "Pan-Negroism."

11. Historian Alex Michael Carter asserts that Omega Psi Phi Fraternity was at the heart of his research on Fort Des Moines Officer Training Camps. This can be seen in *George E. Brice and Francis Mores Dent: Omega Men in World War I* presented at the Sixty-Sixth Annual Omega Psi Phi Fraternity, Eighth District Conference, April 25, 2015, Des Moines, Iowa.

12. *Guinn v. United States* is a US Supreme Court decision that deals with provisions of state constitutions that set qualifications for voters. It found grandfather-clause exemptions to literacy tests to be unconstitutional. *Buchanan v. Warley* is a US Supreme Court decision in which the court addressed civil government–instituted racial segregation in residential areas.

13. W. E. B. Du Bois, *The Souls of Black Folk* (1903; New York: Penguin, 1996), 87; Thomas Jesse Jones, *Negro Education: A Study of the Private and Higher Schools for Colored People in the United States* (Washington, DC: US Office of Education and Phelps-Stoke Fund, 1917).

14. "Jewel" is a term used to connote a founding member of Alpha Phi Alpha. "The Founding of Alpha Phi Alpha," *Alpha Phi Alpha Fraternity Inc.*, https://apa1906.net/our-history/, accessed November 30, 2020.

15. Ibid.

16. "Mission," *Alpha Kappa Alpha Sorority Inc.*, https://aka1908.com/about/mission, accessed November 30, 2020.

17. "A Brief History," *Kappa Alpha Psi Fraternity Inc.*, www.kappaalphapsi1911.com/?page=history, accessed November 30, 2020.

18. *Omega Psi Phi Fraternity Inc.*, http://www.oppf.org/, accessed November 30, 2020.

19. *Delta Sigma Theta Sorority Inc.*, http://www.deltasigmatheta.org/, accessed November 30, 2020.

20. "History of Phi Beta Sigma Fraternity," *Phi Beta Sigma Fraternity Inc.*, phibetasigma 1914.org/index.php/about/history/, accessed November 30, 2020.

21. Ibid.

22. "About Zeta Phi Beta," *Zeta Phi Beta Sorority Inc.*, http://www.zphib1920.org/our -history/, accessed November 30, 2020.

23. "About Sigma," *Sigma Gamma Rho Sorority Inc.*, https://www.sgrho1922.org/, ac-cessed November 30, 2020.

24. "About: Historical Overview," *Iota Phi Theta Fraternity Inc.*, http://www.iotaphi theta.org/about/historical-overview, accessed November 30, 2020.

25. "About the NPHC," *National Pan-Hellenic Council*, https://nphchq.com/ millennium1/about/, accessed November 30, 2020.

26. Ibid. For the purpose of this chapter, Iota Phi Theta is not included because most of the activities of the Black New South and the subsequent Black political empower-ment and electoral politics took place either before or just after Iota's founding. This is not a slight to Iota Phi Theta but an issue of periodization.

27. Langston Hughes, "Merry Christmas," *Humanities and Social Sciences Online*, New Masses, https://lists.h-net.org/cgi-bin/logbrowse.pl?trx=vx&list=h-afro-am&month= 1001&week=b&msg=SmJfPnnfMwNMBCLhBqvg8g&user=&pw=, accessed November 30, 2020; Shae Irving, *Nolo's Encyclopedia of Everyday Law*, 7th ed. (Berkeley, CA: Nolo's, 2008), 68; *Alpha Phi Alpha Men: A Century of Leadership,* Maryland Public Television, Public Broadcasting Service, 2006.

28. *New Negro Alliance v. Sanitary Grocery Company*, US Supreme Court, April 25, 1938, www.findlaw.com, accessed November 30, 2020; "New Negro Alliance's Sanitary Grocery Protest Site," *Cultural Tourism D.C.*, https://www.culturaltourismdc.org/portal/ new-negro-alliance-s-sanitary-grocery-protest-site-african-american-heritage-trail, accessed November 30, 2020.

29. Evelyn Brooks Higginbotham and John Hope Franklin, *From Slavery to Freedom: A History of African Americans* (New York: McGraw-Hill, 2010), 423–427.

30. "De Priest, Oscar Stanton," *Office of Art and Archives, US House of Representatives*, https://history.house.gov/people/Detail/12155.

31. Higginbotham and Franklin, *From Slavery to Freedom*, 423–427.

32. James A. Miller, Susan D. Pennybacker, and Eve Rosenshaft, "Mother Ada Wright and the International Campaign to Free the Scottsboro Boys, 1931–34," *American Histori-cal Review* 106, no. 2 (2001): 387–430.

33. Todd J. Moye, *Freedom Flyers: The Tuskegee Airmen of World War II* (New York: Oxford University Press, 2010), 99; Martin Blumenson, *Eisenhower* (New York: Bal-lantine, 1973), 127.

34. Melinda Chateauvert, *Marching Together: Women of the Brotherhood of Sleeping Car Porters* (Urbana: University of Illinois Press, 1998); Herbert Garfinkel, *When Negroes March: The March on Washington Movement in the Organizational Politics of the FEPC* (New York: Atheneum, 1969).

35. Ulysses Lee, *The Employment of Negro Troops* (New York: St. John's, 2016); Wil-liam H. Young and Nancy K. Young, *World War II and the Postwar Years in America: A Historical and Cultural Encyclopedia* (Santa Barbara, CA: ABC-CLIO, 2010), 1:534.

36. Suzanne Mettler, "How the G.I. Bill Built the Middle Class and Enhanced Democ-

racy," *Scholars Strategy Network*, January 2012, https://scholars.org/sites/scholars/files/ssn_key_findings_mettler_on_gi_bill.pdf; Suzanne Mettler, *Soldiers to Citizens: The G.I. Bill and the Making of the Greatest Generation* (New York: Oxford University Press, 2005).

37. Jacqueline Dowd-Hall, "The Long Civil Rights Movement and the Political Uses of the Past," *Journal of American History* 91, no. 4 (2005): 1233–1263; Sundiata Cha-Jua and Clarence Lang, "The 'Long Movement' as Vampire: Temporal and Spatial Fallacies in Recent Black Freedom Studies," *Journal of African American History* 92, no. 2 (2007): 265–288; Jeanne Theoharis, "Black Freedom Studies: Re-imagining and Redefining the Fundamentals," *History Compass* 4, no. 2 (2006): 348–367.

38. Houston Baker, *Betrayal: How Black Intellectuals Have Abandoned the Ideals of the Civil Rights Era* (New York: Columbia University Press, 2010).

39. Maurice J. Hobson, "But for Bull Connor and Birmingham, We Would Not Have Dr. Martin Luther King Jr.'s 'Letter from a Birmingham Jail,'" *Birmingham (AL) News*, April 13, 2013.

40. David J. Garrow, "The Origins of the Montgomery Bus Boycott," *Journal of Southern Regional Council* 7, no. 5 (1985): 24.

41. Charles H. Wesley, *The History of Alpha Phi Alpha, a Development in College Life* (Baltimore: Foundation, 2008), 336–369.

42. "Unsung Sorors of the Civil Rights Movement Exhibit Timeline," http://unsungsorors.aka1908.com/VeriteCo-TimelineJS-a89ae22/examples/timeline.html.

43. Kazuyo Tsuchiya, "Race, Class, and Gender in America's 'War on Poverty': The Case of Opal C. Jones in Los Angeles, 1964–1968," *Japanese Journal of American Studies* 15 (2004): 213–236.

44. Chris Jenkins, "Omega Psi Phi Brother Celebrate Centennial at D.C. Birthplace," *Washington Post*, July 27, 2011.

45. Aeja O. Washington, "Lady Fortitude," *The Hilltop*, October 26, 2004, www.howard.edu/library/imagesofthecapstone/Lady_Fortitude.htm.

46. Stephen Curtis, "Life of a Party," *Crisis* 113, no. 5 (2006): 30–37.

47. Tai Hicks, "Autherine Luce Foster Returns to the Schoolhouse Door," *Dateline Alabama.com*, 2003.

48. Gregory Parks, *Black Greek-Lettered Organizations in the Twenty-First Century: Our Fight Has Just Begun* (Lexington: University Press of Kentucky, 2008).

49. Southwide 1957–1989, undated, folder 1, box 1; Delta Sigma Theta Sorority, 1969, folder 10, box 64; and Delta Sigma Theta, 1972 and 1978, folder 2, box 112, all in Voter Education Project Organizational Records, Robert W. Woodruff Library Archives Research Center, Atlanta University Center.

50. Maurice J. Hobson, *The Legend of the Black Mecca: Politics and Class in the Making of Modern Atlanta* (Chapel Hill: University of North Carolina Press, 2017).

51. Ibid.

52. "Blacks Return to South," Newsweek Atlanta Telex, February 20, 1974, box 3, *Newsweek Inc.* Atlanta Collection, Stuart A. Rose Manuscript, Archives and Rare Book Library, Emory University, Atlanta, Georgia.

53. Ibid.

54. Ibid.

55. Ibid.

56. "About Us," White House Initiative on Historically Black Colleges and Universities, *US Department of Education*, https://sites.ed.gov/whhbcu/about-us/, accessed November 30, 2020. Historical Black college and universities (HBCUs) are institutions of higher education in the United States that were established before 1964 with the intention of serving the Black community; they consist of public and private institutions, community and four-year institutions, and medical and law schools. "Predominately White institutions" is the term used to describe institutions of higher learning in which Whites account for 50 percent or greater of the student enrollment. However, the majority of these institutions may also be understood as historically White institutions in recognition of the binarism and exclusion supported by the United States prior to 1964. Predominantly White institutions have not been as clearly defined as HBCUs in the federal law, but researchers, to identify higher education institutions where the student population is primarily White, commonly use the term. For the purpose of this study, a predominantly White institution is defined as an institution with more than 50 percent non–Hispanic Caucasian student enrollment.

57. "Quick Facts," *US Census*, https://www.census.gov/quickfacts/fact/table/US/PST045219, accessed November 30, 2020.

58. Juliet Eilperin, "What's Changed for African Americans since 1963, by the Numbers," *Washington Post*, August 22, 2013, https://www.washingtonpost.com/, accessed November 30, 2020.

59. David A. Bositis, *Black Elected Officials: A Statistical Summary 2000* (Washington, DC: Joint Center for Political and Economic Studies, 2002), 6.

60. Ibid., 6.

61. Ibid., 8.

PART IV

IDENTITY AND IDEOLOGY

Introduction

R. BAXTER MILLER

Identity is the way that people perceive themselves in the context of their historical, religious, social, and psychic origins. Through individual distinctiveness, African American citizens recognize themselves in the context of those who would define them and whom they would define as well. By the time of adolescence, both the hypothetical definers and the African American citizens come to terms with what both believe, somewhat differently, about capitalist desire, American democracy, and racial freedom. Their ideologies imply the devices and strategies of the systematic, cognitive, and material ways that Blacks intend to implement their ideas in the world, reshaping their society to their vision. To say that there is African American or Black thought in the regard (the two are not necessarily synonymous) would be an oversimplification, for diverse individuals often think different things, both in their own time and beyond.

Nevertheless, one might chart a communal trajectory of Black intellectual traditions across the twentieth century, accounting for shifting nuances within a few decades of each other, from the emergent nationalism of the 1930s and eventually of the 1960s and 1970s to the more isolationist adaptations of ideologies during the final decades of the century. What becomes obvious is that Black nationalism increases most when the African American middle class believes that American history threatens its life, liberty, and pursuit of happiness.[1] It is important to recognize Black nationalism as it has emerged from the late nineteenth century to the turn of the twenty-first, the rise of the Nation of Islam (Black Muslims) in its various renditions during the early and then late twentieth century, the ascent of the ideology of Black Power by the final third of the twentieth century, and yet the displacement of such political activism by Afrocentricity during the final decades of the twentieth century. Finally, it is important to acknowledge the emergence of post-Blackness, a provocative fantasy during the early decades of the new millennium. The intellectual history of the last century—and, indeed, this section—represents a rich diversity of opinion more than a monolithic racial mind. Nevertheless, racial history produces racial responses. Identity means the developmental compulsion to define oneself and articulate the self to the external world. In this regard, the self declares its own values and aesthetics within historical and cultural contexts. Despite the existence of identity, primarily in the dimension of the humanistic values, the political assertion of Black distinctiveness poses a political challenge to the hierarchy of power.

The essays that follow exist within the diverse context of African American identities and ideologies. The chapter "A New Afrikan Nation in the Western Hemisphere: Black Power, the Republic of New Afrika, and the Pursuit of Independence" by Edward Onaci reports on efforts to establish a Republic of New Afrika (RNA), a nationalist state, in the American south during the Black Power era. At a conference in 1968, the two hundred founders of a proposed government agreed that political sovereignty for Black Americans would assure their freedom. In their efforts to create a polity outside the jurisdiction of the United States, they proposed to acquire ownership of the states of Alabama, Georgia, Louisiana, Mississippi, and South Carolina. Obviously influenced by the ideology of Elijah Mohammed, including a concept inherited from the first Nation of Islam, the founders believed they had achieved communal revelations about European hegemony in the world. As would be true for nearly every ideological school after Elijah Mohammed, the Asiatic origins of the Black Muslims were lost. Rather, the activists who attended would consider the heritage to be Afrocentric, a term yet to be invented by the next generation. There were disagreements in the ranks of Black Power. Especially early on, Robert Williams and Huey P. Newton of the Black Panther Party refused to support the idea of the RNA. They feared that the creation of a Black nation, RNA, within the United States, which was an imperialist power, would place the new polity at risk, as the recently decolonized nations were. Despite the establishment of a provisional government, the RNA seemed to resemble other Black Power agencies. After all, it provided educational classes and facilitated community organizing. Nevertheless, the RNA was unique in theorizing its intellectual foundations as those of an independent nation.

The contribution by Keisha N. Blain, "'A Certain Bond between the Colored Peoples': Internationalism and the Black Intellectual Tradition," on the contrary, documents a century of Black internationalism, highlighting political collaborations by people of color worldwide. From the complementary side of the political spectrum, she traces a century of African American collaborations with Asia initially within the context of the Universal Negro Improvement Association (UNIA) of the 1920s and then the Russo-Japanese War of 1904–1905, the Italo-Ethiopian War of 1935, the Great Depression, and, finally, the concurrent advances of civil rights and Black Power. She clarifies the global strategies of freedom and transcultural partnerships. By the term "internationalism," she suggests interracial cooperation as contrasted with a Pan-Africanism that presumes racial solidarity. In addition to internationalism across race, then, there is a globalism beyond race. Some theoretical clarification would help. Although there are diverse internationalisms, surely a few of them would prove mutually exclusive, provoking a crisis in racial identities.

La TaSha B. Levy's chapter, "Black Conservative Dissent," presents a well-researched historical narrative about Black conservatives of the 1970s. In the impassioned polemics of the era, she observes a presumed minimization of racial impact in American intellectual life. What characterizes such thought most is the opposition to affirmative action, a public policy based on demographic inclusiveness. Conservatives express a visceral disdain (if not hatred) for the welfare state. To them, economic context proves more crucial to individual success than race does. While the well-written essay proposes no argument, it implies a fascinating double standard. Conservative thinkers represent themselves either as those who mystify social history—insisting that racial narratives are entirely divorced from historical production—or those who obfuscate history to invalidate the state's responsibility for social equity. Such thinkers often imply that affirmative action legitimizes a pathological culture of poor African American work habits, excluding the numerous White women on welfare; yet, these same theorists claim an inexplicable, innate supremacy of personal talent. While they embrace no proactive advocacy of their own, they become disingenuous strategists for the status quo. In other words, they define their ideological mission in terms of what they oppose.

Rather than extending the historical narrative of slavery and colonialism, Zebulon V. Miletsky, in "Postracialism and Its Discontents: Barack Obama and the New 'American Dilemma,'" explains the consequence of erasing historical memory. To many, the election of Obama as the forty-fourth president of the United States in 2008 proved the nation had ventured out on new, postracial terrain. Despite the riots that followed the fatal shooting of Michael Brown by David Wilson, a White police officer, on April 9, 2014; of Ahmaud Arbery on February 23, 2020; of Breonna Taylor on March 13, 2020; and later of George Floyd on May 25, 2020, and despite the consequent expansion of the Black Lives Matter initiative, the idea of post-Blackness surged. Conservatives, however, had promoted expedient claims of color-blindness since the Ronald Reagan presidency of the 1980s. Whether the idea of post-Blackness proves true, of course, does not change the danger that the ideology poses for people of color, particularly African Americans. Acceptance of the premise would result in dismissing claims of racial inequality.

There is no disputing the shared impact of these essays, for all illuminate the decisive racial ideologies of the twentieth century. In addition to the presentation of historical concepts, these chapters embed their own ideological postures subtly, and often inadvertently, within persuasive explanations. It is revealing that Afrocentrism represses within itself the Asiatic roots dating from the Harlem Renaissance. Then, too, the proposed Republic of New Afrika took a militant stance toward the US government, at least rhetorically, but was sympathetic to Native American treaties. Subconsciously, those who had been colonized emotionally feared becoming colonialists themselves. Within the complexity of globalism and life, Blacks shared alliances with Asians and Africans, the former in the theory of intercultural internationalism and the latter in the principle of Pan-Africanism. If the duality seems hypocritical today, as binaries become juxtaposed, the reason is that human identity is multifaceted. Only such intricacy accounts for the constant couplings and decouplings within Black intellectual traditions of Asians and Blacks, of Pan-Africans and Americans, of civil rights litigators and Black Power activists, of international partners and nationalistic skeptics, and of Afrocentric educators and neoconservatives. If a trend persists across the essays, it is that the diverse ideologies of globalism and activism challenged European hegemony for a hundred years.

Note

1. Algernon Austin, *Achieving Blackness: Race, Black Nationalism, and Afrocentrism in the Twentieth Century* (New York: New York University Press, 2006), 184–185; Kevin R. Anderson, *Agitations: Ideologies and Strategies in African American Politics* (Fayetteville: University of Arkansas Press, 2010), 1.

CHAPTER 9

A NEW AFRIKAN NATION IN THE WESTERN HEMISPHERE

BLACK POWER, THE REPUBLIC OF NEW AFRIKA, AND THE PURSUIT OF INDEPENDENCE

EDWARD ONACI

The order and meaning of the Republic of New Afrika's (RNA) green, red, and black representative flag illuminate some features of New Afrikan thought that distinguish its ideas and objectives from other Black Power–era formations. According to the article "The Flag of Our Nation," the color black is on the bottom to symbolize the political and economic positions of African people throughout the world. Green takes up the top position of the RNA flag because New Afrikans recognized obtaining land as the most important aspect of their struggle for liberation. Only by gaining land and independence could New Afrikans expect to help rearrange the economic conditions that made African people among some of the poorest in the world. Finally, the thin red stripe in the middle stands in for the blood of people who must secure land through any necessary means, although New Afrikans hoped to lose "as little Black blood as possible" in pursuit of their goal. The goal was full independence and statehood.[1]

During the 1960s and 1970s, a number of African American activists articulated varying notions of "separatism." Specifically (and more accurately), individuals and organizations sought self-determination in a variety of ways, including through control over their children's education, advocacy for Black political empowerment, rethinking the history and meaning of the Black religious experience, and the development of African-inspired cultural practices. Efforts to develop curricula that taught children to value themselves as African people, and struggles for Black Studies programs and the "Black University" rose in prominence in the years following the assassination of Malcolm X. Also, the Gary Convention and various conferences for Black Power and Black economic development brought an array of self-proclaimed integrationists, nationalists, and revolutionaries together to develop agendas that could empower Black Americans. Simultaneously, Black liberation theology framed religious communities' spiritual strivings in terms that did not depend on a White savior. Aside from the reworking of Christian practices, Islam and African spirituality earned noticeable space in the African American religious landscape. Relatedly, the rise of cultural practices like Kwanzaa helped provide rituals and celebrations that centered on the unique experiences of African-descended peoples in the United States.[2] Although important initiatives that helped fortify African Americans' sense of self, none put forth a strong vision of Black statehood. Instead, they sought survival, cultural revitalization, and political empowerment within a more egalitarian (though sometimes revolutionized) American state.

Unlike many of their peers, New Afrikans understood self-determination as choosing where to place their consent of citizenship. Toward that end, they advocated for the creation of an independent Black nation-state that stood apart from the legal and political jurisdiction of the United States of America. Their effort focused on securing control of the states of Mississippi, Louisiana, South Carolina, Alabama, and Georgia. In March 1968 Gaidi Obadele, his brother Imari Abubakari Obadele, and five hundred Black nationalists met in Detroit to pursue independence from the United States and to stake their claim over the five states.[3] At the time, New Afrikans viewed theirs as one of the many nations, not an American minority group, participating in the global effort to end worldwide White supremacy and win independence for colonized peoples. Their ideas added an alternative option to the nationalist thinking of the Black Power era and beyond.

The discontent of anticolonial or independence movements resonated with the RNA's founders, who, following anticolonial and Black American revolutionary traditions, produced similar ideas in their foundational texts. Several documents, including the RNA's Declaration of Independence, Code of Umoja (the RNA constitution), New Afrikan Creed and Oath, and New Afrikan Ujamaa, a document that explains the New Afrikan nation's economic philosophy, articulate these notions, as well as New Afrikans' perceptions of what would lead to lasting racial progress. The desires for revolution and independence were also embedded in the Provisional Government (PG) of the RNA's organizational structure and directed toward alliances with other oppressed nations. Collectively, New Afrikan ideas and actions repackaged common themes of the era in ways that were unique to and for their time and that continue to have some resonance in the twenty-first century.

The RNA's Foundational Documents

New Afrikan political science (NAPS), or RNA ideology, was the guiding light that directed New Afrikan thinking and distinguished them from their Black Power–era counterparts. According to cultural studies scholar Stuart Hall, ideologies are "the mental frameworks—the languages, the concepts, categories, imagery of thought, and the systems of representation—which different classes and social groups deploy in order to make sense of, define, figure out and render intelligible the way society works."[4] Similarly, political scientist Michael C. Dawson considers ideology "a world view readily found in the population, including sets of ideas and values that cohere, that are used publicly to justify political stances, and that shape and are shaped by society."[5] Originally drafted within the first five years of the Provisional Government's founding, the RNA's foundational documents impart a basic understanding of NAPS by defining the RNA, providing characteristics of the ideal citizen, and mapping out the Provisional Government's goals. I distill NAPS into five principles, two of which are important here: first, African people in the United States make up a "captive" nation upon whom United States citizenship was *imposed*. New Afrikans argue that it should have been *offered* with the Fourteenth Amendment to the US Constitution. Second, New Afrikans have been consciously fighting a war against United States imperialism and for RNA (and all oppressed nations') self-determination.[6] The RNA Declaration of Independence and other founding documents have been the cornerstone of NAPS.

Declaration of Independence

The RNA's Declaration of Independence articulates the predicament of African people in the United States and proffers an approach to solving their problems. The document's authors framed the plight as an enduring national oppression that included enslavement and its legacy of racist subjugation that weakened their connection with their African ancestry. When dozens of Black Government Conference attendees, in convention, signed the declaration in 1968, they decided that physical and political independence comprised the only solution to their dilemma in America. They summed up this decision in the opening paragraph in which they proclaim, "Black People in America . . . forever free and independent of the jurisdiction of the United States of America and the obligations which that country's unilateral decision to make our ancestors and ourselves paper-citizens placed on us."[7] As paper-citizens of the United States, New Afrikans used the declaration as their first official statement asserting the right to self-determination. The signatories claimed to desire nothing from the

United States except the basic human rights guaranteed to all people, inclusive of "the right to damages" for the effects of the racial oppression. Addressing the probability that their oppressors would refuse to provide reparations in the form of land and financial restitution, the authors also positioned New Afrikans as revolutionaries prepared to back their demand with military and political struggle against the injustices done to them.[8]

Next, the document specifies particular aims of the New Afrikan revolution. The thirteen goals form three roughly overlapping categories. One category includes social goals that focus on individual rights and responsibilities. These include attaining religious and spiritual freedom, "assur[ing] equality of rights for the sexes," and calling for the end of racial discrimination. The next category reveals practical economic goals that would aid in the development of RNA territory. To this end, the founders wanted to place the means of production under the control of the New Afrikan government, thereby allowing all citizens to benefit from industry. As a factor in and consequence of working together to create "the New Society," New Afrikans would live cooperatively, working together to reach their goals. The final category contains political commitments that sought to overturn global oppression. The document's authors deem all of the aforementioned elements important for the New Society they envision because they insist "self-respect and mutual respect among all people in the Society" cannot exist if the said nation's citizens harm each other and other nations in the very ways New Afrikans protested.[9]

The closing paragraph of the declaration charges signers with devoting all of their physical, economic, and intellectual resources to bringing about a successful revolution and winning independence. The authors believed that only with independence could they create the New Society. Building upon the aspirations set by their predecessors in various abolitionist, emigrationist, and communist formations, the authors believed the New Society would be "better than what we now know and as perfect as man can make it."[10] The vague wording here suggests that the authors left room for future New Afrikans to interpret the document in ways that would meet their specific needs. That way, activists could be flexible and dynamic as they struggled for New Afrikan independence and third world liberation. For example, with the work of Frances Beale, welfare rights organizations, and groups such as the Combahee River Collective and other Black and Brown feminist organizations, a burgeoning critique of heterosexism was gaining momentum.[11] Thus, the RNA declaration's lack of any steadfast description of the New Society theoretically made room for New Afrikans to embrace changes necessitated by such critiques. Also, like many other Black Power–era revolutionaries, New Afrikan founders understood that their ability to gain independence from the United States was both reliant on and instrumental to the success of various third world revolutionaries and their allies in the United States whom scholar Cynthia A. Young refers to as the "U.S. Third World Left."[12] The imprecise wording, therefore, would allow successive generations of New Afrikan freedom fighters to adapt to the changing (neo)colonial situation as it unfolded.

In many ways, the RNA's Declaration of Independence existed within the trajectory of a Black revolutionary intellectual tradition that sought to define African people's problems and have them decide on appropriate solutions for themselves. The tradition was long-standing and spatially diffuse; yet, it was coherent and consistent even as it traveled across multiple contexts.[13] For example, one can see parallels between the RNA founders' intentions and the aims of those who overthrew the French government and created the Republic of Haiti. The 1804 Haitian Declaration of Independence lists Haitians' grievances and committed those who signed on (both literally and ideologically) with the task of creating a better world. It states, "It is not enough to have expelled the barbarians who have bloodied our land for two centuries; it is not enough to have restrained those ever-evolving factions that one after another mocked the specter of liberty that France dangled before you. We must, with one last act of national authority, forever assure the empire of liberty in the country of our birth; we must take any hope of re-enslaving us away from the inhuman government that for so long kept us in the most humiliating torpor. In the end we must live independent or die."[14] Because of their successful revolution against enslavement, Haitians became an inspiration to their contemporaries as well as future generations of freedom fighters and intellectuals, including some African Americans active in political organizing during the Black Power era.[15]

The final portion of the RNA declaration echoes such sentiments as it ends with an agreement that the signers would "pledge without reservation, ourselves, our talents, and all our worldly goods" to bring about a successful revolution. RNA contemporaries, such as the League of Revolutionary Black Workers and the Black Panther Party, also expressed similar ideas. The League, for example, sought to wage "relentless struggle against racism, capitalism, and imperialism." In so doing, it strove to help create a free world for all oppressed peoples.[16] The RNA's statement also parallels Huey P. Newton's concept of "revolutionary suicide," which he summed up in a poem that reads, "By surrendering my life to the revolution / I found eternal life."[17] In agreeing with the pledge, New Afrikan revolutionaries indicated that they directed their lives according to the pursuit of statehood.

The New Afrikan Creed

Another important document in the canon of NAPS is the New Afrikan Creed, which reiterates the declaration's aims and expands the pledge presented at the declaration's conclusion. Written and approved shortly after the RNA's founders declared their intention to pursue independence from the United States, the creed is divided into two sections. The first section contains fifteen commitments to which New Afrikans agreed when they became conscious citizens. With attention given to individual and collective spirituality, moral aptitude, revolutionary discipline, and the pursuit of global liberation, these personal pledges (written as "I-statements") formed the foundation for New Afrikans' collective identity and were intended to guide decisions about everyday life. For example, point number 10 states: "I will give my life, if that is necessary, I will give my time, my mind, my strength and my wealth because this is necessary."[18] Like the declaration's closing pledge, the creed exhibits an idealism matching that of New Afrikans' revolutionary forebears and many of their contemporaries. It envisions a world free from systemic oppression and problems against which the New Afrikan government and its citizens were struggling.

The second section closes out the creed with a statement that summarizes its fifteen points of commitment. The original version reads, "Now, freely and on my own will, I pledge this creed, for the sake of freedom for my people and a better world, on pain of disgrace and banishment if I prove false. For, I am no longer deaf, dumb or blind. I am—by the grace of Malcolm—a New Afrikan." The creed's authors borrowed the phrase "deaf, dumb, or blind" from Elijah Muhammad, who used it to describe "so-called Negroes" who accepted European cultural, spiritual, and political domination. By reciting, "I am no longer deaf, dumb, or blind," the speaker or reader reiterates a New Afrikan identity that directly opposes European hegemony and ignorance regarding Black people's African heritage.[19]

Malcolm X's prominence at the pledge's closing should come as no surprise when considering his influence on the Obadele brothers and many other Black Power activists. When New Afrikans developed the creed, Malcolm X's spirit endured as one of the preeminent forces behind various Black Power ideologies of the period.[20] However, his distinction became subtler when on May 5, 1993, the PG-RNA revised the pledge to state: "I am, by inspiration of the ancestors and grace of the Creator, a New Afrikan."[21] It is likely that with the aging and passing of several important activists whose work preceded and inspired the creation of the RNA, the PG-RNA realized their gratitude should include more than just their most immediate ideological forefather. That is not to suggest, however, that his importance diminished. Since the 1970s, some New Afrikans have gone so far as to base their calendar around the ancestral transition of their patron saint, dating moments following his tragic death as "adm," or after the death of Malcolm.[22]

The New Afrikan Creed, as a statement of commitments and principles, helped cement the foundation of what later cohered as NAPS. The practice of reciting the full list of I-statements, or personal declarations, at gatherings helped solidify a collective New Afrikan identity based on common struggle and goals. The statements guided how they interpreted their everyday actions and life choices. Coupled with the Declaration of Independence, the New Afrikan Creed provides a basic theoretical understanding of how New Afrikans constructed their political identity and goals as distinct from their Black Power–era peers.

The New Afrikan Oath

The New Afrikan Oath reformatted the creed as a concise pledge of allegiance. Through the oath, New Afrikans proclaim:

> For the fruition of Black Power,
> For the triumph of Black nationhood,
> I pledge to the Republic of New Africa
> and to the building of a better people and a
> better world, my total devotion, my
> total resources and the total power
> of my mortal life.[23]

That the oath begins by matching the "fruition of Black Power" with "the triumph of Black nationhood" signals that it attempted to reframe some of the prevailing assumptions about the concept of Black Power.[24] According to a handbill produced by New Afrikans in New York City, "Black power means more than wearing Afros, dashikis, taking or teaching a course in Afro-American history, using traditional names and calling each other brother and sister. [Instead,] Black power means having your own nation. But in order to build a nation [Black people] must begin by controlling the institutions in [their] communities." The author of the flyer's text emphasizes controlling schools and supporting "real Black political candidates, Black community organizations such as the Welfare Rights Groups, and all Black revolutionary organizations."[25] Such goals were congruent with popular emphases of many Black Power–era organizations. The Sons of Watts in Los Angeles, the League of Revolutionary Black Workers, the Third World Women's Alliance, and the Black Panther Party, among others, all articulated versions of these ideas. Yet, in articulating the end goal as the attainment of political and territorial independence, RNA activists reframed seemingly reformist goals as revolutionary tactics for New Afrikan independence.[26]

In contrast, some of the era's notable spokespersons put forth arguments that disclaimed attention to the five southern states that New Afrikans pursued. Stokely Carmichael drew upon Malcolm X's "Message to the Grassroots" speech and Marxism-Leninism to confirm that Black revolutionaries needed to ground their struggle in a land base. However, he argued that the five states that New

Afrikans claimed were insufficient because the states did not provide mineral resources necessary to generate industrial power. Also, because he considered Pan-Africanism to be the highest expression of Black Power, he suggested that African-descended people consider the continent of Africa as their land. Floyd McKissick, former Congress of Racial Equality (CORE) chair, wanted to build a city that would enable its poor and disadvantaged residents to become economically independent, although as US citizens. His plans for Soul City, North Carolina, also sought to work within the established capitalist structure, even if they eventually provided Black residents with the means to exercise some political autonomy. Between Carmichael and McKissick was a variety of urban-focused land claims, attempts to protect African American–owned rural land, and experiments with cooperatives. Although all challenged aspects of racial capitalism and promoted land acquisition as racial progress, none framed their plans for land as paths toward the creation of an independent nation-state.[27]

The Black Panther Party, the single most studied Black Power–era organization, helps exemplify how many organizations regarded independent statehood. New Afrikans within the party tended to accentuate point number 10 in the party's ten-point program. It originally stated that a "major political objective" of the party was to ensure "a United Nations–supervised plebiscite to be held throughout the black colony." The plebiscite would allow "black colonial subjects . . . to participate, for the purpose of determining the will of black people as to their national destiny."[28] When pressed about this matter, however, Newton wrote to then–RNA president Robert F. Williams, indicating that the Black Panther Party could not give support to the independence movement. He reasoned that it would not be in Black people's best interest to seek independence while the United States, "a capitalistic imperialist country," remained intact. Seceding would put Black Americans at risk of enduring oppression that surpassed the conditions experienced by various recently decolonized countries. Newton disclosed that the party was not concerning itself with independence because it was "somewhat premature."[29]

In 1970, after significant changes to his analysis of local and geopolitical conditions, Newton restated his position regarding the independence movement. Instead of considering it premature, he put forth that any land under New Afrikan control was "the people's liberated territory" that "represent[ed] a community liberated." For Newton, however, having liberated territory was not in itself a sufficient end goal in a broader struggle for "revolutionary intercommunalism." He insisted, "It is only ground for preparation for the liberation of the world, seizing of the wealth from the ruling circle and equal distribution and proportional representation in the intercommunal framework."[30] Although Newton signaled some ideological support for the RNA, he ultimately maintained his disagreements with New Afrikan independence. By arguing for intercommunalism, he also criticized the major goal of New Afrikan independence activism, nationhood. According to Assata Shakur, many Panthers either did not understand or disagreed with Newton's arguments for intercommunalism. Perhaps this lack of comprehension and/or difference of opinion helps explain why several Panthers and Black Liberation Army members continued to promote point number 10 of the Black Panther Party's program and platform. New York Panthers Safiya Bukhari and Bilal Sunni Ali pledged their allegiance to the Provisional Government even as they carried out their duties for the party. As former Panthers, Shakur and her comrade Sundiata Acoli also swore loyalty to the PG-RNA toward the end of the 1970s.[31]

The Congress of African Peoples also exhibited fidelity toward the RNA. In a five-point resolution, they decided the following. First, they pledged that Black people in the United States had a right to territory in the Black belt and to "support the efforts of the Republic of New Africa to establish on this landmass an independent, progressive, technically and spiritually excellent nation for those black people who want it." Second, they recognized "the right of the Republic of New Africa [to] organize a peaceful plebiscite among the people living in the national territory and to secede the territory and the people peacefully from the United States should the plebiscite so decide, and the congress explicitly opposes and condemns any efforts of the United States or its political sub-divisions to interfere with the peaceful organization of such a plebiscite or the peaceful execution of its results." Third, the congress urged "the Nixon Administration and a joint Committee of the United States Congress to meet individually or jointly with Representatives of the Republic to discuss terms of a peaceful settlement of the land secession question, and with representatives of the Republic and of the Congress of African Peoples to arrive at the details of a reparations settlement." The fourth point emphasizes the need to provide African Americans with reparations and resettle those who desired independence. Fifth and finally, the congress advised Black troops fighting for the United States against Vietnam to enter a cease-fire agreement with the Democratic Republic of Vietnam.[32] Aside from these examples, as well as the Afrikan People's Party and other New Afrikan formations, the general trend in Black Power seemed to favor solutions that promoted Black empowerment within the United States.

To return to the New Afrikan Oath, pledgees' commitment to Black Power fortified yet another vow to devote one's entire livelihood to the pursuit of that goal of territorial sovereignty. Whether such total commitment was achievable, or even desirable, for most New Afrikans is the topic of broader research.[33] Based on the New Afrikan Oath and the RNA Creed, it is clear that New Afrikan founders did not adhere to liberal individualism in the same ways broader American society did. Although these documents articulate some expectation that each revolutionary would bring unique contributions to the movement, the expectation was that no one person was more important than the nation. In that way, they subscribed to the Southern African concept of *ubuntu*, considering each individual New Afrikan an important part of the Black nation.[34] The fine line New Afrikans drew between the individual and the group helped shape their theorizations about how the New Afrikan economy could function.

New African Economics

The RNA Declaration of Independence, New Afrikan Creed, and New Afrikan Oath all sketch the broad ideological outline of NAPS and create one path for entering the broader discourse about citizenship and Black liberation during the 1960s and 1970s. However, they do not convey in detail what their independent nation would look like. The *New Afrikan Ujamaa*, a booklet that explains New Afrikan economic philosophy, invites deeper investigation into this issue. In concurrence with the aims written in the Declaration of Independence, this document communicates New Afrikans' conviction that an economy based on the principle of *ujamaa* would best serve them in a global society. One-time Minister of Culture Maulana Karenga's definition of "ujamaa" roughly translates it as "cooperative economics." However, the Kiswahili word literally means "family-hood."[35]

The *New African Ujamaa* outlines a plan that, if implemented, could be the economic foundation for a society that nurtures in its citizens the alternative value system explicated in the creed and oath. In fact, the *New African Ujamaa* expressly commits RNA citizens to the creation of an independent society that they envisioned in many ways as the antithesis of American society. Seeking a productive and cooperative—as opposed to consumerist and individualistic—way of life, their "New Community" would serve the basic needs of the New Afrikan people. In turn, once freed from poverty and oppression, New Afrikans would dedicate their work and leisure time to building and maintaining their nation. As written in the document, "those whom [RNA citizens] bring into the New Community will be New Africans: Black people already trained to live with one another as brothers and sisters and willing and capable of putting the New African Creed into practice."[36] New Afrikans' capabilities to live cooperatively in line with the creed "as brothers and sisters" would prove pivotal in making this economic philosophy and system successful. It is important to note that the writer did not naturalize this relationship. Having survived under centuries of subjugation and oppression, people were in need of training that would help them transition more easily into liberated life in the New Community. Nation-building classes (explained below) were the first stage in this retraining process.

The *New African Ujamaa* has eight sections, the first of which is a preamble that defines nation building and Black liberation as sacred duties.[37] "Our supreme purpose in life—our reason for being," the author explains, "must remain a companion-guide, eternally with us, full bodied, and well formed." The author implores New Afrikans to be mindful of "the world revolution until all people everywhere are so free," as he or she deems the end of worldwide oppression as part and parcel to Black liberation from United States domination. Further, the author posits the "supreme purpose of the nation" as akin to economic production, which under the proper system, is supposed to ensure each citizen's basic needs. The author outlines such necessities in the preamble as the six basic principles of ujamaa: food, housing, clothing, health services, and education, along with the element of defense.[38]

The remaining sections of the *New Afrikan Ujamaa* detail the nuts and bolts of providing the "essentials" and managing manufacturing, industry, trade, recreation, cultural production, and New Afrikans' personal incomes. Accordingly, "[t]he principle involved is simple. All the wealth—the Gross National product (the GNP)—created by the work of the Nation shall belong to the people as a whole, to the Nation. . . . Every 'dollar' of the GNP would thus be divided in accordance with a calculated decision of the Government, designed to efficiently achieve national goals."[39] As the *New African Ujamaa* describes, the national economy would secure the nation's needs as well as those of each individual New Afrikan. After the fulfillment of those essentials, the government would distribute any surplus as personal income for spending and saving. In this way, the architects of the plan hoped to furnish a better standard of living for their people than what they believed most experienced in the United States. The RNA system of cooperative economics would also support many of the goals found in the previously mentioned foundational documents, including eliminating class disparity.

As students of the emerging modern nations, New Afrikans likely based much of their *New Afrikan Ujamaa* on the example set by Julius K. Nyerere and his political party, the Tanzania African National Union (TANU).[40] When Pan-Africanism and third world solidarity regained strength during the mid- to late 1960s, some activists regarded Tanzania as an influential model for revolutionary achievement.[41] Black nationalists, students, and Black Peace Corps participants of all stripes from the United States began flocking to the unified republic, partially in response to Tanzania President Nyerere's call to African Americans for assistance in TANU's nation-building project.[42] Furthermore, Black activists, such as Pete O'Neal and Charlotte O'Neal, found political asylum there after fleeing the United States. Nyerere and Tanzania held tremendous influence among the Black Power movement in America and African-descended revolutionaries across the globe. At a moment when having an internationalist outlook was reaching a peak with the Black left, Tanzania represented the possibilities for a successful challenge to global White supremacy and capitalist dominance. RNA leaders, therefore, were among many individuals and political formations galvanized by the breadth of Nyerere's authority and significance. They saw his government as a potential ally in their own struggle for land and independence but also as a model.[43]

Upon reviewing the works of Nyerere, one can discern where New Afrikans borrowed from and modified the African head of state's ideas. For example, Nyerere regarded the accumulation of personal wealth as detrimental to society: "Apart from the anti-social effects of the accumulation of personal wealth, the very desire to accumulate it must be interpreted as a vote of 'no confidence' in the social system." On that premise, he forcefully argued that a healthy society was responsible for each individual and that no one should ever "worry about what will happen to him tomorrow if he does not hoard wealth today. Society itself should look after him, or his widow, or his orphans. This is exactly what traditional African society succeeded in doing. . . . That is socialism."[44] From the president's vantage point, each individual stood equally responsible for the well-being of the broader society. Again, Nyerere aptly summarized the citizen's responsibility: "In traditional African society everybody was a worker. . . . But it is too often forgotten, nowadays, that the basis of this great socialistic achievement was this: that it was taken for granted that every member of society—barring only the children and the infirm—contributed his fair share of efforts towards the production of its wealth."[45] Following Nyerere, the *New Afrikan Ujamaa* predicates the RNA's success on similar ideals. New Afrikans' work, whether in civil engineering, teaching, or as ministers in the Provisional Government, would go toward the betterment of the nation-state they were trying to build. The RNA modification was that individual citizens would reap rewards for contributing time, skills, and labor to the RNA. These included extra cash, as well as the luxury of vacationing at waterfront resorts financed by the Provisional Government with the surplus created by the hard work of its people.

Another modification regarded the RNA's demand for reparations. In addition to land, the PG-RNA sought financial restitution as part of its design for liberation. Collectively, New Afrikan leaders drafted a formal demand for reparations in their Declaration of Independence of 1968. In the statement, RNA founders announce the Black nation's desire for independence from the United States and stipulate the "right to damages, reparations, due us for the grievous injustices sustained by our ancestors and ourselves" as the first item on their list of demands. Placing the reparations claim in the second paragraph, just after establishing the need for independent statehood, was important because its placement evidenced the authors' framing of reparations as essential to New Afrikans' ability to exercise self-determination.

Since the 1968 Black Government Conference, New Afrikans worked hard to research and make the case for reparations. In 1972 the RNA released its antidepression program, a plan designed "To End Poverty, Dependence, Cultural Malnutrition, and Crime" and to "Promote Inter-Racial Peace." Specifically, they wanted legislative acts authorizing the session of five states to the RNA and a $300,000,000,000 payment as restitution "for slavery and unjust war against the black nation." Their efforts continued through the 1980s and eventually contributed to the creation of the National Coalition of Blacks for Reparations in America (N'COBRA). Called for in 1987, N'COBRA formed in 1989 with some of the most recognizable New Afrikan leadership at the forefront (and in the background). Imari Obadele, Chokwe Lumumba, Nkechi Taifa, and many other conscious New Afrikans helped facilitate the coalition's formation, and many of them held high-ranking positions within it. Not only is N'COBRA still active today but New Afrikan independence activists also continue to participate in discussion and activism regarding reparations.[46]

History shows that Tanzania, for various reasons, did not achieve the economic and political goals touted by Nyerere and TANU during the 1960s and 1970s. Nyerere maintains, "Our ambitions do outrun our competence at times. . . . But we are aware of our goals, and we are conscious of the socialist philosophy which we have chosen as the path to them."[47] He also recognized that many of the Tanzanian people were apathetic, if not resistant, to some of TANU's plans.[48] According to former Tanzanian government official A. R. Mohamed Babu, TANU's failure resulted from its inability to learn from former colonies in Asia that, in previous decades, attempted to develop their own brands of socialism in an overwhelmingly capitalist world. Concomitantly, Tanzania's socialist philosophy earned serious opposition from the United States and other nation-states hostile to the African country's policy of "nonalignment."[49]

Although the Republic of New Afrika never gained political independence—something its citizens continue to work toward—New Afrikans based the projected success of their economy on their ability to gain income from reparations, a national bank funded by Malcolm X Land Certificates, taxes paid by citizens, and donations from supporters.[50] Such logic assumed two things: First, they had faith (even if limited) that the United States would eventually pay reparations to the African people whose ancestors European Americans enslaved and brutally excluded from the full rights of citizenship. Second, New Afrikan leaders held that Black people, especially conscious New Afrikans, were able to and would willingly purchase land certificates, pay taxes, make monetary donations, and contribute their labor to building a physical New Afrikan infrastructure. Although the *New African Ujamaa* expresses skepticism regarding the United States' willingness to pay what the RNA demanded, the document conveys more confidence toward the possibility that African Americans, once educated, would vindicate the second assumption. However, because New Afrikans have neither achieved independence nor gained financial reparations, it so far appears their ambitions have outrun what was realistically achievable. The duality of being consciously New Afrikan and paper-citizens of the United States compromised RNA citizens' ability to live out their ideology.

The Constitution and the Organizational Structure

The Code of Umoja became an official part of the New Afrikan canon in March 1970. Its ratification occurred when Imari Abubakari Obadele won the presidency of the PG-RNA through what he argued was a "popular" election. Interestingly, several prominent New Afrikans, including Imari's brother Gaidi Obadele, "Queen Mother" Audley Moore, and Betty Shabazz, boycotted his convention and the vote. The Code of Umoja explains in detail the RNA's various government offices and describes the duties specific to each position. It also delineates the Provisional Government's plans for funding its operations, running the economy, and recruiting and retaining New Afrikan citizens as active workers. The publication of this early document marked an important step in the RNA's efforts to codify its various ideas presented in previous publications, including Imari Obadele's *War in America: The Malcolm X Doctrine*. It also demonstrated how the PG-RNA's goals and strategies departed from those of its Black Power contemporaries.[51]

RNA founders attempted to set up a governmental formation rather than an activist organization. A document titled *Government Administration* explains various government positions and their functions, the chain of command, duties of RNA citizens, and many other legal and functional directions that governed the Black nation.[52] The founders consciously framed their 1968 Black Government Conference as an opportunity for Black people in the United States to begin working toward formal independence from what they viewed as an oppressive colonizer. Therefore, the PG-RNA did not intend to create positions in name only. Instead, they expected to operate as a government with sovereignty recognized by the United Nations and the United States. Thus, the Provisional Government originally organized itself as follows: a president, first and second vice presidents, several ministers, and deputy ministers. An all-star cast of Black nationalists filled the original Provisional Government's ranks, including Robert F. Williams, Shabazz, Jamil Al-Amin (H. Rap Brown), Karenga, Amiri Baraka, Akbar Muhammad Ahmad (Maxwell Stanford Jr.), and Moore. It seemed as if some RNA leaders, including Williams and Baraka, only lent their names to the government and did not actually perform the duties of their positions to any significant degree. Others, including Moore, became lifelong independence advocates.[53]

The PG-RNA founders' initial and enduring intention to act as a self-determined and independent government distinguished New Afrikan activism from the various other efforts of the era. Not only did this aspiration set the RNA apart from most Black Power organizations but it also developed among New Afrikan ranks a nuanced understanding of Black people's relationship to the United States. Their advocacy of political independence and territorial autonomy as the only solutions to Black Americans' problems attested to New Afrikans' profound departure from the objectives endorsed by the mainstream Black Power organizations. Yet, although the RNA's founders stated and agreed upon their desires for independence, disagreements over the best strategy for achieving the end goal caused internal turmoil and led to notable changes in the government structure.

The first change occurred in 1969 following the New Bethel incident, a shoot-out between armed New Afrikans and the Detroit police. The conflict ended with the destruction of New Bethel Baptist Church, the arrest of over one hundred people, and the death of one police officer.[54] Following the incident, acting president Gaidi Obadele reorganized the Provisional Government to include four regional vice presidents as opposed to first and second vice presidents. Within one year, significant internal conflict and Imari Obadele's usurpation of power led to more changes that reorganized the internal hierarchy. For example, a People's Center Council became the top decision-making body in the RNA, followed by the president and then other leadership positions.[55] In addition to the battle at New Bethel, such changes resulted from distrust and contrasting opinions about the best strategy for New Afrikan liberation. Suspicion of the leadership came from a number of sources. The Federal Bureau of Investigation (FBI) infiltrated the PG and New Afrikan cadres across the nation, created interpersonal conflict, and exploited preexisting disagreement. Between the Obadele brothers, for example, there was discord regarding how to organize the military arm, then called the Black Legion (and later the New Afrikan Legion and New Afrikan Security Force). Similarly, the two proffered incongruent strategies for organizing and argued for different paces and tactics for gaining power in the New Afrikan national territory. To exploit such disagreements, the FBI sent false letters about the leadership, such as one from "A Concerned Brother," to increase distrust even as provocateurs used Imari's reputation for seeking a faster and more aggressive approach to suggest that he was a government informant or agent.[56]

Although it was among New Afrikans' original goals, the independence movement's evolution through conflict, repression, and growth also contributed to the pursuit of attaining United Nations recognition. Political scientist James C. Roberts explains that in order for any "political community to be sovereign," it must adhere in some degree to the following principles: It must have territory and a population; it must demonstrate "effective rule over that territory and population"; and it must gain the "recognition of other nation-states."[57] Well-versed in international law and determined to use it to their advantage, New Afrikans attempted to live up to these criteria while seeking support for their objectives.

The New Afrikan Praxis

The foundational documents provide a basic understanding of what producers of NAPS valued in the pursuit of their New Society. They valued Black Power through the attainment of an independent nation-state. To this end, New Afrikans wanted to prepare potential citizenry for the struggles involved in achieving self-determination. Two ways, in addition to their organizational structure, can be considered for how New Afrikans put their distinct ideas into practice. The RNA's "nation-building classes" and interracial solidarity efforts indicate some ways that participants of the independence movement imagined and realized their goals.

Nation-Building Classes

Before a person could become a New Afrikan citizen, the PG-RNA required that he or she go through nation-building classes. Bokeba Trice describes nation-building classes as sessions that "explained the relationship between land and power. . . . How the land basically produced all of the resources that [New Afrikans] needed to be in control of—to survive as a people." He insists until "we could get control of the land then we would always be dependent on outside sources for our power."[58] As political education for local communities, New Afrikan leaders intended to use these classes to prepare recruits for revolutionary struggles and lifestyles that departed from what they had experienced in the United States. To that end, there were several specific goals.

First, class facilitators gave prospective citizens an orientation in which they learned about the Provisional Government and the founding documents. Next, potential recruits learned the "History of White atrocities against Black people in the modern era," as explained in texts like W. E. B. Du Bois's *World and Africa*, Herbert Aptheker's *Documentary History of the Negro People in the United States*, and Ralph Ginzburg's *100 Years of Lynching*.[59] Taken together, such texts provided potential citizens with a historical and theoretical grounding in the circumstances African people faced in the United States and the world. The use of primary documents, as seen in Aptheker's and Ginzburg's edited volumes, indicates that New Afrikan leaders likely wanted recruits to learn to think critically about history by engaging directly with the voices of the oppressor and oppressed. Considering the documents included in those texts, it is conceivable that instructors highlighted their ancestors' multiple attempts to gain the rights of citizenship but to no avail. Instead, they saw kidnappings and (re)enslavement, harsh Black Codes and slave laws, brutal and spectacular lynchings, sexual assault, and more. Such institutionalized viciousness reinforced Anglo-Americans' attitudes toward the prospect of Black citizenship and inclusion. Further, Du Bois's research indicates that although the specific conditions of African Americans may have been distinct, they were not significantly different from what African people throughout the world faced under European and American domination.

Although nation-building classes were critical of White supremacy and the actions of European people, the use of scholars such as Aptheker and Ginzburg, both Jewish, may have allowed participants to focus their major critiques on systems of oppression. Consequently, they would have placed the actions and ideologies of specific individuals and groups within this broader context. Aptheker, Ginzburg, and other White leftist thinkers may have reminded them that some people of European descent made useful and enduring allies. Providing space for potential citizens to develop a clear perspective about the history of setbacks and gains, enemies and friends allowed participants to develop their own analyses about the historical trajectory of Black people leading up to the 1968 Black Government Conference.

After becoming oriented with the need for Black liberation, aspiring citizens delved deeper into NAPS. They studied and discussed Imari Obadele's books *Revolution and Nation Building* and *War in America* and Malcolm X's "Message to the Grassroots." Students also read texts "dealing specifically with the emergence of modern nations (including White racist nations), Algeria, Ghana, Guinea, Tanzania, the Congo-Kinshasa, Australia, Cyprus, Israel, Rhodesia, Union of South Africa, Canada, India, China, and Cuba."[60] Matching such a comprehensive study of contemporary nationalisms with guided investigation of African people's condition in the United States prepared students to think critically about American citizenship and determine their collective destiny.

Finally, instructors taught budding citizens about how the PG-RNA codified the definition of "New Afrikan." The RNA constitution provides that all African-descended peoples in the United States were "deemed to be citizens of the Republic of New Africa unless and until their actions or explicit statements indicate otherwise." Because most African-descended peoples in the United States did not self-identify as New Afrikans, whether by choice or ignorance about the option, RNA members had to find a way to distinguish New Afrikan independence advocates from the Black masses. First and foremost, conscious New Afrikans, or "Citizens of Record," went through "Nation-Building and

Orientation Courses." The *Government Administration* handbook delineated a list of behaviors and actions to aid further in this identification process and provide RNA citizens with guidelines for their daily practice. The sections "A Clear Understanding of What All Citizens Must Do" and "A Clear Understanding of What the Individual Must Do" list nine responsibilities, including paying taxes, studying RNA literature and current world events, selling and distributing RNA newspapers, and being "<u>a missionary</u>" who carries "out the basic, simple RNA message to all Black people with whom one come[s] in contact." Further, a missionary "must set an example in living up to the New African Creed and in industriousness, perseverance, constancy, and revolutionary fervor which [he or she] may then rightly expect from other citizens."[61] In sum, nation-building classes provided an opportunity for potential New Afrikans to educate themselves about a range of historical, legal, and sociological topics and to think critically about their status in the United States. These meetings and the curriculum that guided them also helped New Afrikans think about New Afrikan statehood and begin to form bonds with similarly oppressed nations.

Interracial Coalitions

The identification as a colonized African nation prompted New Afrikans to form alliances with peoples who sought sovereignty, restitution, and/or independence from an outside force. They argued that liberating the RNA from the United States would strike a significant blow to Western imperialism, which would aid in the demise of oppression throughout the world. Simultaneously, they claimed that their liberation was dependent on forming and maintaining alliances with other nations that could aid in the struggle for Black liberation. The PG-RNA was especially concerned with other colonized groups within the United States. The Code of Umoja states:

> It shall be the policy of the Provisional Government to recognize the just <u>claims</u> of the American Indian nations and other oppressed nations for land in North America. It shall be the policy of the [P]rovisional Government to negotiate with the American Indian Nations the claims which conflict with the claims of the New Afrikan nation and to resolve these claims in the spirit of justice, brotherhood, and mutual revolutionary commitment to the human and natural rights of all oppressed nations in North America.[62]

Given New Afrikans' self-identification as paper-citizens of the United States, it comes as no surprise that the RNA Declaration of Independence, creed, and other such documents emphasize New Afrikans' respect for and support of other oppressed groups' struggles for self-determination. As indicated in the passage above, New Afrikans were especially eager to make negotiations with indigenous nations whose claims to land preceded those of the RNA.

As part of their recognition of indigenous nations' struggles and demands, the RNA used precedents set by treaties between Native Americans and the United States to argue for New Afrikan liberation and to strategize ways to fund preliberated New Afrikan communities.[63] Periodicals like the *New Afrikan Journal* occasionally ran sympathetic articles reporting on the historical and contemporary struggles Native Americans have faced. In one notable article, the author details various ways that the Bureau of Indian Affairs curtailed the sovereignty and self-determination of Native Americans through its policies on elections, education, and reservations. Characterizing their struggles as "war," the author seeks to draw parallels between American Indian and New Afrikan battles against a common oppressor. Also along those lines, the Washington, DC, unit of the Provisional Government issued a statement supporting "the Liberation Struggle of the indigenous peoples of North America" and proclaiming African and Native people "shall dwell on the land in prosperity and harmony."[64] Further, the Minister of Foreign Affairs and other PG-RNA officers initiated concrete dialogues and negotiations with American Indian movement activists with regard to New Afrikans' anticipated acquisition of land in the five states.[65]

Similarly, RNA activists and Puerto Rican liberation fighters have had at least some contact and shows of solidarity. In mutually amicable statements, Rafael Cancel Miranda and Imari Obadele identify the rights of New Afrikans and Puerto Ricans to land and independence. Published articles exclaiming "Free Puerto Rico!" and praising the actions of people such as Marie Torres, Oscar Collazo, and Lolita Lebron litter New Afrikan publications. One article lists the various actions Puerto Ricans carried out in the name of independence. The article expresses solidarity by detailing the repressive actions committed against Puerto Rican liberationists, drawing parallels between New Afrikan liberation and a global revolution against imperialism. New Afrikan People's Organization cofounder Ahmed Obafemi brought these claims together in a 1981 speech. In arguing that the New Afrikan goal was to liberate their territory in the Deep South, he also affirmed and pledged to assist Chicanos, Indigenous nations, and Puerto Ricans in the securing the lands that their movements claimed.[66]

The RNA vocally supported many other struggles for self-determination and independence since its founding in 1968. Even though New Afrikans' penchant for thinking of their own liberation in terms of global revolution fits squarely with the mood of the Black Power era, noteworthy nuances distinguished them from their contemporaries. New Afrikans believed a worldwide revolution against colonialism, imperialism, and White supremacy would shift both the world economic structure and the very organization of United States society. Although their solutions to race relations, poverty, education, and many other issues fell within the spectrum of leftist perspectives popular at the time, New Afrikans diverged from their contemporaries insofar as they rejected inclusion within the imagined postrevolution United States. Instead, they argued that they could only achieve true liberation when New Afrikan people controlled their own sovereign and independent territory, the Republic of New Afrika. They also looked forward to independent Puerto Rico, the restoration of Aztlán, and the liberation of indigenous nations.

Conclusion

New Afrikans participated in a revolutionary discourse that was unique to the 1960s and 1970s. They were attentive to the historical trajectory of struggle within the African diaspora, conscious of contemporary independence movements in Africa, and grounded in the immediate needs of Black people in America. This allowed them to draw on the major concepts and symbols of their time while reshaping them to fit their specific agenda. The RNA paralleled some of the formation's contemporaries, but their pursuit of full independence and statehood—not just tactical separation—caused them to stand out. Additionally, everything from the PG-RNA's organizational structure to their political education led New Afrikans to conclusions that distinguished them from the Black Power activists around them.

Notes

From *Free the Land: The Republic of New Afrika and the Pursuit of a Black Nation-State* by Edward Onaci. Copyright © 2020 by the University of North Carolina Press. Used by permission of the publisher. www.uncpress.org.

1. "The Flag of Our Nation," n.d., ca. 1970, Radical Information Project [hereafter RIP], in author's possession, original underline. A note about word usage and spelling: RNA documentation contends that all African-descended people born in the United States are New Afrikans. However, I only use the term "New Afrikan" to refer to "conscious citizens" of the RNA. I designate all other people of African descent in the United States as "Black," "African American," and so forth. The Provisional Government decided on November 30, 1975, to spell "New Afrika" with a *k* rather than a *c*. Because this has been their preferred spelling for most of their existence, I use the *k* spelling to refer to the Provisional Government of the Republic of New Afrika (PG-RNA) and to New Afrikans prior to the actual spelling change, except when quoting texts that utilize the letter *c*. See "Black Nation Day," (Washington, DC) *New Afrikan*, March 1976, 2, Nkechi Taifa's personal papers, private collection, Washington, DC [hereafter Taifa Papers].

2. For education, see Ibram H. Rogers, *The Black Campus Movement: Black Students and the Racial Reconstitution of Higher Education, 1965–1972* (New York: Palgrave, 2012), and Russell Rickford, *We Are an African People: Independent Education, Black Power, and the Radical Imagination* (Oxford: Oxford University Press, 2016). For Black electoral empowerment, see Cedric Johnson, *Revolutionaries to Race Leaders: Black Power and the Making of African American Politics* (Minneapolis: University of Minnesota Press, 2007); Robyn C. Spencer, *The Revolution Has Come: Black Power, Gender, and the Black*

Panther Party in Oakland (Durham, NC: Duke University Press, 2016), esp. chap. 6; and Jakobi Williams, *From the Bullet to the Ballot: The Illinois Chapter of the Black Panther Party and Racial Coalition Politics in Chicago* (Chapel Hill: University of North Carolina Press, 2013). For African American spirituality, see Angela D. Dillard, *Faith in the City: Preaching Radical Social Change in Detroit* (Ann Arbor: University of Michigan Press, 2007); Tracey E. Hucks, *Yoruba Traditions and African American Religious Nationalism* (Albuquerque: University of New Mexico Press, 2012); Jeffry O. G. Ogbar, *Black Power: Radical Politics and African American Identity* (Baltimore: Johns Hopkins University Press, 2004); and Ula Taylor, "Elijah Muhammad's Nation of Islam: Separatism, Regendering, and a Secular Approach to Black Power after Malcolm X (1965–1975)," in *Freedom North: Black Freedom Struggles outside the South, 1940–1980*, ed. Jeanne Theoharis and Komozi Woodard (New York: Palgrave, 2003), 177–198. For information on the origins of Kwanzaa, see Keith Mayes, "'A Holiday of Our Own': Kwanzaa, Cultural Nationalism, and the Promotion of a Black Power Holiday, 1966–1985," in *The Black Power Movement: Rethinking the Civil Rights–Black Power Era*, ed. Peniel E. Joseph (New York: Routledge, 2006), 229–249.

3. "What Is the Republic of New Africa?" n.d., folder 4, bay 1, series 3, box 1, Republic of New Africa Collection, Mississippi Department of Archives and History, Jackson. See also Christian Davenport, *How Social Movements Die: Repression and Demobilization of the Republic of New Africa* (New York: Cambridge University Press, 2015); Akinyele Omowale Umoja, *We Will Shoot Back: Armed Resistance in the Mississippi Freedom Movement* (New York: New York University Press), 186–194.

4. Stuart Hall, "The Problem of Ideology: Marxism without Guarantees," in *Stuart Hall: Critical Dialogues in Cultural Studies*, ed. Kuan-Hsing Chen and David Morley (London: Routledge, 1996), 25–26.

5. Michael C. Dawson, *Black Visions: The Roots of Contemporary African-American Political Ideologies* (Chicago: University of Chicago Press, 2001), 4.

6. Edward Onaci, *Free the Land: The Republic of New Afrika and the Struggle for the Pursuit of a Black Nation-State* (Chapel Hill: University of North Carolina Press, 2020).

7. Republic of New Africa, "Declaration of Independence," [Washington, DC] *New Afrikan*, March 1976, 2, Taifa Papers.

8. Ibid.

9. RNA, Declaration.

10. Ibid.

11. Beverly Guy-Sheftall, *Words of Fire: An Anthology of African-American Feminist Thought* (New York: New Press, 1995), 231–240; Deborah K. King, "Multiple Jeopardy, Multiple Consciousness: The Context of a Black Feminist Ideology," *Signs* 14, no. 1 (1988): 42–72; and Kimberly Springer, *Living for the Revolution: Black Feminist Organizations, 1968–1980* (Durham, NC: Duke University Press, 2005).

12. See Cynthia A. Young, *Soul Power: Culture, Radicalism, and the Making of the U.S. Third World* (Durham, NC: Duke University Press, 2006), 12–15. A debate occurred in the 1970s regarding the idea that Black Americans align themselves with non-Black groups. Even as the PG-RNA, Congress of African People, and Black Panther Party began to consider themselves at the forefront of global revolution, Haki Madhubuti,

Shawna Maglangbayan, and others cautioned against the embrace of ideas and actions that did not focus on the liberation of African and African-descended peoples first and foremost. See Haki R. Madhubuti, "The Latest Purge: The Attack on Black Nationalism and Pan-Afrikanism by the New Left, the Sons and Daughters of the Old Left," *Black Scholar* 6, no. 1 (1974): 55; Shawna Maglangbayan, *Garvey, Lumumba, and Malcolm: National-Separatists* (Chicago: Third World, 1972), 88.

13. Dawson, *Black Visions*, 7–11.

14. Laurent Dubois and John D. Garrigus, *Slave Revolution in the Caribbean, 1789–1804: A Brief History with Documents* (Boston: Bedford, 2006).

15. See, for example, C. L. R. James, *The Black Jacobins: Toussaint L'Ouverture and the San Domingo Revolution*, 2nd rev. ed. (New York: Vintage, 1989).

16. James A. Geschwender and Judson L. Jeffries, "The League of Revolutionary Black Workers," in *Black Power in the Belly of the Beast*, ed. Judson L. Jeffries (Urbana: University of Illinois Press, 2007), 151.

17. Huey P. Newton with the assistance of J. Herman Blake, *Revolutionary Suicide* (New York: Harcourt, 1973), iv.

18. "A Short History of the Black Nation in North America," ca. 1980, 8, Taifa Papers.

19. There has been debate recently regarding whether this line promotes ableism. See "Some More Thoughts on the Creed: What It Means to Be 'Deaf, Dumb and Blind,'" *Re-Build! A New Afrikan Independence Periodical*, Fall 2018, 5–6.

20. Peniel E. Joseph, *Waiting 'til the Midnight Hour: A Narrative History of Black Power in America* (New York: Holt, 2006); William W. Sales Jr., *From Civil Rights to Black Liberation: Malcolm X and the Organization of Afro-American Unity* (Boston: South End, 1994); William L. Van Deburg, *New Day in Babylon: The Black Power Movement and American Culture, 1965–1975* (Chicago: University of Chicago Press, 1992).

21. "The New Afrikan Creed: Fundamental Precepts That Guide the New Afrikan Independence Movement" (New Orleans, LA: Ukali Mwendo, n.d.); "Political and Philosophical Documents of the Independence Movement Which Guide the Work of the Provisional Government of the Republic of New Afrika," n.d., General Kuratibisha X Ali Rashid's personal papers, private collection, Miami, FL [hereafter Rashid Papers]; Provisional Government Republic of New Afrika, "The Republic of New Afrika: Land Independence, Self-Determination," n.d., Taifa Papers.

22. See, for example, Nkechi Taifa, "The Spirit of Author McDuffie," *New Afrikan Journal: The Official Voice of the Malcolm X Party*, 1980, 35.

23. See "The Oath," n.d., Rashid Papers; Republic of New Africa, *Short Official Basic Documents*, n.d., Taifa Papers, 3.

24. There has always been some tension about how advocates and opponents define "Black Power." See Stokely Carmichael (Kwame Ture) and Charles V. Hamilton, *Black Power: The Politics of Liberation* (New York: Vintage, 1992); Peniel E. Joseph, "The Black Power Movement: A State of the Field," *Journal of American History* 96, no. 3 (2009): 751–776; Martin Luther King Jr., *Where Do We Go from Here: Chaos or Community?* (Boston: Beacon Press, 1967).

25. "Message to Our Young Brothers and Sisters," frames 671–672, reel 10, *The Black Power Movement Part 3: The Papers of the Revolutionary Action Movement, 1962–1996*, ed. John Bracey Jr. and Sharon Harley (Bethesda, MD: LexisNexis, 2004).

26. Ashley D. Farmer, *Remaking Black Power: How Black Women Transformed an Era* (Chapel Hill: University of North Carolina Press, 2017), 172–187; Douglas G. Glasgow, "Sons of Watts," and Komozi Woodard, "Imamu Baraka, the Newark Congress of African People, and Black Power Politics," in *Black Power in the Belly of the Beast*, ed. Judson L. Jeffries (Urbana: University of Illinois Press, 2007), 119–124 and 53–54, respectively.

27. Stokely Carmichael (Kwame Ture), *Stokely Speaks: From Black Power to Pan-Africanism* (Chicago: Lawrence Hill Books, 2007), 202; Nishani Frazier, *Harambee City: The Congress of Racial Equality in Cleveland and the Rise of Black Power Populism* (Fayetteville: University of Arkansas Press, 2017), xxvi; Russell Rickford, "'We Can't Grow Food on All This Concrete': The Land Question, Agrarianism, and Black Nationalist Thought in the Late 1960s and 1970s," *Journal of American History* 103, no. 4 (March 2017): 963–972; Christopher Strain, "Soul City, North Carolina: Black Power, Utopia, and the African American Dream," *Journal of African American History* 89, no. 1 (2004): 57–74; Monica M. White, "'A pig and a garden': Fannie Lou Hamer and the Freedom Farms Cooperative," *Food and Foodways: Explorations in the History and Culture of Human Nourishment* 25, no. 1 (2017): 27–29, https://doi.org/10.1080/07409710.2017.127 0647; Van Deburg, *New Day in Babylon*, 132–140.

28. For useful inquiry into this matter, see Spencer, *Revolution Has Come*, 84–85, 141–142; Newton, *Revolutionary Suicide*, 118; Bobby Seale, *Seize the Time: The Story of the Black Panther Party and Huey P. Newton* (Random House, 1970; Baltimore: Black Classic, 1991), 68, citations are to the 1991 edition.

29. Huey P. Newton to the RNA, September 13, 1969, in *The Black Panthers Speak*, ed. Philip S. Foner (New York: Da Capo, 1995), 72.

30. Huey P. Newton, "Speech Delivered at Boston College: November 18, 1970," *To Die for the People: The Writings of Huey P. Newton* (New York: Random, 1972), 33.

31. Safiya Bukhari, *The War Before: The True Life Story of Becoming a Black Panther, Keeping the Faith in Prison & Fighting for Those Left Behind* (New York: Feminist, 2010), 18–19; Assata Shakur, *Assata: An Autobiography* (Chicago: Lawrence Hill Books, 1987), 225–226; Bilal Sunni-Ali, conversation with Paul Karolczyk and Edward Onaci, Jackson, Mississippi, March 27, 2010.

32. Congress of African Peoples, "Republic of New Africa: Proposed Resolutions for Political Liberation Workshop," n.d., folder 13, box 159–11, Civil Rights Documentation Project, Moorland-Spingarn Research Center, Howard University, Washington, DC.

33. Onaci, *Free the Land*.

34. For an explanation of ubuntu, see Desmond Tutu, *No Future without Forgiveness* (New York: Doubleday, 1999), 34–35.

35. Julius K. Nyerere, *Freedom and Socialism: A Selection from Writings and Speeches* (Oxford: Oxford University Press, 1972), 2. For a theoretical explanation and critique of this concept, see Julius K. Nyerere, *Ujamaa: Essays on Socialism* (London: Oxford University Press, 1968), 106–110.

36. There exists an implied distinction between New Afrikans and Black Americans that is important to consider here briefly because it follows in the tradition of African people in the United States trying to adequately define and name themselves in ways that are empowering. Often, the attempt to provide African people with a group name took into consideration their history of being of African ancestry, though also with some

European and Native American parentage. New Afrikans participated in this practice but framed their group-name choice in a way that would allow them to become independent of the American nation-state and culture. See Edward Onaci, "Revolutionary Identities: New Afrikans and Name Choices in the Black Power Movement," *Souls: A Critical Journal of Black Politics, Culture, and Society* 17, no. 1–2 (2015): 67–89.

37. The document's authors discuss the eight sections as though a human being—a revolutionary sage—on a spiritual journey fraught with obstacles challenging that person's ability to stay on his or her chosen path. In his unpublished autobiography, Imari Obadele uses strikingly similar wording to describe his views on New Afrikans' dedication to liberation. See Imari Obadele, *Seize the Land! The Autobiography of the Primary Apostle of Malcolm X Detailing How the Foundations Were Laid for a Black Struggle for Independent Land in the United States,* unpublished ms., ca. 1971, 24, Taifa Papers.

38. *New African Ujamaa: The Economics of the Republic of New Africa* (San Francisco: Marcus, 1970), 1–2.

39. Ibid., 7.

40. Republic of New Africa, *Government Administration*, n.d., 18, folder 1, box 1, series 1, bay 1, Republic of New Africa Collection, Mississippi Department of Archives and History, Jackson.

41. Ali Mazrui, "Tanzaphilia," *Transition* 31 (June–July 1967), 20–26.

42. See Charlie Cobb, *African Notebook: Views on Returning 'Home'* (Chicago: Institute of Positive Education, 1972); David Graham Du Bois, "Afro-American Militants in Africa," *Black World* 21 no. 4 (1972): 4–11; Joyce Ladner, "Tanzanian Women and Nation Building," *Black Scholar* 3, no. 4 (1972); Fanon Che Wilkins, "'Black Power in the Belly of the Beast': Black Power, Anti-Imperialism, and the African Liberation Solidarity Movement, 1968–1975" (PhD diss., New York University, 2001).

43. See, for example, Kathleen Neal Cleaver, "Back to Africa: The Evolution of the International Section of the Black Panther Party (1969–1972)," in *Black Panther Party: Reconsidered*, ed. Charles E. Jones (Baltimore: Black Classic, 1998), 211–254; Seth M. Markle, "'We Are Not Tourists': The Black Power Movement and the Making of Socialist Tanzania" (PhD diss., New York University, 2011); Wilkins, "'In the Belly of the Beast,'" 59–116. Haki Madhubuti, after having an opportunity to speak with Nyerere, decided that instead of seeking independence, it was more fruitful to develop Black institutions in the United States that could then service African Americans and Africans in other countries. Haki R. Madhubuti, conversation with author, Chicago, Illinois, December 14, 2010. Also, Tanzania was a haven for revolutionary activity and a base for forces such as Frente de Libertacao de Mocambique (FRELIMO).

44. Nyerere, *Ujamaa*, 3–4. Elsewhere, Nyerere claims that "it most certainly is wrong if we want the wealth and the power so that we can dominate somebody . . . [To do so] is completely foreign to us, and it is incompatible with the socialist society we want to build here." Nyerere, *Ujamaa*, 6.

45. Ibid., 4–5.

46. Republic of New Africa, "Declaration of Independence," and RNA, *Anti-Depression Program of the Republic of New Africa: To End Poverty, Dependence, Cultural Malnutrition, and Crime among Black People in the United States and Promote Inter-Racial Peace*

(Jackson, MS: Republic of New Africa, 1972), 1; and "N'COBRA Fact Sheet," n.d., Rashid Papers. Malcolm X Grassroots Movement (MXGM), a New Afrikan organization that grew directly from the New Afrikan People's Organization, continues to weigh in on conversations about restitution for enslavement, discrimination, terrorism, and other US harms to African-descended people. When the Movement for Black Lives released its "Reparations Toolkit" in July 2019, MXGM issued an open letter explaining the importance of acknowledging land as part of any reparations agreement. See Movement for Black Lives, "Reparations Toolkit," https://policy.m4bl.org/wp-content/uploads/2019/07/Reparations-Now-Toolkit-FINAL.pdf, accessed July 27, 2019; Malcolm X Grassroots Movement, "Malcolm X Grassroots Movement Position on Reparations," July 23, 2019, in author's possession courtesy of Malcolm X Grassroots Movement.

47. Julius K. Nyerere, "From Uhuru to Ujamaa," *Africa Today* 21, no. 3 (1974): 3–8.

48. Godfrey Mwakikagile, *Tanzania under Mwalimu Nyerere: Reflections on an African Statesman* (Dar es Salaam, Tanzania: New Africa, 2006), 61–62.

49. Abdul Rahman Mohamed Babu, *African Socialism or Socialist Africa?* (London: Zed, 1981), xv, 111. For recent reflections on the successes and failures of Ujamaa in Tanzania, see Mwakikagile, *Tanzania under Mwalimu Nyerere*, esp. chap. 5.

50. *New African Ujamaa*, 13–14.

51. Imari Abubakari Obadele, *The Malcolm X Doctrine*, rev. ed. (Detroit, MI: Malcolm X Society, 1968).

52. Republic of New Africa, *Government Administration*, 32.

53. General Kuratibisha X. Ali Rashid, interview with author, Jackson, Mississippi, March 30, 2009.

54. "New Detroit to Probe Church Raid Charges," *Detroit (MI) News*, April 8, 1969, 2A, 4A, RIP; John Griffith, "Cavanaugh Defends Police Acts," *Detroit (MI) Free Press*, April 2, 1969, RIP. See Al Stark, "'Shot on the Floor': Bethel Raid Victim Talks," *Detroit (MI) News*, April 4, 1969, 3A, RIP; and Lee Winfrey, "Police Tell of Shooting in Church," *Detroit (MI) Free Press*, April 9, 1969, 1A, 8A, RIP. See also the Detroit Police Commissioner's 24th District Reporter: Del Rio—Reports, folder 27, box 188, New Detroit Records, University Archives, Wayne State University, Detroit, Michigan.

55. Provisional Government, Republic of New Afrika, "The Code of Umoja," November 3, 2007, Rashid Papers.

56. FBI director to SAC [special agent in charge], November 22, 1968, Detroit, Michigan, folder 4—Republic of New Africa, box 111, SCRC 173, Liberation News Service Records, Temple University Libraries, Philadelphia, Pennsylvania.

57. James Roberts, "Sovereignty," *The Internet Encyclopedia of International Relations*, Department of Political Science, Towson University, Towson, Maryland, http://www.towson.edu/polsci/irencyc/sovreign.htm, accessed February 26, 2010.

58. Bokeba Trice, interview by author, Detroit, Michigan, March 4, 2009.

59. Republic of New Africa, *Government Administration*, 18.

60. Ibid., 17–18.

61. Ibid., 18–20, original emphasis. If no consulate is established where one desired to become a citizen of record, that person could demonstrate to a PG official that they had educated themselves and then take the oath before such an official. Republic of New Africa, *Government Administration*, 31, underlining in the original.

62. Provisional Government, Republic of New Afrika, "The Code of Umoja," 10–11; underlining in the original.

63. Republic of New Afrika, "Forming Municipal, Country, and Parish Councils in the Kush District, Republic of New Africa," January 1976, folder 1, box 1, series 1, bay 1, Republic of New Africa Collection, Mississippi Department of Archives and History, Jackson; PG-RNA, *A People's Struggle: An Analytical Outline of the Struggle of Afrikans in North America* (Washington, DC, 1986), Taifa Papers.

64. "Sovereignty for Native Americans," *New Afrikan Journal*, ca. 1980, 19. See also "Free Leonard Peltier," *New Afrikan Journal*, special ed., 1980, 20–21; Republic of New Afrika, *Black Nation Day Commemorative Journal*, ca. March 1986, Taifa Papers.

65. Kwame-Osagyefo Kalimara to Robert Robideau, September 7, 1983, Taifa Papers.

66. An image of both incarcerated men clasping hands accompanies the statements. See Rafael Cancel Miranda, "Solidarity Statement," *New Afrikan Journal*, July 6, 1979, and Imari Obadele, "Solidarity Statement Reply," *New Afrikan Journal*, ca. 1980, 15–16, Rashid Papers; "Free Puerto Rico!" *New Afrikan Journal*, ca. 1982, 20, 31; "Puerto Rican Liberation," *New Afrikan Journal,* special ed., 1980, 21; "Re: The Puerto Rico Struggle," *New Afrikan*, December 25, 1976, 9–10; Ahmed Obafemi, "Building Strategic Alliances and People's War: National Liberation Inside the U.S. Imperialist State," New Afrikan Institute of Political Education, *Towards the Liberation of the Black Nation: Organize for New Afrikan People's War!* 1982, 17–22, *Freedom Archives*, www.freedomarchives.org.

CHAPTER 10

"A CERTAIN BOND BETWEEN THE COLORED PEOPLES"

INTERNATIONALISM AND THE BLACK INTELLECTUAL TRADITION

KEISHA N. BLAIN

In his 1937 speech "The Meaning of Japan," W. E. B. Du Bois emphasized the cultural and political exchanges and historical connections between African Americans and Japanese people. In the years preceding World War II, the well-known civil rights leader reminded people of African descent in the United States that the challenges they faced on the national front were deeply intertwined with the struggles for freedom among people of color worldwide. Reminiscent of his earlier statements in *The Souls of Black Folk* (1903), Du Bois brought attention to the global color line, the racial hierarchy that placed people of color at the bottom and Whites on the top.[1] Reflecting his commitment to global racial solidarity, Du Bois emphasized what he described as a "certain bond between the colored peoples because of worldwide prejudice."[2] Building upon a long tradition and history dating back to the era of the American Revolution, Du Bois's statement underscores his global vision and endorsement of Black internationalism—a commitment to "universal emancipation" unlimited by "national, imperial, continental, [racial,] or oceanic boundaries."[3] Du Bois understood that the struggle for Black rights in the United States could not be divorced from the global struggles for freedom in Asia, Africa, the Caribbean, and other parts of the globe. For this reason, he devoted his life to endorsing Black internationalism and urged Black Americans to forge networks and pursue political collaborations with other people of color worldwide.[4]

This internationalist vision, personified by Du Bois, was a fundamental aspect of the Black intellectual tradition during the twentieth century. Like Du Bois, countless Black men and women articulated Black internationalism through various avenues, including journalism and overseas travel. Recognizing that the condition of Black men and women in the United States was "but a local phase of a world problem," Black activists articulated global visions of freedom and employed a range of strategies and tactics intent on shaping foreign policies and influencing world events.[5] The expressions of Black internationalism during the twentieth century were profoundly shaped by the rise of various global movements—the Universal Negro Improvement Association (UNIA) and the Communist International (Comintern), among them. They were also shaped by key historical developments of the period, including the Russo-Japanese War (1904–1905), the Italo-Ethiopian War (1935), World War I (1914–1918), the Great Depression (1929–1939), World War II (1939–1945), and the modern civil rights–Black Power era.

Drawing on various primary sources—archival material, historical newspapers, and government records—this essay highlights Black men's and women's internationalist ideas, emphasizing their engagement with Japan during the early twentieth century. Amidst the sociopolitical upheavals of the period, African Americans from all walks of life deployed internationalist rhetoric to underscore the "shared tradition of resistance . . . and racial exploitation and oppression" between people of African descent in the United States and other non-Whites globally.[6] Through an array of writings and speeches, they articulated global visions of freedom and worked to build transnational and transracial alliances with other people of color in order to secure civil and human rights.

Although the subject is not new, the field of Black internationalism has grown in leaps and bounds in recent years. Since the publication of Robin D. G. Kelley's groundbreaking essay "But a Local Phase of a World Problem" (1999), scholars have been paying greater attention to the global dimensions of the long Black freedom struggle, drawing parallels between the experiences of African-descended people in the United States and people of color in Africa, Asia, Europe, and other parts of the globe.[7] Utilizing a range of sources and methodological approaches, scholars are moving further away from a nation-state level of analysis, situating internationalism as a central feature of the Black experience in the United States. The works of Gerald Horne, Brenda Gayle Plummer, Penny Von Eschen, Michael O. West, Carol Anderson, Nico Slate, Minkah Makalani, and others highlight the myriad ways African Americans historically linked national and geopolitical concerns; these works also shed light on how these men and women often drew on diverse political strategies of resistance from activists abroad.[8] Recent studies by Carole Boyce Davies, Barbara Ransby, Erik S. McDuffie, Dayo F. Gore, Cheryl Higashida, Keisha N. Blain, and others address the crucial role Black women played in leading internationalist movements and shaping Black internationalist discourses during the twentieth century.[9]

Historical works on Afro-Asia—including those by Kelley, Horne, Marc S. Gallicchio, Reginald Kearney, Vijay Prashad, Bill Mullen, Yuichiro Onishi, and Robeson Taj Frazier—have significantly enhanced our understanding of Black internationalism during the twentieth century.[10] These works offer key insights into the historical struggles and strategies of resistance shared by people of African descent and those of Asian descent. These writings chart the varied political collaborations and ideological links between individual Black and Asian activists—on national and international levels—as well as the central role various groups and institutions played in fostering these links. Significantly, these studies also shed light on "how race, nationality, ethnicity, gender, and geopolitics mediated, impacted, and curtailed Afro-Asian solidarity."[11] By centering Afro-Asia as a significant area of scholarly inquiry, these works capture the richness and complexities of internationalism in the twentieth-century Black intellectual tradition.

Building on this body of scholarship, this chapter highlights the key role both state and nonstate actors played in shaping Black internationalist movements and discourses during a tumultuous era of US history.[12] Paying particular attention to how Black intellectuals and activists engaged Japan, this essay expands the existing body of work on Afro-Asia and Black internationalism, more broadly. Although much of the literature on Black internationalism privileges the political activities of the Black middle class and elite, this essay captures the wide array of Black engagement in internationalism during the early twentieth century. The chapter shows how Black activists from various socioeconomic backgrounds—Madam C. J. Walker, John Q. Adams, Marcus Garvey, Hubert Harrison, Mittie Maude Lena Gordon, and Pearl Sherrod, among them—employed a myriad of strategies and tactics to promote Afro-Asian solidarity and Black internationalist politics.

The Roots of Afro-Asia

The historical experiences of peoples of Asian and African descent have been deeply intertwined for centuries. "From the earliest days of the United States," Fred Ho and Bill Mullen explain, "Africans and Asians in the Americas have been linked in a shared tradition of resistance to class and racial exploitation and oppression."[13] In a 1905 speech Du Bois acknowledges the link between the "color line" and "Yellow Peril."[14] The racist "Yellow peril" ideology of the late nineteenth century, which stemmed from White fears and anxieties over Asian immigration, persisted well into the twentieth century and extended beyond national borders. The negative images and stereotypical depictions of Asian cultures that dominated Western mass media mirror the pervasive global racist attitudes toward African Americans and other people of color. Du Bois understood this connection, and during the early twentieth century, he advocated political collaboration and solidarity between peoples of African and Asian descent.[15]

Like Du Bois, countless Black activists in the United States promoted Afro-Asian solidarity as a radical political response to global White supremacy. Japan's victory in the Russo-Japanese War (1904–1905) strengthened this point of view. A watershed moment in the history of Afro-Asian relations, the Russo-Japanese War began in February 1904 over tensions between Russia and Japan concerning territorial claims in Manchuria and Korea and officially ended with the Treaty of Portsmouth on September 5, 1905.[16] For Du Bois and other Black activists, Japan's successful defeat of the Russian military was no small accomplishment. It served as a powerful "example of people who demonstrated the fallacy of white assertions that people of color were innately incompetent or inferior."[17] As a consequence, the Russo-Japanese War sparked a rise in pro-Japanese sentiments among Black men and women across the United States.[18]

These ideas gained increasing currency during World War I (1914–1918), another watershed moment in the history of Black internationalist politics in the United States and other parts of the globe. Far beyond its moniker as the "war to make the world safe for democracy," World War I represented a catalyst for Black internationalist fervor. If the war changed the relationship between US citizens and the state, as historian Christopher Cappazzola has argued, then the war dramatically altered the relationship between Black citizens and the global polity.[19] The millions of Black men and women across the globe who served the war effort—as soldiers and workers—demanded full citizenship rights, recognition, and inclusion in return. Indeed, World War I gave rise to the emergence of a "mobilized" African diaspora—a group of Black men and women in the United States and abroad who maintained a strong sense of race consciousness and who were determined to fight for the democratic rights and privileges they were being denied at home.[20] Echoing the Wilsonian ideals of justice and self-determination, people of African descent in the United States and colonial territories in Africa, Latin America, and the Caribbean demanded the end of discrimination, racism, colonialism, and imperialism.[21]

Significantly, people of African descent understood that the struggles they endured were interconnected with the challenges facing other people of color across the globe. During the early twentieth century, Du Bois, Mary Church Terrell, James Weldon Johnson, and several other race leaders "pushed African Americans to identify their interests with Japanese, Indians, Chinese, and other Asians."[22] This was certainly the case for Black journalist and educator John Q. Adams. Born free in Louisville, Kentucky, in 1848, Adams relocated to St. Paul, Minnesota, in 1886, where he became associate editor, and later owner, of the *Western Appeal* (which became the *Appeal* in 1889).[23] In an open letter to President Woodrow Wilson in December 1918, which was published in the

Appeal in January 1919, Adams promoted Afro-Asian solidarity from his base in Minnesota and called for an end to what he referred to as the "autocracy of color." Through the pages of the *Appeal*, Adams articulated his internationalist political vision and emphasized the links between national and geopolitical concerns. In his open letter to President Wilson, Adams demanded the rights and recognition of people of color in the United States and other parts of the globe: "Through the centuries, the colored races of the globe have been subjected to the most unjust and inhuman treatment by the so-called white peoples." Echoing the rhetoric of self-determination, which US leaders fully supported in words rather than in deeds, Adams called on Wilson to maintain the principles of global democracy—especially in relation to people of color.[24]

In no uncertain terms, Adams articulated a vision of Black internationalism that simultaneously called attention to the problems facing people of color in the United States and abroad. Along these lines, Adams not only appealed to President Wilson to support the political self-determination of India and "all colonies which desire it" but he also brought particular attention to some of the unique challenges facing people of Asian descent in the United States. Adams openly criticized "anti-oriental" immigration policies in the United States and called for the United States to acknowledge the "rights of Japanese and Chinese and Malays to become citizens." He went on to demand the "repeal [of] all laws of the United States, or of any state, in which the words colored, African, Afro-American, Negro, Mulatto, Indian, Japanese or Chinese are used for the purpose [of] making discriminations against the people of any race, nationality, class or creed." Reminiscent of Du Bois's earlier writings, Adams's open letter brought attention to the global color line and called for "the immediate abrogation of any color line restrictions enforced without warrant of law."[25]

The ideas Adams expressed in the *Appeal* newspaper capture the Black internationalist visions of the men and women who helped to establish the International League of Darker Peoples (ILDP). One of the earliest organized efforts to advance Afro-Asian solidarity during the twentieth century, the ILDP was established in 1919 by Madam C. J. Walker, the first African American female millionaire in the United States, along with notable Black leaders, including Jamaican Black nationalist Marcus Garvey and A. Philip Randolph, who later organized the first Black-led labor union.[26] According to historian Judith Stein, the ILDP "proposed to advance the interests of 'darker peoples,' the Third World in present-day language, through 'education, organization, and agitation.'"[27] In January 1919 ILDP leaders met with Japanese editor S. Kurowia—one of the Japanese representatives to the Paris Peace Conference—in which they articulated their unwavering commitment to ending racial prejudice in the United States and abroad.[28]

The ILDP's meeting with Kurowia, while significant, only highlights one aspect of the organization's commitment to Black internationalism. Indeed, the public speeches and writings of ILDP leaders underscore Black intellectuals' global visions of freedom during the early twentieth century. In a 1919 editorial in the *Messenger*, Randolph called on African Americans to "[c]arry the Negro problem out of the United States, at the same time that you present it in the United States. . . . The international method of dealing with problems is the method of the future."[29] Randolph's comments capture his Black internationalist vision—rooted in a belief that the struggle against White supremacy in the United States could not be divorced from the larger struggle against imperialism worldwide.

Garvey, UNIA's leader, expressed similar sentiments during this period. Founded by Garvey in Jamaica in 1914, with the assistance of activist Amy Ashwood, the UNIA was the largest and most influential Pan-Africanist movement promoting Black pride, African redemption (from European colonization), economic self-sufficiency, racial separatism, and political self-determination.[30] While Garvey certainly endorsed Pan-Africanist politics—by emphasizing the belief that African peoples, on the continent and in the diaspora, share a common past and destiny—he maintained a commitment to Black internationalism in the broadest sense of the term.[31] He articulated a global vision of liberation that sought to not only address the concerns of people of African descent but the plight of *all* people of color worldwide.

One of the crucial aspects of Garvey's internationalism was his vision of Afro-Asian solidarity. Through the pages of the *Negro World*, the UNIA's official newspaper, Garvey expressed pro-Japanese sentiments and encouraged political collaborations with Japan. In 1918 the charismatic Black nationalist leader publicly endorsed Afro-Asian solidarity, insisting that the "next war will be between the Negroes and the whites. . . . With Japan to fight with us, we can win such a war."[32] In 1919 Garvey praised Japan's assertiveness and went on to appeal to his supporters to anticipate the "great day . . . of the war of races, when Asia will lead out to defeat Europe."[33] Other Black writers grappled with the significance of Japan in the UNIA's newspaper during this period. In an editorial for the *Negro World*, Harlem radical Hubert Harrison described Japan as "the most powerful" of the "darker nations" and went on to suggest that Japan was "only relevant insofar as it served as 'an index' to advance the ends of black liberation."[34] In another *Negro World* article, "The Line-Up of the Color Line," Harrison endorsed Afro-Asian solidarity and articulated his commitment to Black internationalism: "We need to join hands across the sea. We need to know what they are doing in India; we need to know what they are doing in China; we need to know what they are doing in Africa; and we need to let them know what we are doing over here."[35]

For Harrison, Garvey, and other race leaders, the 1919 Paris Peace Conference provided a crucial space in which to endorse Afro-Asian solidarity and articulate a commitment to Black internationalism. Convened in Paris on January 18, 1919, the conference brought together more than thirty nations for the purpose of establishing peace terms following the end of World War I. Significantly, the conference provided a venue for Black intellectuals and activists to challenge global White supremacy and ensure that the interests of colonized subjects would not be overlooked. In Wilson's Fourteen Points, issued a year before the conference, Black intellectuals found a source of inspiration—they hoped that the peace terms laid out by Wilson would extend to people of African descent and other people of color globally.[36] At the Paris Peace Conference and in the years leading up to it, several race leaders expressed their grievances and demanded the rights and recognition of people of color across the globe. In one instance, leaders of the National Association for the Advancement of Colored People (NAACP) held a mass rally in hopes of bringing "Africa to the attention of the Peace Conference and the civilized world."[37] Linking national concerns to global ones, representatives from the NAACP and other race organizations fought to bring pressure on the delegates at the 1919 conference to address the conditions of colonized people in Africa and other parts of the globe. As historian Yuichiro Onishi has argued, these men and women "were not interested in presenting their political demands without consideration of the rights of Africans and people of African descent to complete their struggle for self-determination."[38]

Visions of Afro-Asian Solidarity during the 1930s

The political demands that activists raised during the era of World War I continued to inform Black political thought and praxis in the decades to follow. The 1930s, in particular, gave rise to the proliferation of Black internationalist political organizations, which provided platforms from which African Americans could build alliances with Asian activists in the global struggle against White supremacy. These organizations included the Pacific Movement of the Eastern World (PMEW), the Development of Our Own (TDOO), and the Peace Movement of Ethiopia (PME). Building on the pro-Japanese sentiments that circulated in Black communities in the aftermath of the Russo-Japanese War, the leaders of these organizations viewed Japan as a model and potential military ally in the struggle against global White supremacy.[39] According to historian Gerald Horne, many Black leaders during this period "looked to Japan as a living and breathing refutation of the very basis of white supremacy, that is, that one had to be of a 'pure European descent' in order to construct an advanced society."[40] The 1931 Japanese invasion of Manchuria, though a source of contention, reinforced these pro-Japanese sentiments. Japan's subsequent withdrawal from the League of Nations strengthened this point of view. After facing mounting international criticism for their invasion of Manchuria, leaders of Japan parted ways with the league in 1933 as a direct refutation of Western control. Japan's withdrawal, combined with the Manchurian invasion and earlier victories in the Russo-Japanese War, amplified the place of Japan in the Black political imagination during the twentieth century. By the early 1930s Japan had become a "symbol of pride for the darker races."[41]

Across the United States, several Black and Asian activists played a key role in sustaining pro-Japanese sentiments in Black communities. In the immediate aftermath of Japan's invasion of Manchuria in 1931, Asian activist Ashima Takis, whose real name was Policarpio Manansala, began spreading pro-Japanese sentiments in various cities across the country. Born in the Philippines in 1900, Takis had adopted a Japanese persona in an effort to secure approval among Japanese sympathizers in the African American community.[42] In the early 1930s he joined forces with a group of Black and Asian activists in St. Louis, Missouri, to establish the PMEW, a pro-Japanese organization that supported the unification of people of color globally.[43] Representing their commitment to transracial unity, Takis and other PMEW leaders designed a banner with the colors black, brown, and yellow—symbolizing the organization's appeal for people of color across the globe.[44] By the mid-1930s, chapters of the organization could be found in several states, including Arkansas, Pennsylvania, Maryland, and Missouri. The organization drew a following of mostly working-class Black activists who came to embrace the vision of Japan as a "champion of the darker races." For example, Burt Cornish, an elevator operator in St. Louis, joined the organization in the early 1930s and later recalled having an interest in Takis's plans to facilitate Black emigration to Japan. With Takis's promise that impoverished African Americans would find better job opportunities in Japan and equal opportunities in other sectors of society, several thousand African Americans in Missouri became actively involved in the PMEW.[45]

Meanwhile, in Detroit, another Asian activist by the name of Satokata Takahashi was collaborating with local Black activists who were determined to combat racial segregation and discrimination at home and abroad.[46] Born Naka Nakane in Japan in 1875, Takahashi relocated to Victoria, British Columbia, Canada, sometime around 1900 until he and his family relocated to Tacoma, Washington, in 1921.[47] Claiming to be affiliated with the Japanese embassy, Takahashi advocated Afro-Asian solidarity during the early 1930s and began to draw a significant following of Black radical supporters across the urban north. As Takis's movement began to wane in the region, Takahashi's influence rapidly expanded when he became involved in the Detroit-based organization TDOO. Established by George Grimes, a local Black worker, TDOO emerged as a significant political site for working-class Black activists in Detroit to ally with other activists of color—"yellow, brown, and black against all white people."[48] Within a year of its founding, TDOO underwent an organizational shift as "Major" Takahashi became its new leader. Under Takahashi's leadership the organization flourished, drawing an estimated following of ten thousand members—mostly Indians, Filipinos, and people of African descent.[49]

The Black men and women who were active in TDOO embraced an internationalist view of the Black freedom struggle. This was certainly the case for Pearl Sherrod, a working-poor Black woman, who joined the organization during the early 1930s and later became Takahashi's second wife.[50] Born Pearl T. Barnett in Alabama in 1896, Sherrod relocated to Detroit sometime between 1927 and 1929, where she was a member of the newly formed Nation of Islam. In February 1934 she married Takahashi—only a few months after joining TDOO. After Takahashi was arrested for a string of immigration violations and ultimately deported to Japan in April 1934, Sherrod began writing in the *Detroit (MI) Tribune Independent*, the city's dominant Black newspaper during the interwar era.

Through the pages of the newspaper, Sherrod promoted third-world solidarity by identifying the common interests and challenges between Black men and women in the United States and non-Whites in colonial nations in Africa, Asia, Latin America, and the Caribbean. In a June 16, 1934, editorial, "Development of Our Own," in the *Detroit (MI) Tribune Independent*, she explained, "Let me remind you that fully three-fourths of the population of the world are colored people and only one-fourth are white. But the greater part of the colored world is today under white political control." Echoing the same sentiments expressed by Du Bois, Harrison, Garvey, and others, Sherrod called on people of African descent in the United States to actively pursue contact and collaboration with other people of color across the globe. Alluding to the need for African Americans to forge transracial political alliances, Sherrod insisted, "We must make success for ourselves by conjugating ourselves close together for racial unity and equality. Then, and only then will we get power."[51]

In Sherrod's view, Black men and women would be able to increase their power and eradicate global White supremacy by forging political alliances with Asian activists. Sherrod envisioned Afro-Asian solidarity as a viable political strategy in the struggle to eradicate the global color line. In the same 1934 *Detroit (MI) Tribune Independent* editorial, she audaciously declared that African Americans need to join forces with the Japanese: "[O]ur minds have been diseased, and we have tried 'Mr. White's' medicine and failed; tried 'Mr. Black's' medicine and failed. *Now we must try 'Mr. Brown's['] medicine.* . . . No doubt he will cure us of the mental disease which was caused from a lack of organization. [T]hen we can develop ourselves."[52] Sherrod's comments offer a glimpse into her internationalist vision and pragmatic approach to combating global White supremacy.[53] Identifying the apparent shortcomings of mainstream civil rights activism and Black separatism—Mr. White's medicine and Mr. Black's medicine—Sherrod urged readers to try a new antidote—Mr. Brown's medicine, or political collaboration with the Japanese. Sherrod's appeal to Black men and women to eschew the political approaches of mainstream civil rights leaders and Black nationalist activists underscores her broader internationalist vision—one that was "connected . . . to an overarching notion of black liberation beyond any individual nation-state or colonial territory."[54]

Sherrod's internationalist vision was consistent with that of other Black intellectuals and activists of the period, including those who were active in the PME, the largest Black nationalist organization established by a woman in the United States.[55] Founded by Mittie Maude Lena Gordon in Chicago in December 1932, the PME attracted an estimated three hundred thousand supporters during the years of the Great Depression. Born in Louisiana in 1889, Gordon became active in the Garvey movement in Chicago during the 1920s. Determined to advance nationalist politics in the aftermath of Garvey's 1927 deportation—and the subsequent organizational split at the 1929 convention in Kingston, Jamaica—Gordon established the PME, which drew mostly members of the Black working-poor. Gordon, her husband, William, and twelve other African Americans drafted the PME's mission statement in 1932, advocating Black emigration to West Africa, political self-determination, and the "confraternity among all dark races."[56]

Like Sherrod, Gordon viewed Japanese people as potential allies in the global struggles for Black liberation. In the months before she launched the PME, Gordon had even collaborated with Ashima Takis—the Filipino activist who posed as Japanese. Sometime in 1931, Takis met with Gordon in Chicago, where he shared his vision for the PMEW.[57] The two activists collaborated in the months that followed, circulating an emigration petition in Chicago and later in Indiana, until their relationship began to unravel. While records from the Federal Bureau of Investigation (FBI) indicate that the source of the conflict was financial, Gordon attributed the conflict to ideological differences.[58] Recounting the course of events years later, Gordon insisted that she parted ways with Takis when he proposed emigration to Manchuria instead of West Africa.[59] Unlike PMEW member Burt Cornish and other local Black activists in St. Louis, who welcomed the opportunity to relocate to Japan, Gordon rejected the proposal. Although Gordon viewed Japan as a model and potential military ally, she was unwilling to support African American emigration to Japan's newly conquered territory.[60] This is especially significant, revealing some of the ideological tensions among Black internationalists during this period. Although Gordon maintained an interest in Afro-Asian solidarity and, certainly, understood its utility in the global struggle against White supremacy, she was also unwilling to abandon her Pan-Africanist vision of uniting people of African descent in "Liberia or some other place or places in Africa."[61] Notwithstanding the desire to forge transracial and transnational alliances, Gordon reasoned that Africa was the only logical destination for people of African descent.

Even after parting ways with Takis and the PMEW in the early 1930s, Gordon maintained pro-Japanese sentiments and believed that the fight for Black liberation was all encompassing, thereby including all other "dark races" battling racial oppression in a White-dominated world. Mirroring the views of Garvey, Du Bois, Harrison, Sherrod, and others, Gordon believed that the struggle against White supremacy in the United States was intertwined with the larger struggle against imperialism worldwide. Drawing a direct link between the manifestations of White supremacy in the United States and Asia, Gordon argued that the "destruction of the white man in Asia is the destruction of the white man in the United States."[62] In one instance, Gordon emphasized the connection between the challenges facing African-descended people and the plight of Indians: "The India situation is somewhat connected, and the complete freedom of India will bring complete freedom to the American black people, because the same men are holding them in slavery."[63] Her comments bear a striking resemblance to what historian Nico Slate refers to as "colored cosmopolitanism," a shared vision that "transcended traditional racial distinctions, positioning Indians and African Americans together at the vanguard of the 'darker races.'"[64]

Maintaining a commitment to Black internationalism and Afro-Asian solidarity, Gordon attempted to forge new alliances with Asian activists from her base in Chicago. In May 1934 she sent a letter to Kenji Nakauchi, then Japanese Consul General in Chicago, introducing her organization and requesting his support. "We are seeking the assistance and cooperation of your people in this our darkest hour," she explained. "We have suffered untold misery in America over three hundred years and now our condition is far worse than ever." Gordon requested a "private interview" and assured Nakauchi that she would be willing to "meet on [his] own terms."[65] In another letter to Sadao Araki, a Japanese military general, Gordon requested a truce between the PME and "the dark skin people of the East[ern] world" in the event of a war between Japan and the United States.[66] Gordon's comments, while emblematic of her interest in forging transnational alliances, also reveal the contradictory nature of her politics. Although she viewed the Japanese as important allies in the fight against racial oppression, Gordon, like many other Black internationalists during this era, overlooked Japan's own military aggression toward other people of color.

Many of these ideological tensions and contradictions are evident on the pages of the *Negro World* during the 1930s. Although the UNIA had succumbed to fragmentation, the organization's newspaper remained in circulation until 1933 under the editorship of UNIA organizer Maymie Leona Turpeau De Mena. Amidst the sociopolitical turmoil of the era, members of the UNIA actively discussed developments taking place in Japan as well as the kinds of activities in which Japanese leaders were engaged. In an April 18, 1931, article "Japs Succeed; Latins Failed," a writer for the *Negro World* emphasized the imperialist successes of the Japanese and criticized the failed efforts of Spanish and Italian leaders: "Where Italians and Spaniards have failed in the colonization of Brazilian forest regions, the Japanese have made brilliant success." After explaining how the Japanese planned to build new towns in Brazil, the anonymous writer concluded by letting readers know that the settlements "have been opened by the Japanese for residence to peoples of any and all nationalities." This article joins many others in the *Negro World* that laud Japan's imperialist ventures. While Black internationalists during this period envisioned Japan as the champion of the darker races, they also had to contend with Japan's military aggression toward other people of color, including the Chinese—another ethnic group that Black internationalists often identified as potential role models and political allies.[67]

While activists in the UNIA grappled with these concerns, a lively discussion ensued on the pages of the *Negro World*. In November 1931, an editorial "Japanese Holdup of Manchuria" appeared on the front page of the newspaper. "It is regrettable that the Japanese militarists have defied their saner civil officers [by invading Manchuria]," the writer indicated. "If Japan's aim was to keep the white powers out of Manchuria, she has made an unwise move in trying to swallow up China, which will certainly prove too big in the end."[68] Although the writer of the article clearly maintained some misgivings about Japan's invasion of Manchuria, this individual also attempted to justify Japan's actions. Importantly, the writer refrained from outwardly denouncing Japan's military actions and criticized Japanese officials simply for being too ambitious. A subsequent article in the *Negro World* newspaper a week later was far more critical. "Friends of Japan have no cause to be jubilant over the antics of Japanese militarists in Manchuria," the writer stated unequivocally. Without mincing words, the writer argued that although Japan had successfully "defied and discredited the League of Nations and made the United States look like 'two cents,'" the nation's "imperialistic aggression in China" was no less "odious, nor excusable." While acknowledging that "white European and American imperialists" employed the same tactics, the anonymous writer insisted that there was no justification for Japan's "mistreatment of China."[69]

If readers of the *Negro World* presumed that the newspaper had somehow shifted positions on Japan, they might have been surprised by a December 5, 1931, article "Garveyism's World Opportunities." Published only a few months after Japan's invasion of Manchuria in 1931, the article attempted to set the record straight on Japan. "No true Garveyite who is instinctively anti-imperialist will show sympathy to the imperialist activities of Japan in China," the article began. "However, Japan's high-handed action in Manchuria has opened new opportunities for the triumphal march of Garveyism." While seemingly denouncing Japan's military aggression toward other people of color, the author proceeded to show how Japan's rise would still benefit people of African descent. Referencing Japan's departure from the League of Nations, the writer pointed out that Japan's military successes reveal the "impotency of any peace organization or peace treaties."[70] Arguing that "world peace will always be threatened as long as imperialists will hold on to their ill-gotten territories in China, India, Near East and Africa," the author contended, "[e]very nation that is sufficiently interested in its own sovereignty will henceforth have to depend on their own well-organized defense."

With these words, the writer advised readers to worry less about Japan's imperialist ventures and focus more on advancing the cause of universal Black liberation: "All this uncertainty of peace, ought to unite all Garveyites to better plan an attack on the problem of redeeming Africa." The *Negro World* writer justified Japan's invasion of Manchuria by insisting that while the actions of Japanese officials had negative consequences on China, these actions fell within the general patterns of imperial behavior. In addition, the writer implied that Japan still served as a model and potential ally for Black activists: "The only way we can make inroads on the common enemy is when he is hard pressed." To that end, the writer concluded the article with a poignant question for readers to ponder—"Will the Garveyites rally to the standard of their leader without delay to prepare for the day of redemption of Africa that is soon approaching?"

The articles in the *Negro World* during the 1930s—written by various Garveyite men and women across the globe—captured the internationalist vision of many Black intellectuals and activists in the twentieth century who admired Japan for its military prowess and envisioned the struggle against White supremacy as a global one.[71] Their visions were certainly fraught with contradictions. While these activists believed that people of color needed to form a united front against racism and imperialism, they were unwilling to fully denounce Japan's aggression toward the Chinese. Partly as a result of the belief that Japan's military skills would prove instrumental for combating global White supremacy, Black internationalists were often willing to look the other way.[72] This is not to suggest that activists did not care about China. However, their vision of Japan as the champion of the darker races certainly shaped their political worldview and strengthened their belief in the inevitable defeat of global White supremacy with Japan's aid.

Conclusion

During the twentieth century, Black intellectuals of all walks of life endorsed Black internationalism as a legitimate response to global White supremacy. Through an array of writings and speeches, these men and women called on people of African descent to link their experiences and concerns with those of people of color in other parts of the globe. In response to Japan's military rise and its growing imperial presence on the globe, Black people in the United States endorsed Afro-Asian solidarity and actively pursued contact and collaboration with Japanese activists. Notwithstanding the complexities and contradictions in their perspectives, especially as they relate to Japan's aggressive policies toward China and Korea, Black intellectuals during the twentieth century envisioned alliances with Japan as a viable strategy for combatting global racism and securing human rights. A diverse group of Black men and women, including Walker, Adams, Garvey, Harrison, Gordon, and Sherrod, articulated global visions of freedom and emphasized what Du Bois had described in 1937 as the "certain bond between the colored peoples because of worldwide prejudice."[73]

In the decades that followed, internationalism remained a major current in Black political thought and activism. During the early 1940s, as the United States entered World War II, many Black activists continued to endorse Afro-Asian solidarity. However, few were willing to publicly call for political solidarity with the Japanese people in the aftermath of the 1941 Pearl Harbor bombing. Individuals like Gordon who were vocal about their pro-Japanese stance faced the consequences for their actions. In 1942 Gordon, along with a group of Black activists in Chicago, was rounded up by federal authorities and eventually charged with the crime of sedition.[74] Government repression during the era of World War II certainly posed a threat to Afro-Asian political movements and Black internationalist politics, in general, but it did not quell them.[75]

During the 1950s and 1950s, a new generation of Black intellectuals and activists, including Martin Luther King Jr., Edith Sampson, Paul Robeson, Eslanda Robeson, and Malcolm X, linked the fight for civil rights in the United States with the struggle for African decolonization and other anti-imperialist movements abroad.[76] Throughout the civil rights–Black Power era, a number of organizations in the United States, including the Council of African Affairs and the Organization of Afro-American Unity promoted the idea that African Americans should identify with colonized peoples all over the globe. Echoing the views of Du Bois, Gordon, Sherrod, and many others before him, Robeson reminded people of African descent in the United States that "[the] fight for Negro rights here [in the United States] is linked inseparably with the liberation movements of the people of the Caribbean and Africa and the colonial world in general."[77] His comments underscore the significance of internationalism in the Black intellectual tradition in the United States during the twentieth century. It is a tradition that has shaped, and has been shaped by, a diverse group of Black men and women, representing varied socioeconomic backgrounds and operating in different locales. Importantly, it is a tradition that remains firmly rooted in Black political thought and thus continues to inform global liberation struggles today.

Notes

1. W. E. B. Du Bois, *Souls of Black Folk* (New York: Dover, 1994); Manning Marable and Vanessa Agard-Jones, eds., *Transnational Blackness: Navigating the Global Color Line* (New York: Palgrave, 2008). Also see W. E. B. Du Bois, "To the Nations of the World," (1900), in *The Oxford W. E. B. Du Bois Reader*, ed. Eric J. Sundquist (New York: Oxford University Press, 1996), 626.

2. Reginald Kearney, "The Pro-Japanese Utterances of W. E. B. Du Bois," *Contributions in Black Studies* 13, no. 1 (1995): 201. For an earlier draft of the speech, see W. E. B. Du Bois, "The Meaning of Japan," March 12, 1937, MS 312, W. E. B. Du Bois Papers, Special Collections and University Archives, University of Massachusetts Amherst Libraries.

3. Michael O. West, William G. Martin, and Fanon Che Wilkins, eds., *From Toussaint to Tupac: The Black International since the Age of Revolution* (Chapel Hill: University of North Carolina Press, 2009), xi.

4. See Derrick P. Alridge, *The Educational Thought of W. E. B. Du Bois: An Intellectual History* (New York: Teachers College Press, 2008); Bill Mullen and Cathryn Watson, eds., *W. E. B. Du Bois on Asia: Crossing the World Color Line* (Jackson: University Press of Mississippi, 2005).

5. Robin D. G. Kelley, "'But a Local Phase of a World Problem': Black History's Global Vision, 1883–1950," *Journal of American History* 86 (1999): 1045–77.

6. Fred Ho and Bill V. Mullen, eds., *Afro Asia: Revolutionary Political and Cultural Connections between African Americans and Asian Americans* (Durham, NC: Duke University Press, 2008), 3.

7. See Kelley, "But a Local Phase."

8. The scholarship on Black internationalism is extensive. The most significant works include Gerald Horne, *The End of Empires: African Americans and India* (Philadelphia: Temple University Press, 2008); Nico Slate, *Colored Cosmopolitanism: The Shared Struggle for Freedom in the United States and India* (Cambridge, MA: Harvard University Press, 2012); West, Martin, and Wilkins, *From Toussaint to Tupac*; James Meriwether, *Proudly We Can Be Africans: Black Americans and Africa, 1935–1961* (Chapel Hill: University of North Carolina Press, 2002); Brent Hayes Edwards, *The Practice of Diaspora: Literature, Translation, and the Rise of Black Internationalism* (Cambridge, MA: Harvard University Press, 2003); Minkah Makalani, *In the Cause of Freedom: Radical Black Internationalism from Harlem to London, 1917–1939* (Chapel Hill: University of North Carolina Press, 2011); Penny Von Eschen, *Race against Empire: Black Americans and Anticolonialism, 1937–1957* (Ithaca, NY: Cornell University Press, 1997); Roderick D. Bush, *The End of White World Supremacy: Black Internationalism and the Problem of the Color Line* (Philadelphia: Temple University Press, 2009); Keisha N. Blain, *Set the World on Fire: Black Nationalist Women and the Global Struggle for Freedom* (Philadelphia: University of Pennsylvania Press, 2018).

9. Gerald Horne, *Race Woman: The Lives of Shirley Graham Du Bois* (New York: New York University Press, 2000); Gregg Andrews, *Thyra J. Edwards: Black Activist in the Global Freedom Struggle* (Columbia: University of Missouri, 2011); Barbara Ransby, *Eslanda: The Large and Unconventional Life of Mrs. Paul Robeson* (New Haven, CT: Yale University Press, 2013); Erik S. McDuffie, "'For the Full Freedom of . . . Colored Women in Africa, Asia, and in these United States . . . ': Black Women Radicals and the Practice

of a Black Women's International," *Palimpsest: A Journal on Women, Gender, and the Black International* 1 (2012): 1–30; Cheryl Higashida, *Black Internationalist Feminism: Women Writers of the Black Left, 1945–1999* (Urbana: University of Illinois Press, 2013); Keisha N. Blain, "'[F]or the Rights of Dark People in Every Part of the World': Pearl Sherrod, Black Internationalist Feminism, and Afro-Asian Politics during the 1930s," *Souls* 17, no. 1–2 (2015): 90–112.

10. Key works on Afro-Asia include Reginald Kearney, *African American Views of the Japanese: Solidarity of Sedition?* (Albany: State University of New York Press, 1998); Marc S. Gallicchio, *The African American Encounter with Japan and China: Black Internationalism in Asia, 1895–1945* (Chapel Hill: University of North Carolina Press, 2000); Robin D. G. Kelley and Betsy Esch, "Black like Mao: Red China and Black Revolution," *Souls* 1, no. 4 (1999): 6–41; Gerald Horne, "Tokyo Bound: African Americans and Japan Confront White Supremacy," *Souls* 3, no. 3 (2011): 16–28; Ho and Mullen, *Afro Asia*; Heike Raphael-Hernandez and Shannon Steen, eds., *AfroAsian Encounters: Culture, History, Politics* (New York: New York University Press, 2006); Vijay Prashad, *Everybody Was Kung Fu Fighting: Afro-Asian Connections and the Myth of Cultural Purity* (Boston: Beacon, 2001); Bill V. Mullen, *Afro-Orientalism* (Minneapolis: University of Minnesota Press, 2004); Yukiko Koshio, "Beyond an Alliance of Color: The African American Impact on Modern China," *Positions* 11 (Spring 2003): 183–215; Yuichiro Onishi, *Transpacific Antiracism: Afro-Asian Solidarity in 20th Century Black America, Japan, and Okinawa* (New York: New York University Press, 2013); Robeson Taj Frazier, *The East Is Black: Cold War China in the Black Radical Imagination* (Durham, NC: Duke University Press, 2015). The term "Afro-Asia" in this essay (as in the extant literature) functions as a theoretical framework that sheds light on the myriad exchanges and collaborations among people of African descent and persons of Asian descent. To that extent, it includes varied perspectives and experiences. The framework is especially useful in this context even as the chapter is chiefly concerned with African Americans' engagement specifically with Japan.

11. Robeson Taj Frazier, "Afro-Asia and Cold War Black Radicalism," *Socialism and Democracy* 25, no. 1 (2011): 257.

12. On nonstate actors, see Brenda Plummer, ed., *Window on Freedom: Race, Civil Rights, and Foreign Affairs, 1945–1988* (Chapel Hill: University of North Carolina Press, 2003).

13. Ho and Mullen, *Afro Asia*, 3.

14. Kearney, "Pro-Japanese Utterances," 201.

15. Erika Lee, "The 'Yellow Peril' and Asian Exclusion in the Americas," *Pacific Historical Review* 76 (2007): 537–562; Eiichiro Azuma, "Japanese Immigrant Settler Colonialism in the U.S.-Mexican Borderlands and the U.S. Racial-Imperialist Politics of the Hemispheric 'Yellow Peril,'" *Pacific Historical Review* 83 (2014): 255–276.

16. Steven Ericson and Allen Hockley, eds., *The Treaty of Portsmouth and Its Legacies* (Hanover, NH: Dartmouth College Press, 2008).

17. Kearney, *African American Views*, xxv.

18. Nicholas Papastratigakis, *Russian Imperialism and Naval Power: Military Strategy and the Build-Up to the Russo-Japanese War* (London: Tauris, 2011); Rotem Kowner, *The*

A to Z of the Russo-Japanese War (Lanham, MD: Scarecrow, 2009); Naoko Shimazu, *Japanese Society at War: Death, Memory, and the Russo-Japanese War* (Cambridge, UK: Cambridge University Press, 2009); Rotem Kowner, *Rethinking the Russo-Japanese War, 1904–05* (Folkestone, UK: Global Oriental, 2007).

19. Christopher Cappazzola, *Uncle Sam Wants You: World War I and the Making of the Modern American Citizen* (New York: Oxford University Press, 2008).

20. See Joseph Harris, "Dynamics of the Global African Diaspora," in *The African Diaspora*, ed. Joseph Harris, Alusine Jalloh, and Stephen Maizlish (College Station: Texas A&M University Press, 1996); Adriane Lentz-Smith, *Freedom Struggles: African Americans and World War I* (Cambridge, MA: Harvard University Press, 2009); Chad Williams, *Torchbearers of Democracy: African American Soldiers in the World War I Era* (Chapel Hill: University of North Carolina Press, 2010).

21. Erez Manela, *A Wilsonian Moment: Self-Determination and the International Origins of Anticolonial Nationalism* (New York: Oxford University Press, 2007).

22. Kenneth C. Barnes, "Inspiration from the East: Black Arkansans Look to Japan," *Arkansas Historical Quarterly* 69, no. 3 (2010): 205.

23. David Vassar Taylor, *African Americans in Minnesota* (St. Paul: Minnesota Historical Society Press, 2002), 24–26.

24. John Q. Adams, "End Autocracy of Color," *Appeal*, January 4, 1919.

25. Ibid.

26. For an excellent overview of Randolph's political life, see Cornelius Bynum, *A. Philip Randolph and the Struggle for Civil Rights* (Urbana: University of Illinois Press, 2010).

27. Judith Stein, *The World of Marcus Garvey: Race and Class in Modern Society* (Baton Rouge: Louisiana State University Press, 1986), 50.

28. Onishi, *Transpacific Antiracism*, 33; Plummer, *Window on Freedom*, 51.

29. Yuichiro Onishi, "How African Americans Forged Cross-Racial Solidarity with Japan, 1917–1922," *Journal of African American History* 92, no. 2 (2007): 199.

30. See Tony Martin, *Race First: The Ideological and Organizational Struggles of Marcus Garvey and the Universal Negro Improvement Association* (Dover, MA: Majority, 1976); Colin Grant, *Negro with a Hat: The Rise and Fall of Marcus Garvey* (Oxford: Oxford University Press, 2008); Adam Ewing, *The Age of Garvey: How a Jamaican Activist Created a Mass Movement and Changed Global Black Politics* (Princeton, NJ: Princeton University Press, 2014).

31. Hakim Adi and Marika Sherwood, eds., *Pan-African History: Political Figures from Africa and the Diaspora since 1787* (New York: Routledge, 2003).

32. Ernest Allen Jr., "When Japan Was the 'Champion of the Darker Races': Satokata Takahashi and the Flowering of Black Messianic Nationalism," *Black Scholar* 24 (Winter 1994): 29.

33. Robert A. Hill, ed., *Marcus Garvey and the Universal Negro Improvement Association Papers* (Berkeley: University of California Press, 1983), 2:42.

34. Hubert H. Harrison and Jeffrey Perry, *A Hubert Harrison Reader* (Middletown. CT: Wesleyan University Press, 2001), 230; Yuichiro Onishi, "The New Negro of the Pacific: How African Americans Forged Solidarity with Japan," in *Escape from New York: The*

New Negro Renaissance Beyond Harlem, ed. Davarian Baldwin and Minkah Makalani (Minneapolis: University of Minnesota Press, 2013), 127.

35. Harrison and Perry, *Hubert Harrison Reader*, 128.

36. Gallicchio, *African American Encounter*, 19.

37. Ibid., 20.

38. Onishi, *Transpacific Antiracism*, 28.

39. Allen, "When Japan Was Champion," 28–29.

40. Gerald Horne, *Race War: White Supremacy and the Japanese Attack on the British Empire* (New York: New York University Press, 2004), 43.

41. Kenneth C. Barnes, "Inspiration from the East: Black Arkansans Look to Japan," *Arkansas Historical Quarterly* 69, no. 3 (2010): 204.

42. Gallicchio, *African American Encounter*, 97.

43. Ibid.; Prashad, *Everybody Was Kung Fu Fighting*, 31.

44. Barnes, "Inspiration," 207.

45. Ernest Allen, "'Waiting for Tojo': The Pro-Japan Vigil of Black Missourians, 1932–1943," *Gateway Heritage* (1995): 38–55.

46. Takahashi was also affiliated with the Black Dragon Society, an ultranationalist organization established in 1901 for the primary purpose of obtaining military information to aid Japan's imperialist ventures. See Allen, "When Japan Was Champion," 31; Kearney, *African American Views*, 76; David E. Kaplan and Alec DuBro, eds., *Yakuza: Japan's Criminal Underworld* (Berkeley: University of California Press, 2012), 24.

47. Allen, "When Japan Was Champion," 31.

48. Ibid., 32.

49. Michael A. Gomez, *Black Crescent: The Experience and Legacy of African Muslims in the Americas* (Cambridge: Cambridge University Press, 2005), 284. The actual breakdown of membership along racial lines is unclear.

50. See Blain, "'[F]or the Rights of Dark People.'"

51. On third-world solidarity, see Darryl C. Thomas, *The Theory and Practice of Third World Solidarity* (Westport, CT: Praeger, 2001).

52. Original emphasis.

53. See Douglass Flamming, *Bound for Freedom: Black Los Angeles in Jim Crow America* (Berkeley: University of California Press, 2005).

54. West, Martin, and Wilkins, *From Toussaint to Tupac*, xi.

55. Blain, *Set the World on Fire*.

56. Mittie Maude Lena Gordon to Earnest Sevier Cox, October 27, 1939, box 5, Earnest Sevier Cox Papers, 1821–1973, Rare Book, Manuscript, and Special Collections Library, Duke University, Durham, North Carolina [hereinafter referred to as Cox Papers]; Peace Movement of Ethiopia, One God, One Country, One People; also, a Brief History, Memorial to President, Funeral Oration and Burial Ceremonies, Battle Hymn of the Peace Movement (United States: s.n., 1941) [Peace Movement of Ethiopia Constitution].

57. See *United States of America v. Mittie Maud Lena Gordon*, US Court of Appeals for the 7th Circuit, Reply Brief for Appellants, box 34, Cox Papers; Allen, "Waiting for Tojo," 38–55.

58. Robert A. Hill, *FBI's Racon: Racial Conditions in the United States during World War II* (Boston: Northeastern University Press, 1995), 524.

59. *United States v. Gordon*, Cox Papers.

60. Allen, "When Japan Was Champion," 28–29; Kearney, *African American Views*, 18–30.

61. Peace Movement of Ethiopia Constitution, 15.

62. Gordon to Theodore Bilbo, January 27, 1942, exhibit 132, Report by Special Agent John Colin Robinson, FBI Investigative File no. 100–124410. All FBI records used in this essay were obtained under the Freedom of Information Act (FOIA).

63. Gordon to Tommie Thomas, August 28, 1942, exhibit 125, Report by Special Agents Francis A. Regan, Aubrey Elliott Jr., and Richard W. Axtell, FBI Investigative File no. 100–124410.

64. See Nico Slate, *Colored Cosmopolitanism: The Shared Struggle for Freedom in the United States and India* (Cambridge, MA: Harvard University Press, 2012), 2, 7; Gerald Horne, *The End of Empires: African Americans and India* (Philadelphia: Temple University Press, 2008).

65. Gordon to Kenji Nakauchi, May 22, 1934, exhibit 164a, Report by Special Agents Francis A. Regan, Aubrey Elliott Jr., and Richard W. Axtell, FBI Investigative File no. 100–124410.

66. Gordon to Sadao Araki, n.d., Exhibit 160a in Report by Special Agents Francis A. Regan, Aubrey Elliott Jr., Andrew J. Rafferty, and Richard W. Axtell, FBI Investigative File no. 100–124410.

67. This point of view is evident in the *Negro World*. See, for example, "Woosung the Chinese Thermopylae," *Negro World*, February 20, 1932. For an excellent overview of Black intellectuals' engagement with China during the twentieth century, see Frazier, *East Is Black*.

68. "Japanese Holdup of Manchuria," *Negro World*, November 21, 1931.

69. "Siding with the Strong?" *Negro World*, November 28, 1931.

70. See Thomas W. Burkman, *Japan and the League of Nations: Empire and World Order, 1914–1938* (Honolulu: University of Hawai'i Press, 2008).

71. Kearney, *African American Views*; Gerald Horne, *Race War! White Supremacy and the Japanese Attack on the British Empire* (New York: New York University Press, 2004).

72. Gallicchio, *African American Encounter*, 59.

73. Kearney, "Pro-Japanese Utterances," 201. For an earlier draft of the speech, see Du Bois, "Meaning of Japan."

74. See Blain, *Set the World on Fire*.

75. Kearney, *African American Views*, 133.

76. Bush, *End of White World Supremacy*, 153–175.

77. Paul Robeson and Philip Sheldon Foner, eds., *Paul Robeson Speaks: Writings, Speeches, and Interviews* (New York: Brunner, 1978), 224.

CHAPTER 11

BLACK CONSERVATIVE DISSENT

LA TASHA B. LEVY

"Being a black 'conservative' is perhaps not considered as bizarre as being a transvestite, but it is certainly considered more strange than being a vegetarian or a bird watcher." This opening line in the August 8, 1976, *New York Times* article "A Black 'Conservative' Dissents," by economist Thomas Sowell, represents, in full color, the controversial rhetorical strategies that would come to characterize his body of work on race, culture, and politics over the next fifty years. In this article, Sowell—a disciple of neoliberal architect Milton Friedman—brazenly rejects the premise that racism or sexism is to blame for persistent inequality in the United States. To prove his point, he invokes the hot-button issues of the day, such as busing, affirmative action, women's rights, and antipoverty initiatives. These were the cornerstones of bankrupt liberal policies, grounded in moral suasion and White liberal guilt, Sowell argues, rather than sound research and commonsense solutions. He claims, "The grand assumption that body count proves discrimination proceeds as if people would be evenly distributed in the absence of deliberate barriers. There isn't a speck of evidence for this assumption, and there is a mountain of evidence against it." Discounting an abundance of Black historical studies and social science scholarship, Sowell turns the spotlight away from structural explanations of inequality. Instead, he emphasizes social and cultural norms, religion, and individual choices as the primary factors underlying racial and gender disparities. His antiliberal tract raises provocative questions about the root causes of inequality, and he chastises both liberals and so-called radicals—those "who take liberal orthodoxy to extremes"—for insisting that discrimination was to blame.

Sowell's public alignment with conservatism as a political ideology signaled a new Black intellectual tradition on the horizon. This tradition rests on a posture of dissent, which challenges the fundamental assertion that racial discrimination continues to stifle access and opportunity, especially for African Americans. In the decades following Sowell's pronouncement, a network of Black dissenters bridged aspects of social conservatism with the politics of civil rights retrenchment and antiliberal backlash of the Republican Party's right wing. Disputing any claims that conservatives seek to "conserve the status quo," he insists, "I have never come across this mythical being. . . . [A] so-called conservative is nothing more than a dissenter from the prevailing liberal orthodoxy." Not only did Sowell destabilize conceptions of political conservatism as inherently racist but he also provided a blueprint for the political incorporation of African American dissidents into the GOP.

This chapter uses the term "Black political conservatives" to refer to a network of intellectuals, politicians, civic activists, government officials, and pundits who propagate antiliberal dissent in alignment with the rise of right-wing conservatism in national politics. The elevation of Black political conservatives on the national stage marks a contentious development in Black politics that illustrates critical distinctions between the *social conservatism* often associated with African American culture and the *political conservatism* of the Republican Party since Ronald Reagan's presidential election in 1980. Certainly, the tenets of Black conservatism in the post–civil rights period extended a tradition of Black political thought dating back to the late nineteenth century. Its tenets include bootstrap theory, racial uplift, Christian moralism, middle-class respectability, and faith in American institutions, including capitalism and the American creed. However, by the late twentieth century, Black conservatism had evolved into a distinct political ideology, a new Black right, that helped to shape the racial politics of the modern conservative movement, firmly anchored in the Republican Party.

To be Black and politically conservative in the late 1970s was strange indeed, bizarre even, given the flowering of Black political consciousness and grassroots organizations as a result of the civil rights and Black Power movements. Black activists and intellectuals theorized the complexities of racial domination through the lens of concepts like institutional racism, racial capitalism, anti-imperialism, and double jeopardy.[1] According to political scientist Katherine Tate, the early 1970s was one of the most radical periods of Black public opinion.[2] Unsurprisingly, only a small segment of African Americans identified as conservative, and African American affiliation with the Republican Party remained pitiable as a result of the GOP's support for anti–civil rights agendas, repressive law-and-order tactics, and the accommodation of White segregationists into the Republican mainstream.[3] Yet, African Americans were also deeply disillusioned with the Democratic Party. While the various expressions of Black politics during the 1960s and 1970s were incredibly diverse, and the Black Left also criticized the reformist policies of White liberals and their Black counterparts, Black political conservatives were, undoubtedly, marginal voices.[4]

What distinguishes Black political conservatism from previous iterations of Black conservatism (such as Booker T. Washington's vision of economic self-help; Marcus Garvey's Black nationalism; or the respectability politics of the Black women's club movement) is decisive opposition to liberal politics alongside unprecedented patronage from a network of White conservative think tanks, foundations, media, and interest groups. In the decades following the decline of the civil rights and Black Power movements, Black conservative intellectuals fashioned themselves as "dissidents" who opposed the so-called civil rights establishment, and they chastised Black culture and identity as debilitating and detrimental to the cause of racial progress.[5] These "new Black conservatives," as they were called in the press, seemed largely disconnected from Black social institutions and organizations. Black political conservatives were individuals based in conservative think tanks such as the Heritage Foundation, American Enterprise Institute, and the Hoover Institution at Stanford University. While Black political conservatism represented a new phase in the history of Black intellectual traditions, all iterations of Black conservatism, from the late nineteenth century onward, raise critical questions for understanding the full scope of Black freedom struggles, including competing interpretations of the root causes of racial inequality.

The collusive relationship between Black conservatives and their White conservative networks also distinguishes Black conservative dissent from a long history of conservative expression in Black political culture. Conservative think tanks and foundations funneled resources into fellowships and publications for Black conservative intellectuals and pundits, giving them a platform and greater visibility to wage ideological warfare. In a 1986 address "Waging and Winning the War of Ideas," Edwin Fuelner, president and founder of the Heritage Foundation, states plainly, "We man the ivory towers as well as the trenches in this war of ideas. We define the objectives, devise the strategies, and manufacture the ammunition. The war of ideas is a war of words—a war of intellect."[6] Conservative intellectuals were deliberate and calculating in mobilizing a popular front to shape public policy, and a relatively small network of African Americans were to play an indispensable role in stimulating ideological struggle. In addition to aligning with the Republican right wing, Black dissenters instigated vigorous debate within Black thought regarding the crisis in Black leadership, social problems in Black communities, and the men and women who get to represent the interests of Black America.[7] Moreover, the fact that many Black political conservatives were awarded fellowships and access to media as "experts" on race (despite lacking expertise in the manner of training) only fueled widespread skepticism, and even hostility, toward the peculiar politics of these Black dissenters.[8]

Of greater significance is the way in which the new crop of Black political conservatives upended a long-standing tradition of Black Republican politics.

Prior to the advent of Black political conservatism in the 1980s, older generations of card-carrying Republicans self-identified as moderate or liberal Republicans, and they often used the terms "Lincoln Republicans" or "Rockefeller Republicans" to distance themselves from the right-wing fringe. Black Republicans fused Republican principles of self-reliance with the expectation that federal intervention was necessary to counter the intergenerational impact of racist exclusions and the reality of White resentment toward racial equality. They forged political alliances with African Americans across the aisle and joined civil rights organizations, such as the National Association for the Advancement of Colored People (NAACP) and the Congress of Racial Equality, in the fight for Black freedom.[9] During the height of the civil rights movement, Black Republican leaders mobilized what historian Leah Wright Rigueur refers to as an "economic civil rights movement," firmly committed to civil rights protections and Black economic development.[10] Certainly, many Black Republicans were fiscally conservative in terms of their support for free-market capitalism and classist respectability. Black Republican leaders also preferred legal remedies and "working within the system" over direct action and radical transformation. Yet, their unbridled support for race-conscious public policies and some form of government intervention placed them at odds with the modern conservative movement. The elevation of Black political conservatives in the post–civil rights period played a vital role in legitimizing antiliberal policies and civil rights retrenchment, but it also displaced—and attempted to delegitimize—generations of moderate and liberal politics among African Americans who had struggled to make the Republican Party responsive to economic and racial justice agendas.[11]

Shortly after the publication of Sowell's "A Black Conservative Dissents," a handful of self-proclaimed Black conservatives had bloomed into a viable network within the modern conservative movement. In 1980 Sowell organized a small network of fellow dissidents to disrupt media attention given to Black liberal leadership following the election of Ronald Reagan. In collaboration with Reagan associates, Sowell convened the Black Alternatives Conference at the Fairmont Hotel in San Francisco, California, to give visibility to a new class of Black leaders and intellectuals who were willing to publicly disavow race-conscious policies and government intervention. More significant, this "alternative" Black leadership waged an ideological campaign to challenge and discredit structural explanations for the nation's persistent problem of racial inequality.[12]

Following this convention, a new Black politics began to take shape in the 1980s. Its professed leaders were more likely to represent themselves as individuals rather than constituencies, and its spokesmen were considered "experts" on race. The new Black conservatives included economists Walter Williams and Glenn C. Loury; sociologist Anne Wortham (who identifies as libertarian); government officials US Supreme Court justice Clarence Thomas and chair of the US Commission on Civil Rights Clarence M. Pendleton Jr.; and Reagan supporters Lincoln Institute cofounder Jay A. Parker, real estate developer Gloria Toote, and Woodson Center founder Robert Woodson Sr. In the 1990s a second wave of Black dissenters flooded public discourse with an oppositional analysis of race, including author Shelby Steele, UrbanCure founder Star Parker, American Civil Rights Institute founder Ward Connerly, political commentator Armstrong Williams, associate professor John McWhorter, and writer Stanley Crouch. This new Black right refuted any claims that White racism was primarily to blame for racial disparities, and they marshalled a body of ideas, concepts, and scripts that would have lasting impact on post–civil rights racial discourse, tilling the ground for a euphemistic postracial society.

In the groundbreaking study of this political phenomenon, *Guess Who's Coming to Dinner Now? Multicultural Conservatism in America*, historian Angela D. Dillard investigates the core ideas and rhetorical strategies of "multicultural conservatives"—the women, racial minorities, and queer Republicans who have aligned themselves with right-wing politics. In her treatment, which extends beyond the purview of African American conservatives, Dillard argues:

> The impact of multicultural conservative style is undeniable. By positioning themselves within the ranks of the Right as both diehard devotees and lukewarm fellow travelers, in both subtle and overt ways they have been steadily expanding the boundaries of the sayable. To be able to preface potentially racist and sexist remarks with the phrase "As Thomas Sowell says . . . " or "As Linda Chavez has argued . . . " is to be able to cannibalize the moral authority of minority voices while skirting responsibility. The presence of women and minorities within the ranks of the movement has also helped to humanize and soften its rhetoric. By saying it first, multicultural conservatives have primed the pump for others.[13]

Dillard's astute inquiry led the way in critical scholarship that seriously engaged the ideologies and impact of Black conservative intellectuals, especially as it pertains to the ways in which they opened pathways for the circulation of anti-Black rhetoric.

Few strategies were more enduring in shaping national racial discourse than the right wing's racialized rhetoric. From Barry Goldwater's racially coded references to the "Silent Majority" and "Forgotten Americans," to Ronald Reagan's public declaration that conservatives were winning the "battle of ideas," the modern conservative movement used both ideology and discourse as key political tools to anchor its ascendancy into the political mainstream. The rhetoric of White conservative intellectuals, such as Russell Kirk, Irving Kristol, Richard M. Weaver Jr., William F. Buckley Jr., Milton Friedman, Phyllis Schlafly, and Norman Podhoretz, to name a few, bolstered right-wing political agendas in the 1950s and 1960s, which reached full bloom with the 1980 election of Ronald Reagan—the first presidential candidate to win the election on an expressly conservative agenda. Through a constellation of publications, college newspapers, student groups, and local and national media, conservative thinkers mobilized a well-funded movement to undermine the welfare state.[14] Their platform, rooted in small government, privatization, deregulation, militarism, anticommunism, and the invocation of traditional "family values," was also unapologetically hostile to the demands of the Black freedom movement.[15]

A Debunking Project

As an ideology grounded in antiliberal resistance, much of Black conservative discourse is overwhelmingly centered on undermining the liberal consensus and discrediting antiracist agendas. In their book *Challenging the Civil Rights Establishment: Profiles of a New Black Vanguard*, conservative authors Joseph G. Conti and Brad Stetson explain, "At its most fundamental level, theirs is a *debunking project*. It is a protestation concerning the dominant, routinized racialist philosophy at work in America. It rejects the conventional wisdom that a liberal political agenda is identical with the best interests of black Americans."[16] As Conti and Stetson illuminate, Black conservative intellectuals contend that the dominant narrative of racial liberalism bloomed in the late 1960s when Black Power challenged institutional racism and inspired visions of Black liberation beyond the legal protections of the US Constitution.

In the late 1960s and 1970s, radical conceptions of "rights" included a right to housing, jobs and decent wages, healthcare, and education. Struggles against racism, capitalism, imperialism, and patriarchy linked diverse expressions of Black Power to international struggles for human rights. However, Black conservatives assailed Black Power for breeding a sense of "entitlement" that made unreasonable claims upon the state and alienated those who did not conform to the "blacker than thou crowd" around Black consciousness and Black radicalism.[17] Black conservatives were, therefore, a "new Black vanguard," Conti and Stetson argue, "a minority within a minority, criticizing certain now-entrenched attitudes that in the 1960s, spoke with romantic passion. The years have transformed those espousing these once-revolutionary viewpoints into what the New Black Vanguard perceives as imperious and doctrinaire sentiments of 'proper' racial attitudes."[18]

In order to steer the mainstream of US politics toward conservative solutions and ideologies, Black conservative intellectuals advanced alternative narratives of the nation's race problem. Although they do not deny that racism exists, they insist that racism is no longer to blame for racial disparities and inequality. In an effort to depoliticize race and downplay the material effects of racism, Black conservative intellectuals derided concepts like "systemic racism" or "institutional racism" as fallacies that rely on abstract definitions and hopeless exaggerations.[19] Sowell, for instance, chides liberals for making structural arguments when he makes a nefarious use of the term "society"—a nebulous concept designed to mask real cultural problems at the heart of racial inequality:

> A prime obstacle is the prevailing intellectual vision which not only insists on a cultural relativism that denies that some cultures are more advanced than others, but which also treats group progress as a function of the way those groups are treated by "society." While the actions of others have often had profound effects, whether on minority groups or on whole conquered nations, peoples are not mere creatures of other peoples—and their *long-run* fate, especially, is seldom determined by other peoples' policies.[20]

The implication of Sowell's theory is that cultural behavior is a better explanation for African Americans' social position in the United States than racism. Throughout Sowell's work is an insistence that the will of individuals transcends prejudice and even public policies. His reference to "other people's policies" does not account for the reality that prejudicial attitudes certainly shape power relations through government, political, and economic institutions as well as in social space. Still, Sowell and others stand firm on the belief that other people's policies (perhaps, racial slavery and segregation?) cannot account for an individual's personal failures to take advantage of educational and economic opportunities since freedom was won.

Loury, considered a "darling of the right" during the Reagan era, echoes Sowell's analysis almost verbatim in his book *One by One from the Inside Out: Essays and Reviews on Race and Responsibility in America*. He explains, "Characterizing the problem of the ghetto poor as due to white racism is one variant of this argument that 'society' has caused the problem. It overlooks the extent to which values and behaviors of inner-city black youths are implicated in the difficulty."[21] Following Sowell's lead, Loury maintains that Black complainants and their White liberal allies take advantage of an emotional investment in the idea of structural racism in order to evade personal responsibility. Human agency, cultural attitudes, behaviors, and individual choices are far more influential in shaping the human experience, say the Black economists. These ideas generated support for the defunding of social services and the criminalization of inner-city Black youth, even as the effects of deindustrialization and high unemployment fueled an economic crisis that reverberated across the nation, especially in urban areas.

Interestingly enough, Sowell grounds his racial theories in comparative studies of inequality and ethnic cultural differences around the world. Not only do these international studies establish inequality as a human tradition of sorts but Sowell's global framework also normalized White domination in the United

States by attempting to recontextualize the nation's race problem—and, more specifically, the Black problem—as nothing more than the normative outcome of competition. Throughout his writings, Sowell draws upon his international experiences to undermine interpretations of the Black condition in the United States as distinctly oppressive or somehow unique in human history. After traveling extensively in Asia, Africa, and Europe for research trips funded by the Hoover Institution, Sowell concludes, "[G]roups with different cultural heritages react very differently to the same current environment and the same objective opportunities."[22] He then points to the history of slavery around the world as evidence that the "same circumstances" have led to different outcomes according to group culture and values.

Even in the case of chattel slavery, Sowell was unrelenting. While he asserts that all human societies practiced slavery, he maintains that enslavement in other parts of the world did not produce a victim-oriented identity that perpetuates itself in generations of freedom, as is presumably the case with African Americans. To illustrate his point, he highlights the differences in economic and educational outcomes between Afro-Caribbean immigrants and African Americans. Slavery was oppressive indeed, but Sowell argues that it was not totalizing. For Sowell, the entrepreneurial spirit among West Indians, along with conservative family values and a cultural emphasis on education, savings, and thrift, dispels any claim that the legacy of slavery in the United States produced racial inequality. That Afro-Caribbean immigrants largely descend from majority-Black slave societies (nations that continue to face grave economic and political challenges despite supposedly cultivating good, wholesome cultural values) mattered little to Sowell. Nor is he interested in comparing Afro-Caribbean immigrants to those African Americans who have emigrated to other countries and tend to outperform local Black populations in education attainment and economic success. Rather, Black conservative intellectuals like Sowell insist that Black Americans have instilled in their children a victim identity in which White racism is to blame for personal failures. Despite the severe blind spots in his arguments, Sowell professes that if Afro-Caribbean immigrants, who are also descendants of a brutal slave system, can achieve economic success in the United States, then "society" is not to blame for Black America's failures.

The "bad Black culture" thesis, though a prominent feature of Black conservative dissent, has widespread currency in both conservative and liberal camps. Even Black nationalists have praised the insular practices among immigrants as a model for Black self-reliance. This theory perpetuates a deeply flawed comparison in which culture accounts for economic disparities, rather than the social and economic conditions underlying any immigrant experience.[23] Notwithstanding, Black conservatives uphold immigrants, including Afro-Caribbeans, Jews, and Asians, as model minorities for Black America precisely because of the presumed political passivity of these groups—not just the assumption they hold superior cultural values. To be apolitical allows a people to invest their energies elsewhere, such as in business development and education—Sowell has argued—and these are surer pathways to assimilation and the achievement of the American Dream. From his "empirical studies," which mostly references data without citation or illustration, we are to deduce that White people are dominant in the United States only because White culture is rooted in hard work, intellectual rigor, thrift, and the development of marketable skills. Apparently, generations of White racial preferences based on rampant racist exclusions in the areas of housing, education, and the workforce have nothing to do with the wealth gap or political dominance. Sowell, therefore, reifies a specious artifice of White cultural supremacy that undergirds both the culture of poverty thesis and scientific racism. Despite Sowell's erroneous claims, his invocation of empiricism and his performance of intellectualism as an economist have garnered widespread respect and admiration among conservatives and liberals of all racial backgrounds, including some African Americans.

To be sure, Black conservative intellectuals are unapologetic in sustaining the "culture of poverty" thesis, which has been negated by sociologists, political scientists, and other scholars since the late 1960s.[24] Sowell, for instance, emphasizes Black pathological behavior as a dangerous and detrimental facet of African American culture. He asserts that culture must be defined not by "music or art" but by "the material requirements for life itself . . . the specific skills, general work habits, saving propensities, and attitudes toward education and entrepreneurship—in short, what economists call 'human capital.'"[25] Certainly, Conti and Stetson invoke Sowell's definition of culture and its deleterious effects on racial inequality: "The New Black Vanguard argues that a chilling silence has been spread around a ghetto-specific culture by black advocates who fear that discussions about it will play into the hands of enemies of the black community."[26] Ultimately, Black conservative intellectuals have maintained that traditional Black leaders of the "civil rights establishment" evade the impact of "an injurious 'culture of poverty'" in order to secure victim status in American society, which leads to ineffective social policies and guilt-driven government funding.[27] Even more, Black conservatives insist that ignoring Black cultural pathologies absolves the real issue, which is personal responsibility, and they categorically deny that racism continues to play a significant role in the development and creation of racial disparities or the Black poor.

Affirmative Action: A Litmus Test

In addition to the routine condemnation of "bad Black culture," Black political conservatives have been among the most ardent critics of racialized public policies, namely, affirmative action and welfare, the twin evils that form the bedrock of their dissent. Justice Thomas has stated plainly that White conservatives expected their Black counterparts to publicly condemn and discredit these two policies, incessantly. In a speech he gave before the Heritage Foundation in 1987, reprinted as "No Room at the Inn: The Loneliness of the Black Conservative," Thomas explains, "For blacks the litmus test was fairly clear. You must be against affirmative action and against welfare. And your opposition had to be adamant and constant, or you would be suspected of being a closet liberal."[28] He goes on to confess having to "become a caricature of sorts, providing sideshows of anti-black quips and attacks" in order to prove his allegiance to Republicans and, by extension, to White conservative elites. Rather than reject this litmus test as "doctrinaire" or as an infringement upon freedom of thought and individualism, Thomas embraced the challenge and has since dedicated his career to eradicating any suspicion that he might be liberal on any issues, especially as they pertain to race.

When it comes to critiques of affirmative action, Sowell is among the preeminent Black critics since the 1970s. In dozens of articles, he rehashes the central arguments of his 1976 *New York Times* article, in which he maintains that "proportional representation" can never be a valid goal for any institution, especially if it discriminates against Whites. In the 1984 publication of *Civil Rights: Rhetoric or Reality?* Sowell argues that a faulty "vision" of civil rights obscures reality by promoting affirmative action as a moral-laden policy based on the premise of Black inferiority. In keeping with the strategies of the Reagan administration, Sowell delineates a critical distinction between merit-based *equal opportunity* versus identity-based *affirmative action*. The former, he argues, applies to individuals who would be "judged on their qualifications as individuals"—a formulation advanced by the Reagan administration, while the latter judges people based on group membership who receive preferential treatment to "achieve a more proportional 'representation' in various institutions and occupations."[29] Black conservative intellectuals including Steele, McWhorter, Connerly, and Yale University professor Stephen L. Carter followed Sowell's lead, ignoring decades of accumulation of wealth opportunities for Whites, in order to posit an argument that more realistic determinates of racial disparities include work habits, educational background, culture, marital status, and age.

Black conservative dissent effectively reproduced mischaracterizations of affirmative-action policies (designed to counter the intergenerational effects of legalized White preferences and racist exclusions in labor and education) as an illegitimate policy of proportional representation. In *The Content of Our Character: A New Vision of Race in America*, author Steele bemoans, "This expansion of what constitutes discrimination allowed affirmative action to escalate into the business of social engineering in the name of anti-discrimination, to push society toward statistically proportionate racial representation, without any obligation of proving actual discrimination."[30] Yet, Walter Williams had already moved the goal post even further when he suggested White racial preferences were not necessarily a bad thing, regardless of the work habits and qualifications of Black candidates. In his book *The State against Blacks*, published in 1982, he suggests a dearth of Black representation in any industry may simply be the result of "racial tastes"—to which Whites are entitled—rather than racial discrimination.[31] Ultimately, Black conservative dissent rested on the uncritical assumption that the eradication of legal barriers was enough and that taking affirmative steps to achieving racial equality, in terms of policy, is beyond what is reasonable, amounting to emotionally driven policies of reverse racism. Furthermore, these "racial quotas" or "racial preferences," as Black conservatives tend to refer to them, perpetuated feelings of Black inferiority, stigmatized Black success, and stirred justifiable resentment among Whites.

Consider Wortham, who spearheaded a spurious practice of psychoanalysis that continues to guide Black conservative dissent against antiracist policies. Wortham paved the way for an intellectual engagement with what she claims are the psychological effects of African Americans' internalization of Black inferiority. In the 1981 publication of *The Other Side of Racism: A Philosophical Study of Black Race Consciousness*, which draws upon the intellectual work of Ayn Rand (an avid supporter of hyperindividualism and free-market capitalism), Wortham expresses, "I am convinced that most Americans are so inundated with cries of freedom from Negro intellectuals and political leaders that they fail to recognize that, more often than not, these apostles of freedom are among its first violators." In this rumination, which forms the basis of her dissertation, she proposes a schema of five types of Black race-consciousness: the conforming integrationist, the power-seeking nationalist, the spiritual separatist, the independent militant, and the ambivalent appeaser. According to her logic, these various expressions of Black consciousness erode individual freedom and are, therefore, a threat to harmonious relations "between individuals and groups in a multi-ethnic society." Wortham insists race-conscious policies, such as affirmative action and other civil rights legislation, which she regards as unconstitutional, were nothing short of "retributive reverse discrimination."[32]

Even though Wortham's work affirmed Reagan's right-wing agenda, she did not receive the same acclaim as Sowell due to her controversial stances and, perhaps, her gender. Beyond her public opposition to civil rights legislation, Wortham, a strict constitutionalist, found common ground with White supremacist and arch segregationist Lester Maddox. In 1964 Maddox threatened some Black customers with a rifle when they attempted to patronize his restaurant following the passage of the Civil Rights Act. In his defense, she declares, "A businessman who cannot serve whom he pleases is not a businessman but a slave."[33] Denying that she suffers from Black self-hate, Wortham underscores her commitment to the concept of individual freedom, which protects the rights of Whites to discriminate according to their preferences and tastes, and she imagined Black consciousness only masks a deep-seated struggle with low self-esteem. Although President Reagan's advisers deemed Wortham too controversial for an appointment within the administration, her work fueled a body of ideas around Black victimization as a barrier to self-advancement and a hindrance to assimilation.

At a time when Black communities suffered enormous economic instability, civil rights retrenchment, and a resurgence of racial terror enacted by the Ku Klux Klan, Wortham boldly describes Black demands for racial equality and social justice as psychosis. She systematically challenged antiracism as "the other side of racism" in which symbolic claims of group oppression cloaked personal failings and fear of competing freely with Whites. Wortham suggests, "Whether he actually has experienced injustice or not, the symbolic victim presents himself as the embodiment of all the real imagined suffering of his membership group as a whole. The symbolic victim asks us to ignore the fact that he is not an actual victim and, instead, treat him as if he were a victim."[34] Like Sowell, Wortham considers racial discrimination to be a relic of the past rather than a present-day reality that continues to shape power relations and individual experiences. She is unmatched, however, in her framing of Black victimhood, or "victimology," as a personality disorder in which Black consciousness disguises an individual's deep-seated feelings of inferiority.

Although Wortham's ideas were too controversial for the Reagan administration and the rebranding of the modern conservative movement, her core arguments continued to inspire the political campaign outside of government, in the realm of ideology and discourse. Her early conceptions of Black victimhood were, undoubtedly, foundational to Black conservative ideology in the early post–civil rights era. Among Wortham's probable devotees is Steele, an English professor who won critical acclaim with the 1991 release of his first book, *The Content of Our Character*. This collection of controversial essays made Steele an instant spokesperson for Black conservative dissent, and he was awarded a fellowship at the Hoover Institution in 1994, serving as a specialist on race relations and multicultural issues for over twenty-five years. Although Steele credits his wife, a psychiatrist who is White, for inspiring his thinking on the links between Black victimization and White guilt, his arguments are classic Wortham.

In addition to theorizing links between the internalization of Black inferiority and the false sense of power that stems from victimization, Steele replicates Wortham's argument that race-conscious policies like affirmative action are safe havens for low self-esteem and a pathological fear of competing on an equal footing with Whites. Referring to affirmative-action policies as "racial preferences," Steele argues, "[P]references only impute a certain helplessness to blacks that diminishes our self-esteem. The self-preoccupied form of white guilt that is behind racial preferences always makes us lower so that we can be lifted up."[35] Here, Steele claims that the interdependence between Black inferiority and White guilt traps Black people into a vicious cycle of racial stigma:

> Even when the black sees no implication of inferiority in racial preferences, he knows that whites do, so that—consciously or unconsciously—the result is virtually the same. The effect of preferential treatment—the lowering of normal standards to increase black representation—puts blacks at war with an expanded realm of debilitating doubt, so that the doubt itself becomes an unrecognized preoccupation that undermines their ability to perform, especially in integrated situations.[36]

Following this line of argument, Steele diminishes affirmative action as an "escapist policy" that institutionalizes Black entitlement and discourages Black people from developing their skills and intellect so that they can compete with Whites and, more important, "develop a faith in their own capacity" to compete.[37]

The mischaracterization of affirmative action as racial preferences that lower "normal standards" erases the fact that generations of Black people exceeded White standards and were categorically denied opportunities due to a ubiquitous White fear of competition with African Americans. Steele, Wortham, and company are particularly silent on the effects of affirmative action as "gender preferences" that have opened up a world of opportunity for White women and, thus, White families. In addition, Steele's sophistic assessments of the psychological health of Black folks are considered credible precisely because of his racial identity. (Notably, he also credits his biracial heritage for his racial ideas.) Despite his objections to race-conscious policies, Steele strategically uses his race as a badge of authenticity and authority, "expanding the boundaries of the sayable" about the mental fortitude of Black people.

Welfare: "The Kissing Cousin"

Black conservative critiques of affirmative action are coupled with contempt for welfare. The orthodox position is that the expansion of welfare policies as a component of Lyndon B. Johnson's Great Society programs, including the War on Poverty, created a vicious dependency among African Americans. Hence, government dependency is the primary cause of inequality and a perverse culture in urban ghettos. One of the most iconic illustrations of welfare perversion was Justice Thomas's infamous stories about his sister, Emma Mae Martin. In 1991 he stated, "She gets mad when the mailman is late with her welfare check. That's how dependent she is. What's worse is that now her kids feel entitled to the check too. They have no motivation for doing better or getting out of that situation."[38] Thomas's personal testimony about the dangers of intergenerational dependency on government handouts proved to be a fabrication, yet the lie reflected a historical "truth" etched in the collective conscious of this nation's racist imagination. The images of welfare mothers and their delinquent children fit squarely within a tradition of blackface minstrelsy. They also reflect more recent racist caricatures that fuel what political scientist Ange-Marie Hancock refers to as a "politics of disgust."[39] These caricatures not only dehumanized Black Americans, they justified racial violence, exploitation, and legalized racism.

No one played up these hackneyed stereotypes of Black womanhood more than Star Parker, a self-proclaimed welfare queen turned conservative activist. Her rise in national prominence within conservative circles in the early 1990s is a fascinating tale of "rags to riches." Conservative talk-radio host Rush Limbaugh was so impressed by her stories of Black criminality, sexual promiscuity, Black racism, and slavish dependency on government that he opened opportunities for her to speak before national conferences and conservative media. Because Parker is a Black woman, her contributions were invaluable in confirming the grotesque portrayals of Black welfare recipients. In her first book, *Pimps, Whores, and Welfare Brats: The Stunning Conservative Transformation of a Former Welfare Queen*, Parker offers her personal narrative as testimony that ultimately affirms vilification of Black women and the Black poor.

In addition to providing her life as the prime example of the immorality of welfare and the abuse of it within Black communities, Parker's book used provocative caricatures of Black life to delineate the nation's race problem. According to Parker, Democrats are "political pimps" who do not believe that African Americans have the capabilities to succeed on their own efforts. (Parker argues that the "pimps" implemented a slew of social programs like food stamps, Aid to Families with Dependent Children, and public housing with the intent to redistribute the wealth and aid White guilt.) If the pimps were White Democratic leaders, then the "whores" were Black leaders, such as Jesse Jackson, Al Sharpton, and Maxine Waters and the other Democratic members of the Black Congressional Caucus, who received "a job in government, a power base in their home district, and plenty of campaign money." Parker insists that the "whores" are the real racists, although she redefines racism as simply talking about racism. "It's not that they hate whites," she explains, "but they frequently accuse them of hating blacks and judge every issue through race-colored glasses."[40] The "welfare brats," as she describes them, are the children of the first generation of welfare recipients. Armed with a rebellious sense of entitlement, they have abandoned the Black conservative principles of hard work and self-reliance that Parker claims "brought Black Americans up from slavery." She argues that the welfare brats demand government handouts like Social Security, Medicare, and aid for college or else they "riot at the ballot box" by threatening to vote out of office those who refuse to toe the liberal line.

Parker's argumentation and writing style may not fit the cast of intellectual work, but her role as spokesperson or "witness" to Black cultural degeneracy aided in the circulation and normalization of racist and sexist ideas that had severe implications for public policy. She also served as an asset to the conservative movement because of her racial identity and gender, and her arguments rehashed a key conservative script: welfare is a new form of slavery that produced multiple "generations of welfare dependents and a younger generation that doesn't give a darn about anything."[41] It is important to note that Black liberals and leftists also criticized welfare policies, along with the demeaning assumptions and surveillance that often shape the experiences of Black folks in need of assistance. Blaming welfare recipients for producing complex economic and social problems (while depoliticizing race) is prototypic of the racialized arguments advanced by a web of conservative think tanks that provide unprecedented financial backing for the reproduction of cultural explanations.

Second to Parker's salacious testimony are the acerbic critiques espoused by McWhorter, a trained linguist who joined the Manhattan Institute, a conservative think tank, as a fellow in 2004. Although he identifies as a Democrat and a liberal, his commentary on Black culture, Black identity, affirmative action, and welfare parallels Black conservative dissent and contempt.[42] McWhorter is often mislabeled a conservative, much like Wortham, Crouch, and sociologist Orlando Patterson, yet their ideas undoubtedly make them "fellow travelers"—as Dillard suggests—given the ways in which their ideas have informed "oppositional ideologies" promoted by the modern conservative movement.[43] McWhorter explicitly pays homage to Wortham in *Losing the Race: Self Sabotage* (2000) and along with his second book, *Authentically Black: Essays for the Black Silent Majority* (2003), expands her theory of Black victimology. In these texts, McWhorter admonishes Black cultural identity and Black political behavior as cultish and debilitating, and his arguments follow the basic architecture of Wortham's scheme, in which Black victimhood trumps *actual victimization*. For instance, McWhorter defines victimology as "the tendency to exaggerate the degree of black oppression regardless of progress" and reiterates the psychological need for African Americans to misrepresent "occasional inconveniences" as systemic oppression.[44]

Not to be outdone by Black conservative innuendo, McWhorter invokes stereotypes of Black deviance to advance his provocations. "Victimology seduces young black people just like the crack trade seduces inner-city blacks," he states, "virtually irresistible in its offer of an easy road to self-esteem and some cheap thrills on the way." Though McWhorter acknowledges that bringing attention to victimhood is necessary and healthy, as in the case of Jews, he maintains Black people profess victimhood in cases where racism barely exists.[45]

At the center of McWhorter's criticism are affirmative action and welfare. In *Authentically Black*, McWhorter defines welfare as handouts that "pay black women to have illegitimate children." He suggests welfare was expanded in the 1960s specifically to benefit Black people, and he reminds his readers (unlikely a Black audience) that welfare was intended primarily for widows, ignoring the economic crisis that produced the Great Depression and the expansion of public welfare in the 1930s. According to McWhorter, it was in the 1960s when "white leftists" supported expansion of welfare only because they believed it would be unfair to expect a formerly oppressed group to rise up the economic ladder on their own efforts. To counter these malevolent trends, McWhorter proposes, "Black Americans must be regularly taught that the expansion of welfare in the late 1960s created the unique desolation of today's inner cities," rather than deindustrialization and unfettered capitalism.[46]

McWhorter was even more flagrant in his proposition that the "true story of welfare" is just as important to Black history as the 1896 US Supreme Court decision in *Plessy v. Ferguson*. He recounts, "Whitey really done us wrong this time: the expansion of welfare created more black misery than any number of brutal policemen, white thugs yelling 'nigger,' real estate agents turning black applicants away, or white teachers not calling on black boys in school."[47] Indeed, the racist and sexist caricatures of Black women as criminal leeches of the state was a bipartisan trope in which conservatives and liberals, Democrats and Republicans, invoked the welfare queen to justify cuts to social services and the expansion of the prison-industrial complex. According to the cultural logic at play, Black "welfare queens" breed children who wreak havoc in their communities, in schools, and eventually in prisons.

Black conservative critiques of welfare and affirmative action are inextricably linked, and conjoining them implicates Black people, across economic background or social standing, in the cultivation of dependency. For instance, business tycoon Connerly, who successfully waged a campaign to abolish affirmative action in California and Washington state, blames welfare for eroding fundamental values that once guided Black culture and identity prior to the onslaught of social engineering in the 1960s and 1970s. In *Creating Equal: My Fight against Race Preferences*, he asserts:

> In a brief thirty years, programs such as welfare had changed all this, replacing these heroic efforts at self-betterment with a culture of dependency. And affirmative action was the kissing cousin of welfare, a seemingly humane social gesture that was actually quite diabolical in its consequences—not only causing racial conflict because of its inequities, but also validating blacks' fears of inferiority and reinforcing racial stereotypes.[48]

While Connerly acknowledges the good intentions that appeared to drive welfare and affirmative-action policies, McWhorter is more brash in his proposition that both policies were forms of Black reparations.

Typical of Black conservative dissent, McWhorter affirms White racism and capitalist greed were wrongly blamed for the predicament of the Black poor, leading to "young blacks' rejection of the establishment in favor of the street."[49] The intergenerational effects of White racist exclusions in housing (denying billions of dollars in wealth to Black families) and in education (stifling Black opportunity for promotion and career advancement) are wittingly absent from Black conservative critiques. Ultimately, the intended impact of centering affirmative action and welfare in Black conservative criticism is that it implicates Black people—including the Black working poor and Black educated elites—as undeserving subjects making illegitimate demands on the state. Furthermore, McWhorter's incessant use of the term "Whitey" throughout his essays reinforces a racist caricature that mocks Black ways of talking and thinking that are illustrative of the anti-White racism he claims is pervasive within Black culture. Broadening what is "sayable," McWhorter in his written work often refers to Black people as children, dupes, and animals.

Conclusion

In 1903 W. E. B. Du Bois prophetically proclaimed, "The problem of the 20th century is the problem of the color-line." By century's end the ascendancy of Black conservative dissent underscored new challenges for the cause of racial equality and social justice.[50] In many ways, Black conservative thinkers propagated narratives of racial progress in which the victories of the civil rights movement had finally settled the race question—leading to unprecedented opportunities for African American success and congenial racial attitudes of Whites. In this vein, Black conservative intellectuals have argued that the Black freedom struggle was won, and equality before the law was enough. Black demands for racial parity or proportional representation were not only superfluous, they were divisive and undeserved. In the post–civil rights decades, according to this logic, the persistence of racial disparities along the color-line are largely due to poor individual choices and Black cultural pathologies.

Elevating Black conservatives in the public sphere not only protected conservative policies that adversely affected African Americans but it also justified the GOP's limited outreach efforts to Black voters in the 1980s and beyond. No longer did mainstream Black Republican leaders urge African Americans to take advantage of the two-party system. Instead, Black conservatives engaged in controversial aspersions that discredited Black leadership and diminished the Black electorate as "slaves on the Democratic plantation." Rather than to offer substantive solutions to pressing social problems, Black political conservatives deflected serious political debate by promoting stereotypes of African Americans as slavish, childlike, and mindless and therefore incapable of evaluating public policy and making sound political choices. More significantly, Black political conservatives were leaders but not of Black community groups or grassroots organizations. They constituted an intellectual class of ideologues, designated as the "new Black leaders" by conservative media, think tanks, and foundations. This client-patron relationship undermined their credibility within Black communities.

Because Black conservative intellectuals rely heavily upon the patronage of right-wing formations, skeptics have raised pertinent questions regarding motives. Who is their audience? Whom do they represent? What have been their role and function within the modern conservative movement? Concepts like "race hustlers," "race baiters," "soul patrol," "the race card," "plantation politics," and "civil rights establishment" are some of the derisive rhetorical strategies, imbued with vilification, that typify Black conservative dissent. Intended to debunk liberal public policy, discredit Black leadership, dismiss antiracism, and decry Black people as culturally deficient, it is no wonder that Black political conservatives failed to generate mass support or attract significant numbers of African Americans to the Republican Party. Black alignment with the modern conservative movement appeared to be delusional, and to some it was traitorous, given the racially polarizing strategies of the right that inflamed White racial resentment toward social change. Although Black political conservatives have had limited influence in expanding African American affiliation with the Republican Party, their ideas have contributed immensely to US political discourse and public policy in the post–civil rights period.

Black conservative intellectuals maintain that the problem of the twenty-first century and beyond is the problem of Black victimhood—a mentality that portrays Black people as perpetual victims of White racism rather than captives of their own faults and insecurities. The solution, according to conservative talk-radio host Larry Elder, is to simply "get off your ass and work hard, stop blaming the white man, stop bitching and moaning."[51] This perpetual denial of actual racial discrimination posed a formidable challenge for Black politics in the post–civil rights decades. Black political conservatives mobilized an alternative mode of identity politics geared toward debunking the saliency of race even as their own standing depended exclusively on the fact of their blackness. This new Black right forged an intellectual tradition, shrewdly made, to dictate the right way forward.

Notes

1. See Abdul Alkalimat, "A Scientific Approach to Black liberation: Which Road against Racism and Imperialism for the Black Liberation Movement?" pamphlet (Nashville, TN: Peoples College, 1974), http://alkalimat.org/writings.html#1970s; Robert L. Allen, *Black Awakening in Capitalist America: An Analytical History* (New York: Doubleday, 1969);

Frances Beal, "Double Jeopardy: To Be Black and Female," in *The Black Woman: An Anthology*, ed. Toni Cade Bambara (New York: New American Library, 1970); Stokely Carmichael and Charles V. Hamilton, *Black Power: The Politics of Liberation in America* (New York: Random, 1967); Angela Y. Davis, *Lectures on Liberation* (New York: Committee to Free Angela Davis, 1971); Cedric Robinson, *Black Marxism* (London: Zed, 1983).

2. Katherine Tate, *From Protest to Politics: The New Black Voters in American Elections* (Cambridge, MA: Harvard University Press, 1993), 52–53, and *What's Going On? Political Incorporation and the Transformation of Black Public Opinion* (Washington, DC: Georgetown University Press, 2010), 1–5.

3. See Leah M. Wright, "Conscience of a Black Conservative: The 1964 Election and the Rise of the National Negro Republican Assembly," *Federal History Journal* 1, no. 1 (2009): 35.

4. See Michael Dawson, *Black Visions: The Roots of Contemporary African-American Political Ideologies* (Chicago: University of Chicago Press, 2001), 281; Ronald Walters, *White Nationalism, Black Interests: Conservative Public Policy and the Black Community* (Detroit, MI: Wayne State University Press, 2003), 230–231.

5. Clint Bolick defines the civil rights establishment as a core of groups and organizations committed to advancing, through political means, a revised agenda, not of civil rights but of social entitlement and privilege. *Changing Course: Civil Rights at the Crossroads* (New Brunswick, NJ: Transaction, 1988), xii.

6. Edwin Fuelner, "Waging and Winning the War of Ideas," Heritage Foundation Report: Political Process, *Heritage Foundation*, December 30, 1986, https://www.heritage .org/.

7. See Martin Kilson, "Anatomy of Black Conservatism," *Transition* 59 (1993): 4–19; Manning Marable, *Beyond Black & White: Transforming African-American Politics* (London: Verso, 1995); Hanes Walton Jr., "Defending the Indefensible: The African American Conservative Client, Spokesperson of the Reagan-Bush Era," *Black Scholar: Journal of Black Studies and Research* 24 (Fall 1994): 46–49; Cornel West, "Demystifying the New Black Conservatism," *Praxis International* 7 (July 1987): 143–151.

8. For studies of modern Black conservatism, see Angela D. Dillard, *Guess Who's Coming to Dinner Now? Multicultural Conservatism in America* (New York: New York University Press, 2001); Corey Fields, *Black Elephants in the Room: The Unexpected Politics of African American Republicans* (Oakland: University of California Press, 2016); Michael L. Ondaajte, *Black Conservative Intellectuals in Modern America* (Philadelphia: University of Pennsylvania Press, 2010); Gayle T. Tate and Lewis A. Randolph, *Dimensions of Black Conservatism in the United States: Made in America* (New York: Palgrave, 2002); and Robert C. Smith, *Conservatism and Racism, and Why in America They Are the Same* (Albany: State University of New York Press, 2010).

9. See Joshua Farrington, *Black Republicans and the Transformation of the GOP* (Philadelphia: University of Pennsylvania, 2016); Leah Wright Rigueur, *The Loneliness of the Black Republican: Pragmatic Politics and the Pursuit of Power* (Princeton, NJ: Princeton University Press, 2015).

10. Wright Rigueur, *Loneliness*, 153, 163.

11. For a discussion on the decline of moderate Black Republicanism, see Devin Fergus,

"Black Power, Soft Power: Floyd McKissick, Soul City, and the Death of Moderate Black Republicanism," *Journal of Policy History* 22, no. 2 (2010): 148–192.

12. See *The Fairmont Papers: Black Alternatives Conference San Francisco December 1980* (San Francisco: Institute for Contemporary Studies, 1981).

13. Dillard, *Guess Who's Coming to Dinner Now*, 20–21.

14. For studies of the modern conservative movement, see Donald Critchlow, *The Conservative Ascendancy: How the Republican Right Rose to Power in Modern America* (Lawrence: University of Kansas, 2011); Nancy MacLean, *Democracy in Chains: The Deep History of the Radical Right's Stealth Plan for America* (New York: Penguin, 2017); David W. Reinhard, *The Republican Right since 1945* (Lexington: University Press of Kentucky, 1983); Jonathan M. Schoenwald, *A Time for Choosing: The Rise of Modern American Conservatism* (New York: Oxford University Press, 2001).

15. Donald T. Critchlow and Nancy MacLean, *Debating the American Conservative Movement: 1945–Present* (New York: Rowman, 2009).

16. Joseph Conti and Brad Stetson, *Challenging the Civil Rights Establishment: Profiles of a New Black Vanguard* (Westport, CT: Praeger, 1993), 9.

17. Glenn Loury, *One by One from the Inside Out: Essays and Reviews on Race and Responsibility in America* (New York: Free Press, 1995), 5–6.

18. Conti and Stetson, *Challenging*, 10.

19. For an analysis of institutional racism, see Carmichael and Hamilton, *Black Power*.

20. Thomas Sowell, *Race and Culture: A World View* (New York: Basic Books, 1994), 10.

21. Loury, *One by One*, 18.

22. Sowell, *Race and Culture*, 228.

23. The immigrant model is a canonical myth in US political culture that enshrines American exceptionalism, romanticizes US history, and obscures the reality that most immigrants are among the working poor, not the business class.

24. For discussion of the "culture of poverty" thesis as a "culture of racism," see Keeanga-Yamahtta Taylor, *From #BlackLivesMatter to Black Liberation* (Chicago: Haymarket, 2016), 21–50.

25. Sowell, *Race and Culture*, xii.

26. Conti and Stetson, *Challenging*, 25.

27. Ibid., 31. See Loury, *One by One*, 183.

28. Clarence Thomas, "No Room at the Inn: The Loneliness of the Black Conservative," in *Black and Right: The Bold New Voice of Black Conservatives in America*, ed. Stan Faryna, Brad Stetson, and Joseph G. Conti (Westport, CT: Praeger, 1997), 9.

29. Thomas Sowell, *Civil Rights: Rhetoric or Reality?* (New York: Morrow, 1984), 38.

30. Shelby Steele, *The Content of Our Character: A New Vision of Race in America* (New York: St. Martin's, 1991), 114.

31. Walter Williams, *The State against Blacks* (New York: McGraw-Hill, 1982), 20–21.

32. Anne Wortham, *The Other Side of Racism: A Philosophical Study of Black Race Consciousness* (Columbus: Ohio State University Press, 1981), x.

33. Ibid., 304–317.

34. Anne Wortham, "Black Victimhood versus Black Individual Responsibility," pamphlet, *Libertarian Alliance*, January 1, 1994.

35. Steele, *Content of Our Character*, 90.

36. Ibid., 117–118. Shelby Steele's twin brother, Claude Steele, advances a slightly different argument about the ways in which Black students, in particular, internalize self-doubt, which has a negative effect on their ability to perform well on standardized tests. See Claude Steele, "Stereotype Threat and African American Student Achievement," in *Young, Gifted and Black: Promoting High Achievement among African American Students*, ed. by Theresa Perry, Claude Steele, and Asa Hilliard (Boston, MA: Beacon, 2003).

37. Steele, *Content of Our Character*, 89.

38. See Clarence Page, "Thomas' Sister's Life Gives Lie to His Welfare Fable," *Chicago Tribune*, July 24, 1991.

39. Ange-Marie Hancock, *The Politics of Disgust: The Public Identity of the Welfare Queen* (New York: New York University Press, 2004).

40. Star Parker, *Pimps, Whores, and Welfare Brats: The Stunning Conservative Transformation of a Former Welfare Queen* (New York: Pocket, 1997), 125–126, 128, 143.

41. Ibid., 127–128.

42. Black dissenters who identify as libertarian or refuse political labels, including conservative, are undeniably "fellow travelers," a phrase used by historian Angela Dillard to characterize Black spokespersons who dis-identify with the label "conservative," although they have been given a platform in media as well as fellowships from conservative foundations and think tanks.

43. Dillard, *Guess Who's Coming to Dinner Now*, 13.

44. John McWhorter, *Losing the Race: Self-Sabotage in Black America* (New York: Free Press, 2000), 212–218.

45. Ibid., 39, 27.

46. John McWhorter, *Authentically Black: Essays for the Black Silent Majority* (New York: Gotham, 2004), 24–25, 90, 210.

47. Ibid., 91–92, 215.

48. Ward Connerly, *Creating Equal: My Fight against Race Preferences* (San Francisco: Encounter, 2000), 3.

49. McWhorter, *Authentically Black*, 216.

50. W. E. B. Du Bois, *The Souls of Black Folk* (New York: Penguin, 1989), 1.

51. Brad Stetson, "The Sage of South Central: An Interview with Larry Elder," in *Black and Right: The Bold New Voice of Black Conservatives in America*, ed. Stan Faryna, Brad Stetson, and Joseph Conti (Westport, CT: Praeger, 1997), 159.

CHAPTER 12

POSTRACIALISM AND ITS DISCONTENTS

BARACK OBAMA AND THE NEW "AMERICAN DILEMMA"

ZEBULON VANCE MILETSKY

All of the stored up bile of white supremacy has exploded
like airborne E-Coli as a result of Obama's election.
—Ishmael Reed, 2010

The election of Barack Obama in 2008 as the first Black president of the United States raised hopes that we were entering a postracial moment in American life. Spurred by the media, thousands of reports were printed, aired, and broadcast that alluded to America's postracial moment, and Americans prematurely congratulated themselves on having moved beyond the hateful legacies of the past. These voices claimed that the legacies of enslavement and imperialism were overcome not only in the United States but globally. The Obama years, however, brought about issues of racial profiling, police terror, heightened mass incarceration, and predicaments of authority caused by neoliberal states, serving as constant reminders that we were living in anything but a postracial era. The election of Donald J. Trump as president in 2016 seemed to punctuate this point. If there had ever been any doubt that postracialism was a myth, the rise of the previously hidden forces of White supremacy proved that we were not only *not* postracial but also perhaps even moving backward as a country. The more frightening question, of course, was had we ever really changed at all?

The Merriam-Webster Dictionary defines "post-racial" as an adjective, "having overcome or moved beyond racism: having reached a stage or time at which racial prejudice no longer exists or is no longer a major social problem."[1] Because postracialism is essentially a creation of the media, it is appropriate to note that its first known usage was by journalists.[2] Even so, the idea has been around in some form or fashion since at least the 1970s. It became a prominent fixture in the debate over race and class launched by William Julius Wilson's game-changing book, *The Declining Significance of Race*, in which he argues that class, not race, would be the defining factor in American life and culture in the latter part of the twentieth century and beyond.[3]

The seeds of the theory of postracialism can be found in earlier iterations of terms such as post–civil rights, an idea that first used to describe African American success and mobility because of the decades-long struggle for racial and economic justice. This concept was later embraced to denote the entrance of African Americans into the middle class and to elected office. By reconnecting postracialism to its earlier iteration of post–civil rights—and reclaiming it to mean something quite different from how the media and the dictionary define it—the concept of postracialism also necessitates an examination of the various generational responses to it. Beginning with the post–civil rights generation, Generation X, the Hip-Hop generation, and finally, the millennial generation, which helped elect Obama to the presidency in 2008, this generational framing is key to understanding its development.[4] The link between multiracialism and postracialism is also an essential part of this discussion. Key features of what scholars such as Heather M. Dalmage call multiracialism, and the larger "mixed-race experience"—require critical engagement with the emerging theory of postracialism.[5]

Using the term "postracialism" as part of a new popular discourse about racism and the African American experience, this chapter examines how the election of Barack Obama *did* move America into new postracial terrain and centers Obama as a representative of the postracial intellectual. At its most basic level, postracialism describes one approach of Black politicians, made possible by the civil rights movement. To be elected in statewide and national elections, this group has been able to appeal to both a Black and White electorate simultaneously and out of necessity.[6] As political scientist Andra Gillespie notes, "With the election of the nation's first Black president, the end of the first decade of the twenty-first century ushered in what journalists commonly referred to as a 'post-racial' era of American politics. The election of Barack Obama supposedly proved that America had finally atoned for centuries of slavery and codified segregation. Black candidates now would be free to run as candidates, judged only by the soundness of their racially transcendent policy proposals and not by the color of their skin."[7]

Introducing the notion of "the new American dilemma" by redefining and reclaiming what postracialism means, this essay draws out some of the many weaknesses of postracialism while also considering its utility by teasing out aspects that help gain a fuller understanding of our times. Indeed, the actuality of postracialism can be said to have both a beginning and an ending point, starting with the electoral campaign of Barack Obama and ending almost immediately upon his first term as the forty-fourth president. As such, postracialism was an idea with limited saliency in American politics. However, it lives on in other representative postracial politicians, such as US Senators Cory Booker of New Jersey and the first woman US vice president, Kamala Harris of California.[8]

This chapter argues that Obama's second term deserves closer examination and consideration. While in his first term Obama took on issues that spoke to a postracial reality, it was in his second term that he appeared to begin to realize the limits of a postracial approach.[9] The most postracial thing about Obama was that he was bold enough and comfortable enough in his ability to try to govern—not as a Black president but as a president who happened to be Black. The first thing his administration did was set about to transform the "third rail" of American politics, health care of all things—as well as remake the new world order, with what would come to be known as the Obama doctrine. He was postracial enough to make war. He was postracial enough to hunt down Osama bin Laden. Referring to Gillespie's definition, Obama was postracial in the sense that he thought he could govern like any sitting president and tackled non-Black areas of life almost exclusively in that first term.

Finally, this chapter suggests that Obama's presidency pushed the limits of what postracialism was and possibly *could* be. Challenging the deconstructive notion that is being applied to race in both popular and political discourse, this essay analyzes efforts to grapple with definitions of postracialism.

The unfolding of events in his second term—such as the shooting of unarmed teenager Trayvon Martin in 2012, who, Obama said, "could have been my son," the shooting of Michael Brown, the choking of Eric Garner in 2014, and the seemingly unending chain of police shootings in 2015 and 2016—reveal that Obama may have simply changed his mind about the possibilities of postracialism.[10] By the end of his presidency, with his US Supreme Court nominee altogether ignored by the US Senate and successive votes to block his policy agenda on issue after issue, it became apparent to many that the president himself may be being racially profiled.[11]

The Obama years themselves can be viewed as a period of continuous racial calamities, the repercussions of which were felt on a seemingly daily basis beginning with the arrest of renowned Harvard University professor Henry Louis "Skip" Gates Jr. for allegedly breaking into his own home in 2009. The arrest of arguably *the* leading scholar of the African American experience—certainly the most well-known due to his television work—may have been an early, if misunderstood, warning at the time of what would become a cascade of Black arrests, with even worse outcomes. Had this been a warning shot across the bow of Black America?

During the summer of 2009, Cambridge police arrested Gates at his home and claimed to be investigating a possible break-in. Obama stepped into the fracas by saying, "[The] Cambridge police acted stupidly," and eventually invited the arresting officer and Gates for an unprecedented "beer summit" at the White House. According to Benjamin J. Rhodes, Obama's deputy national security adviser and speechwriter, "The Skip Gates thing was more impactful than people know." As Rhodes recounts, Obama was asked, "What do you think about probably the preeminent African American academic in the country being arrested in his house? . . . and he [Obama] said it was stupid. The blowback was so insane, and it was like people were so excited to be talking about race on cable television, and it was multiple days of people going back and forth and Fox going into hysteria. And then we have this absurd beer summit where Gates has a beer with the guy, and you know, he [Obama] was trying to fix the economy."[12] Rhodes's observations remind us Obama was dealing with race in a way previous presidents wouldn't have been expected to, even as he attempted to repair the American economy from the worst crisis since the Great Depression.[13]

Unlike so many other ideological positions within the Black intellectual tradition, postracial theory occupies a strange place in the pantheon of Black political thought. Postracialism emanates not from the firmament of the Black community or even Black thought per se but was, instead, foisted upon it by the media.[14] While the lexicon can be traced to Obama, or at least has been done so by media pundits, the source of this shift from idea to embodiment in a singular individual is also up for debate. In so many ways—except where it is connected to more muscular ideologies such as multiracialism—its usage must also be viewed through the prisms of more sophisticated frameworks, such as generational shifts. If we disregard the fact that postracialism has mostly proven to be a myth and consider it seriously as an actual ideology or mode of thought, it is not inaccurate to say that the concept of postracialism is a unique one, indeed.[15]

The Black Presidency

Barack Obama's election in 2008 as the first Black president of the United States supposedly proved that America had finally atoned for centuries of slavery and codified segregation. To be sure, the idea of a postracial body politic is a farcical idea to most people who study race in American politics. However, it requires a more critical examination to more fully understand its implications. Summing up what she characterizes as an almost absurd notion, Andra Gillespie has noted, "Although our nation has indeed improved race relations and reduced inequality, it is in no position to rest on its laurels and proclaim that Dr. Martin Luther King, Jr's dream has been fulfilled."[16]

A somewhat superficial, if commonly held, understanding is that it took the election of an African American to the nation's highest office to unleash a level of racial hatred the likes of which we have not seen in decades. But the cause-and-effect relationship here may be more complicated than that. The Ku Klux Klan—which endorsed Trump in 2016—found a way to reestablish itself in the wake of Obama's election, rebranding themselves as White nationalists under the more normalized title of the "alt-right." This had tragic outcomes. On August 12, 2017, at the so-called "Unite the Right" rally in Charlottesville, Virginia, hundreds of White nationalists and neo-Confederates carrying tiki torches gathered to protest the removal of a statue of Confederate general Robert E. Lee. Massive violence ensued; three people were killed, and thirty-four were injured, with President Trump famously commenting that there were "very fine people on both sides."[17]

And while this rise of White supremacy seemed to have been caused by Obama's election, the cause-and-effect relationship here is not as clear as it may appear. Signs of a resurgence and a more subdued effort to reinstitute White nationalism were happening well before Obama's election. David Duke, a former grand wizard of the Ku Klux Klan, made a successful run in a special election for a Louisiana House seat in 1989, serving as a Republican Louisiana state representative for one term. He went on to endorse Trump for president.

What if the racism that we thought was eradicated by the civil rights movement was simply there all along—dormant, hiding in wait, waiting to pounce—waiting for America to feel just threatened enough to resort to that grandest of American traditions, the use of racial brutality?[18] Who could have guessed that America would reach back to this very old idea—thought to be long since gone—to restore the balance of Whiteness in the twenty-first century?[19]

An analysis of the relationship between ideologies, such as multiracialism and postracialism, as well as how Whiteness operates in the United States, helps us to more fully appreciate what has come to pass. Obama's racial identity put him in the ironic position of having to respond to these events while also being seen as the initiator of these crises. In either case, people wondered aloud how it could be that under the watch of the first Black president, so many Black lives were in peril. How could a movement called Black Lives Matter coexist with what was supposed to be such a triumphant moment for African Americans? The election of the first Black president caused many to rethink what was happening outside of the "Obama bubble." White supremacy was reorganizing to protect itself from the perceived threat of Obama's presidency. But how could such a thing happen in this reputed "postracial" era?

One of the most well-known ideological "cousins" of postracialism is the ideology stemming from the mixed-race or multiracial movement known as "multiracialism."[20] As mentioned earlier, other related terms make postracialism as an idea possible, including the set of strictures and imperatives embodied by the term "post–civil rights." Obama is a member of this post–civil rights and GenX generation and to a lesser extent, millennial generation, because of how he resonated with young people. As such, postracialism is in some sense deeply attached to the millennial worldview—one which dismisses claims of racism through the promotion of a color-blind, multicultural society. This view seeks to jettison essentialist notions of race and differences premised on race-based identities while encouraging cultural diversity. In its removal of legal barriers to full citizenship and its lifting of many African Americans into the middle and upper classes, postracialism is also somewhat paradoxically deeply dependent on, at the very least, the acknowledgment of the existence of those same structures to give it legitimacy.

Of the post–civil rights era, historian Robin D. G. Kelley comments, "The generation that came of age in the '70s, '80s, and '90s has been called a lot of things: the post-soul generation, the post–civil rights generation, the postindustrial generation. But few standing 'at the edge of history,' to use the language of the Gary Declaration, thought in terms of being 'post' anything. Rather, they entered a new period with tremendous optimism. For some, this sense of a better future came because of efforts toward racial integration. For others, it was the hope for greater political and social control of their lives."[21] In his book *White Supremacy and Racism in the Post–Civil Rights Era* (2001), political sociologist Eduardo Bonilla-Silva explicitly characterizes the post–civil rights ideology as one of color-blind racism, which he calls "a system of social arrangements that maintain white privilege at all levels."[22]

The New American Dilemma

In his classic 1944 study of race relations, *An American Dilemma: The Negro Problem and Modern Democracy*, Swedish-born Nobel-laureate economist Gunnar Myrdal argues that political and social interaction in the United States are shaped by an "American Creed." This creed "emphasizes the ideals of individualism, civil liberties, and equality of opportunity." He adds, however, that "there is a 'Negro problem' in the United States and most Americans are aware of it, although it assumes varying forms and intensity in different regions of the country and among diverse groups of the American people. Americans have to react to it, politically as citizens and, where there are Negroes present in the community, privately as neighbors."[23]

Funded by the Carnegie Foundation and coming in at nearly fifteen hundred pages, Myrdal's two-volume encyclopedic study painstakingly details what he saw as obstacles to African Americans' full participation in American society as of the 1940s. At the center of Myrdal's work is his claim that the American creed keeps the diverse peoples of the United States together: "It is the common belief in this creed that endows all people—whites, negroes, rich, poor, male, female, and immigrants alike—with a common cause and allows for them to co-exist as one nation."[24] Indeed, creed is a clue to understanding our current political moment.

In his chapter "Discrimination and the American Creed" (1944), Robert K. Merton describes, "Viewed sociologically, the creed is a set of values and precepts embedded in American culture, to which Americans are expected to conform. It is a complex of affirmations, rooted in the historical past and ceremonially celebrated in the present, partly enacted in the laws of the land and partly not. Like all creeds, it is a profession of faith, a part of cultural tradition sanctified by the larger traditions of which it is a part."[25] To wit, Myrdal observes:

> To the great majority of white Americans, the Negro problem has distinctly negative connotations. It suggests something difficult to settle and equally difficult to leave alone. It is embarrassing. It makes for moral uneasiness. The very presence of the Negro in America, his fate in this country through slavery, Civil War and Reconstruction; his recent career and his present status; his accommodation; his protest and his aspiration; in fact his entire biological, historical and social existence as a participant American represent to the ordinary white man in the North as well as in the South an anomaly in the very structure of American society. To many, this takes on the proportion of a menace—biological, economic, social, cultural, and, at times, political. This anxiety may be mingled with a feeling of individual and collective guilt. A few see the problem as a challenge to statesmanship. To all it is a trouble.[26]

Much like race relations described by Myrdal in the 1940s in which African Americans were seen as somehow being "different" and outside the margins of what constitutes "the American creed," the twenty-first century could also potentially mark a new low in American race relations—or a "new American dilemma."

A More Perfect Union?

In a speech that later came to be known as "A More Perfect Union," Obama, then a candidate for the Democratic presidential nomination, was called upon to publicly denounce his affiliation with the minister of the church he attended, the Reverend Jeremiah Wright.[27] In this moment, in which he tried to salvage his candidacy by distancing himself from a minister known for his punitive Black nationalist rhetoric, Obama delivered a speech that not only highlighted his multiracial heritage but also opened the door to define what could be thought of as a kind of outline of postracialism. His speech, which specifically addressed his upbringing, demonstrates that the racial divide meant different things for Blacks and Whites. In essence, he called for a type of racial forgiveness that was predicated on personal evolution, particularly, among Whites. But Black Americans were uneasy with this new concept, which they saw as undermining the salience of institutional and personal racism. For those who remembered the struggles of the 1960s or earlier, forgiveness had not proved to be an effective political strategy. Instead, it was direct action that had provided structural changes. Therefore, in essence, Whites who heard this message could embrace the concept of a postracial America because in its erasure of historical racial bias, race loses all its meaning. On the other hand, many Blacks could (and did) reject this same construct. "A lot of black people aren't ready to get beyond race, because race puts them in the situation they're in," relates the late Ron Walters, a political scientist at the University of Maryland, who worked on Jesse Jackson's presidential runs. "But many whites want to get beyond the past, they want to support a black person who doesn't raise the past and in fact gives them absolution from the past."[28]

In addition to his youthful appearance and ability to relate to people, much of Obama's overall appeal (to certain segments of the population) stemmed from his image as a postracial politician. His mixed-race background and rhetoric, seen most prominently in the 2004 Democratic National Convention speech, also emphasized the importance of Americans moving beyond political, religious, and racial differences. As a postracial intellectual, Obama was able to deliver this, and more.

The Connections between Postracialism and Multiracialism

Here's an interesting thought experiment. If Obama had not been the offspring of an interracial marriage between a White mother and Black father, would the media have painted him as a postracial figure? That is to say, would the media have been so quick to label the Obama years as postracial had Obama identified monoracially as an African American and not of interracial parentage? One reading of postracialism lies within this appraisal of Obama himself, as a consciously multiracial subject and the degree to which his biraciality augured postracialism.[29]

Postracialism is rooted in the changing demographics of the American population. This has led to another myth of postracialism—that the increase of interracial marriages is somehow emblematic of a change in racial attitudes in the United States and that the rise in those who identify as multiracial has somehow brought us to a point where race does not matter. This, too, is a falsehood. In his work *Amalgamation Schemes: Antiblackness and the Critique of Multiracialism* (2008), Jared Sexton makes the argument that "despite being heralded as the answer to racial conflict in the post–civil rights United States, the principal political effect of multiracialism is neither a challenge to the ideology of white supremacy nor a defiance of sexual racism. More accurately . . . multiculturalism displaces both by evoking long-standing tenets of antiblackness and prescriptions for normative sexuality."[30]

While it is true that there are more interracial marriages than ever before—nearly one in seven marriages in 2008 was interracial or interethnic—a closer look at the ethnic makeup of these marriages reveals that fewer of these are Black-White marriages than one might think. A 2010 Pew Research Center report notes more than double the intermarriage rate of the 1980s and six times the intermarriage rate of the 1960s, yet White-Black couples made up only 11 percent of total interracial marriages. White-Hispanic couplings accounted for the greatest proportion of these intermarriages, at 41 percent.[31] Some 22 percent of Black male newlyweds in 2008 married outside their race, compared with just 9 percent of Black female newlyweds.[32] Among Asians, the pattern is the opposite. Black men and Asian women have the highest rates of intermarriage while Asian men and Black women have the lowest. While many point to the US Supreme Court *Loving v. Virginia* decision of 1967 as the cause of the increase in interracial marriage, as Rainier Spencer, leader of the opposition to the theory of multiracialism and sharp cultural critic, has argued, it is the loosening of immigration laws in 1965 that did much more to increase the rates of intermarriage.[33] This is what allows for higher rates of interracial marriage between Whites and non-White groups, such as Hispanics and Asians, with much less growth in Black-White intermarriage. Two of the leading scholars of critical mixed-race theory, G. Reginald Daniel and Jasmine Kelekay, agree on this point. They write in their influential essay "From *Loving v. Virginia* to Barack Obama: The Symbolic Tie That Binds": "Black-White intermarriages have composed a relatively small percentage of the nation's interracially married couples. Consequently, the *Loving* decision did not result in a significant growth in intermarriages."[34]

Indeed, while the depiction of this rise in multiracialism has informed the postracial discussion, much of the news coverage of multiracial identity from 2000 onward depict it as a new event in American national life. It was not. As Spencer has argued, it was portrayed as a phenomenon that was exoticized as new and different and in need of federal recognition, hence the change in the US Census that allowed people to choose more than one race since 2000.[35] However, this "phenomenon" has historical antecedents. The relaxed immigration statutes of the 1965 Immigration Act and other laws, such as the War Brides Act of 1945, had the effect of bringing larger numbers of non-White groups, such as Asians, to the United States, including Japanese and Korean immigrants. As a result, many of the children of this supposed bi- and multiracial baby boom are Hispanic-White and/or White-Asian—not Black and White.[36] A contemporary example of this would be George Zimmerman, the White and Peruvian man accused and acquitted for murdering Trayvon Martin in 2012. His racial and ethnic background did not reflect the postracialism touted by the media. Instead, as Bonilla-Silva points out, members of these groups are moving toward the status of "honorary whiteness."[37]

Furthermore, as sociologist Herbert Gans has commented, "Over the last decade, a number of social scientists writing on race and ethnicity have suggested that the country may be moving toward a new racial structure."[38] If current trends persist, today's multiracial hierarchy could be replaced by what he calls as a dual or bimodal one consisting of "non-Black" and "Black" population categories, with a third, "residual," category.[39] Gans suggests that racial categories, as currently understood, are undergoing fundamental changes. He argues that the current racial hierarchy will collapse into two categories: Black and non-Black. He continues, "More important, this hierarchy may be based not just on color or other visible bodily features, but also on a distinction between undeserving and deserving, or stigmatized and respectable, races. The hierarchy is new only insofar as the old white-nonwhite dichotomy may be replaced by a nonblack-black one, but it is hardly new for blacks, who are likely to remain at the bottom once again."[40] During Obama's first term, despite the insistence of the media, the president was constantly reminded that postracialism was not a concept that applied to him, even as a biracial individual. Indeed, he identified himself on the census of 2010 in the "Black" category of the "Black/non-Black" binary.[41]

Charles A. Gallagher's notion of racial redistricting is also very useful here. In his piece "Racial Redistricting: Expanding the Boundaries of Whiteness," he explores, through in-depth interviews and focus groups with White college students, the boundaries of racial tolerance in White familial relations: "As whites and other nonblack groups inhabit common racial ground, the stigma once associated with interracial relationships between these groups is diminishing. The shifting boundaries of whiteness have 'important implications' for the Multiracial Movement and, if not careful, the movement will exacerbate anti-black sentiment in the United States."[42] In these, and many ways, the multiracial movement, much like the postracial racial ideal—which is supposedly egalitarian and integrationist—can easily manifest itself as inegalitarian and assimilationist. Consequently, they are seen as inimical in many ways to the priorities, desires, imperatives, and hopes of the African American community.[43] As Dalmage explains, "Gallagher argues that the multiracial movement must acknowledge the 'racial redistricting' taking place in the United States in which whiteness is expanding to include multiracial Asians and light-skinned Latinos."[44]

The Literature on Postracialism and Multiracialism

Two schools of thought in the literature are emerging that give rise to postracialism. One is a selection of pieces that form the crux of critical–mixed race studies literature and argue for multiracialism, and on the other side are selected pieces that offer a critique based on the notion of anti-Blackness and incorporate the one-drop rule more into their analysis. Among these scholars' works, Spencer's stands out. In his book *Challenging Multiracial Identity*, Spencer asserts that the "mulatto" in historical context has been characterized through dysfunction and thus offers a more multilayered identity than any of the previous studies mentioned. He argues convincingly that the mulatto has historically been characterized as marginal and emotionally unstable, with an overwhelming desire to be White. He begins by pointing out that historically, White people considered interracial children an abomination. He compares this to the more contemporary American multiracial and mixed-race movement known as Generation MIX, which, he argues, has a relationship to the "mulatto movement" of days before the historic *Loving v. Virginia* decision.[45] In their more current incarnation, Spencer argues, "mulattos" have been rejected as flawed and retrograde, and yet the mulatto is tied to the African American identity in many important ways. He points to examples such as William Craft and Ellen Craft, who used their racial ambiguity as a way of escaping slavery. This interpretation of the mulatto, Spencer says, is incompatible with the myths reinvigorated by Generation MIX.[46] According to Spencer, these proponents of a multiracial movement are not interested in linking the contemporary movement with the mulatto past, and instead, lay claim to a constructed identity by right of force—by redefining unilaterally what or who is considered Black. He writes, "What is the relation of the black/white multiracially identifying members of Generation Mix to the mulatto of history? Does the American Multiracial Identity Movement embrace the mulatto as a mixed-race pioneer. as a kindred ancestral spirit, as a lineal precursor?"[47]

Some indication of Obama's feelings about mixed race can be gleaned from comments he made in 2006 to members of Generation MIX, a group of multiracial college students that drove around the country in a bus with the words "Generation MIX" written on it, featured in the documentary *Chasing Daybreak: A Film about Mixed Race in America*. Then–US Senator Obama kind of "burst their bubble," explaining to them that the oppression they felt was as people of color, not as multiracial people. His comments in the Generation MIX documentary film offer an interesting glimpse into his thinking on mixed-race identity:

> I don't think that you can consider the issue of mixed race outside of the issue of race. . . . Um I do think that racial relations have improved somewhat and I think to the extent that that people of mixed race are part of those larger movements and larger concerns then I think they can serve a useful bridge between cultures . . . but the thing that I'm always cautious about is persons of mixed race focusing so narrowly on their own unique experiences that they're detached from larger struggles . . . and I think it's important to try to avoid

that sense of exclusivity and feeling that you're special in some way. . . . I think you may be unique in your experiences and that may allow you to reach out to more people but you know ultimately the same challenges that all of you face are the same challenges that a lot of young people face which is how do you have an impact on the world that's positive for the long term.[48]

This aspect of Obama's identity could best be expressed as a lesson for all multiracials; he learned early on that he would have to run and identify as an African American to survive racially and politically. The Generation MIX movement raised many interesting questions about the validity of race but didn't resonate with African Americans because it didn't honor the African American experience.

The Black Imperial Presidency

So complicated was Obama's election in 2008 that it is often overlooked that, originally, fear of Obama's assassination served to limit Black criticism of him. This does bolster the postracial claim—which is to say that we went from a place of being so *not postracial* that we were worried that Obama would simply be assassinated as soon as he got into office, to a place where Obama's daily presence as the first Black president became so commonplace that we began to expect him to do more for the Black community. Meanwhile, Obama used his political celebrity to push for ideas that were very postracial and "outside of his lane" in the view of many on the center and right. African Americans seemed to understand at some level that Obama could not be merely a Black president; he had to be a president for all the people, and, therefore, racial expectations of him were somewhat diminished. This, in itself, is evidence that we are post-something—that African Americans could grow from a place where nothing was expected to one where everything was expected suggests that there has been some kind of tectonic shift. Michael Eric Dyson tapped into this sentiment when he made his famous pronouncement at the Black Agenda Conference in Chicago in 2010: "Obama is not Moses, he's Pharaoh." In tamping down to some extent Black expectations of Obama, while also arguing for Obama to do more for Black folk, Dyson captured brilliantly in that one statement both Obama's potential to do more and the realistic expectation that he might not.[49] Speaking for much of that criticism, political scientist Fred Harris comments:

> The triumph of "post-racial" Democratic politics has not been a triumph for African-Americans in the aggregate. It has failed to arrest the growing chasm of income and wealth inequality; to improve prospects for social and economic mobility; to halt the re-segregation of public schools and narrow the black-white achievement gap; and to prevent the Supreme Court from eroding the last vestiges of affirmative action.[50]

Black adoration of Obama seemed to have waned by the end of his first term. Even his most ardent critics—Black conservatives included—had to admit that the admiration they shared for Obama had suffered due to his handling of issues of race. Although many attributed this to the handling of the Gates arrest or the firing of Shirley Sherrod, former Georgia state director of Rural Development for the United States Department of Agriculture, or Obama's neoliberal policies, one could argue that his misreading of issues of race may have stemmed from his biracial identity, which, perhaps, caused him to think that he was somehow an exception to the rule. As mentioned earlier, that level of comfort in his first term—nay, confidence—was probably the most postracial thing about Obama.

Another phenomenon that was certainly not a new one but one which Obama's tenure, perhaps, accentuated has to do with the politics of respectability. Because of Obama's enormous influence as a role model, specifically for Black youth, his words carried quite a bit of weight, and he was, naturally, in great demand as a speaker and motivator—especially for commencement speeches. Ronald Chennault, a scholar of Black education, has compared two of Obama's commencement addresses—his Barnard College speech from 2012 and his Morehouse College speech from 2013—with a particular focus on how each speech positioned its audience as victims of and/or victors over discrimination. Chennault contrasts the content of each speech, pointing out, as other observers have, the contradictory nature of the speeches to these very different audiences. Obama could certainly get "preachy" when talking to young Black men, exhorting them in ways to "do better" and "reach higher" and other such mantras. His speech to Barnard was quite different, in its approach, however.[51] Should it come as a surprise that the first Black president would be "more comfortable" speaking to an audience of Black graduates from one of the nation's most prestigious HBCUs? That he would use the "vernacular" and draw from the "scriptural" tradition of the Black preacher and "the word"? The question is, how is this different from most speeches given at Morehouse? After all, the motto of Morehouse is: "Et Facta Est Lux" taken from the Latin, "And there was light."

Sharp criticism of Obama has come from many quarters within the Black community. Much of it has emanated from and been driven by leaders and thinkers in Black radical circles whose voices were raised often during the Obama era. For them, Obama, as the first Black president, had not done enough for Black Americans. They felt he could have done more.[52] But what would *more* look like?[53] Perhaps the loudest and most vocal critic is the eminent thinker and race philosopher Cornel West, who once called Obama, among other things, "a republican in blackface." While others were not as vociferous (or personal) in their criticisms, it would be correct to say that there was a vigorous, lively, and spirited Black critique of Obama, including Keeanga-Yamahtta Taylor's brilliant article in the *Guardian*, in which she states, "Barack Obama's refusal to use his position as president to intervene on behalf of African Americans is a stain on his record many activists will never forget." Among intellectuals, the opposition seemed to fall into two major camps.

In the first camp, scholars were self-reflective of their deep appreciation for the realization of the first Black presidency; they often remarked on how their hearts stirred at the meaning of a Black man in the highest office of the land celebrated right along with Black America at that moment. As Milton Vickerman describes in *The Problem of Post-Racialism*, Obama's election in many respects "represented a radical break in American history, a potent symbol of Black progress, and a significant example of the society's ability to move some way toward living up to its higher ideals."[54]

But some had deep disagreements with Obama's policies: the usage of drones in war, his neoliberal tendencies, mass deportations, and his somewhat boiler-plate centrist, even conservative agenda.[55] The second camp could be classified as coming out of an important Black radical tradition, in which it was often pointed out that Obama, while Black, was worse for Black America in many ways and was not as progressive as he appeared to be. Their project seemed to be to point out that it was precisely because Obama was Black that he could get away with such policies and had, thus, pulled the wool over everyone's eyes, racially speaking. It was becoming the second camp's task to call out Obama at every turn, with a vitriolic political tone that at times seemed to verge more on personal hatred than unbiased criticism.

In many ways, both camps had valid points. Obama turned out to be much more centrist, much more neoliberal in his policies than one might have first thought. Although that should have come as no surprise—considering the imperatives of postracialism, Obama's use of drones particularly vexed this mainly antiwar, Black radical voice. However, this public in-fighting among Black leaders, often generational, left many constituents scratching their heads. The heightened language left many to simply dismiss the fighting as "personal."[56] What we did not know then, of course, was that behind all of this, to West's point, White supremacy was reconstituting itself, and the forces of hate were responding in many different ways to Obama's so-called racial conservatism. But it also raised a question: If these forces responded the way they did to a Black president who was this "middle of the road," how would they have responded to someone more radical?

How else was the first African American president supposed to govern, except to make wide concessions, to try to be the president for all people—at least at the beginning of his presidency? Like his predecessors, he would make mistakes. His race seemed to amplify these missteps. Obama was not Dwight Gooden; he was Jackie Robinson. He was the first. While Robinson was spat upon, Obama was heckled during his televised State of the Union address when a Republican House member shouted, "You lie!" after the president denied that his health care plan would cover undocumented immigrants.[57] Rhodes describes it as a kind of "Jackie Robinson ethos," which is, "I'm the first African American to do this, so I have to do this job better, twice as good as a like, white person would have to, and I have to take all this stuff and keep my head down."[58]

Despite the illusion of postracialism, racism in America was still palpable enough that Obama would be limited by the color of his skin. The media's adherence to its belief in the fiction of postracialism often prevented it from calling the words and actions of the Tea Party what they were—pure unadulterated racism.[59] Obama hanged in effigy. Obama depicted as an ape. The so-called birther movement launched by Trump was part and parcel of the same thing. This had nothing to do with a birth certificate and much more to do with discrediting a president named Barack Hussein Obama. As Daniel argues, "birthers were less concerned with the legality of Obama's citizenship than with discursively calling his citizenship into question as a means of delegitimizing his presidency because he is Black."[60]

Despite its apocryphal origins, postracialism remains an important lens through which to understand the opening of the twenty-first century. It is also a viable political and ideological lens through which to examine a new era of Black intellectual thought in this century. But it's one plagued with the illusions of Whiteness and all its attendant issues and problems. One thing is clear, postracialism is inseparable from neoliberalism. The two go hand in hand. Precisely because it coincides with the rise of another "-ism" in America, multiracialism, and a critique of Blackness writ large—what scholars like Sexton call "anti-Blackness"—it is a phenomenon that begs to be better understood in the larger context of American political thought.

Obama and the Black Left: Were Progressives Duped?

In much the same way that Bill Clinton's "don't ask, don't tell" politically galvanized the lesbian, gay, bisexual, transgender, and queer (LGBTQ) community, the presence of a Black man in the highest office in the land did the same for Black progressive forces in America. African Americans did not win statewide elections generally. It had happened in Massachusetts with Deval Patrick. It had happened in an earlier era with Edward Brooke. But it was still quite rare for an African American to win a national election.

Obama did much to reinstate forces of progressivism in America. Probably not since the 1960s had there been such a large mobilization of progressive voices. His campaign has been credited for rebuilding the Democratic Party, for creating the massive movement of Whites to vote not only for Obama but also for Trump's election and the disaggregation of the Democratic party.

But without Obama, would there have been a Bernie Sanders? Did Obama clear the way for an avowed socialist to be taken seriously in his run to head the ticket of one of the two major American political parties? It was Obama who was called a socialist not only by the Tea Party and the extreme right but also by many writers who examined his neoliberal bent toward a European variant of democratic socialism. This connection, of course, became more pronounced with Obama's early push for health care reform in which America and European systems were compared in the public debate. In a 2009 *Chicago Tribune* op-ed piece, Frank Llewellyn, a former national director of the Democratic Socialists of America, and Joseph M. Schwartz, a professor of political science at Temple University, stated, "Over the past 12 months, the Democratic Socialists of America has received more media attention than it has over the past 12 years. The global economic crisis undoubtedly opened some people's eyes to the inequality and insecurity that capitalism generates and rendered them curious about an alternative." And so, it was that the "socialist" label began to stick to Obama.[61]

A 2009 *Newsweek* cover headline proudly, although perhaps prematurely, declares, "We are all socialists now."[62] Although true democratic socialists (and probably Senator Sanders) certainly took exception to the title, one had to admit that Obama had shined a light on an ideology and political force that had dwelled in relative obscurity before his election—at least in the United States. Sanders, who had not yet achieved the national fame he would when he ran for president in the 2016 election, had certainly proved his bona fides as a socialist, independent voice in the US Senate and dating back much longer to his days in Vermont politics.[63]

In a *New York Times* interview, Obama claims that in the early days the administration was very wary of speaking about race. Indeed, in the few times Obama did speak about race—the Gates arrest, the killing of Martin—there was a very big pushback by the American mainstream electorate. Infrequent as it may have been, Obama *had* spoken about race in ways more personal and poignant than any other president in recent memory. And even in light of those somewhat-modest utterances of race, Obama was pilloried by the right.

Later, when Obama tried to stake out a careful middle ground in the wake of Ferguson, Missouri, and other killings, he was criticized for not visiting Ferguson. As is so often the case when it comes to Obama, he was damned if he did, damned if he didn't—handcuffed in a way to the strictures of postracialism—simultaneously bringing about an era in which race was not supposed to be focused on and yet an era, ironically, in which race was being punctuated in a way unseen since the civil rights–Black Power days of the 1960s and 1970s. Much of this has to do with the ways he was "packaged" and pitched by his campaign handlers in both the 2008 and 2012 campaigns, especially by David Axelrod. Daniel describes one example, in particular, that seems particularly shocking in retrospect but is a perfect example of how postracialism is tied to Whiteness:

> This connection to whiteness was strategically emphasized in black educator, activist, political commentator, and Democratic Party affiliate Donna Brazile's appeal to whites who might not vote for Obama simply because he is an African-descent American rather than because they disagreed with his political platform. Brazile stressed that Harvard-educated Obama is "biracial" and "spent nine months in the womb of a white woman. He was raised for the first eighteen to twenty-one years by his white grandparents. He ain't spent no time in living rooms like I spent my childhood."[64]

Along these same lines, in a wide-ranging series on Obama's legacy, the *New York Times* recounts that only weeks after seventy million Americans chose a Black man for president,

> shattering a racial barrier that had stood for the entirety of the nation's 232-year history, no one in the White House, especially the man in the Oval Office, wanted to talk about race. President Obama had made a pragmatic calculation in January 2009, as the financial crisis drove communities across the United States toward economic collapse. Whatever he did for African-Americans, whose neighborhoods were suffering more than others, he would not describe as efforts to specifically help Black America. Mr. Obama made the decision knowing how powerfully his election had raised the hopes of African-Americans—and knowing that no matter what he did, it would not be seen as enough. The fear inside the West Wing was that promoting a "black agenda" and aiming programs directly at African-Americans at a time of widespread economic anxiety would provoke a white backlash—the kind that, years later, White House officials would view as helping to elect Donald J. Trump.[65]

Whither Postracialism?

Demographers predict that Whites will be a racial minority in the United States by 2045. The election of the first Black president as well as this statistical reality, more than any other factor, helps to explain the election of Trump and the reemergence of White nationalism as a primary organizing principle in the second decade of the twenty-first century. However, the argument can also be made that this kind of organizing began well before Trump's election.

As Manisha Sinha, a historian of abolitionism slavery and the American Civil War, commented just after Trump's election, "As a historian, I see uncanny and unsettling parallels between what happened with the overthrow of Reconstruction, America's startling experiment in interracial democracy after the Civil War.

It seems after every period of extraordinary progress, we witness a complete regression to the forces of reaction." As Sinha suggests, "Obama's election was a reconstruction of sorts for the nation, and we are just now seeing the same 'whitelash' that accompanied the end of that widely misunderstood period." She continues, "The historical roots of the 'whitelash' that fueled Trump's victory lie in a prior racial backlash to an unprecedented attempt to grant African Americans citizenship during the period of Radical Reconstruction."[66]

Obama was only the third African American elected to the US Senate since Reconstruction.[67] Activists during the civil rights–movement period called their movement a "Second Reconstruction." Scholars like Manning Marable and Aldon Morris have also helped to popularize this idea among scholars, as well as today's activists, such as Reverend William L. Barber III. However, in light of Sinha's analysis, we may need to rethink the periodization—to include the post–civil rights work of the 1980s, 1990s, and beyond—the generation that Obama brought to a close. It makes sense that postracialism is the outcome of a movement that was essentially integrationist from its outset.[68] Although one may debate the extent to which Obama was truly part of the civil rights tradition, what cannot be denied is the way that civil rights veterans like John Lewis welcomed him as such. Photos of them marching arm in arm across the Edmund Pettus Bridge fifty years after Bloody Sunday evoke this sentiment.[69] If the civil rights, Black Power, and post–civil rights era can be called a second reconstruction, then our current historical moment could be said to be verging on a potential third reconstruction. As such, the first half of the twenty-first century could potentially mark a new nadir in American race relations, and this is at the heart of what constitutes the new American dilemma.

The destruction of Black bodies at the hands of police, the resurgence of White nationalism and White supremacy in the twenty-first century, and the wholesale attempt to "keep the nigger down" as Ida B. Wells characterized an earlier era in the beginning of the twentieth century, where Black bodies were lynched so often, it became commonplace, are features of this new reality. In October 2006, two years before Obama was elected, the Federal Bureau of Investigation (FBI) issued a report warning about White supremacists infiltrating law enforcement and "hiding behind the uniform to terrorize minorities."[70] This report in some ways helps to explain the uptick in the killing of unarmed Blacks in the last several years and why the Obama years felt both like a great celebration and a racial nightmare simultaneously. What has transpired in this supposed postracial era requires an analysis of many factors that have made the first two decades of the twenty-first century a time of great change.

In July 2019 President Trump tweeted that a group of four minority congresswomen—who were feuding with House Speaker Nancy Pelosi and later became known collectively as "the Squad"—should "go back" to the countries they came from rather than "loudly and viciously telling the people of the United States" how to run the government. While many were quick to point out that only one of the lawmakers had been born outside of the country, this response appeared to have missed the point. When Trump made the statement, he was tapping into a long tradition of what Myrdal is referring to—a difference in creed. Although three of the legislators were born in the United States, they are not "representative Americans" in the mind of Trump and his supporters. To them, they're not American because they're not White. The trope of "go back to your country" has been around a long time and reifies the fact that America was started as a White male landowner's country—a White republic; the passage of the Naturalization Law of 1790 specified that naturalized citizenship was reserved for Whites. So when we close our eyes and think about terms like "all-American," we don't see Black, we see White. What it suggests is that American society is not purely a democracy but rather a "raceocracy."[71]

This new effort to redefine (or reclaim) what the American creed is and to proclaim that African Americans and people of color somehow fall outside of it constitutes a crisis in American history. It is precisely this effort to reinstitute a new nadir for African Americans—one in which White nationalism becomes the dominant ideology in American life and culture—that constitutes a "new American dilemma" and threatens to tear down all that has been built through previous movements to bring about social justice and equity in America.

The truth is that we find ourselves at a profound crossroads as a nation today. Many are speaking actively of a new civil war, and the violence that accompanied the conflicts in Charlottesville and other places speaks to this reality. It is how America responds to this new American dilemma that will decide our fate as a nation. As President Abraham Lincoln exhorted, "A house divided upon itself cannot stand." About the impending crisis, Lincoln warned, "I do not expect the house to fall—but I do expect it will cease to be divided. It will become all one thing or all the other."[72]

Historically, African Americans have saved this country from war and chaos—during the Civil War and Reconstruction—then again in the 1950s and 1960s when they helped America remember its ideals by spurring the country, as Martin Luther King Jr. said, to "live up to the true nature of its creed." It was African Americans who helped to expand notions of American democracy by forcing America to "be true to what you said on paper."[73] It was King, that great theorist of American democracy, who said, "We are not wrong in what we are doing. If we are wrong, the Supreme Court of this nation is wrong. If we are wrong, the Constitution of the United States is wrong. And if we are wrong, God Almighty is wrong."[74] The civil rights movement pushed America to live up to its *own* stated ideals like, "All men are created equal." That is to say, the Black definition of America's creed was one that was more inclusive and, therefore, expanded the reaches of democracy and equality for *all* Americans. The question now before us is, will African Americans be able (or willing) to do this again, in what the Reverend Barber calls this potential "third reconstruction"? Will America be able to negotiate this new American dilemma by refashioning and rethinking its basic precepts, now, in the twenty-first century? Will America forge boldly into a brave new future, or will we become like apartheid-era South Africa, where only a minority of Whites ruled a nation of Black and Brown? None of these questions take us to postracialism, which has largely been proven to be a myth. However, since we are *post-something*, we must discover that new meaning together as we move into a future in which racial identities are shifting and uncertain and are taking on new and ever greater importance for African Americans in the twenty-first century.

Notes

1. Merriam-Webster.com, s.v. "post-racial," *Merriam-Webster Inc.*, 2020, https://www.merriam-webster.com/dictionary/post-racial.

2. Clarence Earl Walker, *The Preacher and the Politician: Jeremiah Wright, Barack Obama, and Race in America* (Charlottesville: University of Virginia Press, 2012).

3. William J. Wilson, *The Declining Significance of Race* (Chicago: University of Chicago Press, 1980).

4. As for the concept of "postracialism," if one were to ask the generation that invented it (that is to say, millennials) for a definition, the answers may not be as clear-cut as some may have once believed. In fact, many millennials surveyed reject the term "post-racial" and subscribe to a range of ideological and political positions that some may find contradictory but make complete sense to this seemingly somewhat-mercurial generation. See "Don't Call Them 'Post-Racial': Millennials Say Race Matters to Them," *Race Forward*, June 7, 2011, https://www.colorlines.com/articles/dont-call-them-post-racial-millennials-say-race-matters-them.

5. Zebulon V. Miletsky, "Mutt like Me: Barack Obama and the Mixed-Race Experience in Historical Perspective," in *Obama and the Biracial Factor: The Battle for a New American Majority*, ed. Andrew Jolivette (Chicago: Policy, 2012).

6. In an e-mail discussion in 2015 with G. Derek Musgrove, author of *Rumor, Repression, and Racial Politics: How the Harassment of Black Elected Officials Shaped Post–Civil Rights America*, he explains "postracialism" as

> the postracial Black politician playing a pickup game of basketball—at once alluding to their blackness or connections to black culture—but not in heavily overt ways or in ways that would make white voters uncomfortable. Quite the contrary, black politicians' goal is often to put white voters at ease. In doing so, whiteness and the ability to assimilate are key parts of the way that this ideology manifests itself. Blackness is alluded to lightly in ways that are acceptable to the white mainstream but not necessarily highlighted if they are thought to inhibit in any way the election of the postracial (often neoliberal) politician.

7. Andra Gillespie, *The New Black Politician: Cory Booker, Newark, and Post-Racial America* (New York: New York University Press, 2013), 1.

8. Ibid.

9. Obama's second term is also where a new approach to race was born, one that would bring Obama into prisons and bring the creation of programs, such as My Brother's Keeper, including a renewed focus on historically Black colleges and universities.

10. His insistence upon choosing "Black only" on the census of 2010 also speaks volumes.

11. The rise of the "Tea Party" and Trump demanding that Obama produce a birth certificate (which he eventually did) all speak to this.

12. Richard Prince, "Obama Was More Aware of Racism Than We Saw," *The Root*, June 27, 2018, https://journalisms.theroot.com/.

13. At this point, Obama was being compared to Franklin D. Roosevelt for his New Deal–style government bailouts although he is more comparable to Jimmy Carter, who came into the White House as the recession that followed the Vietnam War was just setting in. That being said, Obama has been compared to many presidents, including Ronald Reagan.

14. Unlike even integrationism, postracialism requires a serious deconstruction of Whiteness. More space is needed to distinguish between integration premised on egalitarian and inegalitarian (assimilationist) tenets. However, that is another piece entirely.

15. Besides multiracialism, one of its closest ideological cousins is a theory known as color-blindness or, more specifically, color-blind racism. See Eduardo Bonilla-Silva, *Racism without Racists: Color-Blind Racism and the Persistence of Racial Inequality in the United States* (Lanham, MD: Rowman, 2010.)

16. Gillespie, *New Black Politician*, 1.

17. "Trump Defends White-Nationalist Protesters: 'Some Very Fine People on Both Sides,'" *Atlantic*, August 15, 2017, https://www.theatlantic.com/.

18. This kind of gaslighting has a long tradition in American life and politics. Governor Orville Faubus of Arkansas, who had been a moderate by southern racial standards, was facing a tough reelection bid during the integration of Central High School by "the Little Rock Nine." Faubus hardened his position on the issue of segregation to remain in office.

19. Although it seemed unfathomable before Obama's election, it does not mean that one necessarily preceded the other.

20. See also "color-blindness" or "color-blind racism" in Bonilla-Silva, *Racism without Racists*.

21. Kelley is referring here to the declaration coming out of the historic Black Political Convention held in Gary, Indiana, in 1972. Robin D. G. Kelley, *Into the Fire—African Americans since 1970* (New York: Oxford University Press, 1996), 133.

22. Eduardo Bonilla-Silva, *White Supremacy and Racism in the Post–Civil Rights Era* (Boulder, CO: Rienner, 2001).

23. Gunnar Myrdal, *An American Dilemma: The Negro Problem and Modern Democracy* (1944; New York: McGraw-Hill, 1964), xlv.

24. Ibid.

25. Robert K. Merton, *Sociological Ambivalence and Other Essays* (New York: Free Press, 1977), 190.

26. Myrdal, *American Dilemma*, xlv.

27. Walker, *Preacher and the Politician*.

28. Perry Bacon Jr., "Can Obama Count on the Black Vote?" *Time Magazine*, January 23, 2007, http://content.time.com/.

29. How does the fact that Obama's parents were no longer alive affect this? Because his parents and grandparents had passed away, in many ways he was a self-made man free from the potentially contradicting interpretations of his parents. As such, he was able to tell his narrative without anyone to oppose him. Lastly, the impact of Michelle Obama cannot be overstated—both in reconnecting him with blackness but also in providing a visible reminder of the symbolic nature of Obama's connection to blackness. If he had, for example, married a White woman, he may have had a major problem.

30. Jared Sexton, *Amalgamation Schemes: Antiblackness and the Critique of Multira-cialism* (Minneapolis: University of Minnesota Press, 2008).

31. Jeffrey S. Passel, Wendy Wang, and Paul Taylor, " Marrying Out: One-in-Seven New U.S. Marriages Is Interracial or Interethnic," *Pew Research Foundation*, June 4, 2010, pewresearch.org.

32. Ibid.

33. Ranier Spencer, "'New Age Multiraciality: Generation Mix and the Fascinating Phenomenon of Non-mulatto Mulattoes," paper presented at the 2008 Conference on Race: Future of an Illusion, Future of the Past, History Department, Monmouth University, West Long Branch, New Jersey.

34. G. Reginald Daniel and Jasmine Kelekay, "From *Loving v. Virginia* to Barack Obama: The Symbolic Tie That Binds," *Creighton Law Review* 50, no. 3 (2017): 647.

35. Spencer, "'New Age Multiraciality."

36. Ibid.

37. "The Future of Race in the United States?" in David L. Brunsma, ed., *Mixed Messages: Multiracial Identities in the "Color-Blind" Era* (Boulder, CO: Rienner, 2006). Under this idea, one can have dark skin and yet still be considered an "honorary white." Much like the Irish, Italians, or Eastern Europeans at the beginning of the twentieth century, who were not considered White but would become so eventually—these groups would be able to subscribe to some of the privileges of being White. "Honorary Whiteness" is a term that originated in the apartheid regime of South Africa. See also "South Africa: Honorary Whites," *Time*, January 10, 1962.

38. Herbert Gans, "The Possibility of a New Racial Hierarchy in the Twenty-First-Century United States," in *The Inequality Reader: Contemporary and Foundational Readings in Race, Class, and Gender*, ed. David Grusky (New York: Routledge, 2011), 304.

39. Ibid.

40. Ibid.

41. While part of this was his personal choice, the non-Black members of his family were often erased during his presidency, as they, perhaps, no longer served any useful purpose or were conveniently ignored by his detractors.

42. Heather Dalmage, *The Politics of Multiracialism: Challenging Racial Thinking* (Albany: State University of New York Press, 2004), 9.

43. Furthermore, efforts to change the census, the penultimate organizing goal of

the multiracial movement, such as a multiracial category, potentially undermine major goals and accomplishments of the civil rights movement, such as directive #15 of the Office of Management and Budget, which is the federal order that created the "boxes" on the census we currently have, not to dictate identity but for civil rights compliance monitoring. Do away with the boxes, and it becomes very difficult to measure how well the government and other entities are doing concerning antidiscrimination and equal opportunity efforts in the real world.

44. Dalmage, *Politics of Multiracialism*, 9.

45. Spencer, "New Age Multiraciality."

46. Rainier Spencer, *Reproducing Race: The Paradox of Generation Mix* (Boulder, CO: Rienner, 2011).

47. Ibid., 102.

48. *Chasing Daybreak: A Film about Mixed Race in America*, dir. Justin Leroy, prod. Matt Kelley (Seattle, WA: Mavin Foundation, 2006).

49. Michael Eric Dyson, "We Count! The Black Agenda Is the American Agenda," Chicago State University, Emil and Patricia A. Jones Convocation Center, March 20, 2010, Chicago.

50. "The Price of a Black President," *New York Times*, October 27, 2012, http://www .nytimes.com/.

51. See "Transcript of Speech by President Barack Obama," Barnard College commencement, May 14, 2012, *Barnard College*, https://barnard.edu/headlines/transcript -speech-president-barack-obama.

52. Michael Eric Dyson, *The Black Presidency: Barack Obama and the Politics of Race in America* (Boston: Houghton, 2016).

53. Obama visited a prison (the first president to do so), and he started My Brother's Keeper. However, on the flip side, police violence escalated under his watch.

54. Milton Vickerman, *The Problem of Post-Racialism* (London: Palgrave, 2013), 1.

55. Serena Marshall, "Obama Has Deported More People Than Any Other President," *ABC News*, August 29, 2016, https://abcnews.go.com/Politics/obamas-deportation-policy -numbers/story?id=41715661.

56. Cornel West's reasons for his political break with Obama had to do with a story involving a misunderstanding over West's 2008 inauguration tickets. See "Cornel West's Continuing Feud with Barack Obama," *Atlantic*, May 18, 2011, https://www.theatlantic .com/.

57. In the Trump era, this act seemed relatively timid—but it was something relatively unprecedented at the time. Acts such as this were precursors in many ways to what would follow.

58. Prince, "Obama Was More Aware."

59. In this sense, postracialism becomes a kind of red herring, released by the media to distract from its continual stoking behind the scenes of racial animosities. See Ishmael Reed, *Barack Obama and the Jim Crow Media: The Return of the Nigger Breakers* (Quebec: Baraka), 2010.

60. Daniel and Kelekay, "From *Loving v. Virginia*."

61. Frank Llewellyn and Joseph Schwartz, "Socialists Say: Obama Is No Socialist,"

Chicago Tribune, November 1, 2009, http://articles.chicagotribune.com/. They go on to say, "As soon as Barack Obama announced his candidacy, Web sites on the extreme right began to charge that he was a socialist, a radical and not qualified to be president. At first Republican officeholders were more muted in their criticisms, charging merely that ideas like national health care and progressive taxation were—to use Dick Cheney's favorite denunciation—European."

62. Jon Meacham, "We Are All Socialists Now," *Newsweek,* February 6, 2009, http://www.newsweek.com/.

63. Mike Davis, *Fire in the Hearth: The Radical Politics of Place in America* (London: Verso, 1990); Howard Brick and Christopher Phelps, *Radicals in America: The Us Left since the Second World War* (New York: Cambridge University Press, 2015).

64. G. Reginald Daniel, "Race and Multiraciality from Barack Obama to Trayvon Martin," in *Race and the Obama Phenomenon: The Vision of a More Perfect Multiracial Union,* ed. G. Reginald Daniel and Hettie V. Williams (Jackson: University Press of Mississippi, 2014), 15–16.

65. Michael D. Shear and Yamiche Alcindor, "Jolted by Deaths, Obama Found His Voice on Race," *New York Times,* January 14, 2017, https://www.nytimes.com/.

66. Manisha Sinha, "It Feels like the Fall of Reconstruction," *HuffPost,* November 22, 2016, https://www.huffpost.com/.

67. Reconstruction saw the election of African Americans to more posts than any other time in American history—previous to the "Second Reconstruction" of the 1960s.

68. Peniel Joseph's characterization of Obama as being a representative of Black Power becomes very important to this discussion. This must also be incorporated in a more substantive way to investigate the interesting ways it fits into postracialism. Mainly, I am thinking here about the aspect of Black Power in the arena of elected politics—which was also part of the movement's original vision, as expressed in the National Black Political Convention in Gary, Indiana, in 1972.

69. Add to this Obama singing "Amazing Grace" after the tragic shooting of the Emmanuel Nine in Charleston, South Carolina.

70. FBI Counterterrorism Division, "White Supremacist Infiltration of Law Enforcement," October 17, 2006, https://oversight.house.gov/.

71. Barnor Hesse, "Raceocracy: How the Racial Exception Proves the Racial Rule," *Youtube,* 2013, https://www.youtube.com/watch?v=QCAyQNWteUA.

72. "Lincoln's 'House Divided' Speech," *PBS* (repr., 1968, Encyclopedia Britannica), https://www.pbs.org/wgbh/aia/part4/4h2934t.html.

73. Martin Luther King Jr., "I've Been to the Mountaintop," speech, Memphis, Tennessee, April 3, 1968, *Stanford University,* https://kinginstitute.stanford.edu/encyclopedia/ive-been-mountaintop.

74. Martin Luther King Jr., "MIA Mass Meeting at Holt Street Baptist Church," Montgomery, Alabama, December 5, 1955, *Stanford University,* https://kinginstitute.stanford.edu/king-papers/documents/mia-mass-meeting-holt-street-baptist-church.

CONTRIBUTORS

EDITORS

DERRICK P. ALRIDGE is the Philip J. Gibson Professor of Educational History and an affiliate faculty member in the Carter G. Woodson Institute for African-American and African Studies at the University of Virginia. Alridge's work examines American education with foci in African American education and the civil rights movement. An educational and intellectual historian, he is the author of *The Educational Thought of W. E. B. Du Bois: An Intellectual History* and coeditor, with James B. Stewart and V. P. Franklin, of *Message in the Music: Hip-Hop, History, and Pedagogy*. He has published numerous articles in journals, such as *History of Education Quarterly*, the *Journal of African American History*, *Teachers College Record*, *Educational Researcher*, and the *Journal of Negro Education*.

CORNELIUS L. BYNUM teaches courses in African American history and writes about progressive impulses among African Americans and authentic and independent strains of black radicalism in the early twentieth century. His first book, *A. Philip Randolph and the Struggle for Civil Rights*, is an analytical intellectual history that explores central aspects of Randolph's thought and activism. In it Bynum argues that Randolph's life and career shaped and were shaped by many of the monumental events, ideas, and developments of the twentieth century and demonstrates that Randolph's firm determination to improve the lives of black workers fundamentally affected core strategies and tactics of the civil rights movement of the 1950s and 1960s.

JAMES B. STEWART is a professor emeritus of labor and employment relations, African and African American studies, and management and organization and is currently based at Penn State Greater Allegheny. He was vice provost for educational equity and director of the Black Studies Program. Research interests include diversity management, globalization, and Africana studies. His ten books include *Black Families: Interdisciplinary Perspectives*; *The Housing Status of Black Americans*; *W. E. B. Du Bois on Race and Culture: Philosophy, Politics, and Poetics*; *African-Americans and Post-Industrial Labor Markets*; *Managing Diversity in the Military*; *Flight in Search of Vision*; and *African Americans in U.S. Labor Markets*. He has published over sixty articles in economics and Black studies professional journals and is a former editor of the *Review of Black Political Economy*, past president of the National Economic Association, and past president of the National Council for Black Studies.

CONTRIBUTORS

KEISHA N. BLAIN is an associate professor of history at the University of Pittsburgh. Her research and teaching interests include black internationalism, radical politics, and global feminisms. She is the author of the award-winning book *Set the World on Fire: Black Nationalist Women and the Global Struggle for Freedom*. She is currently the president of the African American Intellectual History Society (AAIHS) and an editor for the *Washington Post*'s Made by History section.

JEFFREY LAMAR COLEMAN is professor of English at St. Mary's College of Maryland. His research areas include literature of the American civil rights movement, music of social consciousness, protest, and resistance, and twentieth- and twenty-first-century American literature. Coleman is the editor of *Words of Protest, Words of Freedom: Poetry of the American Civil Rights Movement and Era* and author of *Spirits Distilled: Poems*. He is also poetry editor and associate editor of the *Journal of Hip Hop Studies*. His research has appeared in various venues, including the *Cambridge Companion to American Civil Rights Literature* and *Critical Essays on Alice Walker*.

PERO GAGLO DAGBOVIE is University Distinguished Professor of History and an associate dean in the Graduate School at Michigan State University. Among his books are *The Early Black History Movement* (2007), *African American History Reconsidered* (2010), *What Is African American History?* (2015), and *Reclaiming the Black Past: The Use and Misuse of African American History in the Twenty-First Century* (2018). Dagbovie is also editor of the *Journal of African American History*.

STEPHANIE Y. EVANS is a professor of Black women's studies and director of the Institute for Women's, Gender, and Sexuality Studies at Georgia State University. Her research interest is Black women's intellectual history, specifically memoirs, mental health, and wellness. At GSU, she is affiliate faculty in the Department of African-American Studies as well as in the Center for the Study of Stress, Trauma, and Resilience. She is author of three books: *Black Women's Yoga History: Memoirs of Inner Peace* (2021), *Black Passports: Travel Memoirs as a Tool for Youth Empowerment* (2014), and *Black Women in the Ivory Tower, 1850–1954: An Intellectual History* (2007), and is lead coeditor of three books, including *Black Women's Mental Health: Balancing Strength and Vulnerability* (2017). She is editor of the Black Women's Wellness book series at State University of New York Press.

AARON DAVID GRESSON III is professor emeritus of education and human development at Pennsylvania State University. Trained in both sociology and psychology, his research interests include race and oppression in the diaspora, cultural theory and symbolic representation, social theory, clinical sociology and identities (betrayals), sociology of communication, critical pedagogy, and education. He is the author of several books, including *America's Atonement: Racial Pain, Recovery Rhetoric, and the Pedagogy of Healing*, the award-winning *The Recovery of Race in America*, and *The Dialectics of Betrayal: Sacrifice, Violation, and the Oppressed*. He previously taught at Boston University, Brandeis, Colby, Brown, Hershey Medical School, and the State University of New York. Gresson is currently a psychotherapist in Baltimore and teaches sociology at Morgan State University in Baltimore, Maryland.

CLAUDRENA N. HAROLD is a professor of African American and African studies and history. Her books include *The Rise and Fall of the Garvey Movement in the Urban South, 1918–1942* and *The Punitive Turn: New Approaches to Race and Incarceration*, coedited with Deborah E. McDowell and Juan Battle. Her latest monograph is *New Negro Politics in the Jim Crow South*.

LEONARD HARRIS is a full professor in the Department of Philosophy at Purdue University. He has conducted research at the W. E. B. Du Bois Institute for Afro-American Research at Harvard University and as a Fulbright Scholar at Addis Ababa University, Ethiopia. He has published in many areas related to Africana philosophy, including pragmatism, ontology, and community and is the author of groundbreaking texts in Africana philosophy, such as *Philosophy Born of Struggle: Anthology of Afro-American Philosophy from 1917* (1983) and *Alain L. Locke: Biography of a Philosopher* (2009). Dr. Harris is also the founder of Philosophy Born of Struggle, an annual conference for Africana philosophers.

MAURICE J. HOBSON is an associate professor of African American studies and a historian at Georgia State University in Atlanta. He is the author of *The Legend of the Black Mecca: Politics and Class in the Making of Modern Atlanta*, the 2018 Georgia Historical Records Advisory Council's award for excellence. Hobson created a new paradigm, the Black New South, and has served as an expert witness in court cases and as a voice of insight for documentaries, films, movies, public historical markers, monuments, and museum exhibitions. He was chief historian for Netflix's *Maynard* and *Hip Hop Evolution*, ESPN's *30 for 30: Vick*, and Public Broadcasting Service's *Eastlake Meadows: A Public Housing Story*.

LA TASHA B. LEVY is an assistant professor in the Department of American Ethnic Studies at the University of Washington–Seattle. Her research and teaching interests include twentieth-century African American history, Black intellectual history, and Black women's studies. She is a contributor to *Understanding and Teaching the Civil Rights Movement*, edited by Hasan Kwame Jeffries, and *Discourse on Africana Studies: James Turner and Paradigms of Knowledge*, edited by Scot Brown. Her monograph, *Race Matters in the GOP: Black Republicans and the Limits of Two-Party Politics*, is forthcoming.

LAYLI MAPARYAN is the Katherine Stone Kaufmann '67 Executive Director of the Wellesley Centers for Women and professor and chair of Africana studies at Wellesley College. Her books include *The Womanist Reader* (2006), *The Womanist Idea* (2012), and *Womanism Rising* (forthcoming), and she has published extensively in women's, gender, and sexuality studies, Africana studies, and psychology. In 2010, she served as a Fulbright Specialist at the University of Liberia to help develop a model gender-studies curriculum. She is a member of the board of directors of the Global Fund for Women and of the Sustainable Market Women's Fund, which serves Liberian market women and their children.

ZEBULON VANCE MILETSKY is an associate professor of Africana studies and history and a historian at Stony Brook University specializing in recent African American history, civil rights and Black Power, urban history, mixed-race and biracial identity, and Hip-Hop studies. His research interests include African Americans in Boston, northern freedom movements outside of the south; mixed-race history in the United States and passing, and the Afro-Latin diaspora. He is the author of numerous articles, reviews, essays, and book chapters and is currently working on a manuscript on the civil rights movement in Boston. His book "Before Busing: Boston's Long Freedom Movement in the 'Cradle of Liberty'" is forthcoming.

R. BAXTER MILLER is professor emeritus of English and African American studies at the University of Georgia and is a leading black literary critic. He is the author or editor of nearly a hundred publications, including twelve volumes. During 2013 and 2014 at Georgia, he was the Donald L. Hollowell Distinguished Professor of Civil Rights. His new works are *Doc Rivers, Cry of Freedom* (2020) and *Arc of Modernism: The Rise of African American Poetics from Langston Hughes to Gwendolyn Brooks* (2020). His earlier study *The Art and Imagination of Langston Hughes* (1989; 2006) won the American Book Award in 1991.

EDWARD ONACI is an associate professor of history and African American and Africana studies at Ursinus College. His first book, *Free the Land: The Republic of New Afrika and the Pursuit of a Black Nation-State*, explores the history of the New Afrikan Independence Movement and the lived experience of revolutionary activism.

VENETRIA K. PATTON is head of the School of Interdisciplinary Studies and professor of English and African American studies at Purdue University. She specializes in African American literature and diasporic women writers. She is the author of *The Grasp That Reaches beyond the Grave: The Ancestral Call in Black Women's Texts* (2013) and *Women in Chains: The Legacy of Slavery in Black Women's Fiction* (2000), coeditor of *Double-Take: A Revisionist Harlem Renaissance Anthology* (2001), and editor of *Teaching American Literature: Background Readings* (2006, 2014). Her essays have appeared in Black studies and women's studies journals as well as the essay collections *Postcolonial Perspectives on Women Writers From Africa, the Caribbean, and the US* (2003), *White Scholars/African American Texts* (2005), and *Imagining the Black Female Body: Reconciling Image in Print and Visual Culture* (2010).

NIKKI M. TAYLOR is professor of history and chair of the department and specializes in nineteenth-century African American history. Her subspecialties are in urban, African American women, and intellectual history. Taylor has won several fellowships including Fulbright, Social Science Research Council, and Woodrow Wilson. In 2017 she wrote the grant to establish the Mellon Mays Undergraduate Fellowship Program Grant at Howard University (the first HBCU with its own program) and manages that program. Her monographs include *Frontiers of Freedom: Cincinnati's Black Community 1802–68* (2005), *America's First Black Socialist: The Radical Life of Peter H. Clark* (2013), and *Driven toward Madness: The Fugitive Slave Margaret Garner and Tragedy on the Ohio* (2016).

INDEX

THE NEW BLACK STUDIES SERIES

The University of Illinois Press
is a founding member of the
Association of University Presses.

Composed in 10.5/13 Adobe Minion Pro
with Futura display
by Jim Proefrock
at the University of Illinois Press

Manufactured by Sheridan Books, Inc.
University of Illinois Press
1325 South Oak Street
Champaign, IL 61820-6903
www.press.uillinois.edu